Taking
a Stand
Gus John Speaks
on education, race, social action
& civil unrest 1980-2005

Taking a Stand

Gus John Speaks

on education, race, social action & civil unrest 1980-2005

For Zehra

With compliments
& With hope.

Gus John
June 2006

**gus
john**
PARTNERSHIP

First published 2006 by The Gus John Partnership Ltd
4 Ellesmere Road South
Manchester M21 0TE

www.gusjohnpartneship.com

I would like to thank Alex Pascall for his poem 'The Letter' which appears on page 326; and to my daughter, Aisha, for 'Tales of the Ancestors' which appears in the dedication.

British Library Cataloguing in Publication Data.
A catalogue record for this book is available from the British Library

ISBN 0-9547843-1-6
ISBN 978-0-9547843-1-7

Printed by Woolnough Bookbinders, Irthingborough, Northants

CONTENTS

Dedicated to the revered memory of

my parents
      Agnes and Wilfred
          who gave so much
             so selflessly
                with so very little
                    to so many
                        ... including me

and in honour of my dear friend and brother, John La Rose

Tales of the Ancestors

I heard tales about the ancestors
a grandmother and father I never met
but loved
like history-book heroes
X or King
They were just
Agnes and Wilfred.
No films or books written about them
but by any means necessary
they created a dream.
                Aisha Phoenix John

PREFACE

Taking a Stand has its origins in two sets of requests. Over the years, people attending public meetings, seminars and conferences at which some of the papers in this collection were presented have requested copies of other things I had written on the same or related subjects for use in their teaching, professional practice or community activism. The second set of requests arose from discussions between different groups of young people, including my children and their friends, and me. In those discussions they were seeking to draw upon my experience as someone who has been active in community struggles around immigration, policing, education, youth policy and much else besides, and has reflected upon and written extensively about those struggles. Those young people persuaded me that they and people of their generation would be well served by my writing about the series of interventions I made over a number of years on a range of issues and events, some of which they are much too young to have experienced.

What was most striking about those discussions is that young people aged between 10 and 25 have been given and are receiving precious little assistance in understanding the current state of Britain, let alone the impact on the British social, cultural and political landscape of the post-war black presence. Schooling and education distances itself more and more from the task of enabling young people on whom the future of the society rests to be politically literate and providing them with the basis upon which they could become more *secure in their identities*. What passes for the current citizenship curriculum is clearly not sufficient to this task. Neither black nor white young people have an understanding of their place in and the contribution of their parents' and grandparents' generation to the shaping of British social and economic history in the last forty years.

It seemed to me, therefore, that I could do worse than make available to them a collection of speeches, essays and commentaries in which I have sought to analyse critical events between 1980 and 2005 and provide some direction to our struggles.

Ever since the bombings in London in July 2005, the 1970s debate about assimilation versus integration and about the dangers or desirability of multiculturalism has been revived to even less purpose and with even more confused thinking than before. Black communities in Britain are as guilty as the British state itself of projecting to young people, black and white, a view of the society and the way it functions which is dangerously misleading. In essence, it is a view which suggests that the inclusion of black people in managing the affairs of state, in public institutions and in delivering solutions to the situation of black people as determined by the state, represents progress and a fundamental shift in the situation of black people in the country.

Far be it from me of all people to deny any black person the right to be a high court judge, chancellor of the exchequer, foreign secretary, head of MI5, or chief executive of any or all of Mr Blair's trust schools. It is a right I continue to defend. The mistake we too frequently make and the false promise we give to young people, however, is that black people's access to these any number of similar positions in the society actually makes a material difference to the overall condition and status of black people in civil society and the economy.

In the last few years, we have witnessed a mushrooming of black staff associations, especially in the public sector, from the National Black Police Association (NBPA) to The Network in the Home Office. Such formations across public life have grown in proportion to the decline of independent organization and mobilization within black and ethnic minority communities. Few of those associations, with notable exceptions such as the NBPA, are actually empowered or constitutionally able to tackle issues which their very members and their children face daily in their communities as consumers of the same services they provide professionally. What they demonstrate, more than anything else, is the fact that black and ethnic minority staff still have a need, almost 40 years after the 1968 Race Relations Act, to take collective action to tackle the marginalization, institutional and personalized discrimination and basic lack of awareness they experience in those institutions.

As such, those civil service and public sector organizations remain legitimate sites of struggle for their black employees. There are therefore two issues for black and ethnic minority communities, in this regard. One is the extent to which the growth of that professional class, in the civil service or elsewhere, actually advances the interests of the community as a whole, or simply represents the incorporation of a growing number of black people into systems, structures and processes that leave the way the majority of black people experience the society and its institutions pretty much unchanged. The other, equally important, is the extent to which ethnic minority communities are prepared to give support to individual black employees and their black staff networks in a manner that empowers them to challenge institutional practices and workplace cultures and, together with those communities, make those institutions and service providers accountable for the treatment and quality of service communities receive.

Taking a Stand attempts to shed light on all these issues and calls for independent organization and the self-empowerment of our communities. Critically, it emphasizes the massively ignored fact that there is much that we ourselves need to fix within our own house and that, collectively, we have to devise the strategies for so doing.

One advantage of isolating significant moments in that twenty five year slice of our post war history as this book does, is that one sees much evidence of communities themselves, let alone the state, reinventing the wheel or/and failing to learn the lessons from past mistakes simply to repeat them over and over again. Nowhere is this more evident than in the way individual Chief Constables and Governments have dealt with civil unrest in the inner cities in the last quarter century.

The speeches and public lectures in this book were delivered to a wide range of people in audiences across Britain, in Europe and in the United States of America. A number of participants, far too many to mention, wrote or sent email with extensive comments after some of the presentations. Significantly, those comments sought to relate the insights shared in the presentations to their own struggles or to their own analysis of the prevailing situation where they were. I am grateful to them for that and for their critical comments. I am also grateful to Tom Wiley, former HMI, at the National Youth Agency for our many stimulating discussions over the years and for his helpful definition of 'active social exclusion' that I have expanded upon in a couple of these essays. My colleagues, Andrew Johnson, Professor Gerry Finn and the late Stuart Ainsworth in the Faculty of Education, University of Strathclyde, have been comrades in struggle and have provided me with constant intellectual stimulation, support and encouragement in the last two decades. I thank them for that and for their efforts in seeking to mainstream issues of social justice and race equality in the education, training and continuous professional development programmes across the Faculty.

Many generous people helped to prepare the book for publication. The advice of John La Rose and Sarah White of New Beacon Books was invaluable. I thank Anthony Downer, my colleague at the Gus John Partnership (GJP), for helping to recover some of the earlier essays and Shantel Collins for re-typing a number of them. Karl John, Aisha Phoenix-John, Milverton Wallace, Gerry German and John La Rose read and commented upon the introduction to the individual chapters and were thankfully sparing in the amount of extra work they sent me back to do. Alex and Joyce Pascall gave generously of their time, advice and hospitality as we discussed sections of the book and particularly what to exclude. I am grateful to Alex for permission to print his poem 'The Letter' and the photographs he provided. Staff and committee members at the Communities Empowerment Network (CEN) and at Parents and Students Empowerment (PaSE) gave much encouragement and support for this publication, nagging me to 'get on with it because we desperately need a campaigning document'.

Special thanks go first to Glenda Pattenden, my publishing editor, whose advice, encouragement and technical support throughout could not be bettered. Second, to Chief Omilade, Managing Director at GJP who coordinated the publication of the book, and to my other colleagues at GJP on whom I made so many demands and who created the space for me to work on the book, keeping me in good humour throughout.

In *Taking a Stand*, I share what is clearly my understanding and analysis of events, policies and social trends and my prescription as to the action black communities and public institutions in Britain need to be taking, given the history of the interface between black people and the society in the post-war period. In doing so, I declare where I stand, even at the risk of offending some people. That understanding and that prescription derive from my involvement in the struggle for racial equality and social justice since 1965 and my reflections on that struggle as a social analyst. The state we are in requires even more radical solutions than those suggested in this book, as I am sure many would hasten to remind me.

The responsibility for any errors of fact or shortcomings of analysis remains mine. Those apart, however, I would be satisfied if there was evidence in two years, either of a refinement of this analysis and the actions recommended, or, better still, of collective action in the key areas identified within these pages.

Gus John
Manchester
February 2006

INTRODUCTION

There is much that resonates in Gus John's timely book for me and other headteachers working in an education system that continues to fail so many black African and Caribbean children despite our fine ideals around equality and inclusion.

Unlike John's book, the Education White Paper 2005 is confused and obfuscated on how to improve schooling for everyone and it shamefully fails to develop strategy for those most at risk of being failed. High-jacked now by the London-based media and Old Labour backbenchers, both fixated on admissions, the White Paper barely touches upon the sensible recommendations made by the 2004 London Development Agency and hardly even pays lip-service to its own education department's "Aiming High" initiative.

What is significant about John's book is that he is not afraid to cast the blame for the educational underachievement and exclusion of black African and Caribbean children heavily on institutional racism. Sadly, from my own perspective of thirty years in education, through decades of debate not action, I am inclined to agree with him.

Refreshingly, John cuts a swathe through the ideological warfare between the anti-racists and the multi-culturalists, challenging the government's failure to put race on the agenda and address racism explicitly in successive education reforms. Exploring historical and sociological reasons for system failure of black African and Caribbean children and analysing below the surface psychological and political factors in his usual unequivocal way, John also offers more than academic polemic. It challenges black and ethnic minority communities too – particularly fathers – to take more responsibility for the destiny of their children as well as institutional racism in schools and other agencies. It does not only criticise the White Paper for its colour blindness but also offers practical and common sense ideas and solutions that I know can work from my own experience.

No one working in a comprehensive education system could

deny that the range and mean of black African and Caribbean children's achievement should equate with the range and mean of the whole pupil cohort. But many would shy from acknowledging that institutional racism exists – or fear naming it. Too many accept failure with excuses – poverty, social alienation, street and anti-school culture, absent fathers – and too few systematically seek ways of removing barriers to achievement. Like John I know that these factors and influences do affect young black people. They should be acknowledged and worked with by schools rather than used as excuses. Schools are ready with empathy and care when a child has a traumatic experience – accident or bereavement, for example – but not always for the routine racism often experienced by black children in their everyday lives.

The government's initiative "Aiming High" sought to do just that and positive findings are due to be published, I understand. But some of us on the ground floor were dismayed at the disregard of good practice already around in favour of cold-start and kick-start models that could deliver a quick fix with media appeal but with inevitably limited success and sustainability. This remains the government's dilemma in many arenas of school improvement.

How many schools really comply with the Race Relations Amendment Act 2000 requiring all schools to have in place an Equalities Policy and practice that would effectively outlaw over time the inequalities that result in such unhappy under-achievement. Unfortunately compliance with the RRAA has been reduced to a bureaucratic tick-box exercise instead of real life accountability and the kind of awareness raising, training and support that is needed to bring understanding and truly change hearts and minds.

I would not want to see a return to some of the badly handled race awareness training delivered in schools in past decades and I am dubious about whacking schools over the head with more compliance although its effectiveness in changing practice in schools is questionable.

I believe that educational leaders need to take a cool long look at what is right and to open up a dialogue with teachers and children themselves. Their voices are not heard and they are not emotionally equipped to leave their inevitable personal experiences of racism outside the school gates. Speak to children and in their own words they will give you the message that you have to confront teacher attitude and low expectations, insufficient knowledge of pupils' capabilities, let alone cultural backgrounds, discrimination and unconscious but clear fear born of ignorance. Sad to say fear, fear both of the children and their own ability to respond. In their own words, black African and Caribbean children will tell you that they like teachers who respect and praise them, believe in them – and who don't shout.

True equality can only be provided by recognizing difference – social inclusion and cohesion stems from accommodating difference. If we really want all children to succeed we have to identify and specifically target those children who are most likely to be disaffected by gaining a better understanding of them and their needs.

Schools that are fully engaging black African and Caribbean children are actively seeking out successful black visiting speakers, poets and artists, scientists and business people to provide positive role models throughout the curriculum and making extensive use of mentoring and peer mentoring. And where schools have managed to recruit a teaching force that begins to reflect the ethnic diversity of the pupil population, this has had a dramatically beneficial affect on relationships within the school community.

In my experience the common misassumption that Black parents, Caribbean in particular, lack interest in, and support of, education – particularly if they are sole parents – is far from the truth. But many parents' alienation and hostility resulting from their own experiences of schooling in the UK needs to be understood and parents need nurturing to trust schools. As one parent said to me, "Schools can be scarey. I would never have thought that I would become this involved – it was only when teachers explicitly encouraged me and made me feel welcome for the first time ever. All parents want their children to do better than themselves at school but sometimes we don't know how to help them. We don't know what to do and we look to you." John's book gives many useful strategies that schools can adopt both to improve their ability to better engage both young people and their parents.

The gaining of identity, self-esteem and respect – both from self and others – are adolescent pre-occupations, no more so than for black African and Caribbean children, given the dominance of African American popular culture. There is a serious lack – in both initial and in-service teacher training – of training in the understanding of adolescence, let alone race equality and anti-racist issues and strategies. Similarly in national training programmes for headteachers and other senior educational leaders they tend to be subsumed in the warmly glowing concepts like values and ethos.

There needs to be a steer from the top for race equality and anti-racism to be a given in all our institutions. In February 2006 I took part in a priority review of the disproportionate numbers of black and ethnic minority children who are excluded from schools at the Department for Education and Skills. Although it was disheartening to revisit the evidence that the lot of black African and American children in our educational system has changed little in thirty years, it was promising to see this issue on the policy agenda. It remains to be seen whether the government can, like Gus John, take a stand and show leadership.

Andrea Berkeley, February 2006

1.0

EDUCATING THE BRITISH
WHAT IS TONY BLAIR'S AGENDA?

The fact that fundamental freedoms and rights whose purpose is to promote the self-fulfilment of human beings and guarantee their dignity remain empty vessels is all the more alarming and serious since, in the 'global village' which the world has become, the marginalization or exclusion of a particular community or social group or even a particular sector of the population is bound to have an adverse effect, in the shorter or longer run, on everybody's future and progress. The destiny of the few is now inseparably bound up with that of everybody else. — Federico Mayor (1995)

In October 2005, the Government published its 'White Paper' Higher Standards, Better Schools for All. The paper is 'white' in every sense of the word. 'Black and Minority Ethnic Children' are disposed of in three paragraphs that take up half a page in a 116 page document.

The White Paper is completely silent on the issue of schools' and governing bodies' legal obligations in compliance with anti-discrimination and human rights legislation. Nothing is said about how the Government will ensure that these obligations are discharged. Nothing is said, either, about what the Government sees as the role of schooling and education in combating racism and preparing all children for living peaceably in and managing a multiracial society. That, despite the fact that the Government has had various working groups overseeing the implementation of the recommendations of the Stephen Lawrence Inquiry and, since May 2002, schools and local education authorities were required to have in place a race equality policy/scheme and an action plan spelling out how that policy was to be implemented.

The White Paper introduces the section on 'black and minority ethnic' (BME) children by observing that: 'Whilst many black and minority ethnic young people achieve well, a significant number fail to realize their potential. Young Afro-Caribbean people and those from Pakistani and Bangladeshi backgrounds are amongst the lowest achieving pupils in our schools'. The White Paper focuses upon black children's underachievement and providing every school with 'advice and support to meet the aspirations of BME parents and pupils'. In addition to much else that is wrong with this approach, as we shall discuss presently, it is hard to believe that the Government has not yet caught up with the fact that the term 'Afro-Caribbean' is outmoded and that African heritage people from the Caribbean have been referring to themselves for at least a decade as '*African*-Caribbean'

The Government published its White Paper at one of the most volatile periods in the history of post-war Britain. In July 2005, London experienced suicide bombings and attempted bombings by black young men who had been part of settled communities in Britain and whose victims represented a cross section of multiethnic and multifaith Britain. On 29 July 2005, in the City of Liverpool, 18 year old black student, Anthony Walker, was racially abused as he waited with his white girlfriend at a bus stop and then murdered after they moved away from their racist attackers.

In October 2005, violence erupted on the streets of Lozells in Birmingham following a rumour that a black girl had allegedly been raped by Asian men as a punishment for shoplifting.

Across the Channel, in France, cities burned night after night as angry young Africans and Arabs pushed inwards from the ghettoes into the very centre of those cities, protesting police violence, denial of opportunity, their existence on the margins of the society and general neglect of their communities.

Even if the Government were to argue that those events have absolutely nothing to do with education, their failure to acknowledge and say how they would deal with issues of 'race' in education still defies belief. Writing in the *Times Educational Supplement* (TES) in September 1997, Estelle Morris, the then Secretary of State for Education, acknowledged the problems of racism, social exclusion and educational failure faced by ethnic minority pupils and was emphatic that those were not challenges the new Blair Government would shy away from.

In 2000, the Government published the amended 1976 Race Relations Act, placing a general duty on public bodies (including schools, colleges, universities and local education authorities) to eliminate unlawful discrimination, promote equality of opportunity and promote good relations between people of different racial groups. In 2000, also, The Parekh Report of the Runnymede Trust's Commission on the Future of Multi-Ethnic Britain was published, a report which provided no less than 21 recommendations on education alone.

In 2001, the Government published their Green Paper, *Schools – Building on Success*. Those proposals showed no evidence of Government acknowledgment of the problems of racism in education, of the recommendations of the Stephen Lawrence Inquiry or of the Parekh Commission.

I was a member of Jack Straw's Race Relations Forum at the time and in February 2001 produced and presented a discussion paper for the Forum, inviting the Home Secretary and the Department for Education to examine the way 'race' issues in education intersected with the Home Secretary's own areas of responsibility, especially policing, youth custody and prisons (1.1). That discussion paper and an expanded set of proposals were submitted to Estelle Morris a month later, during the period of consultation on the Green Paper (1.2).

The Government introduced a number of initiatives in the period that followed, including *Aiming High*, a pilot project in some thirty schools with the objective of raising the achievement of black and ethnic minority (principally African-Caribbean) pupils.

The current White Paper was drafted at a time when it is

increasingly common for organizations to subject policy proposals to race impact assessment or race equality proofing. Having made it a statutory requirement for public bodies to produce and publish their race equality policy/scheme by May 2002 and to align existing policies to the policy or scheme, it was reasonable to expect that the Government would have led the way and demonstrate good practice by providing evidence of taking race considerations into account in the 2001 Green Paper. It did not. Four years later, it is surely reasonable to expect that the Government would assess the possible impact of the White Paper on black and ethnic minority and on white communities.

The letters to the CRE (1.3) and to the DfES (1.4) pose a series of questions for the CRE and the Government, not least about the CRE's role in ensuring compliance with the Race Relations Amendment Act (RRAA) 2000. Responses to these letters are also included.

Since 1997, the Government has placed education high up on its policy agenda. The emphasis has been principally on raising attainment levels and on pushing up standards in schools and colleges. The rationale underlying Government initiatives for raising achievement appears to be that by improving school standards overall, black pupils' attainment levels would increase similarly. But it does not stop there. Yes, there are initiatives such as Aiming High and the Ethnic Minority Achievement Grant. But, for every such initiative, there is retrogressive action, whether it be in relation to headteachers' powers to exclude pupils and not have them returned by independent appeals panels or 'zero tolerance' of challenging behaviour. Meanwhile, black students continue to be excluded in unacceptable numbers and schools feel under no obligation to prepare white students for living in multiethnic Britain, especially when they are located in all or mainly white areas.

Whether it be in white areas or not, the message every headteacher and governing body is given is that high academic performance is the name of the game. Anything that is not immediately related to that or that acts as a hindrance to it must be excluded. So, the Government clearly does not consider that, in a society where in 1993 and in 2005, 18 year old black male 'A' to know that the fastest growing sections of the British population are the African-Caribbean, Pakistani and Bangladeshi communities and, therefore, that they are more than likely to encounter black people in some area of their life.

Exploring issues to do with 'Antiracist Education in White Areas' (1.6) is something which most schools and LEAs in such areas have been compelled to do in order to comply with the general duty of the RRAA 2000. When this paper was presented at the National Anti-Racist Movement in Education conference in 1987, this was not the subject of discussion even within teacher training circles. Indeed, at that time, any talk of antiracist anything was enough to identify you with 'loony left' councils or with left wing politics. The paper establishes a link between the struggle against racial oppression and against gender, disability and other forms of oppression, arguing that, in all white areas, people come more readily to an understanding of racism and its denial of dignity, rights and entitlements to black people by dealing with the other forms of oppression that are ever present around them. The paper argues for a focus on rights, on combating discrimination against all target groups and on social justice.

For at least three decades, the quality of the engagement between black pupils and schools has been the subject of national debate. That debate has centred, more than anything else, around questions of behaviour and discipline and the extent to which poor behaviour triggers school exclusions. In the same way 'black young males' came to conjure up in police circles notions of rebelliousness, non-conformity, indiscipline, lack of parental control and a propensity to offending behaviour, that characterization is similarly applied in schools. Antiracist education, even among practitioners with a degree of racial awareness, tended to be seen as having to do with making the curriculum more inclusive of black people and giving black pupils pride in the achievements of people of their heritage.

There was little understanding of, let alone sympathy for, the view that for black young people 'school' was but another arena of struggle, just as their neighbourhood was and, often, just as their homes were. Their experience of dealing with the police on the streets, of confronting racists in their neighbourhood, of seeing their parents struggle against discrimination and demeaning treatment, was brought into the classroom. Sometimes it influenced their attitude to the way teachers or their peers treated them, sometimes it governed the way they treated others. In many cases, the many matters affecting them at home or in their relationship with their peers, which they carried with them to school, burdening their minds, were more preoccupying than the things which teachers wished them to give their full attention to. Many young people looked to the school to create space for them to deal with those matters and to help them develop strategies for managing them.

Where teachers developed meaningful relationships with young people and afforded them time and space to share such concerns, much satisfaction was derived from the teaching and learning relationship. The key to successful interactions in such situations was 'talk', students being given the space to talk and be listened to, to share in a safe and non-judgemental environment, to be encouraged to make sound judgements and develop and apply sound values.

But, the notion of the school as a legitimate 'site of struggle' against discriminatory treatment, against oppressive authority, against sexist and racist bullying by students or staff is generally considered to be subversive.

'Antiracist Education – a movement for change in education and schooling' (1.7) is, like so many other essays in this collection, evidence that 'the more things change, the more they remain the same'. Today, antiracist education has as its principal focus not only the curriculum and making it more inclusive, but, rightly, a scrutiny of school practices, policies and procedures which impact adversely upon the academic achievement of black and ethnic minority students. There is much less of a focus on black students, and white, developing the strategies that would empower them to be more socially competent and politically literate in their communities in the struggle against racism, homophobia, religious bigotry and the rest.

Where schools persist in the structured omission of issues of oppression, combating discrimination and promoting social justice, students are less likely to be given the space to air those issues and the assistance in developing strategies for dealing with them. In fact, schools are now so much more focused on test and examination performance that many young teachers, who performed well in their GCSE and 'A' level examinations and were themselves highly successful as school leavers, own up to the fact that, even after their teacher training, they do not feel they have the competence to manage those issues themselves, let alone guide students in so doing.

When Jack Straw set up the Race Relations Forum in late 1997, he and Tony Blair expressed their intention to place 'race' at the centre of the Government's policy making. To his credit, Jack Straw heard the pleadings of Neville and Doreen Lawrence and instituted the Stephen Lawrence Inquiry. The Government later partially amended the 1976 Race Relations Act. However, the one area in which the Government's record on 'race' remains truly abysmal is that of education, and schooling in particular. It is against that background that Mr Blair is passionately championing his latest set of reforms, reforms which he warns us will be 'irreversible'.

For all the reasons set out in these papers and for the sake of present and future generations in Britain, white and black, it is essential that there is the most vigorous opposition to the proposals in the White Paper. Through them, the Government is in serious danger of engineering social unrest and structurally embedding educational disadvantage for black and ethnic minority students. Furthermore, those proposals seem set to kick into the long grass, the efforts of committed white parents and teachers to make schools prepare all children for life in a society and a labour market free of the scourge of racial hatred and race discrimination.

1.1

RACE AND EDUCATION:
Promoting racial equality and social justice through schooling

Home Secretary's Race Relations Forum
20 February 2001

Preamble

The investigation of the murder of Stephen Lawrence by the Metropolitan Police epitomized the institutionally racist culture and the individual acts of white people in authority socialized within a culture of racism, that black people had complained of and campaigned about for 40 years.

The Stephen Lawrence Inquiry Report (Macpherson, 1999) was possible, and had the impact that it did, only because of the hundreds of people who were eager to share their experiences of policing in this particular tragic case, and indeed their experience of living with racism and having it define their everyday reality. The report was therefore as much a comment on policing in the Metropolis, and in Britain, as it was on the way black people have their being at the interface with the racism that runs through society's structures and institutions – including the schooling and education system. As such, it focused attention on the issue of race equality in education and on the role of education in combating racism. An earlier report of an inquiry into another racist murder had that as its principal focus (Macdonald et al., 1989), but was not allowed to have anything like the impact on education policy and practice that the Stephen Lawrence Inquiry Report, with the unprecedented endorsement of Government, was meant to have.

The Stephen Lawrence Inquiry Report made four recommendations on Education, aptly titled 'Prevention and the

Role of Education'. While it is unfortunate that the strategies suggested for LEAs, schools, and governors 'to prevent and address racism' were confined (albeit as examples) to recording and publishing data on racist incidents and on the ethnicity of excluded pupils, the recommendations pointed very clearly to the role of the National Curriculum, LEAs, schools and governors in preventing racism and reflecting the needs of a diverse society.

This Forum has had the opportunity to witness the Home Secretary's robust endorsement of the Report in the House, to discuss his Action Plan and review progress on its implementation after one year, as well as to examine reports of work in progress arising from that Action Plan.

Of some concern among black students, parents, teachers and a growing number of education activists and academics, however, is the record of the DfEE, OfSTED, the QCA and the TTA in the period since the Stephen Lawrence Inquiry Report. This paper seeks to outline those concerns and raise some others in the light of current legislation and recent Government announcements.

Education Policy and the Government's Duty to Promote Race Equality

The Stephen Lawrence Inquiry Report emphasized the need for all institutions, not just the police, to tackle institutional racism. Ever since the Rampton Committee reported in 1981, and particularly after the Swann Report (1985), the then Community Relations Commission highlighted what black communities had maintained for over two decades, i.e., that institutional racism was a major factor influencing the quality of black students' experience of schooling as well as their educational outcomes.

Those of us who in the 1960s and 1970s had campaigned against government sanctioned practices such as bussing, banding and the placing of Caribbean heritage children in lower streams than whites because of their assumed 'language deficiency' in the face of clear evidence of the impact of those discriminatory practices upon our children, have seen patterns of low expectations, underachievement and the problematizing of black school students persist. In an education culture that generated a 'moral panic' about black youth (and black males in particular), where generations of black (and specifically African-Caribbean) young people have been discussed in the language of 'underachievement', 'failure', 'disruptive and challenging behaviour', 'lack of motivation' and 'being especially prone to exclusion', and where they see precious little evidence of themselves being associated with success and the celebration of success, it is small wonder that a worrying number of black young people adopt attitudes to learning and to the very process of schooling which contribute to their alienation and disaffection.

Gillborn and Gipps (1996), and Gillborn and Youdell (2000), have pointed to the relationship between that characterization of black students and teacher expectations, but more importantly to the structural disadvantaging of such students through 'setting' and 'streaming'. Those in the lowest sets or streams are expected to perform less well and are taught a curriculum that reflects those low expectations. They are also entered for the sort of examinations where the highest grades cannot be awarded no matter how well they perform.

All of that was known prior to the Education Reform Act 1988 and before the Blair Government placed Education at the core of its political, legislative and modernizing agenda. What, then, have been the Government's strategies for tackling these endemic racial inequalities? The Government, quite rightly, focused the nation on 'raising standards' and promoting 'school effectiveness'. From the vantage point of those of us who built the black education movement in the last four decades, however, it did not appear to ask the question:

In view of the cumulative experience of black people in the schooling and education system, what must we do to ensure that these historical inequalities do not persist even as schools implement our recommended strategies for raising achievement and enhancing school effectiveness?

Before the Stephen Lawrence Report, where were the messages and prescriptive directions from Government about the evidence of schools' action to combat racism and promote race equality which the report expected to see? What was presumed to be the role of the government for controlling quality and pushing up standards, i.e., OfSTED, and of the QCA, and the TTA in this?

The assumption appears to have been made that by improving school effectiveness and raising standards overall, black students who lost out historically would automatically be pulled up with the rest. This 'colour blind' approach which characterized all the education reforms of the previous Government has resulted in these regulatory bodies treating the issue of 'race', and of the role of schooling in promoting race equality, as an added dimension to their core business, rather than somewhere near the heart of the crisis in schooling. The Government's 'Learning Revolution' and positioning of Education at the centre of its project to build the 'new knowledge economy' is not just about economic competitiveness or some fluid concept of 'social inclusion'. In twenty-first century Britain, it is also about how the nation deals with the 'Legacy of Empire' and the effect of that legacy on its capacity to come to terms with multiethnicity, with globalization, and to build a sustainable future for itself.

Eighteen months after the Stephen Lawrence Inquiry Report and its specific recommendations on education, we witnessed an unworthy spat between Mr Chris Woodhead and the CRE following the latter's report on *Inspecting Schools for Racial Equality: OfSTED's strengths and weaknesses* (CRE, 2000). Despite the review of the National Curriculum and the TTA's programme to recruit more black and ethnic minority teachers and provide guidelines on Initial Teacher Training, there is no evidence of the Government stating what its position is on the role of schools in 'preventing and addressing' racism, and what it sees as the function of the QCA, OfSTED and the TTA in that.

To say that is not to gainsay the specific initiatives the Government has taken, namely, 'Excellence in Cities', 'New Deal for Schools', 'Education Action Zones', City Learning Centres, the Ethnic Minorities and Travellers Achievement Grant, the 'Connexions' programme, the Children's Fund, Local

Strategic Partnerships, 'Learning Mentors'. While all of those come with a price tag and headteachers and governors are clearly delighted at being able to fund in-school programmes and school/home/community partnership working, none of it is being done within an overall policy framework on '"race" in schooling and education', with defined expectations and specific roles for the various regulatory bodies and agencies incorporated in the 'raising standards' agenda. In respect of some of those initiatives, the Government seems content to argue that strategies and priorities for dealing with race equality in Education are for local partnerships to decide.

I argue that a clearly stated Government commitment and a central focus on 'race' is essential for a number of reasons:
As things stand at the moment, most activities to do with race equality are targeted at black and ethnic minority communities. While Macpherson specifically mentioned 'strategies in schools to prevent racism' – his focus was on racist incidents and excluded black students. The fundamental issue of the role of schooling in all white or mainly white areas in 'preventing' racism was not addressed.

The very demands of the 'raising standards' agenda, and of OfSTED in the context of 'naming and shaming', and of market principles in relation to parental choice, are cited as reasons for schools in all, or mainly white areas, 'not wasting time on interesting but frankly peripheral matters like race equality', as one headteacher of an otherwise 'successful' school in a shire county told me recently. Similarly, those very demands are considered legitimate reasons for schools to be 'less tolerant and indulgent of the disruptive practices of African-Caribbean students'. In this climate, the practice of internal exclusions and students spending inordinate lengths of time in breezy corridors or in the 'remove room', 'voluntary' self exclusion (where parents are persuaded to remove the child for an indefinite period), and fixed term and permanent exclusions needs to be scrutinized far more closely. However, despite the findings of the Social Exclusion Unit in their *Truancy and School Exclusion Report* (SEU, 1998), I am not aware that the Government commissioned any research to interrogate the dynamics that result in so many African-Caribbean, and Pakistani students being excluded. The examination I have done of the case files of the Communities Empowerment Network (CEN), of which I am Chair, and my own advocacy work with students and their parents in exclusion cases, fills me with deep concern about the way some schools treat some students and the stereotypes and sheer vindictiveness that often underlies such treatment. In spite of that, the Government only saw fit to set targets for reducing school exclusions by one-third in the wake of the SEU report, and later to capitulate to the headteachers' lobby and make it easier for them to exclude disruptive students.

The model of mentoring on which the role of the 'learning mentor' is based is one that targets the student who has been defined as having a need (and usually as 'a serious problem'). Mentoring typically focuses upon the student, their peer group, and sometimes their parents/carers. What students tell us at CEN is that 'learning mentors' are very reluctant to tackle the issues that concern them most, namely, the dynamic between them and their teachers, the sense of injustice they feel about the way teachers resolve conflict, and the labelling of them that other teachers are then influenced by and upon which they pattern their own relationship with the students. The tendency to locate the problem within the students themselves, and not ask fundamental questions about teaching and learning, and about the teacher/student relationship could very well lead to 'learning mentors' being seen not as 'critical friend' but as 'intermediate treatment agents and an extension of the oppressive regime of schooling'.

The political, policy, and legislative context of schooling should not be the Government's modernising agenda only, but should include I would suggest:

• the Stephen Lawrence Inquiry Report, together with the aspirations Doreen and Neville Lawrence have for all children in the society and including the white children who are being denied opportunities to claim, and receive, informed assistance in dealing with racism and

understanding of what it means for them to be part of a
multiethnic society

- the Race Relations (Amendment) Act 2000 and that specific
  duty to promote it places upon public bodies
- the Human Rights Act 1998 (and in particular Protocol 1,
  Article 2, which enshrines a child's right to education in
  British domestic law, and Article 14 which outlaws
  discrimination on the grounds of race, religion, etc.)
- the Parekh Report on the Future of Multi-Ethnic Britain
  (Runnymede Trust, 2000)

Having regard to the schooling experiences of successive
generations of black school students and the Government's
vision of the 'One Nation' state in twenty-first century Britain,
where and how do current practices, and the proposals in the
latest Green Paper on the reform of secondary education, sit
alongside the above reports and Acts?

Before I turn to some proposals, an observation or two about
the current situation.

It is acknowledged that ever since its enactment, few local
authorities paid any serious attention to their obligations under
Section 71 of the Race Relations Act (1976). It is also the case that
even though many local authorities were lambasted for their
efforts, they at least made attempts to engage with the 'equality'
if not the antiracism agenda. The same could not be said about
the private sector. In the absence of 'Contract Compliance' in the
RRA 1976 and in British Labour Laws, that sector needed to be
coaxed to entertain the notion of 'Equality Pays' and 'Profits
through Diversity'. The question remains, therefore, if the
Government is so eager to hand over the provision of education
services (and the running of individual schools) from LEAs to
the private sector, what guarantees is it giving to black students,
parents, and communities about the capacity of those bodies to
deliver race equality? A capacity determined not by what they
say they will do, but what they have a track record as having
done.

Where, for that matter, is the evidence of what those agencies running education in local authorities did on the issue of combating racism, and promoting race equality, before they were considered suitable candidates for that crucial task of running an education service? To whom are they accountable, and how do students and parents make them locally accountable except by sharing their views with OfSTED inspection teams? Those whose personnel were themselves LEA officers, what evidence is there of them having taken leadership responsibility for and shown personal commitment to the agenda of combating racism and promoting race equality? How successful were they?

Judging from the LEA inspections already carried out by OfSTED, and the resultant transfer of education services from 17 of them into private hands, one can assume that there will be a higher ratio of LEAs in urban areas failing to satisfy the Government that education is safe in their hands, than LEAs in mainly white rural areas. It follows (if Greater London is anything to go by) that the existing dynamics of 'race', class, gender, culture(s), and historically entrenched distrust of the system and those running it, would continue to feature for the private 'knights with armour-plated resolve' – in much the same way that those dynamics have tested the political will and management capacity of politicians and Chief Executives/Directors of Education alike over the years.

What criteria is the Government expecting those private agencies to meet in order that black communities, and the country as a whole, could be satisfied that they are making education provision with an agenda that is informed by those 4 reports and Acts listed above?

Mr Blunkett said in a television interview on Monday, 12 February 2001, that the Government was 'modernizing for a purpose. The purpose is to help kids'. One would hope the Government would demonstrate its earnestness in helping 'kids' by ensuring that the right to quality education of *all* children in the schooling and education system is upheld and delivered. One would also hope, that in order to challenge and put an end to this scandalous and perennial situation, a greater number of parents would use the legislation and resort to 'class action', i.e., mounting a legal challenge as a group, to ensure that the new managerialism does not displace that 'right of children to education' which the Human Rights Act enshrines.

'Lord, make me chaste(ned) ... but not yet!'

Give this Government a second term in office, if you so please, but save us from more madness the while.

The Government is consulting on its intention to usher in yet more radical changes in the structure and management of schooling from 11 to 18. Leaving aside what we already know about the process by which certain parents contrive to get places for their children in denominational schools, evidence from the USA would suggest that it is clearly possible for black students, from disadvantaged backgrounds, to use and develop their talents and 'get on' in 'charter schools', or 'magnet schools', or 'beacon schools'. An emphasis on achievement and narrow educational outcomes, however, does not necessarily sit well with the students' need to develop a capacity to deal with the street, and the often unavoidable dynamics of gang membership, or harassment by peers who are members of gangs, domestic violence, and the general malaise of the dysfunctional communities from which so many children come to school.

Inevitably, the new breed of education managers would be no less committed than the current ones to doing whatever is necessary to demonstrate orderliness, disciplined learning, and a school ethos that is about hard work and achievement. The Government would no doubt expect to see early evidence of its experiment proving to be successful.

Many black students would thrive in that environment and have a right to it. Just as many, however, require programmes of work that could address their more fundamental self-management needs, before they could be focused on disciplined learning or even learn how to learn. Are we to see an expansion of Pupil Referral Units and the return of the 'sin bins' of the 1970s and 1980s? Are we to see a return to 'academic' and 'non-academic' banding and streaming, with students being compelled to accept a place in the 'non-academic' stream as a condition of being allowed to stay in the ('contract') school?

The Government has granted 'Beacon' status to some 150 schools, and to all accounts the schools' efforts in working to an extended programme, to raise achievement and invest time and resource in meeting the needs of their most disadvantaged students, appear to be making a distinct difference to school ethos and educational outcomes. I suspect that it is far too early for there to have been a rigorous, nationwide, evaluation of the scheme and the impact of additional pots of funding on the schools' capacity to do the things they would have done but for lack of resources (even when sound leadership is very much present).

Apart from the evidence of strategies for disseminating good practice locally and nationally which the DfEE rightly expects, what lessons does the Government wish the world of schooling to derive from this experiment? What is the connection between that and the newest set of proposals? How might the 'Beacon' school concept be developed to target, specifically, the issue of promoting race equality and combating racism?

It has long been a matter of controversy whether class size is a salient factor in determining educational outcomes. While accepting that to disestablish the connection between class size and teacher quality is foolish, nevertheless, if the Government wishes to encourage that varied 'menu' of structures and modes of governance for the provision of education, why not tackle the issue of class size? Why not experiment with failing schools, or schools causing concern, and in addition to doing something about the leadership issue, reduce class sizes to no more than 20 in primary and secondary schools?

Why not go one step further and aim to improve standards in thinking, learning, and moral education? There is an increasing amount of work done in schools on 'emotional literacy' (Newcastle and Southampton, for example), and in 'Philosophy for Children' (pioneered by Robert Fisher at Brunel University) (Fisher, 1998, 1999). The DfEE has itself supported the Hammersmith and Fulham LEA *School Improvement through Thinking Skills* project (which produced the video: *Minds of Their Own*, 1997). Given the abiding concerns about bullying, disruptive behaviour, and some students' inability to take responsibility for their own actions and for their own learning putting them especially at risk of exclusion, the relevance of curriculum, the fact that in the main students are not encouraged to challenge teachers, and cannot formally assess teachers' performance on the teaching and learning axis – why should smaller classes not be matched to a 'thinking skills curriculum' and a programme focused around improving the quality of the teaching/learning relationship, with teachers and students learning and discovering together?

The skills and capacities that such a programme could help develop in students, as well as teachers, especially when linked to meaningful and relevant curriculum, could have a significant impact upon the way students see themselves, the way they learn and make sense of the world, as well as the way they manage relationships with others. The available literature suggests that there is absolutely no conflict between that model and the skills school students are expected to develop generally. Indeed, part of the nature of underachievement is that too many students go grudgingly to the process of learning, and neither retain 'knowledge' (what it is determined that they should know at a certain age or stage), nor develop the skills necessary for social and technical competence.

Conclusion
In the immediate aftermath of the last General Election, those of us who had been in the struggle to improve educational outcomes for black and working class children for decades welcomed the new Government's commitment to 'Education', and the explicit relationship it established between education and social exclusion. We waited…, and were encouraged when the SEU produced its report on *Truancy and School Exclusion* in 1998. Again, we waited for appropriate Government action in the face of the overwhelming and disturbing evidence from its own Social Exclusion Unit.

The Stephen Lawrence Inquiry Report challenged the Government to take institutional racism seriously and be seen to be tackling it in all Government institutions. It would appear from the Government's pursuit of its education agenda that 'race inequality' is being given even less prominence than Macpherson intended in a report that was primarily about policing.

This paper has sought to raise some crucial questions about how the Government intends to ensure compliance with the law, work within the spirit of Macpherson and join with those of us who have struggled with this issue for upwards of four decades in saying:

'Enough is enough! The future of this country is in the hands of those young people who succeed in the system no less than in the hands of those who are failed and rejected by the system. If they are to co-exist and share that future (blacks and whites) without societal disintegration and inter/intra group conflict on an unprecedented scale, the Government's investment in their future must take their collective past much more fully into account and deal directly with the need to tackle the structural evidence of racial inequality in schooling and education and its already all too visible societal consequences'.

For, surely, there has to be some connection between Mr Blair's address to the country's headteachers at 10 Downing Street on Monday 12 February 2001 and the speech one day later of his Minister, Mr Paul Boateng, in Harlesden, North West London, in support of 'Mothers against Death' and in condemnation of the spate of senseless murders of young black males by young black males in that district.

I invite the Race Relations Forum to discuss this paper and to support my recommendation:

That the Minister of Education, Jacqui Smith, and the OfSTED Chief Inspector be asked to provide the Home Secretary with detailed answers to the questions raised for despatch to Forum members as soon as those answers are available and preferably by the end of March 2001.

Questions and Issues arising from the paper:
Education Action Zones

- Who runs them?
- How many black people are involved in their management and delivery structures around the country?
- What is their focus on race equality?
- What specific mechanisms do they have in place for empowering those students defined by the system as 'disruptive' and 'unteachable'?

Learning Mentors

- Who are they?
- How many of them are black and have an understanding of the background and context of black underachievement and black struggle in schooling and education?
- What capacity do they have to engage with the dynamics of 'race', gender, class and youth as far as working with black students is concerned?
- In one large city, of some 100 learning mentors in secondary schools, 4 are African-Caribbean, 2 Pakistani, and 1 Indian. Over 90% are white. Two Learning Mentor Co-ordinators have recently been appointed, both are white women. Yet, there is a major issue in that city about excessive numbers of black students being excluded or at risk of exclusion. Some schools are applying fixed term exclusions to the same students over and over again, up to the maximum 45 days. Many of those students drop out altogether and are not pursued unless their parents kick up a fuss.

Teacher Recruitment

- The teacher shortage crisis is affecting black students in inner city schools disproportionately. The excessive use of supply teachers is causing a great deal of disruption to the quality of teaching and learning and, hence, of behaviour and discipline. Black students are invariably the ones sanctioned in those situations.
- Yet, Mr Blunkett in his Press Release recently, announcing the teachers' pay award and Government measures to ease the recruitment and retention crisis, made specific reference to making it easier for teachers from Australia and New

Zealand to come and teach here. No mention of teachers from the Caribbean, India, Pakistan and Bangladesh. No concern about black students' experience at the hands of those Australians and New Zealanders – students who have been in and out of the system for some considerable time.

OfSTED Inspections

As the CRE report of OfSTED's strengths and weaknesses pointed out, schools are being given a clean bill of health while they have serious problems to do with racism.

One example is of a school in which the LEA is itself in 'special measures'. In a report dated February 2000, the reporting inspector stated (paragraph one of 'Main Findings'):

'The school is working hard to meet the challenges presented by the diversity of its pupils, many of whom come from disadvantaged families. It is succeeding in promoting positive behaviour and dealing with anti-social behaviour quickly. It provides a secure environment for its pupils'.

The very next month, the Chief Adviser was writing to the Chair of Governors of that same school and expressing concern about:

- Students not getting an education, especially black children
- Little evidence of collaborative or participative management
- Behaviour management being heavy, oppressive and epitomizing the macho culture in the school
- Widespread concern about the breakdown of discipline, with daily confrontation between students and teachers or between groups of students
- Widespread racial abuse by whites of blacks and vice versa, as well as between 'black and Asian' students

Soon afterwards, the LEA was dealing with a stabbing of a black student (on a fixed term exclusion) by a white student from an adjacent school.

The situation at the inspected school gave such cause for concern that the LEA determined to bring in a group of external consultants to review the school. Teaching unions objected, claiming that certain members of the review team were biased and that their track record would suggest that they would not look at the situation impartially.

1.2

SCHOOLS – BUILDING ON SUCCESS
Proposals submitted to Estelle Morris
Secretary of State for Education and Skills
June 2001

Introduction

These proposals are being submitted after a very careful study of the Green Paper: *Schools – Building on Success*. They have been formulated against the background of a lifetime of work to ensure that white working class and black children are provided with quality educational opportunities for their self development, for achieving academic success, and in preparation for the labour market.

In February 2001, just before the Green Paper was published, I presented the attached paper: 'Race and Education – promoting race equality and social justice through schooling' to the Home Secretary's Race Relations Forum. Attending the Forum to respond to the paper were Mike Tomlinson, Her Majesty's Chief Inspector, and Barnaby Shaw, Head of School Inclusion at the DfEE (representing the Minister, Jacqui Smith). This submission builds upon that discussion and is to be read in conjunction with 'Race and Education'.

It is interesting to note that the asterisk in the title of the Green Paper reminds readers of the Government's priorities as stated in its 1997 White Paper *Excellence in Schools*, viz., *'raising standards, promoting diversity, achieving results'*. The Stephen Lawrence Inquiry Report which the Government endorsed wholeheartedly pointed specifically to the 'disease' of institutional racism, and to the fact that the Inquiry perceived it to be operating in education through the practices and policies that resulted in the disproportionate numbers of excluded black school students and in a National Curriculum which did not encourage the promotion of diversity and race equality. Indeed the Lawrence Inquiry noted that:

If racism is to be eliminated from our society there must be a coordinated effort to prevent its growth. This needs to go well beyond the Police Services ... Just as important, and perhaps more so will be similar efforts from other agencies, particularly in the field of education.

It would have been heartening, therefore, if, at least in the spirit of Lawrence, the subtitle of the Green Paper had read:

Building on Success: raising standards, promoting race equality, valuing diversity, achieving results

This would have sent out the most powerful message about the Government's intention to define and give clear guidance on the role of schooling, and education, in preventing the growth of racism and in promoting race equality. It would have implied, also, that the Government viewed all four corporate priorities as being integrally linked, one to another.

In order to do that, however, the Government would have needed to make sure that the proposals in the Green Paper were themselves subjected to a process of *'equality proofing'*. As it is, the proposals are in danger of reinforcing diversity, but in the wrong direction, thus creating the conditions for greater race inequality even as it achieves dazzling results for some children of black and ethnic minority communities.

Defining the Problem with Schooling – Some Pitfalls

I am a parent of six British born black children, all of whom are classified as 'ethnic minority', and none of whom has ever once referred to, let alone defined, themselves as such. It is a notion totally alien to their consciousness of themselves and their relationship to the society. The Green Paper paints a picture of black and ethnic minority students which suggests they are

collectively incapable of being amongst the best performers in
the schooling system. Thankfully, it is now being acknowledged
that there is a large body of children of African descent who are
gifted and talented, and a growing number who, by their
academic success, help to raise the achievement levels of their
peers and the performance of their schools. I say that in order to
draw attention to the unfortunate and highly problematic
language in the Green Paper, and the stereotypical messages it
sends out. In paragraph 3.16, we read:

*We are determined that all ethnic minority pupils should secure results
that are as good as those for other pupils. Many ethnic minority
children have benefited from the recent rise in school standards, and
children from some minority groups achieve highly. But, for others,
there is still an unacceptable inequality in levels of attainment which
must be reduced ...*

*We will invest over £150 million a year over the next three years in
raising the attainment of ethnic minority children with the aim of
closing the differences that exist between the attainment of different
groups.*   (paragraph 3.17)

How are so-called ethnic minority pupils and parents like me
supposed to interpret that?
   *We are determined that all ethnic minority pupils should secure
results that are as good as those for other pupils.*
   For *all* other pupils?
   Who are these undifferentiated 'other pupils'?
   For *all* other ethnic majority, i.e., *white pupils*?
   Why not *that are as good as those for an increasing number of
ethnic minority pupils*?
   The Government's own Social Exclusion Unit has
acknowledged the research evidence that black students
(Caribbean heritage boys in particular) outperform everybody
else up to the age of 7, some sustaining that high level of
performance up to the age of 11), but are among the worst
under-performers by the age of 14. What specific 'ethnic
minority' factors account for that? Do not working class black

girls perform better on the whole than working class white boys and girls? Do not middle class black girls perform better in most subjects than middle class white boys? Equally disturbing is the statement that *children from some minority ethnic groups achieve highly*. Surely, the reality is that *some children from all ethnic minority groups achieve highly* but more children from some ethnic minority groups (Chinese, West African, Indian) achieve higher levels of attainment than is the case for other ethnic minority groups.

To argue thus is not to indulge in semantics.

The Government cannot hope to succeed in encouraging schools 'to set high expectations for all' if it so carelessly indulges in its own form of stereotyping, thus failing to interrogate received wisdom on this sensitive and complex issue. On the contrary, it will succeed in projecting 'ethnic minority' students as an undifferentiated mass, pathologically defined, as if the lack of attainment with which the group as a whole has come to be identified is somehow congenitally determined.

In paragraph 4.62, the Government states:

Our plans to raise standards will also close the attainment gap for children from Caribbean, Pakistani, Bangladeshi and some other backgrounds, who have tended to be poorly served by their experience of school. There is often no lack of ability or aspiration in these children or their families; circumstances have conspired to limit their attainment. *Through a combination of general and targeted policies, those circumstances can be changed*　　　　　　(my emphasis)

The language here is both euphemistic and worryingly vague. We are not told what factors combine to constitute these powerful 'circumstances'. The Government goes on to spell out the remedies without a clear statement of its diagnosis of the complaint.

Standards, Curriculum, the Teaching and Learning Process, Results

I believe that until such time that we tackle the thorny issues of entitlement, relevance, modes of teaching and learning, and the forms of knowledge we are accrediting, 'circumstances' will continue to conspire to make the schooling experience of far too many white working class and black and ethnic minority children result in the abandonment of hope and the death of aspiration.

In his introduction to the Green Paper, the former Secretary of State for Education and Employment, Mr David Blunkett, states that the Green Paper:

shows how we can create an education service which plays to the strengths of every individual, provides a common understanding of the knowledge base on which our society rests, promotes appreciation of the values which hold our communities together and generates the aspiration to learn from our past in order to contribute to the future

One of the things that provides positive reinforcement and a solid grounding for all individuals is the knowledge of who we are, where we've come from, and how positively others see and value us. These are all crucial antecedents of our self esteem. The knowledge base on which our society rests is not a given, not even when we presume to enshrine it in our National Curriculum. It is continuously being contested.

The National Curriculum as currently exists raises epistemological questions that are pretty fundamental. This is especially so in the context of 'promoting diversity' and 'the aspiration to learn from the past in order to contribute to the future'. For example:

- Who determines what constitutes legitimate knowledge and what does not?
- On what basis is it determined that we should all identify in the state curriculum with what is, after all, a very selective construction of knowledge and its forms of production?
- Despite claims of flexibility of approach and content provided for in the National Curriculum where, in the curriculum and the way it is packaged, is to be found the basis on which white working class students could come to a sense of their own identity and of the profound social and

economic changes, locally and globally, that have reshaped their communities and their aspirations in the last three decades?

- Where is to be found the massive contribution to the evolution of British social, economic and cultural history that so-called ethnic minority communities have made in the last fifty years? Notably, it is not even to be found in most present day Cultural Studies courses in further and higher education.
- Is there a commonly shared set of values that 'hold our communities together'?
- Do the residents of Oldham and Winchester subscribe to them equally?
- Multiethnicity in Oldham, as in the rest of Britain, is a given, but do all the residents of Oldham subscribe to a commonly shared set of values?
- Is schooling and education really assisting our children to learn from the past in order to contribute to the future, and learn to manage this increasingly complex, multiethnic society of which they are the inheritors?
- Whose past, and as recorded and seen through whose eyes?

How, truthfully, are today's young black Britons in our schools being assisted in understanding their past and the struggles of those who went before them?

- struggles to win democratic space for the enjoyment and exercise of rights as well as responsibilities
- struggles to make the Government outlaw racial discrimination and acknowledge the extent of racial harassment and racial murder in our communities
- struggles to make society own up to, and act upon, the widespread denial of justice to black people in the criminal justice system
- struggles to get nominated to safe seats in General Elections by all or any of the major political parties
- most school students (black and white) would have some knowledge of the struggles of the late Dr Martin Luther King and Rosa Parks but not of the nationwide Campaign Against Racial Discrimination (CARD) in this country or the

campaign against the bussing of black children to schools outside their neighbourhood in London in the 1960s.

While the packaged knowledge of the National Curriculum is being assessed through tests, exams and the rest, what acknowledgment is being given to the creativity and range of aptitudes of those considered not to have what it takes to perform well in these tests and exams?

How is their multilingualism, creative capacity in the visual arts, sports, music, caring and sharing amongst their peers and in their community, in ICT, and much else besides, being legitimated and validated as talents, knowledge, skills and desirable personal attributes?

Joined-Up Government and Promoting Social Inclusion and Race Equality

A fundamental question for the Government and for education practitioners is how to engage all children in a process of learning and self development that not only 'plays to their strengths' as Mr Blunkett put it, but acknowledges and assists them in overcoming their weaknesses. This brings me to the critical issue of *entitlement*.

I believe that the Government needs to redefine, within the standards debate, precisely what is meant by a student's *curriculum entitlement* and, as such, the function of schooling and education in respect of *all* students.

This is fundamental to the Government's goal of 'raising standards' and 'achieving results' in the context of *education for all*. For, even an interventionist measure such as the Learning Mentor scheme could give the impression that only the well adjusted, highly motivated, self disciplined, or conformist, have the right to mainstream teaching and support en route to good GCSE grades.

Those whose self development is under strain, and who need to acquire basic social interactive and self management skills, even as they engage with the learning process are effectively to be selected out and put through remedial programmes, either before, instead of, or after, internal or external exclusion.

I believe the Government needs to declare whether or not

children have the right, as part of their *entitlement*, to have time spent on:

- assisting them to be better able to manage themselves, take control of their conduct, learn to manage conflict and, in many cases, learn to manage their disordered lives
- assisting them to develop the coping strategies that would enable them to function positively in the chaotic circumstances that constitute their daily living away from school
- assisting them in learning to unlearn the behaviours and strategies that in many cases characterize 'normal' conduct in their homes and in their neighbourhoods, e.g., bigotry, racism, and anti-Semitism, homophobia, the subordination of women through physical and emotional violence, resorting to violence as a means of resolving conflict, insistence on settling scores
- assisting them in developing positive self identity and in dealing with the psychological impact of living with violence, bullying, rejection, low self esteem, sexism, racism, homophobia, including their own behaviour to others
- engaging with them in negotiating relationships and power structures within the school itself, including their peer groups

Were the Government to redefine school students' entitlement in those terms, it would be attending to the process by which the schooling experience compounds the social exclusion of too many students. It would mean revisiting notions of teacher and headteacher competence, measures for assessing quality and school effectiveness, students' education outcomes and the way in which schools are resourced to produce intended outcomes.

One of the many 'circumstances' that conspire to limit the attainment of black, ethnic minority, and working class students, is the increasing requirement that teachers teach subjects rather than students. All sorts of measures are introduced, therefore, to deal with those who thwart the teacher's ability to teach their subject.

Even when it is considered inappropriate to resolve problems with discipline or student/teacher interaction in the teaching situation, once the student is exported from the class, invariably no opportunity is provided for the teacher and the student to revisit the incident that caused the expulsion and examine how they both dealt with it.

Sadly, the reality for most schools and for the category of students who typically are among those permanently excluded, is that they are neither encouraged nor facilitated to embrace that more inclusive definition of entitlement. Indeed, this is matched by the structured omission of issues of inequality and of rights which should be part of the normal working of schools.

The Director General of the Prison Service noted in an address recently that 'the 13,000 young people excluded from school each year might as well be given a date by which to join the prison service some time later on down the line'. He noted that of 400 young offenders in a Young Offender Institution (YOI), over 200 had been permanently excluded from school. The Home Office's own research has revealed that two-thirds of the population of YOIs had left or been put out of school at age 13 or under.

The Chair of the Youth Justice Board, Lord Warner of Brockley, noted at a recent seminar that '80% of young offenders of school age are out of school, either through exclusion or refusal to attend'. He noted that mainstream schooling was not willing, or able, to deal with children with challenging behaviour. It was difficult to get young people back into education and training post-custody. Those excluded from school stay out of education, drift into crime and end up in custody. This was compounded by the very uneven quality of education and training across the 'secure estate'.

That seminar emphasized that for young people in school, especially those at risk of exclusion, and those in YOIs, the motivation to want to learn is fundamental to everything one attempts to do with them in the area of education and training. Unless that issue is tackled, resistance to schooling and to teachers would continue to lead to more of those young people swelling the ranks of the 'secure estate'. When one considers that young black people are up to seven times more likely to be excluded than all other students, the implications of what the most senior people in the penal system are saying must be addressed with urgency.

Contrast, for example, the very real concern about the career path of young offenders in the 'secure estate', with the pleadings of the major teaching unions at their annual conferences earlier this year for an end to the right of students and parents to appeal against headteachers' and governors' decisions to exclude. Headteachers have made it very clear that they regard the Government's intention to reduce exclusions by one-third by 2002 as both unrealistic and undermining of their efforts to meet other Government targets.

Far from capitulating to these demands (and turning Human Rights on its head), the Government should make it compulsory for each school that excludes a student to accept an excluded pupil from another school or from a pupil referral unit and commit itself to delivering that student's personal development plan.

I have long maintained that:

Education is for equipping people with skills for the workplace no more than it is for developing in them the skills and competence to take control of their own lives and to function as responsible social citizens, demanding and safeguarding their own rights and having due regard for the rights of others.

The Government needs to be much more specific about and consult upon the 'targeted measures' it wants to put in place to address the issue of black underachievement and low aspirations, matched by teachers' low expectations, among white working class students.

I fear, however, that the proposals in the Green Paper would lead to a creaming off of able students and more qualified and able teachers into desirable schools, with the rest struggling to contain the category of students (and parents) that those select schools would consider not at all conducive to them becoming the quality institutions the Government favours.

As a Director of Education, headteachers and governors tired of hearing me plead that:

Our mission has to be to make every school a good school, for you can improve and increase parental choice only by improving the quality of education on offer in all schools. Only thus does the notion of quality education for all as an entitlement of all become a reality.

The Government needs to take the lead in promoting the notion of a *good school* as one that delivers a curriculum of entitlement as defined above as well as the academic curriculum, such that parents of able and motivated students as well as those with challenging behaviour could have the confidence to send their children to such a school. If the proposals in the Green Paper provide even more incentives for schools to select parents and children who would cause them no problems but would guarantee their success according to the Government's criteria, the Government itself will have succeeded in its second term of office in extending the basis of the social exclusion it set itself to combat so vigorously in the last four years.

This means that schools should be resourced according to need and with the scope to have teaching groups of varying sizes. Where the needs of students are considered to warrant it, the school must have the capacity to establish teaching groups of no more than 15, or less where appropriate.

The Government proposes extra funding for schools with students facing 'exceptionally challenging circumstances'. It is also set to extend the Learning Mentor scheme and measures to support schools to deal with those students who do not conform to the 'norm'. I am arguing that schools should not be encouraged to view such students as exceptional. Rather, it should be taken as given that they represent that cross section of young people in the community with all their varied backgrounds, experiences, capacities and needs, but all having the same *entitlement to quality opportunities for self and academic development.*

Each student must be following a personal development plan

with self assessment as well as teacher assessment written into the plan. Each student would be entitled to a personal tutorial at least once per fortnight. This should preferably take the form of a 'Student/Teacher Conversation', with both the student and the teacher coming with their programme of issues, including the student's assessment of the teacher's role in facilitating their learning and self development. The student's self assessment, and the teacher's assessment of the student's progress and of the quality of the teaching and learning relationship, should include an assessment of the development of the student's aptitudes outside of school and of the contribution s/he makes to the community.

This would provide opportunities for students and teachers to attend, together, to the process of teaching and learning, including learning how to learn. Together, they could address the following questions:

How is learning taking place for the individual students in the group?

What learning is taking place?

How could it be made more enjoyable and more relevant?

What is the relationship between that and the learning they derive from all other areas of their lives outside school?

How can teachers' teaching objectives be jointly assessed in the light of learning outcomes as defined by students?

How can students be assisted to grow in confidence in sharing the learning they derive outside school, including the teaching of specific skills?

What is the impact upon the above of the modes of planning and delivery of lessons?

Schools should therefore be inspected and 'classified/ranked' not in relation to the number of 5 A*-C grades their students achieve but according to their overall contribution to children's personal, moral and academic development, including certification through tests, exams, etc.

'Promoting diversity' will then be not about building a diverse selection of elite schools, whether based on Arts, Sport, Information and Communications Technology, Astrology, or upon the special characteristics and ethos of denominational schools. It will be about ensuring that every school offers students *quality opportunities for self and academic development for all as an entitlement of all.*

The delivery of the student's plan would be not solely the responsibility of the teacher. Dramatists, artistes, counsellors, speech therapists, professionals in the community, business partners, past students who have come through similar challenges as those in the class and have 'overcome', would all be entitled to make planned interventions in delivering a negotiated curriculum.

The proposals in the Green Paper even as they stand make it necessary for the Government to review admissions policies, not just for schools in direct LEA control but for denominational, Foundation and other selective schools.

If the Government is serious about parental choice, it needs to address the issue of those parents who are left with no choice but to send their children to the local 'sink' schools after those who have the ability to do so, position themselves to obtain places in the more desirable schools.

To further extend the practice whereby schools choose students and parents, thus leaving certain groups of parents with little 'choice', is to promote diversity and achieve results at the expense of equity and social justice.

To do so in the full knowledge of the way the schooling system has historically failed black students and has set a disproportionate number of them on the route to youth custody and prison, is to condemn generations of young Black Britons to an existence on the margins of society, with dire societal consequences.

Implications for Government Bodies
Just about everything in this paper so far has implications for the Qualifications and Curriculum Authority (QCA), OfSTED, the Teacher Training Agency (TTA) and the DfES.

Whilst exempt from the 'specific duty' to promote racial equality and eliminate unlawful racial discrimination, embracing the 'general duty' to promote the role of those bodies in owning and taking forward an agenda to promote racial equality and social justice through schooling and education, should feature centre-stage in the Government's 'delivery' plan in this its second term.

QCA

The first stage review of the National Curriculum hardly begun to address the relevance of the curriculum to a growing percentage of the nation's children, let alone question the cultural supremacist assumptions on which much of the National Curriculum is constructed.

The QCA needs to address the issue of relevance, as well as the implications for schools, of operating with a negotiated curriculum as proposed above. Similarly, it needs to consider and make recommendations with respect to acknowledging and validating students' learning and skills development outside school in order to build upon learning and relationship building in school.

TTA

For their part, the TTA will need to consider the implications of the proposals above for teacher education generally and Initial Teacher Training in particular. Insofar as schools are among the public bodies that have a 'specific duty' to promote race equality, a duty that goes beyond the drawing up of institutional plans, the TTA needs to consider how teacher training would equip teachers with the skills and competencies necessary to take forward that agenda.

In the light of the Race Relations (Amendment) Act 2000, the TTA needs to set clear criteria for teacher training institutions to satisfy before their courses could be validated and those they train given Qualified Teacher Status. This should be followed up by an inspection programme to ensure that trainee teachers across the country are receiving the quality teacher education that would equip them to add capacity in this field to the schools they eventually join, irrespective of where in the country they find work.

OfSTED

The OfSTED framework of inspection has been strengthened to include an interrogation of the effectiveness of schools' policies and practices with respect to some aspects of race equality. Specific issues such as the recruitment, retention and progression of black and ethnic minority teachers, and listening to those teachers' narratives about their experiences, need to be given a clearer focus.

One particularly critical issue for OfSTED, and even more so for the DfES, is headteachers' treatment of black staff, invariably supported by governing bodies. The question of white headteachers' capacity to manage black staff is one that needs to be addressed urgently. Similarly, the obvious question as to why so many black teachers are experiencing difficulties with headteachers, or being put through capability procedures after as many as ten years in the same school.

The fact that such schools could be given glowing OfSTED reports and even awarded 'Beacon' status demonstrates yet again how peripheral to the quality assurance process considerations of race equality and racial injustice are.

In the light of the arguments above, the Government needs to revisit its intention to let 'successful' schools get on with their business, with the odd 'light touch' inspection now and then. Those suffering indignities at the hands of the management of these schools would be applying somewhat different criteria of 'success' than OfSTED in this regard.

A preoccupation with 'problem' schools and their 'problem' students that is geared towards making them like the rest would, in my view, achieve the complete opposite of what the Government intends with its education reforms.

One would wish to see OfSTED using the sort of school I am proposing above as a 'beacon' for those that exclude students who do not fit in, feature high up in the league tables as 'successful', while demonstrating very little evidence of promoting racial equality and social justice.

DfES
Learning and Skills
The focus on skills as evidenced by the Department's name change is welcome, but it will have meaning only if 'skills' are defined inclusively and not solely in relation to labour market skills. The social and self management skills that young people need to develop, especially those experiencing social exclusion and at risk of school exclusion, must feature highly on the Government's agenda for Learning and Skills.

The work of personal advisers in the Connexions programme and learning mentors in schools will necessarily involve them in some aspects of young people's skill development. It is essential, however, that the social and self management skills to which I refer here are not seen solely in the context of compensatory or remedial interventions.

The School Inclusion, School Effectiveness, and other such divisions in the DfES with an agenda for 'raising standards' and 'achieving results', would need to examine the implications for them of taking forward this more inclusive definition of students' entitlement and of 'skills' which lies at the heart of these proposals.

Private Sector Management of Education Services
On page 5 of the attached paper to the Home Secretary's Race Relations Forum, I posed a number of questions in respect of the growing privatization of education services formerly run by LEAs. In spite of the recommendation at the end of the paper, I am not aware that the DfEE provided any answers to those questions, questions which were anything but rhetorical.

Private contractors are typically being commissioned to run education in boroughs and cities with urban, multiethnic populations. Part of the 'failure' of the LEA in those areas has been the fact that they had failed over-representative numbers of black and white working class students, and their parents before them.

In the light of the duties placed upon public bodies by the Race Relations (Amendment) Act 2000 and the Human Rights Act, given that most of those companies have little or no experience in promoting race equality, managing diversity and dealing with black communities and managing black staff; and since they (not unlike the DfEE in the Green Paper) would mostly be given to similar stereotyping and muddled thinking on the issue of 'race' and achievement, it is essential that the Government puts in place mechanisms for ensuring that they are up to the task.

Each existing and new private contractor should be subjected to 'Race Equality Proofing' along criteria that encompass:

- Staffing in the education directorate or relevant establishment and policies and practices with respect to recruitment, retention and progression of black staff
- Staffing policies and practices in individual providing institutions, including schools
- Procedures for 'race equality proofing' of governing bodies and their policies and practices in relation to admissions, staffing, curriculum, exclusions, promoting social inclusion, and working in partnership with black and ethnic minority communities
- The 'Local Curriculum' and the School Curriculum in relation to the National Curriculum and the Government's various measures for promoting school effectiveness
- The priority that is given to dealing with the incidence of school exclusions and the approach that is taken to schools' excluding practices
- Measures for dealing with complaints and for proactively inviting feedback from students and their parents
- Measures by which they discharge their accountability to students and parents

This requires the engagement of professionals with the relevant expertise to investigate existing contractors and to put at the disposal of the DfES' Contracting Unit a set of criteria and guidelines for applying them which should be used to vet would be contractors.

Conclusion
Some of the issues addressed in this paper have been the subject of debate for some considerable time, not least of all that of class

size and its relationship to students' attainment levels.

Towards the end of its first term in office, the Government launched its New Prison Education Strategy and established the Prison Learning and Skills Unit. Her Majesty's Crown Prosecution Service Inspectorate, Prison Inspectorate and OfSTED, as well as the Youth Justice Board, all share major concerns about the schooling experience of the nation's young offenders, as observed above.

The Stephen Lawrence Inquiry Report highlighted institutional racism and personal racism but signally failed to address 'structural' and 'cultural' racism. The disproportionate number of young black offenders about which these Inspectorate have justifiable concerns are increasingly the result of structural racism in the society.

The last four years saw a Labour Government, after many years in the political wilderness, placing 'race' on the political agenda – with Jack Straw's commissioning of the Lawrence Inquiry and reviewing of the 1976 Race Relations Act – in a manner totally unprecedented in British government and politics.

The Secretary of State for Education, Estelle Morris, has an opportunity to place 'race' firmly on the schooling and education agenda and to do for education what, hopefully, Lawrence has done for policing, criminal justice and much else besides.

This would require the Government to be upfront about what it sees as the role of schooling and education in promoting race equality and, in the words of the Lawrence Inquiry, 'preventing the growth of racism' in the society. That, above all else in my view, ought to be the true legacy of the Stephen Lawrence tragedy to this and future generations of children in this country.

The Government prides itself on being a listening Government that seeks to keep faith with the people. Were it to push through the proposals in the Green Paper (with the usual few cosmetic amendments) it will be doing a huge disservice to the children of this country, and young Black Britishers in particular. The consequences of that, not least in terms of systematically creating a Black British underclass, will impact upon the society for generations to come.

The biographical narratives of black people in the 'secure estate', particularly young men, would not make comfortable reading for any government. If we accept that they are in our penal institutions in disproportionate numbers, not because they are congenitally prone to evil and lawlessness, we have a duty as a nation to restore hope and purpose in the lives of those on the road to swelling their ranks even further. To fail to do that would be to subscribe to a 'survival of the fittest' theory of schooling and education, and their connectedness with life chances, rather than affirming quality education as a fundamental entitlement of all.

I therefore urge the Secretary of State, before the Green Paper is progressed, to give due consideration to these proposals and to appoint a body of people, including leading thinkers and practitioners in this field outside Government, to advise her as to their policy and resource implications.

LETTER TO CRE

3 November 2005

3 November 2005

Farzana Hakim
Head of Corporate and Government Services
Commission for Racial Equality
St Dunstan's House
201-211 Borough High Street
LONDON
SE1 1GZ

cc: Anthony Robinson – Director of Legal Services

Dear Ms Hakim

DfES White Paper: Higher Standards, Better Schools For All

I refer to Linda Bellos' letter to you of today's date and wish both to endorse her arguments and to add some concerns of my own.

Linda had informed me and other colleagues of her intention to ask the DfES for evidence of the Race Equality Impact Assessment to which the White Paper had been subjected. I have to say it came as no surprise to me that none had been done prior to the publication of the White Paper.

I find it utterly incredible that the CRE could be co-operating with the DfES and conducting such impact assessment after the White Paper has been published for consultation. Surely, among the things the DfES should be consulting about is whether or not the way in which it has woven in equality and diversity issues and aligned its proposals with anti-discrimination legislation, especially the Race Relations (Amendment) Act 2000, is robust and comprehensive enough, given the radical changes in the provision of secondary schooling it is proposing.

I say 'especially the RRAA 2000', first because it is the area of legislation with which the CRE is primarily concerned and second, because no other issue has preoccupied governments since the late 1960s as that of 'race' and ethnicity in relation to schooling and educational outcomes.

A number of obvious questions suggest themselves:

1.   Did the DfES consult with the CRE about collaborating with them in ensuring that the proposed White Paper was race equality proofed?

2.   Did the CRE take proactive steps to ensure that the DfES was having due regard to the RRAA and indeed to the findings and recommendations of the Stephen Lawrence Inquiry and of the Parekh Commission's 'Future of Multi-Ethnic Britain' when drafting the White Paper?

3.   At what point did the CRE become aware that the White Paper was going to be issued in its present form?

4.   Did it register its objections with the Secretary of State for Education?

5.   Why did it not go public and raise the concerns that Linda Bellos, I and others no doubt are now able to raise only after the document was published for consultation?

6.   Do the black communities of Britain and the white population with a concern to ensure that their children are equipped to manage a multiethnic, multifaith society not have a right to expect that from a watchdog body like the CRE that has itself often entered the fray with such high visibility on the question of schooling and black and ethnic minority children?

7.   Once the CRE has worked with the DfES to carry out the race equality impact assessment on the White Paper as it stands, will the DfES re-issue it for consultation as a document that by then will be legally compliant and on which the nation could be expected to have a view?

8.   Inasmuch as those who welcome the White Paper and its provisions will assess their capacity to operate schools on the basis of what is contained in the document, rather than questioning their competence to engage with all 3 strands of the General Duty of the RRAA, why should they not assume that, at the end of the consultation period, any Bill constructed by that same DfES will be broadly in line with the contents of the White Paper?

9.   Does the CRE consider itself to be sufficiently independent of the various arms of Government to be able to hold Departments to account as it clearly should have in the case of the DfES and that abysmal White Paper?

10.   Should the CRE not be insisting, even at this stage, that the DfES extend the period of consultation and issue a Supplement to the White Paper which does the following things? :

• Demonstrate how the provisions in the White Paper are aligned with the RRAA 2000, the Human Rights Act, the Disability Discrimination Act and other relevant legislation

• Identify the criteria would-be providers of secondary schooling would need to satisfy before they could be considered eligible to run schools in accordance with the requirements of the RRAA and other relevant legislation (e.g., RRAA & admissions; RRAA & curriculum, teaching and learning; RRAA and the profile of governing bodies; RRAA and policy on school exclusions; RRAA and headteacher/teacher competences; RRAA and monitoring educational outcomes; RRAA and partnership working with parents and communities, etc.)

- Set out the matters to be addressed in considering the White Paper as identified through the Race Equality Impact Assessment process

I believe the CRE must be seen to do that, at the very least.

There is growing concern across the country, judging from the work that I do and the networks I link with, about the lack of CRE scrutiny in relation to public bodies' compliance with the RRAA, schools and education providers in particular. The CRE stands to lose whatever credibility it still has if it is not seen to be taking a public and robust stance on the matter of that White Paper. It would be presumptuous of it to want to influence the education debate at all, and in relation to black and ethnic minority communities in particular, from now on if it fails to do so.

Turning now, briefly, to the White Paper itself. It beggars belief that a document such as this, in 2005, contains all of 4 paragraphs under the heading: Black and Minority Ethnic Children, half a page in a 116 page document.

The White Paper fails to deal with the most vexing issues in schooling and education for black communities, i.e., the exclusion of black children and the composition and conduct of independent appeals panels. It makes a series of untested assumptions which we are asked to take on trust in relation to: learning mentors, pupil referral units, city academies, foundation schools, parental participation, parent power, cultural competence and antiracist principles and practice of operators in the education 'market'.

Above all, it says nothing about the role of education in building the future of multiethnic Britain and laying the foundations for peace and for pluralism.

For all of those reasons, and more, the CRE should not be seen to be collaborating with Government in some 'post hoc' assessment of the race equality implications of the White Paper.

I would appreciate a full response, especially to the 10 questions posed above.

Yours sincerely

Professor Gus John
Visiting Professor of Education – University of Strathclyde
Interim Chair – Parents and Students Empowerment (PaSE)

Response 1

Linda Bellos
Director
Diversity Solutions Consultancy Ltd
63A Surrey Road
London
SE15 3AS

Tuesday, 06 December 2005

Dear Linda

RE: White Paper on Higher Standards and Better Schools for all.

Many thanks for your letter of 3rd November 2005 and apologies for the delay in responding.

I am grateful to you for raising your concerns regarding both the content of the above White Paper and the need to conduct a Race Equality Impact Assessment of the proposals.

The Chair, Trevor Phillips and other colleagues from the Commission met with Ruth Kelly, the Secretary of State for Education, on 21 November 2005. During this meeting Trevor outlined the Commission's expectation that this proposed policy, in line with all other relevant policies developed by DfES, should be subject to a rigorous and robust Race Equality Impact Assessment. The Secretary of State agreed and promised to keep the Commission informed regarding progress of the assessment.

I would like to make it clear that the Commission would not wish to undermine its potential enforcement powers by assisting any public authority to carry out a Race Equality Impact Assessment. The Commission is firmly of the view that the duty to carry out a Race Equality Impact Assessment of new and proposed policies sits firmly with the public authority concerned. The Commission's legally defined role is to ensure that Race Equality Impact Assessments are being systematically undertaken and to determine whether such assessments are sufficiently rigorous. As you will be aware, our key focus is to determine whether the assessment has identified all of the potential adverse impacts of the proposed policy and where it has done so, that it has identified action to mitigate or remove the adverse impact.

The Commission can, and does, provide guidance and clarifications to public authorities on a daily basis in order to enable them to meet their legal responsibilities in respect of race equality. It would appear that it is this support which colleagues in DfES have referred to.

In line with the above approach, the Commission will not comment on the specific content of the proposals, however we have made it clear that the Race Equality Impact Assessment of the policy should include consideration of all issues relevant to race equality, including impact in relation to all three strands of the duty.

In relation to your concern that public authorities are not making sufficient progress because they perceive that there 'are no consequences for inaction'. I can assure that the Commission is proactively working to ensure that all listed public authorities are meeting their legal responsibilities and this includes appropriate enforcement action. The Commission has issued in excess of 200 'Minded Letters', which have resulted in the necessary remedial action being taken by the authorities concerned. The task of ensuring that all listed public authorities are meeting their legal responsibilities in relation to race equality is central to the work of the Commission. The Commission will continue to use all of its legal powers to ensure that public authorities are delivering in relation to race equality.

I would like to thank you again for raising this issue with us.

Yours Sincerely

Faz Hakim
Director of Corporate and Government Relations

Cc: Professor Gus John

Response 2

Commission for Racial Equality
St Dunstan's House
201-211 Borough High Street
LONDON SE1 1GZ

25 January 2006

Dear Professor John

I am writing in response to your initial letter to Faz, and subsequent email to my colleague Brid Scanlon about the DfES White Paper: Higher Standards, Better Schools For All. I know you had raised some concerns, so I hope that the following will clarify the points you raised.

1.   Did the DfES consult with the CRE about collaborating with them in ensuring that the proposed White Paper was race equality proofed?

No, on this occasion it would have been inappropriate to help the DfES in this way given our regulatory role.

2.   Did the CRE take proactive steps to ensure that the DfES was having due regard to the RRAA and indeed to the findings and recommendations of the Stephen Lawrence Inquiry and of the Parekh Commission's 'Future of Multi-Ethnic Britain' when drafting the White Paper?

At the meeting that Trevor (Phillips) had with Ruth Kelly, the CRE said that we expected a Race Equality Impact Assessment (REIA) to be done and that we would like to receive a copy when it was published.

3.   At what point did the CRE become aware that the White Paper was going to be issued in its present form?

At the meeting, the CRE was informed that the White Paper was being published the following Monday (a matter of days).

4.   Did it register its objections with the Secretary of State for Education?

Trevor made it clear that there should be an emphasis on identifying potential adverse outcomes and mitigating them. We have raised particular concerns about the underachievement of ethnic minority pupils, concerns around exclusions, admission practices, and racial harassment of both pupils and teachers. We hope they will take these issues on board when carrying out their REIA.

5.   Why did it (the CRE) not go public and raise the concerns that Linda Bellos, I and others no doubt are now able to raise only after the document was published for consultation?

We will not comment on REIA while the DFES is carrying it out in order to preserve our regulatory role.

6.   Do the black communities of Britain and the white population with a concern to ensure that their children are equipped to manage a multiethnic, multifaith society not have a right to expect that from a watchdog body like the CRE that has itself entered the fray with high visibility on the question of schooling and black and ethnic minority children?

The CRE must, like all other interested stakeholders, assess what the white paper will do for those groups of children from some ethnic minorities whose fate seems sealed the moment they enter school. That's one reason why we've insisted that the Government subject whatever it proposes to the most rigorous and testing assessment of its impact on race equality. Currently, there are lots of claims and counter-claims about whether these proposals would create a more segregated education system or would leave some ethnic communities behind. The truth is that we just don't know at this stage. But what we certainly don't want to do is make a bad situation worse.

7.   Once the CRE has worked with the DfES to carry out the race equality impact assessment on the White Paper as it stands, will the DfES re-issue it for consultation as a document that by then will be legally compliant and on which the nation could be expected to have a view?

As I mentioned further up, we are not working with the DfES in this way. We took the same stance with the Department of Health who asked us to help them in relation to the Draft Mental Health Bill. Stakeholders also asked us to comment on the proposals. We raised concerns about the REIA and subsequently the DoH informed us that they would delay the introduction of the bill until enough time had been given to producing a proper REIA. We will take the same approach with the education white paper.

8.   Inasmuch as those who welcome the White Paper and its provisions will assess their capacity to operate schools on the basis of what is contained in the document, rather than questioning their competence to engage with all 3 strands of the General Duty of the RRAA, why should they not assume that at the end of the consultation period, any Bill constructed by that DfES will be broadly in line with the contents of the White Paper?

This white paper has been controversial as you know, and it is unlikely that all its provisions will survive beyond the consultation. What will continue beyond this point, however, is the duty on schools under Section 71 of the RRA to have due regard to the promotion of race equality. We urge other organisations and individuals to express their concerns also.

9.   Does the CRE consider itself to be sufficiently independent of the various arms of Government to be able to hold departments to account as it clearly should have been in the case of the DfES and this abysmal White Paper?

We believe that we are. I refer you to my answer to question 7.

10.   Should the CRE not be insisting, even at this stage, that the DfES extend the period of consultation and issue a Supplement to the White Paper which does the following things?:

• Demonstrate how the provisions in the White Paper are

aligned with the RRAA 2000, the Human Rights Act, the Disability Discrimination Act and other relevant legislation

- Identify the criteria would-be providers of secondary schooling would need to satisfy before they could be considered eligible to run schools in accordance with the requirements of the RRAA and other relevant legislation (e.g., RRAA & Admissions; RRAA & curriculum, teaching and learning; RRAA and the profile of governing bodies; RRAA and policy on school exclusions; RRAA and headteacher/teacher competences; RRAA and monitoring educational outcomes; RRAA and partnership working with parents and communities, etc)

- Set out the matters to be addressed in considering the White Paper as identified through the Race Equality Impact assessment process

We have made clear our expectation that the REIA should be rigorous and robust, covering all aspects of the proposals that are relevant to promoting race equality.

11.   Has the CRE been given a date by which the DfES would conclude its race impact assessment?

The CRE wrote to the DfES on January 13 to formally request a copy of the REIA on completion. We are awaiting a response.

12.   Will the CRE examine the results of that exercise and publish its evaluation?

The CRE will examine the results of the REIA as we have done previously with other proposed government proposals, such as those to introduce ID Cards.

13.   Is the CRE satisfied that the White Paper which did not comply with the requirements of the RRAA 2000 before Government published it, could be considered by Government

to have been properly consulted upon?

We fully expect that the DfES will consult as part of carrying out a REIA. Once we receive the report, we will be able to determine whether there has been appropriate consultation.

Please feel free to get in touch if you have further queries.

Yours sincerely

Bernie Aryeetey
Senior Policy Advisor
Corporate & Government Relations

LETTER TO DfES

4 November 2005

---

4 November 2005

Inderjit.DEHAL@dfes.gsi.gov.uk
Cc: fhakim@cre.gov.uk, arobinson@cre.gov.uk,
lindabellos@diversity-solutions.com

Dear Inderjit

Linda Bellos very kindly shared with me the exchange of correspondence between you and I am writing in that connection.

You will see from the attached that I have written to Farzana Hakim at the CRE to express some concerns about the whole process of relating the White Paper to current race legislation. Perhaps you could point out to me the logic of publishing the results of race equality impact assessment of the White Paper separately from the White Paper itself and after it has been consulted upon, because I simply do not get it. Given all that has been said and done about schooling and black and ethnic minority children in the last 5 years, not least by Government itself, does the country not have a right to expect the DfES to issue a composite document that clearly incorporates the race equality implications of the radical proposals the Government intends to enshrine in law? Or are the provisions of the Race

Relations Amendment Act and of the Human Rights Act in respect of the rights of the child simply there for show?

I invite you to address some of the questions I pose in my letter to the CRE as, clearly, they concern the DfES even more than the CRE itself.

I look forward to hearing from you.

Yours sincerely

Professor Gus John
Visiting Faculty Professor – University of Strathclyde
Interim Chair – Parents and students Empowerment

Response

1 December 2005

Linda Bellos
Copy: Prof Gus John

SCHOOLS WHITE PAPER
Apologies for taking some time to respond to your email. I have addressed the issues that you raise below:

On the 'working class' issue:
The White Paper proposals are explicitly designed to provide less affluent pupils with the opportunities that have previously been available only to the middle-classes. These include:
- A more personalised approach, supported by small group and one-to-one sessions – including additional resources for those schools with the greatest proportion of pupils who have fallen behind in literacy and numeracy;
- Access through extended schools to opportunities beyond the school day to develop particular aptitudes and interests;
- Targeted choice advice to help more deprived families make

the right choice for their child – with an extended offer of transport to overcome situations where the cost of transport is a barrier to taking up a good school place;

- More support for parents in terms of better information, advice on how they can engage with their child's learning and access to parenting classes through extended schools;
- Action to tackle weak and coasting schools, which predominantly serve the most disadvantaged pupils.

The White Paper does not mark a return to a two-tier system. Trust schools, unlike GM schools, will be subject to fair funding, fair admissions (including priority for children in care and with statements of special needs) and full accountability – they will form part of the local authority family of schools.

On joint working with the CRE: we will take your views on board.

On location of race equality advice: the department has an Equality and Diversity Unit, which has responsibility for corporate equality issues and leads on providing advice to senior officials. In addition, there are a number of specialist units located across the Department, which provide specific advice on issues related to the directorate in which they are based. The Ethnic Minority Achievement Unit plays this role in Schools Directorate, for example.

Inderjit

Inderjit Dehal
Department for Education and Skills
Sanctuary Buildings
Great Smith Street
London
SW1P 3BT

RACISM, RACIAL VIOLENCE AND BULLYING IN SCHOOLS

Annual Conference of Hackney Education Managers
November 1993

Introduction

Hackney became a local education authority in its own right in 1990, and in a very real sense the annual conference of Hackney Education Managers has been an exercise in 'Getting to know ourselves', bringing our collective experiences to bear, and using one another as resources.

We have addressed ourselves to: defining a shared vision of the purpose and function of education and schooling in Hackney, identifying the barriers to making that vision a reality, and agreeing upon a set of performance indicators by which both the Education Directorate and individual institutions and services could assess whether or not we are achieving our declared goals.

This year we are joined for the first time by colleagues from the former Leisure Services Directorate, who are already engaged with us in the process of determining a new set of service goals for the combined Directorate of Education and Leisure Services, goals consistent with the three 'E's' of our vision, namely, education for life, equality and excellence.

At this year's conference you have asked me to be a resource and to assist the conference in exploring the issues of racism, racial violence and bullying in schools. I would like to think that this will be an exercise in 'Getting to know ourselves ... better'.

I would therefore like to invite you to 'inquire within' as we approach this vexing issue. We will examine issues and use words, which are generally considered out of place in respectable company and you will hear things which will no doubt stir your emotions. Come what may, in addressing this issue we need to look not just at the management challenges posed by racism, racial violence and bullying in schools, but at ourselves also, and at the structures we operate.

I want to locate my contribution on this topic very much within the theme of this year's conference, 'Raising Achievement in the Context of Curriculum Change – the next steps'.

In doing so, I would draw upon a number of reports, notably the Elton Report (1989), In the Service of Black Youth, (John, 1981), Learning in Terror (CRE, 1988) and, principally, Murder in the Playground (Macdonald, et al., 1989).

What, though is the relevance of a session on racism, violence and bullying to a conference on raising achievement in the context of curriculum change?

At last year's conference we reaffirmed the LEA's vision, that is to achieve high quality education for all, underpinned by principles of equality. We agreed that we needed to be much more focused on quality and equality as we seek to build and support a learning infrastructure in the borough that is responsive to the disparate needs of all Hackney's residents.

The 190,000 residents of Hackney encompass a multiplicity of ethnic groupings who stand in widely variant relationships one to another, and indeed to the society as a whole. We need constantly to remind ourselves, however, that the way those various groups define themselves, and are defined by others, is predicated to a large extent upon the dominant political and ideological processes which confer a certain status upon different groups in society.

As such, 'race' and 'ethnicity' become factors on the basis of which structural relationships and arrangements are constructed, and around which institutions are organized. They serve as a basis for structural marginalization, cultural denial and deracination, as well as systematized forms of oppression.

Racism and Xenophobia in Post-war British Social History

Those of us involved in black struggle in this country in the late 1960s, used to say that one of the critical functions black people perform in this society is 'to interpret the society to itself and encourage it to see itself as mirrored through our experience'.

I believe that to be even more the case now, some 25 years or so later, and with the experience of two generations of black Britishers to draw upon.

It is worth reminding ourselves of certain landmarks in British social history in the post Second World War period. For one thing, a whole new language developed which was totally alien to us black people prior to our arrival in Britain. We had known the language of apartheid, and of racism in the United States of America. We tended to forget, however, that the racialization of oppression, which characterized British imperialist and colonialist exploitation, had provided the society with a language of racism and racial hatred which was equally brutalizing and dehumanizing, and which was a central component of the British cultural heritage.

As we look in some detail at the incidence of racism and racial violence in schools, I would like you to keep very much in mind some aspects of that language and the practices they denoted, as follows:

Dark strangers	the alien wedge
Darkies	coloured immigrants
Coloureds	ethnics
Ethnic minorities	minority ethnics

Those were the terms used in official discourse and in 'polite' company, especially the term 'coloured'. You knew you were done a favour when you were called 'coloured'. And even when you insisted on being called 'black', you were chided for encouraging people to be offensive towards you, and told that, whether you like it or not, it was more correct to refer to you as 'coloured'. So much for self-ascription of 'identity'.

Those who preferred to 'call a spade a spade' and had no time for pussyfooting around used more crude language, but knew that effectively their treatment of you was the same as and more straightforward than that which you received from 'polite company'.

Available to them were terms such as:

Niggers	nig nogs
Coons	sambos
Wogs	pakis
Apes	beasties

Some among them developed a penchant for horrendous pursuits such as:

Nigger hunting, paki-bashing

Whites who stood up in defence of blacks were condemned as 'nigger lovers'. Blacks seeking accommodation, employment, or food and drink from restaurants and bars were invariably met with notices, which warned:

No coloureds, No dogs (and sometimes) No Irish

Immigration, in Britain and across Europe, was racialized such that it was impossible for the term to be used without the connotations of blacks in their thousands, implying a society experiencing immense difficulties in keeping them out:

Immigration	Coloured immigrants
Immigration laws	Commonwealth Immigration Act
1st generation immigrants	2nd generation immigrants
Illegal immigrants	Another wave of immigrants
3rd generation immigrants	Illegal immigrants
A new wave of immigrants	An influx of immigrants
Growing numbers of immigrants	

Researching a book on Police Power and Black People in the early 1970s, I found that policemen in Liverpool and in the Metropolitan Police were eager to boast of running a 'Department of Agriculture and Fisheries' within their police stations.

In 'agriculture', they planted drugs on young blacks and on unsuspecting black workers in their cars and in their homes. In 'fisheries', they went on 'fishing' expeditions, raiding premises (usually factories and hostels) at random in search of illegal immigrants.

Another notorious and widespread form of 'fishing' was the police operation of the 'Sus' laws, in which they picked up young blacks indiscriminately and provocatively, under suspicion of being about to commit an arrestable offence. Robbery from the person, or other forms of street crime, which were a social phenomenon in Britain long before the regular police were established as organized constabularies in the country, were racialized in the 1970s, and 'muggings' became a particular crime committed by young blacks. (See Hall et al., *Policing the Crisis*, 1978).

The criminalization by the police and the courts of thousands of young blacks through 'Sus' arrests reached the same scandalous proportions as the nationwide practice of shunting black children into schools for the educationally subnormal. Moreover, it was to make a significant contribution to the experience of group oppression which inner city black people had, and which erupted so dramatically into the uprisings in Britain's urban centres in the early 1980s.

Black people have been at the receiving end of all of the above, both from institutions and individuals. The culture of racism it all signifies has been matched by a culture of resistance to racist and class oppression, which we have generated and nurtured. Both the culture of racism and the culture of resistance have their manifestations in our lives and in the communities we inhabit.

Both act upon the students, parents, and teachers in our schools, no less than they influence us as managers. I would be very surprised, for example, if anyone can tell me that their teacher training prepared them adequately for dealing with the issues arising from all of the above; or indeed for work in a multiethnic environment, let alone for combating the effects of the culture of racism on her/himself and on their school community.

How many of us still feel very uneasy dealing with the issue of racism, and unable to express our feelings about the subject. Yet, as managers, we are called upon to make decisions every day regarding the conduct of students, parents, and teachers, including the challenging of our own conduct. On what are we basing these decisions, especially given the fact that as managers we hold a great deal of power in our hands and exercise it in a manner which highlights the relative powerlessness of students and parents, particularly those who are not 'professional' like ourselves?

Given the fact that the government is expecting schools to provide the greater part of the teacher education and training that the new teacher recruits will receive, and that the responsibility is being placed upon them in the same period that we are experiencing a resurgence of racism and fascism in the society, the capacity of schools to deal with the issue of racism and racial violence must surely be a matter of enormous concern.

The Challenge Facing Schools

In so far as schools are microcosms of society and places in which values, mores, and beliefs are contested, the question that arises for us as education managers is how to create a secure, safe but challenging social and educational environment in which these contestations could take place as part and parcel of the normal process of teaching and learning.

Irrespective of our abiding faith in the human condition, few of us would assume an automatic commitment to racial equality and social justice in society as a whole. Yet, we tend to assume that by virtue of operating within the well-ordered environment of a school, students and teachers would be more disposed to buck societal trends and conduct themselves in ways which uphold and respect the rights of others, regardless of race, gender, or anything else.

How often do we hear, for example, schools describing their ethnically diverse communities in terms of cultural richness, multiracial understanding, religious tolerance, and the rest? 'Harmony' is thus celebrated as the absence of conflict. To further promote that harmony, any number of steps is taken to project and foster unity in diversity and to stamp a seal of approval upon those cultural preferences and practices which typically are marginalized or denied legitimacy in the wider society.

Few schools are equally upfront about the not altogether pessimistic expectation that the school would mirror the nastiness of the world outside its boundaries, and that precisely because it seeks to give so much space and respect to those whom the world outside denies it, that it would inevitably expect conflict from some sections of its community of students and parents.

Precisely because schooling and education are assumed to take place in non-political, non-ideological, or, in these times, politically correct enclaves, many schools simply get by, guaranteeing conformity by coercion, but without necessarily tackling the fundamental predispositions or conflicts students have. Consequently, students continue to indulge their racism and bigotry, without let or hindrance, away from the controlled environment of school and in situations where they could usually expect either indifference to their activities or positive support from others in their neighbourhoods.

The challenge for schools is therefore not simply to ensure that every student and every teacher could operate in a safe and secure environment, free from bullying and from racial violence, physical, verbal, and psychological, but to address fundamentally the issue of the racism, or sense of being denied their moral right, of those who genuinely feel it is normal and necessary to treat black staff and students in racially oppressive ways.

Raising Achievement, Curriculum Change and Racial Violence

It is worth recording that the biggest culprit as far as disestablishing a relationship between the schooling agenda and the persistence of racism and fascism in society is concerned, is the state. I say 'the state' rather than the government because this has been a constant in the post-war period, common to all sorts of state apparatuses, and irrespective of the particular political party in power.

Nowhere is this more evident than in the raft of education reforms that we have seen since 1988. The 1980s saw the worst social uprisings in Britain in the twentieth century. Concentrated predominantly in urban centres, they were a metaphor for the entrenched and institutionalized forms of racism, discrimination, disadvantage and oppression that black (mostly young) people had suffered in the education system and at the hands of the police and the courts for two decades.

In 1969, the all-party Select Committee on Race Relations and Immigration (the Siamese twins of British social policy) published their report on the 'Problem of Coloured School Leavers'. The report concludes that black parents and their children had been improperly and incompletely socialized into the British class structure. As black, working class and alien, they were judged to have totally unrealistic aspirations for their children, wanting them to be lawyers, doctors, engineers, accountants, and not just nurses and workers on London Transport. Worse still, they tended to equate the length of time spent in school and in formal education with assumed levels of attainment, and the right to good, high status employment.

Effectively, what we were being told was that the white working class had long since learned not to have high aspirations and ideas above their station. The system accommodated them accordingly, so much so that the daughters and sons of railwaymen and miners making their way into universities were seen as extraordinary, if not as committing 'class suicide'.

In the majority societies from which we came, in which not even the handful of expatriate whites were designated 'ethnic minorities', (we considered neither ourselves nor them as 'ethnic' anything), social class was not seen as a structural barrier to academic achievement and to entry to the professions or to high status jobs. Poor children of illiterate parents in tiny villages were able to gain scholarships from the government school and progress to the secondary schools and colleges, going on to win Island Scholarships to Oxford or Cambridge, Edinburgh or the London School of Economics.

Against that background, therefore, black parents were not prepared to come to a settlement with the British State on the same terms as the white working class. Thus it was that a vibrant black working class education movement was built in defence of the right of our children to high quality education, untrammeled by racism and cultural denial and displacement.

It is worth us remembering how the situation we now have in most of our inner cities came about, and what the origins are of the now historical over-representation of black school leavers among the underachieving and unemployable in the country. Speaking at a rally in 1986 during Keith Joseph's war of attrition with the nation's teachers, I observed as follows. I was describing our earliest encounter with the British schooling system:

The fact that children were black and therefore assumed to be stupid, with a brand of stupidity that was thought to be contagious, meant that teachers treated them as stupid, expected them to perform as if they were stupid, and even when they performed academically well, they were still dealt with as if some momentous freak of nature had occurred. Some white parents, leaving nothing to chance, removed their children from local schools or removed themselves from the neighbourhood to which black migrants had come so that the value of both their children's education and of their properties might be preserved.

Some white teachers joined with black parents and black school students in challenging racist practices in schools, and in organizing within the community. Most teachers, however, assaulted black kids with their ignorance, bigotry and racism; headteachers did likewise to black parents; and local education committees and the Department of Education and Science (DES) issued guidelines and passed rules which confirmed all the above practices as legitimate.

Black parents had no experience of white parents which suggested that it was possible for parents to influence fundamentally how schools were run or how teachers behaved. What was clear, however, was that at the time, politicians, local and national, worried only about the white vote regardless of whether it was racist or not, and would further undermine the situation of black kids and pour scorn on their origin, their culture, their history and their homes.

Black parents formed themselves into parent committees in North London and elsewhere, waged lengthy battles with various town halls to prevent and put an end to the practice of bussing black kids away from their neighbourhoods into other areas in order to ensure that the number of blacks in any one school could not be a source of danger either to the image of the school, the education of white children or the physical and mental health of the teachers. This was to conform to the DES rule that no school should have more than 30% black students. They, like the rest of the society, sought to make pariahs of us all, and to turn our children into imbeciles.

In the borough of Haringey, black parents won historical campaigns against the 30% rule which a Labour Education Authority tried to introduce, and against banding when the incoming Conservative Authority brought in that form of selection and grading in 1969. In 1969 also, the Caribbean Education Association was formed. That body, renamed the Caribbean Education and Community Workers Association (CECWA), waged campaigns against the police treatment of our children, the practice of placing most black kids in the lowest streams, blaming the home for what schools and the DES were patently failing to do and, most historic of all, against the nationwide practice of placing vast numbers of black children into schools for the educationally subnormal.

A conference organized by the CECWA in 1970 gave rise to the publication of a book entitled: 'How the West Indian Child is Made Educationally Subnormal in the British School System'. This book was to have a profound impact on black parents, black youths and school students across the land, and a shattering effect on the whole educational establishment. Grave injustices in educational practice against black kids and white kids were exposed. Racial bias and class bias in the determination of educational ability was found to be endemic within the education system. Here, as in so many other areas, the struggles waged by the black working class movement were to have the effect of revealing the way the white working class had been treated for almost a century, since the Shaftesbury Act which guaranteed popular education in Britain, and were to lead to a shake up of schooling practices for all school students, black and white.   (John, 1986)

During the following two decades the struggle in education, and for black rights in the country generally, intensified and institutionalized forms of racist oppression were met with more and more sophisticated forms of resistance. And, of course, we had the ideological warfare between the multiculturalists and the antiracists.

However, the fact that white working class organization declined or was defeated in inverse ratio to the growth in strength, self confidence and social power of black self organization effectively meant that blacks were seen as having their demands met, and as being much more assertive about their rights to decent housing, better education, equal access to employment opportunities, and justice under the law. Moreover, it was felt that they generally behaved as if they owned the place and had always done so, having an impact on popular culture (sports, music, the arts generally) way out of proportion to their numbers.

Margaret Thatcher led the pack, in 1979, eleven years after Enoch Powell, in declaring that there was an enemy within, growing in size, and with the capacity to 'swamp the British culture'. Two years later, in 1981, her government passed the most draconian piece of anti-black legislation to date, the 1981 Immigration Act.

But like soldier crabs, we see the world differently from inside our respective shells. As far as black people are concerned, British society did not capitulate and hand over the goodies on sufferance in the last quarter of the century. What are seen by others as advances for the black population in social, economic and political life were all hard won in the face of relentless odds.

The state and certain sections of the society continued to pile on the pressure. The criminal justice system continued to work against the interests of the blacks; police brutality and discriminatory practices abounded, endorsed by the judicial system; immigration legislation became more and more draconian, with the police enlisted to enforce it; and discrimination in housing and employment, promotion prospects, and in business and finance continued. The state, in a multitude of ways and guises, continued to send powerful signals to the nation that Britishness equalled whiteness, and that despite the number of native born black British in the country, blacks 'per se' were still a problem.

In a paper entitled 'The Resurgence of Barbarism – Europe, 1992 ... and all that' I argued as follows:

Laws relating to immigration, the right of dependants of whatever age to join their parents or families, nationality, citizenship, the status of residents and of aliens, were all racialized in the 1960s and 1970s.

That racialization of immigration across Europe set boundaries around those who 'belong' and those whom the nation states decide 'do not belong'. It commensurately sends out messages to the whole society as to who is desirable and who is undesirable or simply to be tolerated. How those who are deemed undesirable are to be treated becomes a matter for control apparatuses and other institutions of the state no less than for organized racists and fascists, or the disposition of other individuals and groups in the society.   (John, 1990)

Immigration comes to be a 'social problem' caused by the visibility and alien ways of black and other minorities; a 'problem' which the state on behalf of the white majority and in the interest of social cohesion must regulate. What is seen to be at issue is the level of tolerance of the majority white society as they see 'the British character in danger of being swamped' (Margaret Thatcher, 1979), and prospects of 'rivers of blood flowing like the Tiber' (Enoch Powell, 1968). In other words, if the nation state by not taking firm enough action caused that level of tolerance to be breached, there would be bloody racial wars as the majority society sought to defend its sovereignty from the ravages of the alien within.

In Britain, at the peak of the process of racializing immigration, successive governments published annually the number of live births to people from the Commonwealth and Pakistan living in the United Kingdom. In the discourse on race relations and immigration, the purpose of such statistics was not to demonstrate how much of a fully integrated, multiracial society we were becoming, but the strain and stress put upon the society, its institutions, and particularly its level of tolerance by the increase in the size of the black population.

This serves as yet more reason for the state to introduce stricter immigration control measures or, heaven forfend, place limits on the number of children black mothers could have, or the number, similarly, white mothers could have by black men.

The liberal justification for this development is then introduced, in Britain at least, by a Labour Home Secretary, Roy Hattersley, in his famous attempt at racializing: 'Integration without control is impossible, but control without integration is indefensible' (Hattersley, House of Commons, 1965).

In the last twenty-five years, the society has witnessed the phenomenon of paki-bashing, nigger hunting, and a year on year increase in the number of racial attacks, currently estimated to be running at some 150,000 per year. In the last five years, there has been a sharp increase in the number of racist murders, and attempted murders.

Irrespective of how we define ourselves as black people, or how much more superior than other blacks we think we are, the one thing that unites us, whether we call ourselves black or brown, is the certainty that we are all susceptible to racial abuse and to racist attack. Racists and fascists do not concern themselves with niceties such as whether or not you are a Guyanese Indian, a Trinidadian Indian, or a Goan. It is all the same to them. You are still 'a stinking paki'.

In the summer of 1990 during the primary school teacher supply crisis, two of the forty-five teachers we recruited from Trinidad experienced British racism at first hand within ten days of arriving in London. Some racists chased one teacher of African descent as he used the London Underground on his way home. He had to run for his life.

The other, of Indian descent, was walking with his family along Homerton High Street when he was hit in his head by a short plank from a builder's pick-up truck. As the plank connected with his head he and his family heard the assailant's venomous cry, 'Go home, you stinking paki'. A teacher who had come some 4000 miles to teach children in Hackney schools, including quite possibly the children of those who would sooner see him dead than see him here, collapses on the street in front of his petrified family simply because he happened to be black.

The Lessons of Burnage

By now, I am sure some of you are asking yourselves, what has all that 'old hat' historical stuff got to do with racism, bullying, and violence in schools, let alone raising achievement and curriculum change? When will we be told how to manage racial attacks and racial violence in our schools?

The obvious point to be made is that the current focus of curriculum change is such that all those issues continue to be ignored. What is more, those of us who, despite that fact, are inclined if not determined to put them back on the agenda are finding that the space available to us is being increasingly eroded.

Many teachers who were either disinclined to tackle issues of racism or multiculturalism in the curriculum, or were simply unsure of their capacity to do so, used the National Curriculum as an excuse for avoiding consideration of non-white European issues in their teaching. The fact that the National Curriculum is overloaded has been an added factor in teachers' resistance to seeing curriculum planning and delivery as an appropriate locus for combating racism.

It remains to be seen whether the 'slimming down' proposals of Sir Ron Dearing of the Schools Curriculum and Assessment Authority would create some more space for teachers to exercise choice about what is taught, and, if so, how that space will be utilized.

The management challenge is therefore how to re-cast 'the curriculum', in order to ensure that neither white nor black young people are denied an understanding of the major socializing and identity forming influences in their lives, or are displaced from their cultural groundings in recent British social history or in the evolution of human history and knowledge.

According to Mrs Thatcher, the period up to 1963 could now be classified as 'history'. Anything after 1963 is simply 'current affairs'. Be that as it may, it is absolutely crucial that both through the formal and pastoral curriculum we are able to engage students in the development of awareness of the manner in which they construct their identities and have expectations placed upon them, in the context of the evolution of British social history in this last period.

For example, the one question which we need to ask ourselves over and over again in relation to the racist murder of Ahmed Iqbal Ullah at Burnage High School in 1986 is, how could a 13 year old white student be so obsessed by the fact that a 13 year old Bangladeshi student got the better of him in a fight that he could premeditate, and carry out, a fatal stabbing.

Darren Coulburn had been bullying and humiliating younger (first year) Bangladeshi boys. Ahmed had stepped in to stop him, challenging him to take on someone his own size, and thrashing him. Darren vowed that 'if that paki picks on me again, I'll kill him'. When, the following morning he and Ahmed met, no sooner had Ahmed got up to him than he plunged the knife into his stomach and said: 'take this, you stupid paki'. Then, half withdrawing the knife he thrust it into Ahmed's stomach again saying: 'you want it again, paki, there's plenty more where that came from'. He then proceeded to drop the knife down a drain and run to the upper school shouting, 'I've killed a paki. I've killed a paki'...; shouting, not to black students, but to any white students he encountered. He appeared to be seeking affirmation. They kill paki's don't they? What I did was ok, wasn't it?

It is obvious that Darren Coulburn was not born a racist murderer, unless of course one believes in the 'Damien' theory of reincarnation and the human life cycle. Racism is a learned thing. It is not inherited, even the children of the most rabid racists were not born racist.

The question that arises is how does a 13 year old white working class boy acquire the language and odium of racism, such that a black boy, identical in age, in the same year group, becomes nothing but an object of hatred, of such little worth that he could kill and announce the fact to the world with less compunction, one suspects, that he would have had were it a dog he had accidentally killed.

Darren Coulburn was socialized into a culture of racism throughout the thriteen years of his life before becoming a murderer. For him, racism was not an analytical tool or theoretical construct. It was very real. It had its manifestations in the way 'paki's' were treated in his community and in the society as a whole, and in the value he saw society placing on black lives.

The culture of racism was also manifest within the school as was the macho, white, English chauvinism, that he in turn sought to assert in his encounters with Bangladeshi students and Ahmed in particular.

The school, on the other hand, preened itself on the quality of its antiracist policy, but failed to demonstrate to black students that it took their lived experience of racism seriously enough to obviate the need for them to defend themselves against racial aggression.

Time and time again during the Macdonald Inquiry black students told us that they used to complain regularly to the school about bullying, name-calling, and general racist humiliation. Some teachers advised them to ignore the perpetrators and 'take no notice', others said 'leave it to me, I would deal with it', others warned them that if they dealt with it themselves they could get into serious trouble. The major and most frequent complaint from the students, however, was that *they never knew what action the school took* – if any.

The same two or three sympathetic teachers would reassure them, but if, according to the hierarchy and the division of responsibilities in the school, it depended upon a third party to take action on the basis of what the students had reported, the system seemed to gobble up and digest the complaint with nothing whatsoever being done to investigate the source of those complaints.

Students, effectively, had been telling the school: 'we are experiencing this school as an oppressive institution, the discrimination and oppressive acts we are experiencing are hurting us. This is not a safe and secure environment in which we can learn. We feel under threat. By your not taking action you are colluding with racism and leading the perpetrators to believe that what they are doing is acceptable and has the tacit approval of the school. You are not showing us that you value us as students in this school community'.

The school ignored the pain, the hurt, and the totally reasonable pleas of the black students for many years. Four years earlier another black student nearly lost his life when white students set upon him in an unprovoked attack in the school's careers library. The school failed to take notice and learn the lessons of that near fatal incident.

Against that historic background, it was unbelievable, but for witnessing it with our own eyes and ears, to hear a senior teacher with many years service in the school tell the inquiry panel that he was aware that the term 'paki' was widely used in name calling in the school, but that he saw nothing wrong with it, because as far as he was concerned it was an abbreviation of 'Pakistani'.

In other words, black students were complaining to the school about the oppressive and racist language, a language with which the culture of racism in the society had equipped white students. That teacher, a member of the school's senior management team, was unilaterally reconstructing the students' experience of racism into something which he found acceptable. Ahmed Ullah should have been able to say to that teacher in his capacity as an adult in the school, a teacher, and particularly a senior teacher: 'Darren Coulburn is calling us nasty names and bullying us, and he must be stopped', in the clear expectation that the teacher would take appropriate action. Ahmed was right to assume that as an adult living in Britain in the last 20 years, the teacher would know that 'paki' was a nasty word, and a term of racist abuse, that 'paki-bashing' was a murderous pastime engaged in by racists for their amusement, and that people from the sub-continent, from Sri Lanka, and elsewhere, were regularly attacked by racists in the streets and in their homes, that their places of worship were frequently desecrated, and their shop windows pelted with bricks.

As a student coming from a community in which those occurrences effectively placed him, and families such as his, under siege, Ahmed had a right to expect that his school would guarantee him a safe environment in which to learn and to socialize with his peers. It beggars belief, therefore, that nine months after his death, and after evidence was adduced at Darren Coulburn's trial for his murder, giving details of the racist utterances that punctuated the murderous deed, that that teacher could still sit in front of an investigating panel and say 'as far as I am concerned, paki is simply an abbreviation of Pakistani'.

Name-calling and Bullying in a Culture of Racism

When Ahmed Ullah was murdered, his friends at Burnage High School, his family and the black communities in Manchester had no difficulty in coming to the conclusion that his murder was racist. The media and many sections of the public, however, were equally quick to charge that black extremists were seeking to make political capital out of 'this very tragic event' which in their view was a case of bullying that had gone badly wrong.

Leaving aside the question: when does bullying ever go 'right', and for whom, that line of argument had much more to do with a stunned public and a hypocritical (and generally racist) media having difficulty in coming to terms with the harsh reality that a 13 year old student could stab to death another 13 year old because of the colour of his skin, than with any even superficial understanding of the nature of bullying.

On the day before he murdered Ahmed, Darren had lain in wait for a younger Bangladeshi student whom he had threatened to beat up simply because that boy and three other Asian boys had demanded that he give them back their ball. He had been in the habit of calling them 'paki' and humiliating them, and it was known that he disliked Asian children.

It is a well known fact that bullies choose as their victims those whom they perceive as being weaker than themselves, not simply in terms of physical strength but by virtue of the standing they believe members of a certain group to have in the society. The phenomenon of 'queer-bashing' is a particular case in point. People are thought to be vulnerable both because it is assumed that they are among society's undesirables for whom little sympathy is generated, and because bullies assume that they have moral if not physical superiority over them.

In a culture of racism such as that within which Darren

Coulburn and his peer group were socialized, Asians are already socially and culturally constructed as unwanted, unacceptable, intolerable, docile and ready targets for racist attacks. Darren's bullying, like his name-calling, is racially constructed, and is therefore on a continuum with all those other societal acts, which set aside 'paki' in his eyes.

Having premeditated and then stabbed Ahmed, he did not wait to see whether or not Ahmed would be taken off to hospital and given a chance to survive, he ran off proclaiming, 'I've killed a paki'.

To fail to contextualize name-calling and bullying, is to suggest that they do not assume varying gradations of seriousness, and that it is the gloss placed upon all those dangerous practices by onlookers or third parties that is important – rather than the purpose and intent of the perpetrator, and the pain and damage caused to the victim.

Having failed to address the issues as the school's management, and individual teachers, when calamity dawned in the face of its well-crafted antiracist policy, Burnage High School heaped a great deal of collective guilt and suffering upon the white students in the school, and placed the deep friendships and mutual solidarity between some of them and their black peers under considerable strain.

How Does Your School Match up?

I want to make two more essential points, and to develop them briefly. The first is that however crass you may think the organizational culture of Burnage High School was, Burnage is not particularly weird or extraordinary. The constellation of circumstances, characters and events may be peculiar, but there is potential tragedy waiting to happen in any school.

What you need to ask yourself, therefore, is this: Is conformity by coercion enough to safeguard vulnerable black students from such physical racist attacks? How can you be satisfied that those white students who conform to the school's code of conduct while on campus, would not be disposed to joining others, including organized groups of racists, in attacking blacks in their communities? Would you see that as your concern, or would you, like the then headteacher at Burnage School, seek to distance the school from such activity on the grounds that it is taking place outside school hours and away from the school's premises?

If indeed the antecedents of the poor self-esteem of white students, such as Darren Coulburn, include not just their socialization into a culture of racism, but also their view of blacks as denying them a 'place', and as not 'belonging', how does the school begin to tackle that? Similarly, what should the school do about the deep sense of inferiority and resentment that so many young white male students feel as they match themselves up against young blacks?

With the resurgence of fascism in society, especially in the East End of London, it is conceivable that our schools would be called upon to educate the children of professed racists and fascist activists. What challenges do you see that posing for teachers, especially allowing that the children of such people are likely to be encouraged to attempt to win the minds and hearts of other students, and to undermine teachers' or school practices which they perceive as pandering to 'the blacks' and their cultural or religious preferences?

My next point is about your school itself as a source of institutionalized and/or indirect forms of racism, and of racial violence in its psychological form. How do you know that your staff, or indeed your students, are not experiencing your school as a racist institution?

My experience over the years, in different management positions and as a social analyst, in positions where I could assess the capabilities and the performance of white managers and white frontline staff, and as a consequence see how blacks are treated at all levels within majority white situations, confirms to me that we live in a society which validates white people automatically, and which is forever requiring black people to prove themselves.

Excellence in performance, integrity in the conduct of professional and social affairs on the part of whites are seen as the confirmation or fulfilment of society's normal expectations. In the case of blacks, they are seen as a cause for celebration and a source of amazement. Conversely, mediocrity, incompetence, bungling, a lack of commitment, or sheer laziness on the part of whites are seen as part of the flotsam and jetsam of daily living, irritating perhaps but not characteristic or extraordinary.

In the case of blacks, they are seen as characteristic, as conforming to expectations, and as virtually inevitable if not totally so.

That form of validation on the one hand, and pathologizing and racial stereotyping on the other, runs deep in the psyche and cultural consciousness of the nation, and invariably determines the quality of the experiences we as black people have in our day to day work and our day to day living.

Let us take, for example, overseas teachers. What does that connote for us? How many of us automatically have visions of New Zealanders and Australians when overseas teachers are mentioned? Is it not the case that what immediately comes rushing to mind are black teachers without qualified teacher status and with a track record some of us would sooner forget?

New Zealanders and Australians have been given unlimited entry by the immigration authorities for some years now on six-month contracts. They have been used widely in ILEA and post-ILEA schools. The prevailing attitude towards them is, and has always been, that of 'kith and kin' sojourning in far away places but fundamentally 'belonging to us'.

Headteachers could rest assured that white parents are most unlikely to raise doubts about their capacity to teach their children and to hand on the right values, traditions, etc. The notion of 'white overseas teachers' came to be seen almost as a contradiction in terms.

As far as black overseas teachers were concerned, it was an entirely different picture. A large number of those teachers were recruited by the ILEA and deployed in schools as unqualified teachers, instructors or supply teachers. They appeared to receive very little induction, and the identification of their training and support needs, backed up by action to meet those needs was totally idiosyncratic. It appeared to depend on the predisposition of an individual headteacher, inspector, or officer within the divisional education office.

Consequently, most of those teachers found themselves filling gaps, working in situations to which they were entirely unsuited, and having precious little scope for professional development. Without proper mechanisms for assessing their capabilities, headteachers simply gave impressionistic accounts of their performance, invariably unflattering accounts, often affected by parental comments, in response to which the teachers would be moved, only to have that same experience repeated all over again. And the whole sorry mess did a disservice to all the children and no doubt increased racist opinions in the minds of some.

Inevitably, they came to be seen as teachers who could not teach, or could not control a class, or who did not understand, or could not be depended upon to apply the National Curriculum. Rather than demanding a concerted effort to put in place remedial action, headteachers simply took steps to protect their schools and to warn their colleagues. Soon enough, a rich and professionally damaging folklore developed in relation to those teachers who became known 'on the circuit'.

Come the Local Management of Schools, and the critical issue of determining who was, and who was not, on the schools' teaching establishment, many of those teachers found themselves displaced and surplus to requirements. In Hackney, black overseas teachers constitute the majority of teachers who have been identified as being above authorized numbers (TAANS), and feel quite justifiably that they have been dealt a major injustice by the ILEA and by individual schools.

I would be most surprised if you did not have in your schools white teachers whose general capability, classroom management and quality of teaching gave you cause for concern. In fact it would be virtually impossible for that not to be the case. I don't have white parents clamouring about their concerns for their children's education at the hands of those teachers, nor, to my knowledge, are they the subject of headteacher gossip or discussions 'on the circuit'.

That is a form of validation which, if we are not careful, becomes its own justification, leading you to defend the indefensible.

It is against that background that our initial attempts to place the group of teachers recruited from Trinidad in 1990 were so problematic. Firstly, the government decided that by virtue of having two rather than three years full-time initial teacher training they could not be classified as qualified. As a result, teachers whose classroom practice outshone that of many of their colleagues, including their mentors', and who had more years of teaching experience than a great number of them, were given the status of unqualified teachers and were required to teach under license for two years while they studied to acquire Qualified Teacher Status.

The fact that the LEA chose not to acknowledge their many years of teaching experience and reward them accordingly, created many tensions, not least of all among those who equated their 'unqualified' status with that of those other 'overseas' teachers and harboured equally negative expectations as regards their capability.

Notions of 'overseas' meaning backward, behind the times, learning by rote and generally unprogressive, still linger on in the minds of headteachers, however. As an example, in the same period that a furious debate is raging in the country about reading and literacy, about number and the development of concepts of numeracy, in primary age children, some Trinidad teachers are being debarred by their headteachers from using teaching methods which clearly work for children and which, far from being wrong or unsound in themselves, simply offend against the current rigid and stubborn orthodoxy.

The irony of it all is that those same Trinidadian teachers, who came here with their families, worry daily about the evident regression in their children's educational progress, and work with them consistently to ensure that they are performing to their abilities.

The Trinidadian teachers would be the first to admit that through the induction the LEA provided for them, the work on the Licensed Teachers Scheme, and their own classroom practice, they have learnt a great deal about the British schooling system, its strengths and its weaknesses. That has enabled them to develop a healthy eclecticism, combining the best of British teaching methods with the well tried and highly successful methods that characterized their teaching and made them such excellent teachers in Trinidad, with the highest standards of education and educational success for their students in that country.

They would have welcomed an open and healthy debate about pedagogy, about unstated and therefore unchallenged assumptions with regard their pedagogical skills, about teacher expectations and the expectations they encourage students to have of themselves, and about school/home liaison, during the course of the last three years, as I am sure they would welcome it now.

However, on the contrary, without any such sharing of perspectives and approaches to teaching and to children's learning, headteachers are telling those highly experienced teachers that they should not use the chalk board, that 'we do not teach reading here', that 'the formal teaching of hand writing simply isn't on', that 'parents are complaining because children are being given too much homework, and you're already working the kids hard enough at school'.

Is it so inconceivable to think of Hackney schools collectively using 45 primary teachers from Trinidad, as a resource to interrogate systematically issues around the quality of primary teacher training in Britain, and primary students' learning in Hackney?

Had those teachers been from Australia and doing equally successfully in Hackney schools, would there not be any number of seminars in Hackney, at the Institute of Education and elsewhere, considering comparative methods, the experience of the English classroom, etc?

What status, then, do you afford the black staff in your institution? How in your opinion do white staff, students, and parents, black and white, perceive those staff, and what is the extent to which you value them? What subtle messages are sent out to students about cohesiveness of the staff group as far as tackling racism and racial incidents is concerned?

Where black teachers are performing commendably well and bringing a repertoire of teaching skills and a wealth of experience to the organization and delivery of the curriculum, and to school/home liaison, is that acknowledged, and are those staff given opportunities to disseminate good practice among other colleagues? Do you even indicate that you can learn or have learnt anything from them?

And again, lest you are wondering what the relevance of this is, it is a well known fact that racism flourishes in certain environments much more than others. The ethos of an institution, and the extent to which it is seen to value or oppress those whom others are predisposed to harassing and oppressing, is often a powerful determinant of the levels of racism and racial violence within that institution.

This is as true of the British State and the resurgence of racism and fascism in this society, in the last three decades, as it is of a school or college.

Conclusion

I chose quite deliberately to interpret my brief not as providing you with a bag of tricks so you could feel more secure in dealing with racism, violence and bullying in your schools, nor as meaning that racism, violence and bullying reside only with, or are perpetuated solely by, the students of your institution, whether directed towards other students or towards staff.

Each school needs to ask itself: what sort of institution am I? What position(s) exist among the staff on the issue of racist ideology and its relationship to social policy, institutional structures and practices, and individual acts and experiences?

How do the black staff and students experience the institution, and me as a manager?

What is our approach to the curriculum in respect of racist beliefs and practices among students?

One approach, recommended by Lord Elton as late as 1989, was that of winning respect and tolerance from whites for blacks by providing them with evidence of the achievements of the blacks:

It seems clear that racist attitudes among pupils can lead to anything from name calling to assaults resulting in serious injury or even death.

Schools must counter these attitudes. Head-on confrontation is likely to be counter-productive. It may alienate as many pupils as it wins over. We believe that using the curriculum to emphasize the importance of tolerance and respect for other cultures are a more productive approach. A variety of subjects can be used to point out the achievements of different cultures. Where possible these achievements should be linked to cultures represented in the school as well as to the principle of mutual respect in the school's behaviour policy.

(Elton, 1989)

This is based upon the totally dodgy premise that people who are ill disposed towards blacks for a variety of complex reasons would grow in tolerance and respect for them simply by being fed new information. But it also begs the question: which 'other cultures', or cultures other than what? Other than unified, homogenous white British culture? If so, where is that to be found? Who and what is the embodiment of it?

As we observed in the Burnage Report:

After hearing the evidence of the Parents' English Education Rights (PEER) group of parents in Manchester, one gets the sense of white working class parents who have little basis on which to root their own experience as English working class and who, therefore, react angrily and resentfully to a school which, in sharp contrast to their experience, caters directly for the needs and preferences of Asian students, thus indicating the extent to which they and their culture are valued.

(Macdonald et al., 1989)

A balance clearly needs to be struck between:

- taking sanctions against a student involved in racial harassment or racial attacks in order both to deter others and to reassure victims and would be victims that the school would always deal with such matters promptly and robustly, and
- dealing with the context and motivation of the attack in a manner that addresses the realities of that student, if only to understand the wider influences that may be giving rise to their conduct.

I am firmly of the view that schools need to engage all students in a whole school approach to these issues, and, in secondary schools especially, seek to involve students in the formulation and operation of management strategies to tackle them both proactively and in response to specific incidents.

Whether or not there is a functional Students Council within the school, the school would need to invest some quality time, human and financial resources in working with the student body to arrive at a set of commonly agreed strategies and procedures, being careful to delineate where the management/student initiatives exhaust their mandate, and where the legal and statutory powers of the governing body come into play.

In so far as the activities of individual students or groups of them contribute significantly to the ethos and character of the school, students must be encouraged to take ownership of the problems and conflicts that arise, and to work in tandem with the school's management to recover a situation or improve the school's ethos. For one thing, that will provide a much needed opportunity for discussion, learning, and planning as the principal players within the school determine effective approaches to combating racism and devise appropriate methods for communicating them to the body of students and parents.

At the very least, it must be crystal clear both to perpetrators and victims what the school would do in response to any given situation, and in response to the reporting of incidents of verbal or physical abuse. The expectations that students could have of teachers, or non-teaching staff and helpers, and vice versa, and that students could have of one another, must be clearly stated.

Effectively, therefore, the whole community of staff, students and parents should contract into the school's agreed plan, and should receive termly or twice yearly reports on the operation of the plan. It is important to encourage the involvement of parents to ensure that they are working to the same agenda as the school, and are committed to exercising a degree of responsibility for students' development in the home, and their out of school activities, alerting the school as necessary if they feel problems are arising at home or in the context of the students' activities in the neighbourhood. This is especially important for parents who may be concerned that their children are coming under the influence of local facists and racists or are hanging around with groups that harass black people.

Finally, let me say that many of the issues which I have barely touched upon in this paper are explored in much fuller detail in the Burnage Report, 'Murder in the Playground'. That book, although published in 1989, is arguably still the most authoritative single text on racism, racial violence, and effective school management. I would urge you to read it and make it your very own document for in-service education and training (INSET), planning and the sharing of ideas.

If, indeed, we are entrusted with the care of the present, so that our children could inherit and take care of a future, then, as schools and educators, we have a responsibility to ensure that we do not simply leave young people to be impacted upon by the forces of racism and fascism in the society, but provide them with the tools with which to combat those odious forms of oppression. We won't succeed, however, if we ourselves are not seen to be leading by example – not just by paper policies.

As an LEA, we have come a very long way since April 1990 and since our first conference. We have had a year on year percentage increase in our attendance levels, in the number of students being entered for public examinations and in the number receiving A–C and A–G grades at GCSE, and high grades in 'A' levels and progressing to university.

Within the limits of the resources available to us we have efficiently stabilized your budgets and are exploiting to the full the inward investment opportunities available within the authority. The LMS process and its funding regime hold no new surprises for you, and I am confident that as you approach full delegation your management capacity will more than match the tasks ahead.

From that much more footsure base, therefore, I have no doubt that we can begin to tackle racism, racial violence and bullying in our schools more robustly in pursuit of an education of high quality with equality.

To this end, let us set an agenda for now and towards the year 2000.

ANTIRACIST EDUCATION IN WHITE AREAS:
'A Movement in Search of a Focus'
National Antiracist Movement in Education (NAME) Conference
14-16 April 1987

The task I have been given in summing up this conference is to provide 'some key themes and ideas for progress in white areas', as the conference programme states.

Before I do that, I feel it necessary, first, to explore some definitions and to state what I believe to be the assumptions underlying the concern for or commitment to antiracist education in white areas.

Second, I wish to say what I believe to be the nature of education *'per se'* in white areas and, therefore, what it is that needs to be addressed, how, and by whom.

Third, I will demonstrate that the setting up of a hierarchy of oppressions which need to be prioritized in approaches to curriculum change or structural changes within education and schooling as a whole, as is indicated by various equal opportunity policies, is as damaging as it is diversionary and divisive.

Finally, I give some examples of the sorts of activities I consider to be necessary and appropriate to confronting educational practice and the structural underpinnings of that practice in white areas.

By then, I hope that the reasons for my choice of a title for this talk, 'A MOVEMENT IN SEARCH OF A FOCUS' will have become obvious.

Let us turn to the notion of antiracist education in white areas. I assume that this refers to the application of a range of strategies to combat racism in all sectors of the education service, primary, secondary and tertiary, in localities or educational institutions with few, if any, black people. Another, unstated but nevertheless implicit, assumption is that antiracist education as a philosophy to which folk subscribe, and as a practice, is alive and well, or at least is positioned firmly on the map in institutions and localities with a greater or lesser black population.

'White areas' are seen as spatial locations having a particular character because of the absence of blacks. And precisely because of such absence, it is assumed that introducing notions of antiracist education is an up-hill and hazardous task for those with the temerity to attempt it. This, of course, is not just an assumption but a lived experience for many individuals.

Two things are worth remembering about all this. The first is that because of the progress made in challenging racist education providers, structures, and practices in the inner cities, we tend to forget that not so long ago it mattered not one jot whether you were in a black area, a mixed area, or an all white area. The colour and thrust of education and schooling were the same – white and eurocentric, so that black people and progressive whites in so-called 'black' areas were challenging white power structures both within the local state, and inside of education and schooling. The same struggle continues today in the majority of our inner cities and towns. Many local authorities and their staff have had their race awareness training, they've acquired the language of antiracism and can now play the antiracist game with commendable political adroitness – not one thing has changed except perhaps some more jobs for a larger number of black people and for some whites who could now use their antiracist credentials in aspiring to higher positions.

To sum up this first point, then, for 'white areas' you could easily read 'white power structures' or 'white run, white led institutions'.

My second 'thing to remember' is that those white power

structures and white led institutions within the local state machinery in the inner cities and provincial towns have shifted, however little and however cynical the reasons for the shift, because of the black working class movement in education and because of black struggle in the political arena generally. That movement, those struggles, have made these institutions more accountable to the black masses and more responsive to the struggles which black students themselves have waged and are waging within schools and colleges.

The impetus for the struggles inside schools and other educational institutions arises from the political gains the black working class have made within our communities. Those gains and the struggles from which they arise create space for teachers, black and white, multiculturalist and antiracist, to challenge systems, reform curriculum and seek to alter the culture of the school or college.

The question then is, in the absence of those forces impacting upon the system in white areas, who cares, and why should they care?

But before we are lulled into feelings of satisfaction about the choice of antiracist education in white areas as a legitimate concern, let us pause and examine how far we've got with antiracist education in mixed or black areas.

Antiracist education has done nothing to stem the tide of excessive numbers of black school students suspended from schools or spending extraordinary lengths of time in sin-bins or standing in corridors. It has not influenced the rate of under-achievement by black students in the schooling system, nor enhanced their prospects within education or within the labour market more generally. It may well have sanitized or be sanitizing the education system of racism, ensuring that children, black and white, don't get a racist education.

However, it does not seem to be able to guarantee that they receive *an education* as a fundamental human right. Even in those antiracist schools which serve as flagships for their local education authorities and their antiracist policies, 'education for some' remains the reality, if not the guiding principle, and structures, cleansed of all racism, operate effectively to guarantee that.

I return to the second of my four main points, the nature of education '*per se*' in white areas.

The black working class is located within Britain's political and economic relations and in British social history first and foremost through labour. Our relationship to labour and capital constitutes us as a class, a fraction of the working class.

The British state employs 'race' as a justification for denying blacks equal access to political rights and to material and other resources. The black working class movement in education has been about not simply confronting racism, but ensuring that the education system did not, and does not, oppress and disadvantage blacks because of class location. We struggle, therefore, on an axis of class as well as of 'race'. And while the British state and British social and ideological relations have placed the racialization of our oppression very high on the political agenda, black parents particularly have been concerned that the schooling and education system should not re-colonize our children as a pliant and subordinate labour force within the society. It is for those reasons, I suggest, that an increasing number of working class black parents without classical 'petit bourgeois' allegiances are finding fee paying schools in the white highlands, in 'allwhite areas', to send their children to. Such parents are firm in their belief that even if they turned their backs on the antiracist education in the inner city, their children would survive racism and be guaranteed the sort of education that does not add to their oppression because of their class.

They are therefore prepared to buy in, literally, to an education system trading in racist beliefs, notions of white cultural supremacy, the glories of imperialism, the values of a capitalist economy, and all the rest, and encourage their children to turn a blind eye to assaults on their dignity, their identity and their person on the grounds that such things 'can't break your bones' and that those indignities, in addition to the fees, is the price you have to pay for a 'good education' and for the privilege to be able to 'compete with the best of them' in the big wide shrinking world.

Education and schooling in white areas, regardless of whether such areas are working class or middle class, has never concerned itself with the way working class people, and particularly women, are disadvantaged within, by and through education and schooling. It performs a specific function *vis-à-vis* labour and capital and therefore *vis-à-vis* the working class. It has always produced those who would rule and lead and constrain the opportunities and life chances of the working class majority. That working class has always been predominantly white and living in situations spatially and geographically distanced from the rulers.

No headteacher, governing board, nor parent of a student in an all white area should therefore be expected to give a monkey's toss about the fact that with increased mobility students in Chichester might well end up managing a black or multiracial workforce in Birmingham, and that they should therefore be preparing for that eventuality.

To seek to begin with antiracism in all white or mostly white areas, therefore, is often to risk having otherwise sober minded colleagues screaming to have you certified or at best sent on sabbatical or to the doctor to rid you of the virus, particularly after conferences such as this.

In most of those situations there is a high degree of fit between the culture and practices of the educational institution, the beliefs and aspirations of parents and community interests, and their perceptions of the way the dominant culture reflects reality within the society. The curriculum content, the educational practices and structures, the dominant values to which this tripartite partnership gives rise is seen as inevitable, functional and pre-ordained, if not totally necessary to the continuation of the society as they know it.

Whether the white areas concerned are rural, urban, industrial or semi-industrial, there is no evidence of a movement among whites, similar to the black working class movement in education, that is posing any form of challenge to such oppressive education.

The schooling and education system in such areas not only feed upon that rich racist heritage of British history and contemporary socio-political relations that this country provides, it obliterates the historical struggles of women and of the working class, it defaces and denies the culture born of those struggles, and presents a view of knowledge, of culture, and of what is desirable and legitimate which is constructed in the mould of sexist, racist, elitist, colonialist and supremacist white power structures.

Such education is both imperialist and colonialist in the context of labour, capital and national identity. And it is within that framework that the activities of blacks and progressive whites in combating racism is seen.

My contention is, therefore, that in the context of white areas, a movement for change in education has to focus upon attempts to transform the current system into a genuine 'education for liberation', that sees education as a basic and fundamental right for all. It is not a privilege that can be bought or that is dependent upon age, sex, ethnic origin or economic or social status. One's access to it should not be dependent upon your ability to manipulate the property market or use your wealth and social standing.

Moreover, it needs to be seen as a process through which people are empowered and enabled as groups and individuals to take control over their own lives.

Attention needs to be paid, therefore, to identifying, enabling and working with or alongside those oppressed groups in white areas who are being disadvantaged and rendered powerless by the system of education and schooling. The more such groups fail to activate themselves on the question of education in relation to their own condition, the more they acquiesce not only in their own oppression but in that of others. Moreover, their inactivity in itself encourages those who feel they occupy the ideological highground to target the blacks and the antiracists and vilify them for demanding too much, acting 'above their station', or as representing a threat to educational standards or to the very fabric of the society itself (cf. Ray Honeyford, in Bradford, BBC Panorama on Brent, etc.).

This brings me to my third point, i.e. the establishing of a hierarchy of oppressions.

If we accept the notion of the racialization of oppression, if we accept that 'race' is not a scientific concept and that racism operates in society to the detriment of us all, then we need to place the oppression that other groups within society suffer and have suffered historically in proper relation to the very fight against racism. This suggests that the fight against racism could be better served in a number of respects by other groups confronting the system in relation to their own felt discrimination and systematic oppression, and pointing up the extent to which the fertile ground on which the roots of their own oppression flourish is the same ground that spawns such virulent strains of racism.

If we accept then that the 'class' is not homogeneous and never has been, and that fractions within the class include those oppressed groups whose social movement has precipitated change in the structure of class relations within the society, we therefore have a responsibility to locate 'race' in education within the wider context of the purpose and functions of education and schooling in relation to 'class'.

The focus should therefore be laying bare the various forms of oppression orchestrated by and through the schooling and education system for well over one hundred years and acting separately and together to combat those oppressions and put an end to such systematic and institutionalized oppression.

Finally, a word about strategies.

The question 'What does all this mean for me in my particular situation?' is already buzzing around the room. It seems to me that whoever you are and wherever you may be located within the system of education and schooling, whether as parent, teacher, line-manager, governor or student, you have some power you can use to begin to effect the sort of change I am suggesting as necessary.

Whether it be in educational work in white areas or in other areas, we are asked to operate structures which underpin oppression and contribute to the denial of space and of power to those whom education should empower. We need to examine the precise ways in which this occurs and begin to unlock that system, using those very people as allies.

If one is operating a system that contributes to the denial of respect and status for white working class people, their culture and their traditions, or for white women students and parents, then you can only ask them to share your zeal for promoting antiracism if you believe that to be intrinsically good for their souls.

It is not axiomatic that racism is evil and that it hurts and in too many cases actually kills people. Racism functions very well for the majority of people in this country, and they have an amazing capacity to indulge it and live with it as a society.

Antiracist education, or rather de-racialized education, does not, by itself, constitute education for human liberation, and, as such, it need not have anything to do with human liberation, let alone the transition to socialism.

If there are no blacks in the institutions in white areas, then it does mean that apart from challenging how, in certain cases, the structures and racist culture of those institutions might operate to exclude blacks, you need to be active in your concern for how those structures oppress others within the institution. I suggest that if more of that sort of challenge and organised activity were evident, the task of challenging racism would not appear to be such a lunatic activity.

Having talked about structures, a brief word about curriculum. Because the curriculum is inevitably racist, colonialist and supremacist as well as being sexist and heterosexist in the areas we're discussing, it means that ample opportunities exist to confront that curriculum. Examples of this in relation to history, geography, humanities, etc. are now fairly commonplace. Numerous other examples suggest themselves, like science, new technology, media and communication studies, music, etc. The work of the Association for Curriculum Development in Science, the Antiracist Strategies Team of the Inner London Education Authority (ILEA), and a number of other similar bodies around the country, provide ample evidence of what needs to be done and can be done.

We as black people waged long struggles against colonialist and neo-colonialist education in our countries. We are in the vanguard of the struggle against racist education here in Britain. But the colonialist nature of that education must not be forgotten. It is an education that seeks to recolonize us on the twin axes of race and class within the political and economic relations of British capitalism.

Until the white working class, and until women as a class fraction, activate themselves in their essential movement as a force in history confronting the oppression they face in and through the education system, antiracist activity in white areas will remain marginalized and risky, and the education which is thought to be uncontaminated by nasties such as multiculturalism and antiracism in such areas will continue to be colonialist, sexist, and oppressive.

Before I conclude, permit me to say a brief word about ourselves as blacks. We seem to spend so much time talking, to, with, or about white people, or posturing for their benefit on matters to do with race and antiracism; the whole system has got us so caught up in this activity that we begin to assume the existence of some sort of a consensus amongst ourselves on all the above issues *based on our being black.*

More importantly still, we seem to have lost the capacity to talk amongst ourselves, by ourselves, to and about ourselves in an open and democratic manner, and, above all, with respect for one another. Such debate is essential to the building of an anti-autocratic, anti-authoritarian democratic society, as well as being essential to the task of clarifying for ourselves how and where our particular historic experience of oppression and racism as black and working class people intersects with the oppression faced by other groups within the society, and where our responsibilities lie, now.

This task is as critical as it is urgent. And if we were to put half the time into learning to talk with and listen to one another in free, open and democratic discourse that we put into leading the thinking of white folk, or operating the structures into which we are incorporated on the race ticket, our struggle would be considerably more advanced.

One assumption with which most white people begin and end is that blacks know and have the answers. And while we're busily buying into that and seeking to provide those answers (or add to the confusion as the case may be), we neglect to recognize that there are a range of ideological positions, class aspirations and a host of other tendencies amongst us as amongst any other section of the community.

And while our common experience of racism might presuppose a universal commitment amongst us to combat racism, how we approach that task is determined largely by those tendencies and ideological positions, on the question of race, of class struggle, of oppression, and of whether or not we believe that the task of eradicating racism is something which can be accomplished by blacks and/or whites in isolation from the struggle for human liberation and against class oppression.

Until such time that we confront such issues, however much we continue, as we must, to take action within our particular situations and based upon our particular tendencies, we mislead others and confuse ourselves by seeking to provide a 'black perspective'.

For this reason, and this is my very last point, I am suspicious of the impatience of those people who decry open discussion ('jaw, jaw', 'talking shop', etc.) and want to spur us into action before we know who it is we're taking action with, never mind what it is we agree about.

In this paper I have kept to the brief of 'setting out key themes and ideas for progress in white areas'. Those of you expecting to go away with a package of antiracist prescriptions to apply after Easter must look elsewhere.

ANTIRACIST EDUCATION
A movement for change in education and schooling
Manchester
1985

I have chosen to give this title to this discussion paper for two reasons.

One is that I firmly believe that an antiracist approach to education and schooling is essential to the future of education in Britain, not least in terms of assisting Britain in understanding itself and the role of antiracist education in helping it transform itself. The second reason is that there is so much ground to be made up that antiracist education should not be seen as an esoteric project that the zealous could pursue if they wish, while the rest (the policymakers, practitioners and learners) get on with 'the real business of teaching and learning'.

Let me begin by sharing a couple of quotations:

From the period of post-colonial struggle in the Punjab, in Pakistan, in Gujarat, in East Africa and in the Caribbean, we [as black parents] brought with us two distinct attitudes to education. One, that it was a way out of slavery, a step or stirrup to mount the wage differential. Two, that education has something to do with culture, with identity, and so with strength. We were right, 'education' has both potentials, but schooling in Britain is an institutional system which for us has very little to do with either.
... The problems of black people are neither themselves nor white people. The problem of schools does not lie in their percentages [i.e., the ratio of black to white pupils], but in their functions at the junction of labour and capital. Different communities display differing potentials

in their ability and willingness to challenge these functions

(Dhondy, Beese, and Hassan, 1983)

The purpose of flagging these quotations at the head of a discussion paper on antiracism is not to focus on blacks as the *'sine qua non'* of any debate on antiracism, or as victims, or indeed as the cause of the crisis in British education in the last two decades. Rather, it is to highlight the contribution made by black school students and black communities in Britain to a radical examination of the functions and purposes of schooling *'per se'*.

One of the important tasks black people have performed historically, in our colonial enclaves at home, and particularly here at the very heart of British society, is that of interpreting Britain to itself, thereby demonstrating the nature of its institutions, of its cultural assumptions, and of its economic and social relations. Our experience at the receiving end of those institutional arrangements and practices has enabled us to understand and challenge them, and to seek to build the alternative forms necessary for our own survival and the task of humanizing the society.

One of the first, basic, truths we learned was that Britain was not a homogenous society, unified in terms of class, history, and political and economic relations, with a predominantly white population seeking to advance its collective interests by exploiting blacks wherever its jurisdiction over them extended. In other words, British society as a whole may have benefited in one way or another from the imperialist and colonialist exploits of the builders of the Empire. Nevertheless, those gains were very unevenly distributed and ensured the ascendancy of one social class or several classes over the majority British working class.

An ideology of racism developed commensurate with the growth of mercantile capitalism in Europe, and the British working class themselves, in shaping their identity 'as British' and inculcating a sense of Britishness were nurtured like everyone else in the society on that ideology of racism. Even as they struggled to build a workers' movement and win some control over the production process, and over their lives and the fruits of their labour, they, for the most part, saw it as right and proper that the blacks in the colonies should provide, under the colonial yoke, the very stuff that guaranteed them a thriving industrial base in the major cities and towns of Great Britain. There have been, therefore, three dynamic factors at work in British social, political and economic relations, those of race, class, and gender.

Gender is now nudging race in the centre stage of British politics, largely as a result of the persistent struggles waged by women themselves. 'Race' has occupied the centre of the stage for decades if only because through a process of crude reductionism, the internal malaise in the body politic in the post-war period has been explained in terms of the black presence. Race problems came to be equated with the presence of blacks. Conversely, the absence of blacks in any part of these islands was, and still is, taken to imply that a problem of racism does not exist. Does not exist, that is, for as long as the blacks keep out. Once they begin to appear, racism suddenly gains expression and the blacks are more likely than not to experience it in a whole variety of forms, from the subtle, benign and ever so polite variety, to the 'in your face', direct and aggressive.

Class as a feature of social stratification in British society, which like 'God', many might try to argue is now dead, has yet to be included as a key feature of British social relations, and as an issue in society's response to black people.

At best, race and class are conflated in more or less the same way that many now seek to conflate race and gender. At worst, class is seen as irrelevant, and as a consideration that serves only to confuse further the issue of 'race relations'.

Underlying the best part of the 'race' debate in the last three decades, therefore, has been the assumption that blacks have entered a political arena in which institutions are structured to function for the good of everyone, where there are no competing interests, and where the ideology of the state and its institutions embody and reflect the commonly shared values of an undifferentiated mass of the population. As Stuart Hall observed as early as 1978:

*There is ... an overwhelming tendency to abstract questions of race
from what one might call their internal social and political basis and
contexts in British society – that is to say, to deal with 'race' as if it has
nothing intrinsically to do with the present 'condition of England'. It's
viewed rather as an external problem which has been foisted to some
extent on English society from the outside it's been visited on us, as it
were, from the skies ...*

*Racism is not [considered to be] endemic to the British social
formation. It has nothing intrinsically to do with the dynamic of
British politics, or with the economic crisis. It is not part of the English
culture, which now has to be protected against pollution – it does not
belong to the 'English ideology'. It's an external virus somehow
injected into the body politic and it's a matter of policy whether we can
deal with it or not – it's not a matter of politics*

(Hall, 'Racism and Reaction', 1978)

The body politic, of course, apart from being steeped in an
ideology of racism is also characterized by class divisions and
class conflict. There is no undifferentiated mass. The dominant
values of the society are not shared by, nor do they reflect the
lived experience and the aspirations of the majority of the
population. Consensus and social cohesion are guaranteed by
coercion. The institutions of the state are part and parcel of that
coercive process.

In this context, then, notions of 'equality of opportunity', of 'a
free society' and especially of 'the British way of life' are both
grossly misleading and highly suspect. When policymakers set
a goal of ensuring 'equal opportunity' for blacks, it is being
implied that the 'rest' already have and do utilize equal
opportunity. Blacks, on the other hand, are debarred from doing
so by virtue of their 'race'. It clearly is the case that black people
suffer racism and are discriminated against on account of 'race'.
Nevertheless, the fact that competition and selection are quite
often presented as processes for guaranteeing equality of access,
and only marginally have anything to do with 'opportunity', is
often missed both by policymakers and black people
themselves.

Black people have a responsibility to enquire as to the

function of the state and its various institutions and systems, *vis-à-vis* the population as a whole, and specifically in relation to the working class, prior to the post-war black presence. To fail to do that is to internalize the definition of 'the problem of race relations' as something for which we are primarily responsible and, as such, must be seen to be rectifying ourselves.

It seems nonsensical, for example, to question the fact of massive black underachievement in the education and schooling system, and to suggest that one remedy might be to train and employ more black teachers, without stopping to clarify the function and purpose of schooling in Britain prior to the post-war black presence. The fact that the workers employed to assist the school in fulfilling its purpose are black, does not in itself alter the main functions of the institution of schooling.

Most people find the argument that calls for such an enquiry as to function and purpose *vis-à-vis* the British police convincing enough. Yet, many are reluctant to ask the same questions in relation to the function of education and schooling, of social work and of youth work. In other words, what in the context of British social history and the class structure of British society, has been the function of the police and the criminal justice system, and of social welfare *vis-à-vis* the British working class?

Assuming that one accepts that 'English ideology' and the notion of what it is to be British is imbued with racist ideology, and that the state and its institutional framework, legislative and administrative, projects blacks as a 'pollutant' to be excised or at least treated and sanitized; assuming, further, that one accepts that the majority of black people were ascribed working class status in this society and were expected to accept and abide by the same standards as the white working class had done for generations, is it any wonder that the education system, operating on a nexus of 'race' and 'class' would severely underdevelop and disadvantage black young people?

Few readers would contest the argument that education transmits and reflects society's values. What has that meant specifically in relation to race? What has it meant in those parts of Britain where there is no black presence?

Although teacher training institutions, education departments, school inspectors and headteachers still operate for the most part in ways which suggest that education takes place in ideologically neutral spaces, successive education ministers have demonstrated quite clearly, not only that education and schooling are subject to widespread political interference and executive direction, but that what goes on in schools and other educational establishments must be geared to serving the needs of the economy as defined by that executive.

From Shirley Williams and James Callaghan, through to Rhodes Boyson, Keith Joseph and Margaret Thatcher, all have been unapologetically upfront on this issue. All, in one way or another, have given credence to the view of schools as commodity producing factories in the capitalist economy. What the schools fail to produce, despite the Raising of the School Leaving Age, or what the labour market fails to absorb through programmed unemployment as a main plank of the present Government's economic strategy, the Manpower Services Commission (MSC) is primed to work upon as a tertiary commodity producing factory complex.

As early as 1975, Crowther-Hunt, then Minister of State at the Department of Education and Science, emphasized the necessity of 'man-power planning'. 'Man-power planning', he said, 'was already established in medical schools, where places are limited to estimates of the country's future need for doctors, even though hundreds of students wanting medical courses have to be turned away every year'. The burden of Crowther-Hunt's thesis was that the output of manpower from the educational institutions must be subject to firmer direction and tighter control from the state which operates education on behalf of employers. As Teachers' Action Collective observed at the time:

The Minister was merely trying to accelerate the already planned productivity of the schooling process. He was saying that with the expansion of state intervention in the whole productive and reproductive process of society, the schooling industry which produces skilled, graded and disciplined manpower, must be subject to the strictest cost-effectiveness considerations.

(Teachers and the Economy, Teachers Action Collective, 1976)

Some ten years on, Keith Joseph took the cost-effectiveness model to its logical conclusion and warned of his intention to reward the productivity of teachers within the 'planned productivity of the schooling process'.

The shutting down of whole University and Polytechnic departments, the retrenchment of lecturers and teachers, and the coercion of others into engaging in politically acceptable pursuits in the field of research, added to what seems to be clear moves to constitute the Department of Education and Science a branch of the MSC, constitutes a very clear message.

It surely does not leave any teacher, lecturer or college principal an inch of ground to believe that education and schooling are politically neutral processes being carried out in politically neutral spaces by professional educators who are above 'political indoctrination'.

Education and Schooling and Antiracist Education

What, you may well be asking by now, has all of that got to do with antiracist education?

I shall come to the point presently.

Young black people and their parents have known and have charged ever since the 1960s that education is not the wholesome, sanitized process that it is made out to be. There is now widespread concern, not least within Government circles, about the fact that the wageless now number 3.5 million, with their ranks swelling apace. If one were to add that array of conscripts that the MSC caters for, the national picture would be even more horrendous. But, the black communities across the land, long before 1973 and 1974 and all that followed after the 'boom years', had been organizing around the issue of education, and particularly in response to the high level of underachievement of West Indian school leavers and Asian school leavers and their subsequent wagelessness.

They constituted a large flank of the unemployed not because their poor achievement rendered them less employable, but because they themselves refused to accept the consequences of the commodity-producing, skilling, grading and selection agenda of the school system.

Commenting on that stance, Dhondy, Beese and Hassan (1983) noted:

The creation of these Educational Guidance Centres [which first appeared in 1970 as the brain-child of the ILEA] shows at once that the State has located the rebellion of West Indian youths as beginning within the schools. Today's Sin Bin kids are tomorrow's wageless. They represent the most rebellious section of young blacks in the schools. They are the ones who have understood that they are not being educated but schooled, that is, given the minimum training necessary to be churned out at the end as unskilled workers. Once they leave school, they then refuse to do the menial jobs for which they have been designated, and daily battle with the police against their attempts to force them into such work. It is this section which has been identified by Sir Robert Mark, Chief Commissioner of the Metropolitan Police, as 'the greatest threat to public order'.

Since then, of course, that section of the working class have taken their battles against police repression and against coercive state institutions to the streets in the form of mass insurrection in Britain's cities in 1981 and various skirmishes ever since. The response of the state has been to criminalize one whole section of the community, to introduce a series of liberal, social patchwork measures on the one hand, and a range of draconian measures on the other.

The latest of these is the Government's determination to 'starve' into submission those who reject both menial work and the MSC, and those who cannot find work of any description and see the MSC as a hideous substitute and a con. For them, social conscription of an increasingly regimented and disciplinarian nature is ruled to be the order of the day.

The stance taken by young blacks was indicative of a refusal to be re-colonized as a labour force within the bowels of British society. Because of the society's insistence upon marrying up race relations with immigration, [to paraphrase Roy Hattersley's famous words: without integration, control would be inexcusable; without control, integration would be impossible], the stigma of black = immigrant = problem =

pollution and trouble, is visited upon every British-born black. Moreover, the same racist systems, beliefs and practices which operated against the black migrant, act with equal force and consequence against native black British.

A wide body of research has shown that the vast majority of employers expect black school leavers to aspire towards the same jobs that have traditionally been reserved for their parents as migrants and settlers. The Careers Service, long before it became a clearing house for the Youth Training Scheme (YTS), also traded in those sets of expectations, and often complied with, rather than confronted, the stipulations and the entrenched positions of would-be employers, both in the public and the private sector.

The response of officialdom to the stance adopted by young blacks and to the protestations of their communities was, largely, to blame the victim. The DES circular 13 of 1969 [the product of the very first Parliamentary select committee on race relations and immigration] charged that West Indian parents in particular had totally unrealistic aspirations for their children. Moreover, it was argued, by virtue of the defects of their home and cultural backgrounds, young blacks were just not the material from which schools could mould the successes which those parents felt they had a right to expect.

The state's response to the incessant demands and challenges of those young people and their parents has since taken students, teachers, librarians, and not least of all the black communities themselves through the hoops of:

- compensatory measures to deal with the perceived deficits of black pupils and their background
- motivational measures to encourage the belief in black pupils that there have been famous and successful blacks, and that they too could succeed if only they were more highly motivated
- multicultural education to demonstrate a belief in cultural diversity, and a commitment to cultural pluralism and to an attack on ethnocentrism and eurocentrism

When all that failed, when the balance of forces within education and schooling and within the labour market and the wider society remained constant, with blacks still at the bottom of the heap, a kind of collective 'road to Damascus' conversion gripped the nation, particularly those bits of it controlled by the Labour Party, and 'equal opportunity' and antiracist policies and programmes were placed high on the political agenda.

This 'return of the prodigal' type of political commitment with all its trail-blazing exercise of political will, new found wisdom and apparent orthodoxy, at least in the eyes of black communities, leaves those of us who have been active in the education struggle with feelings of deep scepticism.

Antiracist strategies

Before I begin to examine the City of Manchester's *Antiracist Education Policy Statement* and *The Inspectors' Institutional Policy on Racism* and go on to discuss the implementation issues arising therefrom, I need to make some observations about the concept and context of antiracism.

The language of antiracism bears a striking resemblance to that of multiculturalism. There are those who would argue that multicultural education in its truest sense is essentially antiracist and that antiracist education, at its best, is truly multicultural. The debate about the respective merits of the two approaches will preoccupy many for years. Whatever the claims for either, however, the critical issue is the objectives that those who are committed to one or the other set for themselves.

Antiracism concerns itself with structural issues in a way that multicultural education does not. Moreover, it seeks to challenge institutional practices and individual acts which derive from an ideology of racism. Nevertheless, antiracist education like multicultural education operates within a political and ideological framework which leaves the organizational structure of education and the power relationships embodied therein more or less intact.

It is for those reasons that headteachers, and particularly inspectors, find it possible to deal with racist incidents or with racial conflict as if it were some temporary deviation from the norm, something outside of the true day to day concerns of the school which, if 'treated' or, even better, if not fussed about will go away as suddenly as it manifested. I will return to that later.

Antiracist education is concerned with ensuring that recruitment, remuneration and promotion practices are themselves non-discriminatory. Like multicultural, it is geared towards enhancing due respect for non-white and non-British cultures and to ensuring that the curriculum reflects such a commitment. Education is seen as having a major role in combating racism and 'promoting better race relations'.

But, what does an antiracist approach really mean, in the context of education and schooling? Who determines the 'curriculum' of antiracist education? Is that curriculum to be an adjunct to that inviolable 'sacred cow' that guides and structures the day to day efforts of teachers in and out of the classroom, or is it to be transfused into that animal and enter its bloodstream?

Unless the curriculum of antiracist education is transformed from the clinical sanitizing of existing nasties, with the occasional addition of newly constructed material, to one in which the experiences of students, white and black, the multifarious manifestations of racism at an institutional and individualized level, and people's attempts to understand and deal with those experiences become central, antiracism would be seen to be useful as a tool of conflict management and little more.

In writing this section, I was assisted by two documents, *The Inspectors' Institutional Policy on Racism* (IPOR) and *A Curriculum Statement in Response to DES Circular 6/8*. If my information is correct, the Inspectorate debated and produced both documents. However, the documents bear very little or no relationship to each other. The language and general thrust of the IPOR is 'heretical' in comparison with the measured and 'catholic' pronouncements of the curriculum statement.

Despite careful reading, I could find no reference to 'class' or to 'the economy' in the latter document, although there are passing references to 'structured youth unemployment' and to 'the new technology'. Nor are there any explicit references to the relationship between education and productivity or schooling and the labour market. Rather, the document reiterates some well worn shibboleths which are presented as taken for granted and unproblematic.

For example, the Curriculum Statement states in relation to 'teaching objectives':

These objectives go beyond the learning of additional subjects and must include those elements of personal and social education which emerge from the shared values of our society.

Many would find this assertion highly problematic. There is an assumption that there exists a core set of values which are commonly shared and to which the society subscribes in some undifferentiated fashion. It is a problematic assumption because it fails to take account of the fact that huge swathes of the society see absolutely nothing wrong with greed, nothing wrong with the flaunting of obscene opulence in the face of the most extreme poverty, and nothing wrong with denying people fundamental rights and their intrinsic value as human beings simply because of the colour of their skin.

Similarly, the Curriculum Statement makes the rather audacious claim that:

The formulation of objectives for teaching and learning is the product of the partnership between school, the home and community, and the needs of a wider society

Here is a bold, categorical assertion which I find very troubling and not at all true for the majority of homes and communities who would no doubt be surprised to hear that such a partnership was possible, let alone that it exists. Would that 'objectives for teaching and learning' were formulated on the basis described. It would result in a more relevant and holistic curriculum for one thing, and in some fruitful contestations about how to define 'the needs of a wider society', if only because we do not all experience the society in the same way.

Before I am accused of carping, let me illustrate what I mean.

In the middle and late 1960s, as part of those motivational measures I mentioned earlier, schools in some urban areas in

Britain introduced Black Studies programmes. The rationale, understandably, was that black students would have their self esteem enhanced by learning about the achievements of blacks in history, learning that black could indeed be 'beautiful' and that we are not intrinsically backward. Characters from history and the particular struggles they waged against all odds were identified and discussed. Many such historical figures became household names.

Young black parents even started to name their children after Tshaka, Malcolm, Harriet Tubman, Marcus Garvey, Queen Nefertiti. Black Studies occupied its rightful place on the curriculum shelves.

But when those same students, inspired by the example of those historical giants, decided to bring their own contemporary experience of racism and of the exploitation of ordinary working class people, e.g., their parents, into the classroom, the schools started to see danger signs. Rather than viewing those historical figures simply as icons, the black students were asking themselves, quite properly, what is the relevance of Malcolm X to my situation, how did Marcus Garvey influence the prevailing situation in his day and what learning might I derive from that for our condition as a people today? They wanted their contemporary experience and the interface between black people and British society discussed, and the Black Studies programme used to help them formulate appropriate responses, including strategies for dealing with their experience of schooling itself.

Teachers took fright, charged those school students and the communities that supported them with seeking to politicize schooling and education (a charge that had already been laid at the door of the black supplementary school movement) and, before very long, the in-school variety of Black Studies gave way to multicultural education.

British born blacks were/are nurtured within a culture of racism. Their lives outside school and the experiences of their peers and their parents are often impacted by the effects of institutional and individual actions and practices, from deportation threats to having firebombs thrown through their windows. For many, the need to learn how to survive and to evade police attention as highly visible, unemployed, or excluded young blacks, often overrides anything a teacher might have to offer in her or his curriculum area. Yet, they invariably have problems making their voices heard and having issues that are clearly critical to them considered in the curriculum. Where is the 'partnership' here?

Who determines the needs of the wider society, and what if sections of the wider society see it as inescapable that, given the dominant ideology, blacks must always receive such treatment? Is it not the case that there are many people in the society who believe that Parliament is trampling upon their rights when it legislates to make it unlawful to treat black people and those from other historically oppressed groups in a discriminatory manner? They are not all card-carrying members of the National Front, the British National Party or Column 88, either.

The degree of fit implied by the 'partnership' as described might well exist for some people in some communities. It is a degree of fit that is assumed in most middle class areas and in the relationship between home and community and the providers of private schooling. In the majority of communities, however, where the very existence of the school itself let alone its internal culture is seen as an anomaly, community involvement in curriculum planning will be viewed as a massive irrelevance.

Where in that Curriculum Statement, then, is there any room for a genuinely antiracist approach to education? Yet, this is no doubt the statement with which governing bodies, headteachers and teaching staff generally will be more at ease. It is also a statement which, unlike the other, allows for greater manageability in terms of the role of the Inspectorate.

But if antiracist education is not to become a hybrid of multicultural education, with the added facility of a fire engine service in respect of racial incidents, a curriculum statement that is fit for the purpose will need to challenge a whole range of taken for granted assumptions that are made in the one under discussion and be constructed on a different set of premises.

Most importantly, schooling itself should be regarded as

problematic and 'the school' as one of the institutions which young people, and young blacks in particular, see as part and parcel of the overall problem they face in this society.

Let me illustrate this point and lend some substance to my claim that the antiracist education lobby could represent a movement for change in education and schooling. I shall do so by drawing upon the response that I and other members of the Antiracist Teacher Education Network (ARTEN) made to DES Circular 3/84, the document of the Council for the Accreditation of Teacher Education (CATE).

In language not dissimilar to that of the Manchester LEA Curriculum Statement, paragraph 12 of 3/84 reads as follows:

Students should be made aware of the wide range of relationships – with parents and others – which teachers can expect to develop in a diverse society, and of the role of the school within a community. They should also acquire an appreciation of the way in which the education service is structured and administered. They will also need to have a basic understanding of the type of society in which their pupils are growing up, with its cultural and racial mix, and of the relationship between the adult world and what is taught in schools, in particular, ways in which pupils can be helped to acquire an understanding of the values of a free society and its economic and other foundations. *Opportunities should be provided for students to reflect on and learn from their own classroom experience, and to place their role as a teacher within the broader context of educational purposes.*   (my emphasis)

Our response risked stating the obvious, and because it was so very obvious, we could reach no other conclusion than that the Department for Education and Science took a deliberate decision to omit certain considerations because they did not square with its political and ideological education agenda:

Circular 3/84 falls within the political and ideological framework which serves to preserve and reinforce a particular concept of 'education' which pays no regard to the ways in which society and the education system are structured by class, race and gender and the power relations that these embody.

The fact is that Britain is not and has never been a homogeneous or mono-cultural society. Rather, it is structured in relations of power and these relations limit and distort the freedom of individuals and groups on the basis of race, class and gender. Economic relations in society are based on systems of exploitation which presuppose inequalities of race, class and gender. These 'economic and other foundations', therefore, cannot be taken as unproblematic but should be understood in terms of the inequalities that they engender and perpetuate. The power relation of the classroom reflect and perpetuate the power relations of society. Student teachers are presently trained to preside over those power relations. They should be brought to see ways in which they can transform classroom relations, informed by an antiracist perspective. The relationship between the adult world and what is taught in schools should not be conceived of in terms which reinforce stereotyped racial and gender inequalities.

The absence of an antiracist perspective in this document is not an accident or an oversight. Its view of knowledge and the teaching process inevitably means that teaching must be regarded as non-ideological and non-political. In this context, racism could only be seen as an external factor occasionally impinging on 'the ordinary school', presumably as a product of students and teachers 'failing to guard against their preconceptions'.

Finally, to return to the beginning.

Despite a number of initiatives to encourage school students to 'participate' in the running of their schools, official documents such as the CATE review and the Manchester 'Curriculum Statement' concentrate heavily on the triad of school, home, and community, with 'the wider society' being invoked now and again for good measure. The 'sine qua non' of schooling, i,e, the pupils, are planned for, catered for, or are organized around certain limited areas. Their centrality to schooling is thereby compromised and they are relegated to the role of passive receptacles of stuff other people have deemed beneficial to their development.

In general terms, and specifically in relation to the schooling of working class whites and of blacks, I would argue that the wider society has forfeited the right to determine educational objectives or plan curriculum. In that sense, I support the contention that schools and school students in working class areas could achieve 'a state of collective power in which these very schools will have to take on a different shape and serve the lives of their pupils as defined by themselves'.

If, by exploring the ways in which an antiracist approach to education could challenge the functions and purpose of schooling and its very organizational framework, forces with a firm commitment to education for liberation could be released, the education system might well become relevant to the deep crisis in which this society is and will be gripped for some time to come. It is a crisis that manifests in the extent to which the nation is ill at ease with itself, in the growing incidence of racist attacks and racist murders, in the link between unemployment, domestic violence, and other crimes in communities that are already poor and excluded from the opportunities and benefits in society that others routinely take for granted.

Through a process of interpreting the society to itself, and encouraging whites in the education stable to confront their cultural assumptions, beliefs and societal structures, British born blacks, working in solidarity with progressive whites, might just set in motion a movement for change in education and schooling that not even the microchip era seems set to precipitate.

This paper has turned out to be much more analytical and less prescriptive than some of you would have wished. However, given the state of the industry just now, I see this as no bad thing. It is for those charged with the business of implementation, management and curriculum design and delivery to own it, hopefully, and allow it to guide your thinking and inform future practice.

ENOUGH TALK
TIME FOR COLLECTIVE ACTION

Introduction

For over forty years, black communities in Britain have organized around the schooling experiences of black children. There were three sources of inspiration for the early responses, of African Caribbean parents particularly, to the way the schooling and education system dealt with our children.

First, there was the recent memory of what our own education systems in countries of origin had given to generations of our people, the political activism and popular struggles against imperialism and neo-colonialism that had been part of that recent history, and therefore what we were capable of. Second, there was the broader struggle of our people against racism in the society, as experienced in seeking employment and housing, in the way the police related to us, in immigration legislation and especially in the hostile postures and utterances of leaders of State and politicians across the political spectrum with regard to our presence, and the 'strain' they felt that 'coloured immigration' was putting upon the tolerance of the British people. Thankfully, there were notable exceptions to such pandering to the racism endemic within British society; people like Fenner Brockway MP, Eric Lubbock MP (Lord Avebury), Tony Benn MP. Third, there was the 'Black Power' and the Civil Rights and 'Black Panther' movements in the United States of America, and the work of the Students Non-violent Co-ordinating Committee (SNICC), all of which had a profound impact upon, and helped give focus to, our struggles here in Britain.

We encountered a working class movement that was itself not devoid of racism, that focused predominantly upon struggle in the workplace around wages and working conditions, with the major trade unions punching their weight, and exerting huge influence upon the way the Government organized the economy and related to 'the captains of industry'. We struggled in the workplace, too, against racism and arbitrary and dehumanizing treatment, against lower levels of pay and lack of promotion, and against appalling working conditions.

Unlike the white working class, however, our struggles in the workplace were but an extension of our struggles in the community, as indeed were our struggles in relation to schooling and education.

Black communities have sustained what is arguably the highest and most consistent level of involvement in struggles around schooling and education of any group in the society. That involvement is summarized in 'Black Communities Securing the Future' (2.1). The huge attendance at the conferences organized by Diane Abbott MP is testimony not only to the extent of grass roots involvement in education provision within our communities, but to black communities' impatience for change and to see an end to the perennial underachievement of black people as a group in the schooling system.

Sadly, however, those conferences epitomize the paralysis of collective action within our communities. They are organized without any consideration as to the action the people attending in such numbers might wish to see arising from them. The agenda remains in the hands of the organizers, especially linked as it now is to the political agenda of the Mayor of London. When in May 2002, therefore, the 2,300 people attending tried to come up with some resolutions and to indicate what they wished to see happen after the passion and zest for action that had been displayed at the conference, the organizers would allow no such assertiveness. So, no resolutions, no plan of action for the future, no indication as to how what the conference had agreed would be progressed, particularly the question of passing some firm messages to the Government from the conference.

There have been other conferences since, and in 2003 the rather clumsy and questionable award by the Mayor of London of a contract to the Black Londoners Forum to set up a Black Parents Forum.

In that forum and in many others, small and large, across the country, the incessant talking and reiterating of problems goes on apace. I believe it is time for black communities across Britain to commit to some action, organize independently of Mayors, MPs, LEAs and the rest, and embrace our responsibility for the future of our children.

Black Communities Securing the Future reminds us that there are solid foundations upon which we could build a mass movement across the country.

The 'Parents and Students Empowerment (PaSE)' proposal for a national development programme (2.2), targeted principally at our young people, is designed to empower young people and create space for them to exercise their voice and operate as a positive force across the nation, in their interests and for the benefit of the generation coming after them. Some groundwork is already in train to spur this along, and PaSE is seeking to extend its activities with young people and parents in local communities across the country.

Our communities have focused, rightly, over the years on the failings of schools and the absence of a strategic approach to 'race' in schooling and education on the part of Government. We have not been as good or as vocal in respect of the things we need to fix in our own houses and in the very heart of our communities. For example, despite the excessive numbers of young black men, and thankfully, the fewer number of women, who have lost their lives across the black communities of Britain at the hands of other black men in the last decade, we have tended to treat that phenomenon as a local matter, specific to Harlesden, or to Moss Side, or to Chapeltown.

But those events are not confined to individual areas any more than they are confined to the families that lose loved ones. They also have repercussions in all areas of the lives of the people caught up in the tragedies, including the impact upon young people and their schooling.

'Family-centred Approaches to Youth Conflict' (2.3) explores the way conflicts affect communities and the helplessness some parents feel about the challenges they are facing. The paper explores a range of conflicts and their origins. It further examines issues around parenting and the way we guide and support young people in acquiring and giving expression to sound values and principles in their dealings with others. The programme set out in the paper includes building models for resolving conflicts between young people, between young people/families and schools, and between groups in the community.

'Male Participation in the Education of their Children' (2.4) examines ways of working with our men to get them more actively engaged in supporting their children's education. It extends some of the arguments in Family-Centred Approaches and focuses on assisting men in examining their attitudes to parenting, their values and how they could play a greater role in reversing the damaging trends in schooling and education that have impacted so massively on black young men.

'Living with Dignity' (2.5) explores with the Young Mediators Network, the context in school and society in which they would be increasingly carrying out their mediation and conflict resolution activities. The Young Mediators Network is a national body of school students who have been trained in mediation and conflict resolution skills. They operate in their schools to tackle conflict in peer groups, bullying, and other forms of intimidating practices. Living with Dignity was presented at the first biannual conference which some two hundred young mediators attended.

'Reclaiming the Past, Shaping the Future' (2.6) examines the role of education, and schooling in particular, in empowering young people for political action. The paper notes the absence of a clearly articulated statement of the rights of school students and how they might be prepared for the active exercise of such rights. It points to the fact that there is little attention paid in the school curriculum or in Cultural Studies programmes to the impact of the black population on British social history since the Second World War.

'Widening Access from Both Sides' (2.7) addresses the issue of student progression from state schools to Oxford University. The paper introduced a discussion between Oxford Colleges' Admissions Tutors and Heads of Sixth Forms in state schools. The paper anticipated the Government's 'widening participation' agenda by some six years and was presented in support of the work of the Oxford Access Scheme. It proposes a model for partnership working between Oxford Colleges and inner city state schools with a view to increasing the number of students from such schools progressing to Oxford, and in particular the number of British born African-Caribbean students. There were at that time approximately 40 such students out of an overall student population of 15,000.

The Oxford Access Scheme was but one of a number of such schemes supported by Hackney Education in that period. That same year, Professor Ian Kennedy, Dean of Medicine at St Bartholomew's, invited the Director of Education to have discussions about partnership working between Hackney secondary schools and Barts to try and increase the number of African-Caribbean students choosing medicine as a career, irrespective of whether or not they opted to study at the Barts Group of teaching hospitals.

The Hackney secondary schools rose to the challenge and introduced a number of initiatives to encourage more African-Caribbean students to see entry to Oxbridge as something within their grasp and to prepare for a career in Medicine and Dentistry.

Since 2002, however, Universities, including Oxford and Cambridge, have been developing a much more strategic approach to widening participation in the context of specific Government proposals and of their duty under the Race Relations (Amendment) Act 2000. The monitoring and impact assessment that Universities are conducting as part of their implementation of the Act should provide evidence of the sort I was suggesting that Oxford University should collect to assess whether or not their procedures were having an adverse impact on black applicants.

'Parental and Community Involvement in Education' (2.8) is an intervention in the debate about teaching black boys in 'segregated groups', which the media sparked following Trevor Phillips' report of his visit to a school district in the USA. The paper argues that there have been some fundamental flaws in Governments' responses to the underachievement of black children in the schooling system and that black parents should themselves be more proactive in equipping their children with strategies for surviving schooling and should work collectively and independently to effect better outcomes for their children in schooling and education.

2.1

BLACK COMMUNITIES SECURING THE FUTURE
Building on strengths, eliminating weaknesses
Manchester
9 May 2002

Introduction
There is a vibrant black movement in education with a history that dates back to the middle 1960s. The Caribbean Education Association (CEA) and later the Caribbean Education and Community Workers Association (CECWA) were both formed in the middle to late 1960s and encouraged the growth of numerous community based education initiatives in areas of significant black settlement throughout the United Kingdom.

Black Saturday/Supplementary Schools have their origins in that movement, a movement which has spawned the expansion of supplementary education and a range of voluntary education and community arts projects in our communities. Over time, the black working class education movement was supported by the campaigning activities of, among others:

The West Indian Standing Conference
The Campaign Against Racial Discrimination
The North London West Indian Parents Association
The Black Parents Movement and The Black Youth Movement
New Beacon Books
Bogle L'Ouverture Publications
The Abeng Centre
The Keskidee Centre
Various societies of Caribbean nationals (the Jamaica Society, the Guyanese Overseas Association, the Grenada Overseas

Association, the Trinidad & Tobago Association etc.)

In 1988, the National Association of Supplementary Schools (NASS) was formed, with a mission:

- to record the origins, growth and advances of the black supplementary education movement
- to research and disseminate exemplars of good practice
- to build a library and archive
- to provide guidance and support to community groups wishing to establish new supplementary schools
- to influence Government and LEA policy and decision making in respect of the education of black children nationwide.

Although the NASS had a national reach, its activities and prime movers were mainly London based and belonged to long-established projects which were sustained for the most part by funding from the Inner London Education Authority. With the demise of the ILEA in 1989 and the consequent lack of funding for those projects from the new London LEAs, most of the employees whose salaries derived from ILEA grants lost their jobs or sought alternative employment. By 1992, the NASS was struggling to survive and eventually ceased to function.

What that demonstrated was its failure to build a mass base among black students and parents (who numbered thousands in the supplementary schools in London alone) and its over-dependency on local authority funding.

I was the convenor of the Library & Archives Committee of the NASS throughout its life (including while I was Director of Education in Hackney) and can attest to the fact that the supplementary education movement provided then, as it still does today, the finest examples of:

- black teachers' capacity to motivate children to aspire to high levels of achievement, including those children that mainstream schools reject as being 'unteachable' or 'uncontrollable';
- curriculum planning and delivery celebrating the contribution of black people to the evolution of human knowledge and the development of civic society, to enhance, in black children, the growth of positive self identity and

high self esteem;

- students, parents, teachers and community groups working together in partnership, with common aspirations and a common belief in our children's capacity to succeed academically, and to adopt values that make them fit for living more socially competent and fulfilling lives.
- supplementary school teachers equipping school students and parents with appropriate strategies for surviving in mainstream schools and breaking the cycle of low expectations, high order frustration, and poor educational outcome.

Building on Our Strengths

It is that collective experience, derived over some forty years of life experience in Britain and with the British schooling system, that gained expression so forcefully at the Focus on the Black Child conference, organized by Diane Abbott MP at the Queen Elizabeth II Conference Centre, London, on 16 March 2002.

At that conference, there was unanimous support for the proposal that an independent organization of black parents, of black students, and of black teachers be established, with invitations being issued to all the participants at the conference to join the organization appropriate to them. There was a plea that the situation of black governors be taken into account, and a similar organization involving them be formed.

A majority of participants at the conference called for those proposals to be formulated into resolutions and for the conference and its organizers to commit to a timescale for implementing them. It was felt that given the presence of the Education Minister, Cathy Ashton, as a speaker at the conference, those resolutions and the messages coming from the conference generally should be communicated to the Secretary of State for Education.

The conference organizers were unbending as far as alterations to the programme were concerned. Consequently, there was no space created for the formulation of resolutions or for the key messages from the conference to be distilled for later publication. The organizers assured participants, however, that the conference report, soon to be produced, would contain the proposals and the key messages from platform presentations and workshops alike.

The Communities Empowerment Network (CEN), of which I am Chair, is of the view that until active steps are taken to establish those formations, no further conferences should be arranged. That view has the support of the vast majority of the 2,300 people who attended the *Focus on the Black Child* conference.

Instead, the next conference should be organized by, or in conjunction with, the newly constituted and democratically established Independent Black Parents Organization, and the Independent Black Students Organization, and should be focused around their agenda for work in communities, in and with schools and in relation to Government policies and practices.

At that March conference, CEN offered, that given its infrastructure, the experience of its Management Committee and staff (most of whom have themselves been part of that forty year education history), and the network CEN has established around the country, it would be willing to take the lead in bringing about the formation of the above independent organizations.

For their part, the GLA in the persons of Ken Livingstone, Trevor Phillips and Lee Jasper, committed to supporting the establishment of these formations in Greater London. It was felt that since the focus of the conference had been 'London Schools and the Black Child', the London based organizations when formed could act as a hub to support the developmet of similar organizations across the country.

What are the foundations on which such organizations can be built?
Parents
Most of the people involved in the running or on the management board of voluntary education projects in our communities are parents themselves.

They act as facilitators, supporters, and 'counsellors' to an even larger body of parents who are not necessarily involved with organizations, but who nevertheless share deep concerns about their children's education and their own experience of dealing with schools.

We envisage an Independent Black Parents Organization made up of:

- individual parents
- groups of parents formed around the school their children attend, though not necessarily involved with the Parents Teachers Association
- voluntary education projects joining as affiliated bodies
- representatives of the Independent Black Students Organization (and of the Black Teachers and Black Governors Organizations when formed)

For the above purposes, 'black' parents are parents of African, African-Caribbean and South & East Asian heritage, other ethnic minority parents defining themselves as 'black', as well as white parents of black or dual/multi heritage children.

Aims & Objectives

The aims and objectives of the organization would encompass:

- enabling black parents in Greater London (and across the nation) to bring together their power, and to influence policy and decision making, in the education of black children
- to be an effective advocate on behalf of parents and students in respect of education rights and the damaging experience that many children and their parents have of schools
- to provide parents with knowledge and information about changes in education legislation; schools' policies, guidelines and practices; parents' and students' rights and responsibilities in relation to those, and, generally, about what groups of parents in London and elsewhere are successfully doing to intervene in the situation facing black students and teachers in schools
- to seek involvement in impact assessment at local level of the implementation of race equality policies in schools, colleges and Universities, in accordance with the requirements of the Race Relations (Amendment) Act 2000, and to monitor

outcomes for black and ethnic minority students

- to give support to one another in respect of dealing with challenging children and supporting them through personal and schooling crises pre- and post-16
- to share examples of good practice and collaborate with schools in finding appropriate ways of supporting children's self-development and academic progress
- to intervene in respect of schools' exclusion of disproportionate numbers of black students
- to give active support to black teachers, governors and education officials
- to celebrate black students' achievements and help the growth of a culture of educational excellence within our communities
- to forge alliances nationally and internationally with other progressive movements in education

Students

Unlike parents organizations, there have not been many examples of independent formations of black students in London or elsewhere at any point in the last forty years. Notable exceptions to this are the Black Students Movement, and the Black Youth Movement, established with the active support of the Black Parents Movement that grew out of the work of the George Padmore Supplementary School, in response to police attempts to criminalize a group of progressive black students in North London in the early to middle 1970s. Organized black students groups have been a very rare development.

This is in spite of the fact that it is black students and especially black males who, historically:

- have been failed by the schooling system and have been excluded in largest numbers
- have failed to receive education otherwise than at school, following exclusion
- have been the target of the notorious 'Sus' laws and of police 'Stop and Search' practices
- have been through the criminal justice system and ended up in custodial institutions in disproportionate numbers

- have suffered unemployment for the longest period upon leaving school.

There is a body of black students who, in conjunction with their parents, organize themselves voluntarily and develop an identity as a discrete group – those who attend Saturday or Supplementary Schools. Their ages range from 5 to 19. In addition, there is that large and increasing body of black students who, thankfully, progress to further education post-16. Black and ethnic minority students make up 16% of the student population and 6% of the working population. 26% of the black and ethnic minority population aged 18-24 are studying or have studied for a degree, compared to 14% of the white population in that age cohort.

We anticipate that students, teachers, and young and adult volunteers, as well as parents in most of the supplementary schools, would wish to be involved in the formation of these two organizations. We therefore recommend building the students' organization from that base, especially as one would expect their parents to be supportive of the rationale for having an independent black students' organization.

We would wish to approach parents groups formed around, or meeting under the aegis of, particular schools and assist them in encouraging their children to join the students' organization. Similarly, we would approach black students in Sixth Form and Further Education Colleges in their own right.

Students may also wish to organize themselves on a school by school and college by college basis and affiliate to the Independent Black Students Organization as well as exercising the option to join as individuals.

The Aims and Objectives of the organization might be

- to support black students' personal, academic, moral, spiritual, and social development
- to support black students at risk of exclusion and those excluded, especially permanently
- to examine and critique Government and LEA policies that impact upon the condition of black young people both inside and outside of the schooling system

- to record and disseminate good practice in terms of innovative work in conjunction with schools that is focused upon:
  - motivating disaffected students
  - strategies for conflict resolution
  - collaborative working on issues such as bullying and intimidation
  - dealing with difficult students and with dysfunctional teachers
  - developing and delivering relevant curriculum
  - promoting pride in effective learning and in achievement
  - effecting a positive triangular relationship between the student, the home, and the school
- to seek involvement in impact assessment at local level of the implementation of race equality policies in schools, colleges and Universities, and to monitor outcomes for black and ethnic minority students
- to review the relationship between school exclusion and youth crime and the experience that excluded black students have of the police
- to devise ways of encouraging black students to abandon the negative stereotypes that accompany the general concern about black male underachievement
- to challenge the anti-academic, anti-learning culture that is becoming more and more prevalent amongst girls as well as boys, where in a growing number of cases students are afraid to demonstrate that they have high aspirations and a capacity and desire to work hard and be academically successful
- to celebrate black students' creativity and achievements and help grow a culture of excellence within our communities
- to work with school students, parents, community organizations and other relevant agencies to tackle the impact of the drug market on our young people, including the growing incidence of gang activity, and death by gunshot of young black males
- to support the work of Saturday/Supplementary Schools
- to support young black people in youth custody institutions

and establish networks within our communities to assist their rehabilitation on release

- to lobby and work in partnership with employers' organizations, local authorities, development agencies and the like in order to confront the barriers facing young black people, including ex-offenders, in their search for employment
- to support the expansion of opportunities for creative expression for black young people in our communities
- to encourage the growth of cultural industries in order to link cultural creativity with the economic development of our communities

Embracing the Agenda

The organization, when formed, would need to determine its own priorities. We believe, however, that rather than approaching students and their parents with a clean slate, we should seek to involve their participation around these aims which, from our experience, we consider to be the burning issues facing young people in our communities.

It is essential that both the Parents and the Students organization are democratically constituted, democratically managed and democratically run. As such, we would suggest that, in addition to drawing up an appropriate Constitution, the *Principles and Method of Organization* adopted by the Black Parents Movement when it started some twenty-five years ago, be revisited as an exemplar of good practice and a template for ensuring the democratic organization and operation of those bodies.

Neither organization is meant to replace or displace the work of existing organizations in our communities. Rather, we expect that these independent organizations of parents and students (and of black teachers and Governors) would work in partnership with existing groups. Such groups would be encouraged to provide information about themselves and their services to the independent organizations who will in turn refer parents and students to them, as appropriate.

We envisage that the twin organizations will perform a more

strategic function, representing the interests of parents, and students, and of constituent organizations working with them in our communities; lobbying Government at central and local levels; providing training for capacity building; interpreting and providing digests of relevant Government legislation, guidelines, policies, etc.; conducting or commissioning research; documenting their interventions and evaluating the impact of their work in the short and longer term.

Conclusion

Successive governments have signalled their concern about the entrenched levels of black underachievement, over-representation in school exclusion statistics and in Young Offender Institutions, increased involvement in neighbourhood gangs and increased incidence of gun related crimes among black young males.

There have been many education reforms and interventionist measures. Yet, nationwide, the situation facing black school students and school leavers remains as critical as ever.

We believe that there is clear evidence of black communities wanting to take ownership of this issue and work with the authorities to tackle it. Notwithstanding the efforts of local groups over the years, a solid national infrastructure is needed to tackle the problem in a concerted manner, both in respect of parents and of students.

More large conferences at which people vent their anger at yet more talk and rehearsing of problems are not what is needed.

We believe that the Government should see the aims and 'raison d'être' of both these organizations as being consistent with its own commitment to race equality and building community cohesion and should fund such developments in partnership with others, without requiring the organizations concerned to compromise their independence and dance to its tune.

2.2

PARENTS AND STUDENTS EMPOWERMENT (PaSE): A development programme for students and young people

January 2005

The Proposal in Context

Ever since the middle 1960s, Government has identified problems as far as schooling and the educational entitlement and career aspirations of black school students are concerned. An analysis of government interventions and community responses to this issue in the last four decades would expose the extent to which racial stereotyping and institutional beliefs and practices in respect of black people, African Caribbean males in particular, have led to the current situation in which 'black males' conjure up notions of underachievement, aimlessness, irresponsible parenting practices, criminality and social disorder. Successive Governments have stumbled and bungled from one sorry initiative to another: Section 11 (of the Local Government Act 1966) funding, to Ethnic Minority Achievement Grants, to an Aiming High programme for African Caribbean students currently being piloted in some thirty schools nationally.

The one thing those programmes have in common is that they locate 'the problem' with black young people themselves and make assumptions about deficits caused by ethnicity, background, low aspirations, negative peer group influences, poor language development, absence of positive role models and a whole lot more besides. Those programmes seldom ask fundamental questions about teacher expectations, teaching quality, the quality of leadership provided by headteachers, or the institutional practices that result from racist discourses about black people in general and black males in particular.

The fact that those problems have persisted for so long, such that they have become systemic, is an indication of how marginal black communities' concerns are to the political structures and the political leadership in this country. In our community struggles over the past four decades, we have essentially activated a commitment to racial equality and social justice. Despite the rhetoric of social inclusion, diversity, community cohesion, and the rest, successive Governments have signally failed to demonstrate a commitment to racial equality and to eliminating the many structural barriers to social inclusion for black people, despite the belated provisions of the Race Relations Amendment Act with all its enforcement challenges.

What is worse, their incorporation of a growing number of blacks into state apparatuses and decision making arenas, including Parliament and the Lords, gives the veneer of inclusiveness and of open access based on merit. There is evidence of three generations of massive casualties created by the system among African (incl. African Caribbean) communities, as reflected in

- The over representation of blacks in youth custody institutions and in prisons
- The constantly low attainment of African Caribbean school leavers
- The underrepresentation of African Caribbean males in higher education and of African-Caribbean students generally on high level courses in HE (e.g., Science, Engineering, Dentistry, Medicine)
- The high levels of unemployment and underemployment among black males (including University graduates)
- The incidence of mental illness among young black people (15-25)
- The high murder and suicide rate amongst black young people (13-35). Black people are 5 times more likely than whites to be victims of a homicide. The risk for whites is spread across both sexes and all age groups. Black victims

are predominantly young men, one third of whom are victims of firearms. Asian people are twice as likely as whites to be victims of homicide. Between 2001 and 2004, 31% of black victims of homicide had died from shooting as compared to 7% of white victims. (Home Office Section Statistics)

The Government's own report on *Ethnic Minorities and the Labour Market* (produced by the Strategy Unit in the Cabinet Office in 2003), identifies African Caribbean, Pakistani and Bangladeshi groups as having the lowest educational attainment and lowest occupational status. The report notes that African and Asian people make up 1 in 13 of the UK population and that over the past twenty years they have accounted for two-thirds of the growth of the total UK population. Similarly, in the coming ten to twenty years, the British labour market will be dependent, increasingly, on the supply of labour from those communities. That knowledgeable and skilled labour force will not be available if the current pattern of underachievement, school exclusions, and youth offending within African and Asian communities persists.

Yet, tackling racism and actively promoting race equality as a fundamental pre-requisite for social justice in the society are not high on the Government's agenda. Indeed, as we have seen in repeated pronouncements by Government and those in opposition on matters such as school exclusions and headteachers' powers to exclude; parents and students' right of appeal; city academies, and the right of such institutions to operate their own admissions policies and admit students on the basis of how acceptable they find their parents; the fact that the development of such academies and 'magnet' schools leave a rump of poor and struggling schools in the area to which, inevitably, black and poor working class parents have no 'choice' but to send their children; black children, on whom the very future of this society rests are low down on the Government's list of priorities.

Moreover, the measures the current Government proposes in its increasingly centrist, populist, and knee jerk manner will impact adversely on black young people more than on any other group in the population, from identity cards, to legislating for 'respect', to 'zero tolerance' of poor behaviour, and the rest.

All of this points to the urgent need for a radical change in the response of black communities themselves to these issues and to the Janus-like way Government deals with them, looking in both directions at once. That is why we need to do what we have to do, and do it in such a persuasive and decisive manner, that Government would have no choice but to take notice and seek us out in their search for solutions, rather than having us react decade after decade to what they devise.

It is transparently obvious, in my view, that what they devise is in keeping with their vain attempts to be seen to be doing something without affecting fundamentally the way things are arranged and delivered for the majority. In that sense, our interests, our aspirations, and our pain at the relentless production of those casualties remain marginal to their concerns and to their political project. So, issues around criminality and violence within black communities become a matter of 'law and order' rather than the result of the denial of legitimate means of access to opportunity, to status and to success. Black student disaffection from the schooling process becomes a matter of 'zero tolerance' of indiscipline, rather than a matter of curriculum relevance, teacher expectations, and schools' failure to confer value on black students, their aspirations and prevailing issues, and their construction of reality.

That, in essence, is the context in which PaSE is seeking to intervene and go forward with the agenda outlined in the attached proposal. We are seeking to build a mass movement such as this country has not seen since the new post-war black presence. Our past, present and predicted condition as black people in the society, especially the condition of being young, black and male, demands that we energetically pursue this agenda.

PaSE

A Three Year Development Programme for Students and Young People

Aim

To work with school and college students, including those permanently excluded, and with young people not in education, employment or training to build a national movement to influence policy making and service provision locally, regionally and nationally.

Objectives

a. To provide young people with the support to articulate their concerns, share their experiences and to work together to bring about change

b. To provide a forum for young people to examine school practices and the processes that lead to exclusions and underachievement

c. To provide a forum for young people to share experiences of surviving schooling and becoming high achievers, despite being faced with the same challenges as those who are failed by the system

d. To examine with students and young people issues in relation to access to, and participation in, further and higher education, especially:

- participation of British born black males in higher education
- entry to high level courses in HE (e.g., Science, Engineering, Medicine, Dentistry) by African-Caribbean heritage men and women

e. To work with young people to equip them with peer and community leadership skills such that they could:

- build a student and young people's movement locally, regionally and nationally
- provide support to one another in relation to a wide range of challenges in their lives
- have an effective, collective voice and influence the policies and decisions that affect their lives

The programme will be delivered in four phases over a period of three years, as follows:

Phase One – Building on PaSE

- Work with young people in local areas to lay the foundations for involvement in the programme and preparation for active participation in a national working conference.
- Those areas would include: Peterborough, Luton, Bedford, Oxford, Bristol, Northampton, Birmingham, Leeds, Huddersfield, Manchester and the London boroughs, all of which are places in which PaSE has already had some success in working with students, parents and voluntary education projects

Phase Two – PaSE National Conference

Organizing the first PaSE national youth and students conference, preferably in collaboration with a major University. The conference to be held over a weekend, Friday to Sunday, utilizing the University's conference and accommodation facilities. The programme to be a combination of an examination of national issues impacting upon black young people, presentations by local groups arising out of the work done in Phase One, and widening participation in further and higher education from the perspective both of the further and higher education sectors, and of black students and young people. It is envisaged that the programme would include drama, poetry, music and 'rap' items pertinent to the issues under consideration. There would be an exhibition of visual arts, video films created by young people, book stalls and other displays throughout the weekend.

The conference would elect a National Preparatory Committee to work with PaSE and build towards the extension of PaSE's work in local areas and the establishment of a national movement of students and young people.

Phase Three – Future Leaders Programme

Work with 25 students and young people in each of 12 local areas, including members of the National Preparatory Committee, to develop peer leadership and community leadership skills and build their capacity to be effective organizers and agents of change. The leadership programme would be delivered over a period of 20 weeks and will include a practice element. The programme will be accredited and would be delivered preferably in collaboration with the local FE college and with relevant schools/departments in the University serving that local population.

Phase Four – A Period of Consolidation

- providing support to the National Preparatory Committee in consolidating the work of PaSE in local areas, building a national organization and influencing policy and decision making at local, regional and national levels
- drawing upon the experience of supplementary schools and voluntary education projects in supporting young people and their parents, especially those in the process of overcoming the effects of school exclusion, and developing models for 'family' approaches to supporting young people's education and development
- supporting the committee in planning a second national conference at which reports on the work done since the first conference could be given, common issues identified, and an agenda set for the period to follow.

This would ensure that a second conference has focus and purpose and that students and young people could see real evidence of genuine empowerment and of their capacity to use their collective power to make their voices heard, influence decision making, and make a difference, eliminating barriers and bringing about change in their circumstances.

Target group

Principally, but not exclusively, African (including Caribbean and Somali), Pakistani, and Bengali, school and college students and young people not engaged in education, employment or training. The focus is on these groups because they are by far the most disadvantaged in schooling and education. There is as yet very little evidence of those groups working together to share experiences and find solutions.

Background

PaSE was established in 2003 as the campaigning arm of a registered charity, the Communities Empowerment Network (CEN). CEN was established some six years ago and grew out of the work of an education charity, The Working Group Against Racism in Children's Resources (WGRCR). As the title suggests, WGRCR worked to promote antiracism in the school curriculum and to provide guidance to nursery, primary and secondary schools in relation to teaching and learning resources that could help promote race equality, a respect for difference and an understanding of how racism is learnt through socialization and through the beliefs and behaviours of adults, including parents.

An increasing amount of the work the Working Group was called upon to do concerned black (principally African-Caribbean) students being excluded from school. In 1998, for example, black school students aged 6-16 were 12 times more likely to be excluded than their white counterparts. That trend has continued, albeit the Government's targets for reducing school exclusions have led to a marginal decrease in the number of black students being excluded.

In the last five years, the Youth Justice Board has highlighted the correlation between school exclusion, youth offending, and the high number of black young people in youth custody. The following quotations provide a clear justification for the work of PaSE.

The 13,000 young people excluded from school each year might as well be given a date by which to join the prison service some time later on down the line

    Martin Narey – Director General of the Prison Service (2001)

Of 400 young people in a Young Offender Institution (YOI), 200 had been excluded from school.   Martin Narey

Two-thirds of the population of YOIs had left or been put out of school at age 13 or under.   Home Office Research

Speaking about the link between school exclusion and social

exclusion, Lord Warner of Brockley, former Chair of the Youth Justice Board, noted:

80% of young offenders of school age are out of school, either through exclusion or refusal to attend; .....mainstream schooling is not willing and not able to deal with children with challenging behaviour.

We in PaSE believe, as a famous sociologist remarked over half a century ago, that for many socially excluded groups:

Crime results from exclusion from legitimate means of achieving success.   Robert Merton (1949)

As Professor Gus John observed at a PaSE public meeting in 2004:

Social exclusion is a process. It is a dynamic process. It is the systematic and structural deprivation of the individual's opportunity to participate in society and consequently a denial of dignity, self-esteem and self worth.

It is a process that creates a cumulative set of circumstances in which the individual is unable to achieve the quality of life to which s/he aspires, and that is consistent with dignified living.

PaSE is committed to taking action to tackle active social exclusion, i.e., 'the form of exclusion that comes about when young people lay claim to particular identities and make choices about lifestyles which compound their disadvantage and their existence on the margins of the society'.

Social exclusion (passive and active) for a growing number of young people results in 'the abandonment of hope and the death of aspiration'.

Rationale for the First PaSE National Conference

There have been umpteen conferences over the last three decades dealing with:
- The underachievement of black boys
- Strategies for raising achievement of African-Caribbean school students

- Excessive numbers of school exclusions (especially of black boys)
- Under-representation of black students on various high level University courses, e.g., science, medicine and dentistry
- The gang and gun culture among young black males
- Teenage pregnancies

Each year for the past six years, Diane Abbott MP, has hosted conferences, first on 'Hackney Schools and the Black Child' and latterly, with the sponsorship of the Mayor of London, on 'London Schools and the Black Child'. Out of some 2,000 people attending each of these conferences to talk about young black people and their education, *less than twenty have been young people themselves.*

PaSE has been working across the country in collaboration with CEN and targeting young people, their parents/carers, learning mentors, counsellors and other significant others in the lives of those young people. Some of that work has involved case work in relation to school exclusions, strategies for avoiding conflict, and for focused, disciplined learning, as well as work around involvement in gangs and dealing with bullying by members of gangs.

PaSE wishes to bring young people together from across the country

- to debate the issues confronting them
- share experiences and strategies for positive engagement with school, community and society, and for developing businesses
- to work towards the formation of a national organization of young people committed to working together to tackle those issues, share good practice and influence government policy at local and national levels.

Method of Organization

PaSE believes that the conference should be organized largely by the young people themselves with the support of the PaSE secretariat and of Professor John as Interim Chair and Convenor of PaSE.

In order to ensure that the conference does not become yet

another talking shop, work will be done locally, and regionally, throughout England in order to connect with what young people are doing, link with the young people and the parents with whom CEN/PaSE have been working, and arrange what their contribution would be to the conference. (Phase One)

The conference would aim to bring some 1,000 young people together over a weekend at Easter on a University campus, preferably hosted by a major University in a large city. Easter is typically the time of year when the major teaching unions meet for their annual conference and, increasingly, influence Government policy, not least in relation to the most vulnerable people in the schooling system. We believe it would be highly symbolic to have 1,000 young people meeting for a working conference at a higher education institution at the same time.

The organization of the conference would involve a core group of fifteen young people from across the country, working in tandem with the PaSE secretariat. Planning meetings will be held in Manchester and other cities/towns and members of the organizing committee will be facilitated to attend by having their travelling expenses paid.

Young people have already expressed a desire to have the conference chaired by a sports personality or someone from the world of popular culture and entertainment. Ideally, the programme will include a live performance on the Saturday evening involving a variety of well known artistes. Parents, volunteers and friends would be invited to join the young people for that event.

The intended outcomes of the conference are as follows
- to provide young people with the opportunity to share experiences of the key issues facing them, and of working locally to tackle those issues, with an emphasis on what has worked previously
- to isolate overarching themes (e.g., self management and the disciplined learner; combating bullying, gang cultures, and the fear of crime; realizing creative potential; dealing with school exclusion and staying focused on learning; preparing black young people with the skills and aptitudes to take their

place in a labour market that will be increasingly dependent upon them in the coming two decades; exploring economic activity by young people, especially in the area of business development; peer mediation, advocacy and representation; etc.)

- to highlight the link between education and the national economy and the fact that by 2021 (next Census but one) the British labour market will be highly dependent on a black and ethnic minority workforce, such is the rate of growth of the black and ethnic minority youth population
- to encourage, with support from PaSE nationally, the creation of self sustaining youth movements on a local and regional basis, with a focus on self development, social enterprise, developing young entrepreneurs, combating discrimination and promoting social justice
- to agree an agenda for building an Independent Youth/Students Movement nationally and to elect a National Preparatory Committee to pursue that agenda

Phase Three will build upon the work done in phases one and two, with a focus on building the capacity to develop and sustain a student and young people's movement locally, regionally and nationally.

The work in Phases One to Four will be facilitated by regionally based student/youth co-ordinators employed by PaSE or seconded by a partner organization but managed by PaSE.

2.3

FAMILY-CENTRED APPROACHES TO YOUTH CONFLICT

Manchester
March 2004

We, as facilitators of children's learning and self development, must be seen to model by our own conduct and by living our values, the behaviours and principles we wish to see our children exhibit.

These sessions have been planned in conjunction with young people and their parents to whom I have been giving support, during the last six months, in developing strategies for resolving conflict. They have also been informed by my discussions with learning mentors working in secondary schools.

The conflict situations that have caused pain and distress to whole families, and that have involved the police and the Court system on occasions, include:

- Parents being banned from entering school premises because of physical aggression towards teachers over schools' treatment of their children;
- young people's revenge attacks upon one another;
- verbal aggression, escalating to physical violence, in and around their schools and in the community;
- physical aggression by young people against their mothers;
- parents and other family members at war with one another over incidents involving physical harm to their children.

The issues that have been identified in the sessions we have had so far include the following, as reported by parents and young people:

- Some parents gave examples of the efforts they had made to work in partnership with schools, including telephoning the school on a regular basis to enquire about their children's progress, or to inform the school about events in the family which they felt might have a bearing on the child's mood and conduct. In spite of those efforts and the relationship the parents felt they had formed with teachers, children would be given fixed term exclusions without the parents being alerted that anything was wrong at school, or that the school was about to send the child home.

- African-Caribbean boys, as young as 10, were being bullied and harassed by older boys to join gangs and to tell a web of lies to their parents about their whereabouts. When their parents went to complain to the parents of gang members, they were met not just with denial but with hostility and aggression because those complaining were 'calling their children criminals'. Hostility developed because the relatives of the gang members started going about in the community saying nasty things about those who had complained about their children's conduct.

- Girls in school were in conflict with one another over boys, a not unusual occurrence. The conflict took on a more sinister dimension, however, because the black girls and boys were harassing those other black girls about how black they were. Girls were being viciously bullied for being 'too black' and 'too ugly'. If the latter were also very bright and hardworking, they were ostracized even further. That caused misery not only to the girls themselves but to their families. When parents and other siblings saw those girls becoming more and more miserable, unable to sleep, demotivated and hating the very idea of going to school or college, they decided to take action. That resulted in confrontation with the ringleaders of those bullies and the opposing sides getting their 'posse' involved, thus prolonging the conflict.

- Mothers complained about being 'manhandled' and physically assaulted by their sons, either because of the mother's protest at the boy's treatment of his sister or because of the mother's insistence that he should not come and go as he liked, sometimes not coming home and not saying where he was or who he was with.

- Other mothers were distressed about conflicts between them and their sons as a result of forming a relationship with a new partner, typically after many years of bringing up children on their own. They felt they were being bullied by their sons into choosing between them and the new man in their life.

- Young people complained about not being listened to by parents and teachers, and therefore 'giving up' on trying to share what's going on for them. For them, this had serious consequences when conflicts arose between their parents, typically mothers, and their school, or between them and their peers.

The one thing all participants agreed upon, however, was that nursing conflicts was hard work and an obstacle to progress and meaningful living. The other thing that was generally accepted by all was that 'we heap as much misery upon one another as the system piles upon us' and, therefore, we have to devise methods within our own communities for sorting out problems, avoiding conflict and building peace. We all had to take responsibility for that, because every young bully comes from a home, often with very protective parents, however much those parents might themselves be indulging in bullying behaviour.

Parents talked passionately and at length about how much more difficult we make it for our children by not providing them with the skills to manage themselves in school and in the face of the pressures facing them in the community. Some parents readily admitted to being too stressed, 'too busy trying to make ends meet' to even know how to prepare their sons to handle what they're facing out there in school and in the community around them. Those parents paid tribute to those learning mentors, black and white, who were plainly very committed to helping their children do well, in whom those children confided, and who made a point of visiting them at home to discuss how they as parents could support their children better, and help them make schooling a more positive and productive experience.

A theme which everyone kept returning to, therefore, was the need for us to find ways of supporting one another within our communities, sharing one another's burdens and taking collective responsibility for the development and safeguarding of our children.

Arising out of those discussions, therefore, I have summarized the things we said we would deal with in these sessions, as follows:

Parents as their children's teachers

We agreed that we teach our children from birth and that, for better or for worse, they learn and pattern themselves more upon what they experience at home than what they are taught in school. We agreed that schools are not natural units of social organization and that many children find them quite frightening and alienating places.

Since we are so crucial in our children's development of a sense of what is right and wrong, what is acceptable and not so desirable conduct, we, as facilitators of children's learning and self development must be seen to model by our own conduct, and by living our values, the behaviours and principles we wish to see our children exhibit.

That means we need to be clear about our own values, where they come from, and how we express them in our dealings with our children and with all others with whom they see us interacting.

Some parents spoke about the way they saw their children changing before their very eyes because of how they saw them being treated by their partners. A number of women said that as a result, they had made the decision to throw out their partners, even though they knew it would cause those partners' biological children some heartache.

Talking and Encouraging Children to Talk

We agreed our 'Number One Priority' was to have a session on 'talking':

- Encouraging children to speak and to share by showing them we are keen to know what's happening for them and

that we are *listening*
- Valuing their point of view
- Encouraging their friends, with whom they typically share so much, to get to know the attitudes we have to our child's upbringing and the values we seek to have her/him develop
- Demonstrating that we could disagree with them without being judgemental
- Encouraging them always to consider how they might have handled any given situation differently
- Encouraging them to weigh up the benefits or disadvantages of their different responses, and the values that are reflected in their choice of response
- Assisting them in decoding their schooling experience and in developing strategies for surviving schooling
- Being honest with them and owning up to not having the knowledge or experience to deal with any and every particular situation
- Understanding that if children see us being upfront about our need for help and more informed guidance, they would themselves see it as normal to seek help and not believe they could always sort things out for themselves. That asking for advice/help is not showing failure
- Encouraging positive relationships between our children and significant others in their lives so that we know there are reliable people they feel comfortable about going to, even if, for whatever reason, they feel awkward about coming to us with the heavy stuff

We have agreed to explore those ten issues further in the session after this, which will be devoted exclusively to considering the value of 'talk', and how to encourage it and create space for it.

We will devote the third session to looking at 'International Human Rights Standards' governing the rights of children, namely:
- The best interests of the child must be paramount (Article 3)
- Children have a right to be heard (A.12)
- Children have a right not to be discriminated against on the basis of, for example, class, race, ethnicity, religion/faith or

gender (A.2)
- And we could add, 'OR because of the failings of either parent'.

We would relate this to the way children are treated in our homes, in school, in the community and by providers of public services. We would look at the implications of that for the attitudes children adopt towards one another, towards what they share with us, in their interactions with teachers, towards resolving conflict and in relating to fairness and justice. We would also examine how we can ensure our children are not discriminated against or exploited.

Children also have a right to guidance and support in developing the positive and holistic SELF.

We discussed this briefly in an earlier session and agreed to return to it over a couple of further sessions. We agreed that in doing so, we would explore a range of 'Factors in Constructive Self-building' and we would prepare for that session by reflecting upon the following and bringing our suggestions as to how we relate to each of them and could support our children in developing them. The notes that follow are meant to stimulate discussion and to assist each participant in identifying factors that have worked for them.

Factors such as:–

Positive identification with those that look like you

- Why do so many of us have difficulty respecting our black brothers and sisters, but instead heap negativity upon them by rejecting them for being as black as us and as the parents that gave birth to them?
- Why do we put ourselves in harm's way by trying to bleach out the blackness in the skin that God gave us so as to conform to some spurious notion that whiteness or near whiteness constitutes 'beauty'? How do we reconnect our people with the struggle to revalidate our ebony blackness for which so many of our brothers and sisters gave their very lives over the years, especially in the 'negritude' and civil rights movements of the 1950s through the 1970s?

Positive attitude to your own body and all your characteristic features

- How can we guide and assist our children in forming positive attitudes to themselves as black women and men, by demonstrating that we have positive attitudes to our black skins and black facial construction and body build?

Positive acknowledgement of your roots

- How can we assist our children in understanding that they have a history that is longer than the period since their birth in this country, or elsewhere for that matter? How can we connect them with the values that preserved that generation whose migration to these islands made their birth in and adoption of Britain possible? How, as parents and collectively, can we assist them in developing a historical sense of their rootedness in the Caribbean and Africa such that they do not continue to harbour notions of the 'backwardness' of those countries and their people, and by implication, of themselves?

Positive feedback about how you are and about what you do

- We know how much it matters to us to be told how well or

how badly we are doing? How can we give encouragement to one another and to our children? How can we encourage them to be more positive towards one another and their achievements, and not feel that they should automatically display attitudes of hostility and resentment towards one another? How can we show more evidence of joy, and celebration at one another's achievements, and not give expression to the belief that 'we can't bear to see one another prosper'?

Positive examples of how you should be and how you should act

- How can we, by living our values, sharing one another's burdens, taking individual responsibility for our own conduct and acting collectively to support our youth and build our communities, provide examples to our young people as to how they should be and how they should act?

Being listened to and having your point of view taken seriously, especially when you are hurting and crying out for help

- How can we encourage active listening and 'emotional listening' in our homes and in our interactions with one another, so that we don't have to suffer in silence, and so our partners, children, relatives, friends or work colleagues don't take us for granted?

Identification of personality traits and character

- How well do we know ourselves and what we are like, the kind of 'character' we have? How well do we assist our children in identifying their own personality traits and building sound character?

Acknowledgment of what you are predisposed to do because of them

- You come to know that by being conscious of yourself, but also by what others tell you about how they experience you. Therefore, learning to nurture and cultivate some of those traits and to bring others under control

- That's about sifting the ones that are conducive to personal development and growth, from those that could obstruct your progress and make you socially abhorrent in the eyes of others

Capacity to make mistakes and not be defeated by them
- This means being prepared to take risks and to accept that 'to err is human', however much of a perfectionist you consider yourself to be.

Learning that no one *fails* once they've genuinely done their best, but that that 'best' could be built upon and made even better
- If we develop that positive attitude towards our own performance, on whatever front, we encourage those around us to strive to be the best by acknowledging their individual effort and hard work. This is especially important in giving support and feedback to our children. If we look only at the mark they are given and compare it with that of their siblings or their friends, we could discourage them hugely by not acknowledging the progress they have made and the fact that they may have surpassed the target they set against themselves. Their siblings or friends may have a higher mark but failed to move an inch.

Capacity to see what went wrong and learn from mistakes
- It is one thing to make mistakes and not be defeated by them, it is quite another to keep repeating them and failing to learn any lessons from them. It is by putting ourselves through the discipline of self scrutiny and being honest about what it is that causes us to choose the same path over and over again, that we are able to change course, to enable our children, friends and others in our lives to learn from our situation, and guide them on the basis of our experience.

Capacity to develop a sense of humour
- Do we take ourselves too seriously? Do we react in ways which encourage our children to see every disappointment

as a cause of deep frustration and every joke as being at their expense?

- If we have a tendency to be uptight and ready to take on the world, we invite or search out conflict. Anyone unfortunate enough to step on our toe could well be risking 'life and limb'. It also prevents us from seeing adversity as the imposter he is.

Capacity to show compassion

- That is expressing our basic humanity and having the ability to reach out to others in situations which would test us similarly, were we to find ourselves in such situations. Here, again, this is about living our values and giving example to our young people about the importance of being able to attach value to others, and treat them as they themselves would wish to be treated.

Capacity to understand other people's reality and not judge on the basis of your own

- What is that famous saying: Never judge a man until you have walked a mile in his moccasins? Adults and young people alike engage in various forms of bullying and destructive tittle-tattle by passing judgement on others on the basis of their own reality. How can we encourage children to see people for what they are and respect their realities, and not harass them directly or cause them damage by saying all sorts of hurtful and prejudiced things about them?

Capacity to express one's innermost feelings and not blame oneself for having those feelings

- That's a tricky one. Blocking off the space in which you or your children could express such feelings without being made to feel guilty about sharing them could be a form of oppression. Here, again, laying the foundations for talking and sharing in a safe and secure environment is critical. Too often, even people who live under the same roof pass each other every hour of the day like ships in the night.

Relationships and interactions become contaminated and progress is possible only when individuals make the space to talk openly about the weight they are carrying.

- Why is it tricky? It depends on time, place and audience, and the feelings one feels impelled to express. We all have to accept responsibility for the effect that our conduct, and what we say, has on others. Our innermost feelings could be feelings of anger that are designed to hurt. They could also be feelings of hatred towards particular individuals and groups. Expressing innermost feelings of hatred of homosexuals, of disabled people or of Muslims, is clearly not the same as summoning up the courage to tell your partner fifty reasons why he is a chauvinist pig.

Capacity to manage one's emotions

- How well do we manage our emotions, especially the more extreme ones? How do we manage loss, anger, frustration, ecstatic joy? How do we manage our emotions with sensitivity, having regard to the emotions of others around us and the possible impact of ours on them? What signals are we sending out to our children by the way we respond to their emotions, especially as they don't always take the temperature of ours before they boldly and sometimes demandingly express theirs? How are we assisting them in developing emotional literacy and handling their emotions in their interactions with others in a multiplicity of settings?

Having your confidence reinforced by your successes

- Like it was when you learnt to ride a bicycle. Or did you give up after the third tumble? Success breeds success. Remember what we said earlier about 'when you've done your best'. Your 'best' could always be built upon and the more you succeed, the more you have the confidence to take on new challenges.

Having your confidence reinforced by evidence of learning from your mistakes

- This was raised in a discussion about parenting and how

parents encourage children to learn from their mistakes as parents. Making serious mistakes could often lead to a desire to 'shut down' completely. In relationships that go pear shaped it can sometimes lead to bitterness and a corrosive anger. The man or woman leaves, but you hang on to a load of emotional baggage ten times heavier than their body weight. And then, just when you think you are turning the corner and getting back in control of your own life, you hook up with someone who turns out to be not unlike the one before.

- In an earlier session, we discussed the difficulties some of us have with our sons and daughters, especially our sons, because of new partners. Some of you wanted to discuss this further because of one specific reason, that is, children rebelling because parents take up with white partners. We heard of one boy blowing his lid because, in the presence of the new white partner, his mother shouted at him in frustration: 'you're just like your miserable father'.

- The issue here was not just that this child was being compared to his father. His mother had done that several times before. The issue was that his mother had got into the habit of telling others in his presence, especially her women friends, that she chose a white man because, as far she was concerned, 'black men are rubbish'. Her teenage son lost it because he felt his mother had gone one step too far, putting him down and calling his father, as the boy said: 'in front of her white partner with his superior attitude that was already getting right up my nose'.

- Things went from bad to worse when the man intervened to protect his partner from her angry son and his physical aggression.

- In that session, the boy said how fed up he and his friends were about mothers who used their experience in relationships with black men as a justification for taking up with white men. One of them expressed his frustration passionately, saying: 'If a black woman falls in love with a white man and they want to be with each other, that's their and nobody else's business. It becomes my business, as a black man, when I am made to listen to black women boasting about choosing white men because black men are this and that. That tells me they would be equally happy with those white men who murdered Stephen Lawrence and those that rape and murder. This country had a history of wife-beating long before we came here. You don't hear white women saying they're going to look for a black man because white men are such rubbish. But, it's true isn't it? If our mothers say they're choosing white men because black men are useless, then any white man should qualify for their love and attention!'

- We need to spend some time looking at failed relationships in our community and how we manage them, especially given the number of single mothers who are reporting conflicts between their sons and their 'step fathers'.

Capacity to accept praise

- Some people are very awkward about accepting praise, especially when they are not accustomed to being praised. We come to believe that 'we are not worth it', or 'I was only doing my duty', or 'I can't see what's so special about that'. Those reactions could easily become an invitation to others to take you for granted, especially those around you for whom you do so very much daily. There are times when it is legitimate for you to say, to your children and your partner especially: 'I am glad you appreciate what I have done. I would see it as an even greater mark of appreciation if you tried to do the same more often'.

- We talked before about our children's tendency to 'diss' one another and be negative about how they look, how they dress, who they're with, and all sorts. We therefore need to be careful about our own behaviour, about what they see us do, how they see us react to others, how they hear us speak about others. If giving and accepting praise becomes the norm and they grow up with that from an early age, if that is reinforced by us as adults taking responsibility for how we speak about others and about their achievements, our children, more than likely, would go out there with more positive attitudes to themselves and others.

Capacity to accept other people receiving praise when you are not

- If we did the things we've just noted, it wouldn't be so difficult to rejoice with others and help celebrate their achievements. It wouldn't be so difficult to bask in their sunlight.

Capacity to give praise

- If we did those things, we, and especially our children, would learn to give praise more readily and more genuinely. How often do we hear some of our young people boast that they never say thanks for anything. One young person argued with me when I told him he had no manners, that: 'thanks belongs to God'. He was not too impressed when I told him: 'I am God, and if you cannot see and acknowledge me, then God doesn't want your thanks'. If we don't ensure that our children learn and are at ease with these values, we are encouraging their development as amoral people, without respect for themselves or for others.

Capacity to criticize in a sensitive manner

- Do we criticize in order to indulge ourselves and show off how smart we are, or do we criticize in order that the other person might learn, or might be encouraged to see things from a different perspective? When we criticize in a destructive manner, we invite people to ignore the message and, rather, react to our anger, meanness, or whatever. They take on the messenger and miss the message. They feel the need to respond defensively and, sometimes, to restore their dignity which you stripped away by the manner of your criticism. Furthermore, we fail to allow space for the person to improve when we criticize in those ways. Again, the first place children see how such things are done, badly or well, is in the home and at our side as parents and carers. If our conduct isn't right, and if we celebrate our poor conduct and elevate it to a level of acceptability, that is what our children see as appropriate in their dealings with us, and with others.

Capacity to respect yourself

- If we don't learn to respect ourselves, we cannot see the value in respecting others. Respecting one's SELF is about acknowledging that we are special and born to be great. We have a capacity for good and for evil. Since we have the capacity to nurture our potential for good as well as for evil, we have a corresponding duty to embrace values which make us fit for living in a civilized society. Respect is one such critical value.

- Some of us see, and encourage our children to see, having 'respect' as a sign of weakness. We encourage them to model themselves on our behaviour which, often, is a sign of a total lack of respect for ourselves and for those around us. That, however, does not stop us from demanding 'respect' from others. In other words, we don't show that we respect ourselves, but demand that others show us respect. This is a constant cause of aggravation in the family conflicts we deal with. Parents talk to children in the foulest of language and in the most aggressive manner, and then protest when those children talk to one another, and talk back to them, in the same manner and using the same language.

- That manner of communicating then becomes the only one the children are comfortable with. They take it to every situation, especially in their interactions with their peers. Furthermore, those same parents would go mad with rage when schools exclude their children for persistent verbal abuse of teachers.

Capacity to respect others

- If we don't know how to respect ourselves and why we should, we would hardly see the point in showing respect to others, however respectful they are towards us. Some people who find our conduct disrespectful or unacceptable would remain silent and put it down to a lack of manners. Others might protest and not rise to our anger and abuse in reaction to their protest. Others would see us as wanting to be 'wrong and strong' and see it as their duty to cut us down to size, sometimes literally. 'Why did you shoot him?' Because 'He had no respect', or, 'He disrespected my woman'. 'To teach him some respect'. We have a generation of young people in our communities who are so much at ease with mindless, gratuitous violence that it leads them to commit all kinds of barbaric acts in the name of 'respect', and yet, they have no 'respect' for life itself.

- Respect for oneself and for others grows by giving it expression in all aspects of daily living. Living without 'respect' dehumanizes us and renders us capable of barbarism.

Capacity to demand respect for yourself and safeguard your rights

- Each of us has a right to be treated with respect and dignity, and a responsibility to treat others in a similar fashion in order that we can earn their respect.
- Some people choose to disrespect us and deny us our rights because of who we are (poor people, gays and lesbians, women, or black people, unemployed and claiming benefit), or they think they have a right to do so because they see us as inferior to them. They do so more often than not without knowing the first thing about us and we, naturally, react out of a desire to uphold our dignity and assert that we have no intention of allowing ourselves to be treated in such a manner. In doing so, we have anti-discrimination legislation to assist us.
- In relation to some of the issues highlighted at the beginning of this paper, however, how does our conduct measure up? Do we routinely show respect to one another in our homes and in our communities? How do we prevent our boys and men from engaging in various forms of gender subordination and disrespect of mothers, siblings, and other female members of the family? How do we discourage those women and girls from putting up with it? What signals do we send out to our men that such conduct is unacceptable and would not be tolerated? How do we ensure that we are

giving our boys the right messages about how to treat women, especially girlfriends and future female partners or wives?

Capacity to see disagreements as normal and healthy

- How do we have our disagreements about matters great and small, and make them constructive so that we move forward? Are we able to deal with them in a manner that does not result in aggravation and short or longer term conflict? Do we have the capacity to deal with matters and not let them fester? Do we have the capacity to set them aside once they have been dealt with, and not keep the embers burning so we can reignite them when it suits us?

Capacity to deal with conflict without resorting to verbal and physical violence

- How do we have our disagreements and retain respect for ourselves and for those with whom we are in conflict? How do we continue to give expression to that respect by taking responsibility for not allowing the disagreement to get out of hand, irrespective of what the other party to the conflict does? How do we take control of the situation and avoid verbal aggression, while at the same time putting our position across? How do we avoid being provoked to physical violence?

Capacity to make demands on oneself and meet the legitimate demands of others

- It is a natural tendency to do what we like best and put off, or avoid altogether, those things which we find less satisfying. How do we develop the capacity to set targets for ourselves to enable us to achieve our goals? How do we make changes in our routine and free up time for our self development; time to talk to our children, listen to them, and guide them in facing the many challenges confronting them; time to go to their school and talk about their progress; time to do the many things we keep postponing, while stressing ourselves out about not having done them? How do we build up sources of support so that we are not struggling with making those changes on our own? How do we encourage our children to not settle for the minimum, but to demand more of themselves? How do we assist them in developing the discipline necessary for their own progress, so that they could see the positive results of their efforts and of the sacrifices they make?

Capacity to hold one's own and demand one's rights

- How can we inform ourselves about our rights in order to be more confident about demanding them? How can we identify the responsibilities that we have so as to ensure that we do what is required of us, even as we make others accountable? How can we develop the capacity to be assertive with people, and in relation to systems and structures, that fail to respect our rights as parents, as consumers, as citizens? How can we work collectively with others to make such people, systems and structures more responsive to our needs? How can we take our children through that same process so that they learn to be more socially responsible, socially competent and politically aware?

Capacity to have due regard for the rights of others

- How do we make sure we act in a way that acknowledges and respects the rights of others, in the same way as we expect them to respect our rights? What do we do when those rights conflict? What does 'do unto others as you would have them do unto you' mean in the context of rights and responsibilities? How do we deal with the protests of our children and others around us when they object to us denying their rights and acting in a manner which suggests: 'Do as I say, never mind what you see me do'?

Capacity to compromise, even when you're in the right

- Nothing prolongs conflict more than a refusal or incapacity to compromise. If we believe that to give an inch is a show of weakness and a transfer of power to the other, we displace all room for progress and for resolution of the problem. Sometimes, we box people in to the extent that they see no option but to lash out, never mind that they might be the cause of the conflict. How can we feel confident enough to allow our opponent some space to retreat, some space to see how they might go forward out of the stalemate and not be totally crushed?

Capacity to keep the goal in focus and resist pressure to be like the rest

- Keeping the goal in focus means 'not cutting off your nose to spite your face'. It means giving way on the small things because you have greater things in your sights. It means not insisting on fighting, never mind winning, every single battle. It also means not allowing yourself to be distracted from what your main purpose is. It means persevering with the pain and the hardship in the full knowledge that the end is in sight, and when you reach your goal it will all have been worth every minute of it.

- This is yet another area where the example we show to our children is crucial. We need to discuss these matters fully and regularly with them, because the attitude they adopt would determine: their capacity to remain focused and motivated; their capacity to not allow themselves to get distracted by trivialities or by their friends' lack of focus. One young man said to me and a learning mentor recently, that he doesn't believe in this business of 'no pain, no gain'. As far as he was concerned, 'it stands to reason, no pain, no tears'. Needless to say, he passionately disagreed with my view that that was a recipe for mediocrity and a willingness to settle for anything but the best.

Capacity for deferred gratification: graft today, jam tomorrow

- This is another take on the 'no pain, no gain' philosophy, which so many of our children plainly reject. We live in a fast food, fast movies, fast success, culture. Some of us give in far too readily to our children and we encourage them to believe that it is unreasonable to make even the simplest demands of them. We work ourselves to the bone, feed them, clothe them, give them shelter, provide them with every 'mod con' the electronic media tell them they need, and yet some of us treat them as if to require them to do some chores is a form of child abuse. We thus encourage them to make few demands of themselves, to shirk responsibility and to take, take, take. Consequently, children of high ability coast along, settling for mediocrity, and, in the case of boys, especially, adopt attitudes to self presentation that simply serve to mask their insecurity and lack of social and academic competence. In those circumstances, their masculinity becomes a weapon of power and dominance, a weapon they learn to use indiscriminately, even against their very fathers, mothers, and sisters. It serves them equally badly in school, in their relationship with their peers, in forming relationships and generally in their belief in what they are capable of in life.

The above factors are the result of reflection on the mediation and conflict resolution sessions I have conducted in a variety of settings over the last couple of years. I believe it sets out an agenda for us to follow as we seek to determine where our own values and principles come from, and, as parents, how we give expression to them and guide our children in adopting them.

It will be pretty obvious by now that all of the above have a bearing on our capacity to support our children's personal, spiritual, social and academic development, and to work in partnership with their school. It would be clear, also, that the home, school, peer group and community, all contribute to the development of those factors, factors which I see as reflective of: *values and principles of human conduct.*

All four, home, school, peer group, and community, contribute to building our capacity to engage with and live the values that make us fit for living in an ordered society and in an increasingly disordered world.

Home – School – Peer Group – Community

Each has a culture or cultures of its own. None of them operates in a neutral, value-free environment. Each has the capacity to engender behaviour that is conducive to harmony and order, as well as behaviour that is destructive and that detracts from the individual's capacity to act as a responsible social citizen. Each has the capacity to induce in the individual a state of equilibrium and well being, as well as varying degrees of stress.

Intended outcomes

The sessions should:

- provide opportunities for participants to examine their own values base and the principles that govern their day to day living, as parents/carers and as students
- provide assistance with managing current conflicts, drawing upon the learning that all participants will have derived from examining values and behaviours
- facilitate the development of models for resolving conflicts between groups of young people, between families, and between young people/families and schools
- facilitate the development and trialling of models for resolving conflict in communities
- provide a support network for parents and young people, and particularly for single mothers parenting teenage children
- lay the foundations for the development of a confidential counselling and support service for young people living with bullying and in fear of crime

Recovery Strategies

Throughout our work, we will seek to devise strategies for supporting our young people's progress in schooling and education and reversing the persistent patterns of underachievement and underrepresentation in key areas of the labour market, especially the professions. Strategies in relation to our communities:

- projecting high aspirations and high expectations as the norm
- combating the growing anti-learning culture amongst our young people
- reclaiming black youth culture
- getting more black young people into HE than into HMP

Finally, in working towards a model for conflict resolution and peace building, we would address seven principal themes, and they are:

a.   Understanding Existing Conflict
b.   Managing Conflict
c.   Building on Progress
d.   Sustaining Change
e.   Avoiding Regression and the Re-occurrence of Conflict
f.   Evaluation of the Application of the Model(s)
g.   Ongoing Capacity Building and Skills Development

MALE PARTICIPATION IN THE EDUCATION OF THEIR CHILDREN
Parental participation in raising achievement
The CarAf Centre, London, 1 March 2003

Preamble

I have been asked to speak about male participation in the education of their children and I want to do three things:

- define the males in the population that I shall be talking about
- say what I mean by 'education' as it relates to parents
- make some suggestions as to how we might increase the level of men's participation and interest in their children's education

Who are these males?

One can approach this issue by commenting on the role of men, generally, in supporting their children's education. In doing so, however, you immediately come face to face with the reality that 'men' or 'males' is not a homogenous, undifferentiated group.

Whether one is talking about the black or the white population in Britain, there are:

- middle class men, some of whom have had high levels of educational attainment
- working class men, some of whom are barely functionally literate and are awkward about their inability to engage with their children's school work
- gay and bisexual men trying to come to terms with their own sexuality and to develop meaningful relationships with their children

- men who live with their children and their partners and attempt to be equally engaged with their children's schooling or college experience
- men who live with partners and are parenting other men's children
- men who see their children infrequently
- men who have contact with their children weekly or monthly, by arrangement, according to the directions of a court of law
- men whose own educational experience has engendered a deep dislike and distrust of schools, teachers and especially headteachers
- men who regret not handling teachers and schools differently, and not staying in control of their schooling experience and their educational aspirations, but who are now determined to assist their children in not allowing the system to fail them also
- men who have an unhealthy obsession with making of their boy children replica, or carbon copies of themselves
- men who react violently when their children's mothers attempt to get them to take an interest in their children's schooling and general upbringing
- men who are interested but are in prison and cannot therefore be actively engaged
- men who are in prison but develop meaningful relationships with their children for the first time, through reflection, soul searching, and even conversion to higher levels of consciousness of what it means to live with dignity as a socially adjusted human being
- men who just couldn't give a toss

So, we are not talking about an undifferentiated mass of people called 'males'.

Males in focus
For the purposes of this talk, I want to concentrate on black males of Caribbean and African heritage, and white males fathering black children.

Why the latter?

It is estimated that 51% of Caribbean males are in long term relationships with white partners, whether married or unmarried. There is similarly a growing number of white males in long term relationships with black women of Caribbean and African heritage, whether married or unmarried.

For those white parents of black children, particularly, the steep learning curve about the true nature of British society and its endemic racism begins to level off by the time they have suffered the insults, the racist hostility, often the rejection of friends and family, and come face to face with the misery that racism causes their children in school and community.

But I want to concentrate here on black males.

Black people's experience of the schooling system in the last four decades has been such that among today's fathers of black school age children are men who themselves

- have been failed by the schooling system and been excluded in large numbers, or segregated into schools for the educationally subnormal
- have failed to receive education otherwise than at school following exclusion
- have been the subject of the notorious 'sus' laws of police, 'Stop and Search' practices, or other attempts by the police to criminalize them
- have been through the criminal justice system and ended up in custodial institutions
- have suffered unemployment for the longest periods after leaving school
- have opted for further education rather than employment post-16
- have supported their female partners through college courses and university degrees
- joined Access Courses and progressed to Polytechnic or University
- above all, have been defined by society in an especially negative way, usually on the basis of damaging stereotypes, and been subjected to the behaviours and discriminatory treatment to which such definition gives rise

We need to be careful not to fall into the practice of subscribing to theories of black male pathology and be equally careful to identify ways in which men could support one another, and women could support men, in effectively participating in their children's education.

The 'good book' exhorts us to 'Love ye one another'. And, God knows, we as black people need to learn what that really means and practise it. But, in order for us to love one another, at an individual and deeply personal level, no less than in our communities, we must first understand ourselves, learn to respect and love ourselves, and engage in the never ending task of confronting and eliminating those things that prevent us from so doing. It is those very things that encourage the tendency to project our misery onto others.

One of the things that provides positive reinforcement and a sense of self worth for all individuals is the knowledge of who we are, where we've come from, and how positively others see and value us. That is the beginning of respect, for our own selves and for others.

Valued individuals, accepted for who they are and for what they bring, are more positive, productive and focused than those who feel excluded, insecure, threatened, discriminated against or just tolerated. That is as true in our partnerships, marriages or relationships with one another as it is in our organizations, in the workplace and in society generally.

We derive enormous strength and motivation from our own sense of identity and self esteem.

We all have a right to live with respect and dignity, and to operate as partner, parent, child, student, worker, in an environment in which that right is upheld.

So, in order to be able to tackle what is going on in school for our children, there's some stuff we need to put right among ourselves:

- as men in relation to other men
- as men in relation to our partners and the mothers of our children
- as men in relation to our children generally and our boys in particular
- as men in relation to other men's children

- as women in relation to our men
- as women in relation to other women's men

So, why am I getting into all this stuff in a talk that is supposed to be about male participation in their children's education?

I am reminding us of all that stuff in order to underline a very simple point.

The child's first teacher is its fundamental instinct for survival. It follows, therefore, that the child's foremost teacher is its mother. She provides succour, she provides food, she provides security, all of which are essential to the child's survival. The child's best teachers are its parents.

As my wise and functionally illiterate father used to say: *Education is not about book.*

Education is first and foremost about children's spiritual, moral, social, cultural *and* academic development. A child is capable of gaining that rounded education without going anywhere near a school. Indeed, there are many who believe passionately that the only way to ensure that black children receive that type of education in this country is by not sending them to those schools and handing them over to the existing schooling regime.

What then, is the contribution we make to those key aspects of our children's development?

We are a diverse population of black people, with diverse needs, behaviours, styles and values. We suffer collectively from negative stereotyping and patterns of exclusion in a society that automatically validates white people.

We, therefore, need to continuously restore dignity and self worth to ourselves and especially to the most marginalized and devalued amongst us. There is no question that, for us, that means black boys.

In order for black males to participate meaningfully in their children's education, therefore, we need to agree:

- that that does not just mean supervising homework, taking the child off to a bookstore now and then to buy a book, or attending the parents' open evening once a term
- that it particularly does not mean going down to the school

every time a teacher tells your child off and trying to outdo
George Bush in your appetite for war
- that there is not currently a culture amongst us actively
promoting and supporting male participation in their
children's education

One in five families in this country right now is headed by a
single parent. Of those, about 3% are male. Not so long ago, the
phenomenon of the single parent was seen as an aberration only
amongst so-called promiscuous black communities where men
just dropped children (or, to put it more precisely, biological
substance that gave rise to children) all over the place and never
looked back. There was a myth that an aversion to marriage was
the exclusive preserve of these blacks who have never really got
over the impact of slavery on family and social organization.
You do not hear that same theory being expounded these days
in relation to white women's choices about the type of
arrangement they want with men.

Increasingly, however, schools are having to set aside the
expectation that dealing with the home involves dealing with
mother and father. They are more likely dealing with mother
and grandfather.

The black and ethnic minority population in the UK is said to
be 7.1%. National surveys suggest that it is the fastest growing
section of the overall UK population, growing some 15 times
faster than whites, with an increase of 1 million between the
1991 and the 2001 censuses. But, as more of our young people
reach child bearing age, so, too, the likes of me are growing
older. In 3 years time (2006), there will be more 55-64 year olds
than 16-24 year olds in the population.

Increasingly, in my experience, grandfathers are taking
primary school age children to school and developing
relationships with the schools. That interest in the children's
schooling is usually sustained throughout the young person's
secondary schooling, unless, of course, the students themselves
render the grandfathers redundant, or 'diss' them, for taking too
close an interest in their affairs.

If we accept that education is about the spiritual, moral,
cultural, social and academic development of children, then, I

suggest, participation in our children's education is an activity that has to be learnt.

I cannot assist my child with algebra if I don't know my 'a's from my 'x's.

Similarly, I cannot participate in my children's spiritual, moral, social, cultural and academic development if I am not engaging with where I am, myself, spiritually, morally, socially, culturally and academically. The reason is simple.

By the time I begin to take an interest in my child's education, even as early as the nursery school, the child has already formed views about my interactions with him/her or with their mother and siblings. If I am kind, loving, patient, encouraging with praise and make the child feel secure, I would have already laid the foundations for the child's positive self image and self esteem.

On the other hand, if I am aggressive, disrespectful to child, mother and siblings alike, dealing with my frustration through anger, emotional or physical violence, or have a permanent appointment with a television screen or a mobile phone, then I would have sent out an equally powerful message to that child. Indeed, that message could be so powerful that the child couldn't give a sausage whether or not you're interested in their schooling. What matters to them is that you do something about 'you' and stop being such a pain in the neck. As a matter of fact, they could easily take to praying that you would not come anywhere near their school to embarrass them with your unreconstructed ways.

I cannot impart what I do not have.

In failing to attend to our own spirituality, our own values, our own moral compass, our own social development and basic social conduct and manners, our own cultural awareness (including an understanding of the culture of schooling), our own learning needs, we fail to attend to the quality of our relationship to ourselves and with our children. Parents have power. Some fathers seek to exercise power and authority long after they have forfeited the right to say 'boo', let alone to behave as if dem run tings.

Children rarely have the opportunity to discuss their feelings about these matters with their fathers without provoking some massive confrontation and long running conflict, following which the man disappears (again) until another couple of years have passed.

What am I proposing, therefore?

I believe that, as men, we support our children's education:

- by reconnecting with ourselves, first and foremost
- by reconnecting with ourselves spiritually, morally, and culturally
- by being clear about our values
- by living our values
- by demonstrating that we have respect for ourselves, for our children and for their mothers
- by letting them see that respect grow because you give expression to it in all aspects of your interactions with them
- by not heaping all sorts of negative and oppressive stereotypes upon their mothers
- by endeavouring to be the kind of examples we would like our children to follow
- by giving them the confidence to come and share with us what is going on for them, in school, relationship with their peers, in their attempts to make decisions about their careers, in their growing up generally
- by encouraging them to talk about their schooling in the full knowledge that you would listen to them without being judgemental, that you won't condemn them and, above all, that you won't be tempted to go down to the school and deal with the teacher

As I noted earlier, we are a diverse body of people, with diverse dispositions and beliefs. Some men would have made that journey and are reaching for higher levels of consciousness. They are able to be positive role models for their own children, boys in particular, and for other people's children. Others will be struggling. Some might even dismiss all of this as Gus John talking through his rear end.

We will make an impact on male participation in their children's learning only if we act collectively. Only if we take collective responsibility for this project. Only if we commit to securing the future for our children and the generations of black boys to come, by giving up the time to share, the time to encourage and nurture our men, whoever they are and wherever they are ... especially those in youth custody and in prison. Only by demonstrating that we are done with heaping oppressive stereotypes upon one another. Only by collectively tackling the situation our children face in schools and colleges.

That means:

- being prepared to mentor fathers and their children, together, where appropriate
- being prepared to meet, as men, in small groups and share with one another how the school system operates, the information we could legitimately expect schools to provide about what our children are being put through
- being prepared to forge alliances with black teachers and education officials to aid that process
- being prepared to develop trust and confidence in such groups that would allow men to talk about themselves, their aspirations and their anxieties, and work things out collectively
- being prepared to visit and give encouragement to our young people in youth custody institutions and our men in prisons
- being prepared to welcome them into our networks on release from prison
- being committed to ensuring that through our own small efforts we transform the image of black men as being detached from their children's schooling and education and as poor role models

Conclusion

If the projected growth in the black and ethnic minority population I mentioned earlier means anything, it is that the current status of black people in the education system heralds the growth of a massive underclass of black people in British society in the coming decades. That will inevitably result in higher percentages of black men in prison, more of our communities imploding and more of our young black men having a life expectancy of 25 or under.

The issue we are discussing today, therefore, is not just about school/home partnerships or parental involvement in their children's education in any general sense. It is very much about setting an agenda to reverse some deadly trends, to restore dignity and value to ourselves and to challenge the relentless and corrosive mental and psychological attack on the power and potential of the black man.

Let's do it!

LIVING WITH DIGNITY
Leap confronting conflict
Young Mediators Network Conference, London
11 July 2001

Introduction

It gives me enormous pleasure to be able to join you here today, to acknowledge and applaud your efforts and to share some thoughts and experiences. I trust you will find them both meaningful and challenging, and that they will impact upon you as individuals. I hope, also, that they will inspire you in your collective efforts to make a difference by letting change begin with you.

The thoughts I am about to share have derived from many a source

- From my reflections of what it is that made my youth a period that I recall with joy and gratitude, in spite of the incredible poverty with which I grew up. It was a material poverty but by no means a poverty of spirit.

- From the many elders back home, in this country and in the African Diaspora, who inspired me by their wisdom, their love of life, their determination to be allowed to live full and dignified lives, and by their struggles for bread, for freedom and for justice. I stand erect upon their shoulders in order to better understand where I have come from, evaluate where I am now, where I am going, and determine what road would get me there.

- From my own self scrutiny, my own reflections and attempts to make sense of my world, inspired and guided by the Universal Spirit of the Most High God and by the Spirit of

my glorious ancestors.
- More concretely, those thoughts have been inspired by my parenting of six British born black children, each of whom has taught me as much about myself as I have come to learn about them.
- Last, but not least, those thoughts derive, also, from my work as an educator and friend of young people, aged between 3 and 33, for some 35 years in this country.

I want to suggest to you that there has been a crying need for the work you do, and for more people to be involved in it. I also believe that, now more than ever before, growing a culture of mediation amongst young people, growing a practice of resolving conflict by peaceful means, and restoring dignity to the damaged lives of individuals, are all very urgent goals.

I believe in the dignity and worth of the human person.

I believe that everyone has a right to live with respect and dignity.

I believe that everyone has a right to work, study, and enjoy their leisure in an environment in which those rights are upheld.

I believe that respect for oneself and for others grows by giving it practical expression in all aspects of daily living.

Sadly, however, these basic and fundamental rights are routinely denied every day. They are denied to individuals and to the groups to which they belong. These rights are denied to black people, to poor people, to women, to refugees and asylum seekers, to people who are lesbian or gay, to people with disabilities, to sufferers of mental illness, to ex-offenders wishing to rebuild their lives in the community.

These forms of oppression and the social exclusion that results from them impact upon whole communities in ways that are deeply troubling. Take the consequences for African and Caribbean communities, for example:
- the rate of homicides and suicides among black males in the 13-25 age range
- the percentage of black males in the youth custody and prison population relative to their numbers in the population overall
- the disproportionate number of those who were

permanently excluded from school less than five years before ending up in youth custody or in prison

- the population of black males in mental institutions or/and released unwell into the community
- the disproportionate number of black males unemployed, especially in large cities like London
- the percentage of black males who are totally dysfunctional as fathers, except biologically, and who have had no role models on whom to pattern positive approaches to fatherhood, and to their relationship with women; and who, in turn, perversely celebrate the signs of their own male offspring becoming clones of themselves

A reconstructed brother said at a conference I attended recently:

there's no such thing as a 'baby mother', just some woman whom you have abused and a woman and child whose life chances you have compromised'

- the short and long term impact of all that on girls and women, especially because of the power and dominance males continue to exercise in their relationship with women, on all levels of life and the ease with which women have historically betrayed one another because of men

History has taught us, ever since slavery and its legacy, that economic and social structures have created cultures (Caribbean, North American, Black British) in which succeeding generations of black males come to define their black identity by indulging in behaviours which compound their alienation from Self and community, and are oppressive to both.

As I have observed elsewhere

Social exclusion is a process. It is a dynamic process. 'It changes over time and space and affects different people in different ways'. Social exclusion has causes and effects. It is both passive and active. It is the systematic and structural deprivation of the individual's opportunity to participate in society, and, consequently, a denial of dignity, self esteem and self worth.

It creates a cumulative set of circumstances in which the individual is unable to achieve the quality of life to which s/he aspires, and that is consistent with dignified living.

For the purposes of this discussion, I am especially concerned with the active form of social exclusion in which a growing number of our young people indulge:

I mean by that 'the form of social exclusion which comes about when young people lay claim to particular identities and make choices about lifestyles and social behaviours which compound their disadvantage and their existence on the margins of the society'.

Too often, that is then glorified as aspects of youth culture or expressions of black identity to be celebrated ... Too often, also, it constitutes the 'givens' that schools have to deal with, regardless of the more sanitised view of the world preferred by the Government's inspection body, the Office for Standards in Education (OfSTED).

The Purpose and Function of Schooling and Education
There are five principal dimensions to the planning and process of schooling and education, namely:
Community, Spirituality, Culture, Economy and Politics
    In the system as we know it, and as present and past Governments have designed it, there is a very clear relationship between Politics, Education and Economy. Culture is generally seen as being subordinate to those three. The main reason for this is the assumption that schooling and education is about the promotion of white, middle class culture and the displacement of working class, black and other cultures.
    As for spirituality, that seems to be a word that one should not utter in public or in polite company. Before the Lawrence Inquiry, 'race' was another such word. If you talked about 'race' in an upfront manner, you provoked a reaction as if you had just exploded a loud fart. Spirituality is usually confused or fused, conflated, with religion. At best, it is promoted among young people as aesthetics, the appreciation of music and art as having

'a spiritual dimension'.

Even in the more imaginative approaches to Personal, Social and Health Education, little direct reference is made to spirituality in everyday life. Little emphasis is placed upon the relationship between the values that render people fit for living and the consequences for society of the failure of the schooling and education system to assist people in acquiring them.

Consequently, most young people complete their schooling – even with the highest levels of attainment – without having developed any real sense of spiritual awareness.

There is a growing tendency of governments to marry up education and training, or, in the most recent shotgun marriage, 'education' and 'skills', and to see them as being related first and foremost to the national economy and to the nation's economic competitiveness. This reinforces the view that education is primarily about the pursuit of academic excellence and technical competence. That it is about equipping individuals with high level skills that can be sold in an increasingly competitive global marketplace.

Schools, therefore, become factories for the mass production of a potential workforce that has been trained and groomed to conform and to respect authority, to believe in competition rather than collaboration, and to see 'merit' as meaning society's conferment of rewards for disciplined effort.

They are rarely about equipping students with the skills:
- to take control of their own lives
- to be self-managing individuals dedicated to Truth and having the inner strength to be true to their Higher Self
- to function as responsible social citizens, demanding and safeguarding their own rights and entitlements, and having due regard to those of others

The sort of compliance that is based upon discipline and behaviour management, in a system that depends upon sanctions and punitive measures (fixed term and permanent exclusions), is not guaranteed to produce self-regulating individuals who assume personal responsibility for the quality of the learning environment they help to create, as well as for their actions and behaviours outside school.

'Principles are guidelines for human conduct.
They are deep, fundamental truths that have universal application'

Schooling and education should be about
- assisting students to establish their principles
- inspiring students to choose their own personal, social, moral, and spiritual values, and to be aware of the practical methods for developing and deepening them
- providing students with a philosophy of living so as to support their overall growth and development as rounded individuals
- providing them with the basis on which they could make choices and integrate themselves into the community with respect, with positive self esteem, with confidence and purpose

Schools should be providing the guidance and giving students the confidence to ask
- Who am I?
- Why am I here?
- On what should I pattern my relationship with others?
- What values do I need to adopt if I am to live up to and fulfil my highest potential?
- What are my responsibilities to my Self, my family, community, society?
- How can school provide opportunities for me to negotiate learning such that I construct a personal development plan that is appropriate to my needs and will help me develop my Self?

I believe that at the root of many of the challenges facing young people in the community is the question: what is meant by curriculum entitlement in schools?

The Government has a focus on raising standards and achieving results. But, if we believe in *education for all* as a fundamental principle, we need to challenge the notion that only the well adjusted, highly motivated, self disciplined and conforming students have a right to mainstream teaching and support en route to good GCSE grades.

Those whose self development is under strain and who need

to acquire some basic social interactive and self management skills, even as they engage with the learning process, are effectively to be selected out and put through remedial programmes, either before, instead of, or after internal or external exclusion.

We need to insist that the Government affirms the right of children, as part of their entitlement, to have time spent on:

- assisting them to be better able to manage themselves, take control of their conduct, learn to manage conflict and, in many cases, learn to manage their disordered lives
- assisting them to develop coping strategies that would enable them to function positively in the chaotic circumstances that constitute their daily living away from school
- assisting them in learning to unlearn the behaviours and strategies that, in many cases, characterize 'normal' conduct in their homes and in their neighbourhoods, e.g., bigotry, racism, anti-Semitism, homophobia, the subordination of women through physical and emotional violence, resorting to violence as the only means of resolving conflict, insistence on settling scores, insistence on 'winning the fight'
- assisting them in developing positive self identity and in dealing with the psychological impact of living with bullying, violence, rejection, low self esteem, sexism, racism, homophobia
- assisting them in identifying and eliminating any tendency to bullying, sexism, racism, and homophobia they themselves might have
- engaging with them in negotiating relationships and power structures amongst groups of their peers and within the school itself

I am arguing that schools should not be encouraged in their view that such students are exceptional. Rather, it should be taken as *given* that they represent that cross section of young people in the community with all their varied backgrounds, experiences, aptitudes and needs, but all having the *same entitlement to quality opportunities for self and academic development.*

The way schools are funded at the moment prevents the

organization of small size teaching groups where needed, and the introduction of tutorials. In most inner city schools and especially those where truancy and school exclusion are a problem, schools should have the means of organizing classes of no more than 10 students. Each of those should be entitled to a 'Student <> Teacher Conversation' once per fortnight, to look at the process of teaching and learning and at the progress students are making in their self-development, in their personal as well as their academic development. This is because, for an increasing number of students, a preoccupation with personal issues hampers their ability to focus on learning and, therefore, their academic performance.

This would give students and teachers the space and the motivation to address the following questions:

- How is learning taking place for the individual students in the group?
- What learning is taking place?
- How could it be made more enjoyable and more relevant?
- What is the relationship between that and the learning students derive from all other areas of their lives outside school?
- How can teachers' teaching objectives be jointly assessed in the light of learning outcomes as defined by students?
- How can students be assisted to grow in confidence, in sharing the learning they derive outside school, including the teaching of specific skills?
- What contribution to the formal learning programme and to students' personal development could other professionals make, e.g., youth workers, musicians, footballers, dramatists, poets, business partners, journalists, etc.?
- How can all of the above be made to impact upon the planning and delivery of lessons?

I am arguing that such a model allows the possibility for schools to offer students quality opportunities for self and academic development for all, as an entitlement of all.

It also allows for the development of skills for principle-centred living and building a values-based environment. Skills such as

- Active listening
- Conflict resolution
- Collaborative rule making
- Encouraging positive behaviour
- Dealing with disruptive behaviour
- Managing anger
- Avoiding the negative cycle of inadequacy, low self esteem, resistance, blame, anger, and retaliation

We carry a lot of baggage around. We burden ourselves with things we refuse to put down and walk away from. We besiege ourselves with unfinished business that blocks our spiritual arteries and robs the spirit of the oxygen by which it might grow.

It robs us of peace, we harbour a corrosive anger. Anger induces loneliness and deep frustration.

Forgiveness is liberating. It can truly make you free, especially when you develop the capacity to forgive yourself. And it is by forgiving yourself that you find the strength and the humility to seek the forgiveness of others.

It is by forgiving yourself that you are able to love those who insist on bearing the load and the pain that you have already put down; those who continue to isolate you; those who burn up inside when they set eyes on you; those who carry you in their hearts (or in their craw, as the old people used to say back home) and are so weighed down by it that they cannot take off to spiritual heights.

Some one once said that *'the greatest strength is gentleness'*. If you don't believe that, just go and observe the black panther, or the grace of the lioness tending her cubs.

Gentleness helps you conserve energy so that you could redirect that energy to resist aggression and to deflect the negativity that is being directed at you. And if you have that inner strength and it gains expression in that gentleness, you can resolve conflict without the need to resort to violence, verbal, physical or emotional; without the need to depend on brute force.

Now I am not trying to transform this generation, descendants of a long line of proud black warriors, into a generation of wimps and pushovers. Have no fear, when the situation really calls for it, I could kick arse more fiercely than anyone else. Too often, though, we incite the third world war for trivial reasons. Brothers pass out one another for nothing, or next to nothing.

Iyanla Vanzant, that powerful black woman and spiritual counsellor wrote:

When we have peace in our hearts and minds, we draw peace into our lives

It enables us to reach towards the Higher Self by working to banish all those things that prevent us attaining that higher level of consciousness. Our elevation to the Higher Self is obstructed by our failure to deal with anger, with hatred, with the lust for revenge and the insistence on settling scores, with jealousy, with hypocrisy, with greed, with envy.

It means that we need to take responsibility for what we do and what we say; personal responsibility for what our actions do to others. It means understanding the relationship between what we do, what we say, and how we think.

As one writer put it:

If I have positive thoughts, I go in a positive direction.
If I harbour negative thoughts, I move in a negative direction.
If I have no thoughts, I go nowhere.

Someone else said

The happiness of your life depends upon the quality of your thoughts. If you don't care where you're going, any road would get you there.

It is for that reason we stress the importance of self respect, the importance of *living with dignity*.

If you do not respect yourself you would have precious little respect for others. If your life lacks meaning and purpose, you think nothing of ruining other people's lives, or even of denying them life itself. So, we endure the phenomenon of what is called 'black on black' crime. Brothers gun down one another as if they're killing flies. They use bullets against their girlfriends or wives to express anger, jealousy, inadequacy, and their own worthlessness. Some who know they have Aids go and wilfully sleep with others and have unprotected sex because as far as they are concerned they have nothing left to lose and they don't care who they bring down with them.

The system emasculates them as black men now, in the same way as it did their forefathers in shackles and forced labour. What is worse, the system has programmed us to do the enslavement of ourselves. So, we are persecuted by crime and by the fear of crime within our very own communities. It induces a moral paralysis. It puts us in fear of our own selves. And yet, there is usually not one single white person in sight doing any of this to us. That is what I call structural racism. It is a racism that is a product of certain systemic arrangements, and a consequence of the racist stereotyping and racist expectations of us as a people, expectations which become self-fulfilling.

That is why, however comfortable we may be with ourselves, however safe we may feel because we do not get in harm's way, if we do not uphold and fight to defend everybody's right to live with dignity and respect, we put our own rights and our own safety at risk.

Therefore, if I want to change my life, I need to change my actions. If I want to change my actions, I need to alter my thinking.

The system will not do it for me. Neither will any messianic figure such as a Malcolm X or Martin Luther King. All such Beacons that once in a generation shoot across our skies can ever do is to raise levels of consciousness, and create a climate in which individuals make a change for themselves, and act collectively to bring about change in society. The process has to begin with each and every one of us.

If I want to change my life, I need to change my actions. If I want to change my actions, I need to alter my thinking. I need to challenge my own mindset and will myself to do and act differently.

Those of you who are believers (of whatever Faith) would no doubt seek Divine guidance and help in changing course and sticking to the new plan. Believers or not, however, the challenge is a deeply personal one. And unless we all face up to it, we would forever be expending vast amounts of energy dealing with conflict.

I am reminded of a favourite saying of the Cree people, one of the First Nations of Americans in the USA:

Never let things slide:
Keep a steady hold, each of you, upon yourself
– do not throw away your life simply to spite another.

Permit me to end with a quote from Iyanla Vanzant, part of which I mentioned above:

There are times when we find ourselves at odds with someone.
It may seem that our only choices are to get caught up in the situation
or to walk away.

The ego tells us we must prove we are right.
If we walk away, the other person will win.
The ego keeps us from recognising there is another choice.
Whatever situation confronts us,
We must recognise our right to be at peace.

The need to be right and meet discord head on begins within.
It is a need that stems from feelings of powerlessness,
Unworthiness and a lack of love.
It shows up in life as arguments and confrontation.

When we have peace in our hearts and minds
We draw peace into our lives.
When discord and disharmony present themselves
We can stand firm

When we let go of the need to prove ourselves
Nothing and no one can disturb the quiet and peace of our minds.

Let me salute you once more and wish you a very successful conference and every success in your ever so timely endeavours.

2.6

RECLAIMING THE PAST, SHAPING THE FUTURE
Handsworth Girls' School
Awards Evening
17 November 1994

Year of '93, students, parents, staff, governors, friends all
It gives me enormous pleasure to join you this evening in celebrating your achievements and in reaffirming your aspirations as individuals and as a school community. I am particularly pleased to have been called upon to do so in the final term of Elaine Foster's headship of your school.

Elaine would be the first to remind me that this is your evening, Year of '93, and that I should be dealing with your business. Well, I am sure you will agree with me that part of your business here this evening is to celebrate Elaine Foster's achievements as the headteacher and friend you have been privileged to have. Your achievements are her achievements, and the measure of her success as team leader, parent substitute, bossy boots, whip-cracker, and a constant source of inspiration, encouragement, and faith in what is achievable by the whole school community, staff, students, parents, and governors.

I want to express my personal thanks to her for being my mentor and friend, as well as a highly valued professional colleague for many years; for the massive contribution she has made to effective schooling in this institution, and to British education in general. Elaine Foster is truly a rare specimen in British education and in British public life. Thank you, Miss.

I have called this talk 'Reclaiming the past, shaping the future' because I want to share some thoughts about the role of education in empowering young people for political action.

I am one of those old-fashioned types whose historical sense tells me that I have a responsibility to safeguard and to extend the hard-won rights and entitlements that generations before me have secured through their struggles, and their blood, sweat and tears, even to the point of sacrificing their very lives. I feel it is given to me to do something with that, and within the political and social space it has provided, to take those struggles forward so long as there are at work in society systems of oppression that are an affront to humanity itself.

'*A luta continua*' (the struggle continues) is not the exclusive refrain of revolutionaries. If it means anything, it is about the responsibility of us all to ensure that we do our damnedest to take care of the world we inherit, and pass it on in a state that hopefully enhances the human potential and quality of life of its inheritors.

One does not have to be Marxist to celebrate the fact that the struggles of others before us led to our enjoyment of our childhood without the ravages of child labour, and to the day divided notionally into eight hours for work in which you sell your labour, eight hours for rest and recreation, and eight hours for sleep. The new technological revolution presents to my generation and yours a new imperative, i.e., to join forces in the fight for a shorter worker day, a shorter working week, a shorter working life, and more time for rest, recreation and cultural creativity.

Mind you, I have yet to find a modern day teacher, headteacher or director of education who enjoys eight hours of recreation and eight hours sleep, but at least that is what generations before us fought for.

As an educationalist and a socialist I am guided by certain basic beliefs; that, for example

- Education is a fundamental human right. It is not a privilege to be granted on the basis of social class, racial or ethnic origin, wealth, religion, age, sex or physical ability.
- Education is for life, and, as such, it should be possible for individuals to key in and out of education at all ages of their lives.
- Education is not just for equipping people with skills for the

workplace. It is for developing in people the social skills and competences to take control of their own lives and to function as responsible social citizens, demanding and safeguarding their own rights, and having due regard to and respect for the rights of others.

Whatever denies access to education for individuals, and groups in society, effectively denies them their fundamental human right, and contributes to their oppression.

Education and schooling should be about, among other things, assisting disadvantaged groups in society, and people in general, in understanding the roots and the persistence of racial and social injustice, of gender subordination, and providing them with the individual and collective tools with which to combat these forms of oppression.

The thirty-five years between the 1944 Education Act and the start of this deep winter of Conservative government witnessed many contestations in policy making circles, in communities, within the teaching profession and in boardrooms around these themes. Debates about education priority areas, comprehensive education, the eleven-plus, access to quality schooling and to higher education by working class students, especially women, and by black people, multicultural and antiracist education, access to education across all the phases for people with special education needs, the relationship between schooling and the economy, have all been major preoccupations in the last thirty-five years.

In one way or another they have all been about the purpose and function of education and schooling in society and in relation to the economy, and about fundamental rights and entitlements.

Sadly, however, in all of those debates, young people have been talked about or talked at, but hardly listened to. More absurdly even, young people have been denied opportunities to understand and to learn from the experiences of struggle that people like them have had previously.

One of the principal reasons for that in my view is the tendency in British society to see young people as either dumb, politically uninterested, rebellious, or naturally prone to destructiveness and to apathy. You are all shining examples of the very opposite of all that, and true ambassadors for youth.

It has always puzzled me that young people are seen as rebellious and naturally wayward. As far as I am concerned, the opposite is true. They are boringly conformist. It is that conformism that gives us as parents such headaches: designer clothes, brand name trainers, electronic games, certain noises that are classed as music ... I am sure you get my meaning.

The commercial exploiters of the young, the raiders of the lost art of deferred gratification, the raiders of your pocket and mine, all know that only too well. That is why if there wasn't something called youth they would have had to invent it.

Far from being rebellious and requiring elaborate systems of control, therefore, most young people represent a predictable, sometimes amusing conformity. How different it would be if the norm was to see young people as creative, visionary, critical, caring, as having a deep sense of justice and of fairness, and the right to protest when they experience injustice and unfairness.

I find it interesting, for example, that the so-called Great Debate in education in this country, led by former Prime Minister James Callaghan and Education Minister Shirley Williams, was taking place at the same time as a massive uprising of school students and young people in Soweto.

They were protesting about the apartheid system of education, an education that prepared them to take their allotted place within an increasingly repressive apartheid society. Hundreds lost their lives then, and tens of thousands of young people below the age of twenty-five gave their lives over the years in vehement opposition to that crime against humanity called apartheid. That crime was punctuated by massacres, genocide and the systematic denial of human rights.

Yet, despite the horrendous human cost, the apartheid regime could not extinguish that fundamental instinct for freedom, that spirit of resistance, which has spearheaded the political emancipation of the black people of South Africa.

And I say: Long live the revolutionary spirit of all oppressed people, everywhere.

Whatever views the British state and British schools may have had of the school children of Soweto laying claim to their country and its future with nothing but their bare fists and their defiant voices, always in the face of the military might of the South African army and police, they certainly did not see British youths in similar roles.

The education reforms introduced by the Labour government in 1976 and built upon with a vengeance by the Conservatives from 1979 to the present day, have all had one thing in common. They make no provision for young people to demand accountability from those who educate them.

Parental rights and entitlements are clearly stated in the various education acts and in the Parents Charter. School students' rights, however, are inferred rather than clearly defined. Consequently, too many schools emphasize their expectations of students, the responsibilities they expect to see them carry, and not the rights and entitlements the students have.

It is my belief that were those rights and entitlements to be defined more clearly, with systems put in place to guarantee their delivery, many of the problems that arise between students and schools would be eliminated. Issues such as the quality of teaching, the quality of learning, the quality of educational outcomes, exclusions, racial harassment, bullying, behaviour and discipline generally, all become very relevant in this context.

I know of no better place to begin empowering young people for political action than the school. For one thing it allows opportunities for 'controlled experiments'. For another, it could provide the information and intelligence on the basis of which young people could engage in purposeful action for change.

Let me cite a few examples:
a. The campaigns we waged in the 1970s against the practice of placing scandalous numbers of black children into schools for the educationally subnormal.
b. Campaigns against 'sus', the police practice of criminalizing young blacks for suspicion of being about to commit an arrestable offence.

c. Black parents and students' concerns, registered over a number of years, about the excessive rate of exclusion and expulsion of black students, especially boys.

d. Black youths' struggles in respect of the New Cross Massacre, the racist murder of thirteen young people at 439 New Cross Road in Deptford, South East London on 18 January 1981, while they attended a sixteenth birthday party and the death of a fourteenth youth subsequently.

e. The New Cross Massacre Black People's Day of Action that followed on 2 March 1981. In that march, 25,000 people took to the streets and brought that centre of commerce, central London, to a standstill on an ordinary working Monday. They were mainly black, predominantly young, with a fair representation of progressive whites. Those progressive whites were joining us in saying 'no' to the kind of society the police, the state and the neo-fascists had created around us.

f. The mass uprisings that erupted across Britain three months later, and were to be repeated annually up until the middle of the 1980s. I am sure you hardly need reminding of your own local campaigns.

g. Labour disputes at Imperial Typewriters in Leicester, and at Mansfield Hosiery, in which Asian women for the very first time in British labour relations exercised their workers' rights and took on the management, despite the opposition of their men-folk who insisted on selling them out and managing disputes on their behalf.

In her day, Mrs Margaret Thatcher issued edicts about a number of things, including how we should define history. There are those of us who dearly wish she hadn't. Anything up to thirty years ago should not be called history, she said, but is really current affairs. This means, in effect, that a huge and important slice of British social history in the post-war period is being ignored in the school curriculum, and there is no formal way in which the student generation is being assisted in locating and learning from that history. What is equally serious is that the government itself constantly fails to acknowledge that history and use its lessons in making policy and legislation.

I started with the notion of rights, and this is where I wish to end. I have a major concern about the number of rights we enjoyed prior to 1979 which have been steadily eroded, often without protest and sometimes without the general public even noticing. If it is given to us to take care of the present so that generations to come may inherit a worthwhile future, then we really need to redouble our efforts to safeguard our rights. The Criminal Justice Bill, soon to become law, the laws relating to refugees and asylum seekers, the laws relating to access to social security and welfare payments, the laws relating to the movement of people across European boundaries, increasingly repressive immigration laws, all point miserably to the state we are in and the sort of future that we face.

I would like to think, however, that the future we want is not the future we face. I am convinced that through the prism of the experience of young people, and of young black people in the inner city in particular, we can liberate a massive potential for creativity, for growth and for change, so that together we can build the future for everyone.

Year of '93, I offer you hearty congratulations on your achievements, both academic and in terms of personal growth and development. I wish to congratulate all those who supported you in your learning and hopefully learned a lot from you in the process: your teachers, your parents, your peers. I hope your children, those of you who intend to have them, give you as hard a time as you have given your teachers and your parents. As a matter of fact, history tells me that they certainly will.

Continue to reach for the stars, and let nothing or no one render you less than you know you have the capacity to be, and to become.

In the words of another inspirational headteacher, on an occasion such as this:

Your future lies ahead of you like a carpet of fresh fallen snow. Be careful how you walk in it for every step will show.

Go forth in confidence and with your heads high, always! I wish you well for a bright future.

WIDENING ACCESS FROM BOTH SIDES
Teaching in the Inner Cities – A preparation for excellence?

Keble College – Oxford
30 June 1994

I want to begin by offering an alternative title for my talk. I assure you that the message will be the same, but I put to you that what we are required to do both as teachers and tutors in order to widen access and eliminate barriers is to 'Create an Alternative Education Culture'. We have to begin with that urgent imperative in order to end up, in a reflexive sort of way, with the happier and more just and equitable situation we desire. So, I shall be talking about: 'Creating an Alternative Education Culture' and arguing that it is a task for teachers and tutors, for students themselves, for their parents, and for whole communities.

But 'alternative to what?' Alternative to existing culture, nurtured and systematically cultivated within the last four decades, a culture which results from the state we are in, and results equally in the mess we are in.

What do parents want from the schooling and education system?

My experience tells me that all parents, irrespective of their background, want more or less the same basic things

- they want their children to succeed, to do well, to do better than they themselves did, especially if they are working class parents with the most rudimentary educational attainment
- they want their children to more than just hold their own
- they want them to be equipped, through their education and schooling, for a decent job even if, given the current rate of

unemployment, it might take them some time to get any sort of job

• they want them to develop their particular aptitudes, skills and abilities, and to do so to the point of excellence

They expect 12 years of compulsory schooling to enable their children to achieve, or be well on their way to achieving most, if not all of that, and to do so irrespective of their ethnic background, their sexual orientation, or the particular side of town in which they live.

Moreover, they expect 12 years of compulsory schooling to do so without requiring their children to feel debased and lacking in worth because of their home language, who their parents are, their parents' own standard of education, the predominant life styles that obtain within their communities, or the reported incidence of crime in their particular neighbourhood.

To have those aspirations, however, is to make assumptions, legitimate assumptions about education as a fundamental human right, essential to the proper functioning of a liberal democratic society. But it is also to imagine an education that is facilitative, liberating, predicated upon high expectations, and one that projects such expectations as legitimate because the system produces ample evidence of those high expectations being fulfilled. It is to imagine an education culture, furthermore, in which success is seen as the norm. It is to imagine an education culture in which teachers have high expectations of themselves, not least of all with respect to the quality of their teaching, high expectations of their students, whose learning they expect to be commensurate both with the high expectations they are actively encouraged to have of themselves, and with their teachers' own high quality teaching. It is a culture within which schools seek constantly to satisfy themselves that there is a high degree of correlation between the quality of teaching, the quality of children's learning, and the quality of educational outcomes.

Sadly, however, it is questionable whether such an education culture ever existed for all groups and classes within this society in the last hundred years.

There is strong evidence to suggest that the schooling and

education system was organized for the structured reproduction of both privilege and failure. The natural relationship that was and is deemed to exist between the playing fields of Eton and the spires of Oxford is perhaps relevant in this particular context. Equally relevant is the expectation that generations of certain groups of students from private and independent schools have had that Oxford would be their 'finishing school' at the end of a predictable line of progression in their educational career.

I want to suggest that the structured failure and underachievement in the state system, the culture of low aspirations, and correspondingly low expectations, that characterized the schooling and education of white working class people in this society for well over a century, has been racialized in post Second World War Britain.

What form has this racialization taken?

For black communities across Britain over the last three decades, it has assumed the following characteristics:

- the nationwide and scandalous practice of placing vast numbers of children into schools for the educationally sub-normal (ESN) in the 1960s and 1970s
- the equally widespread practice of placing most black kids in the lowest streams, bands, or sets.
- the failure of the schooling system to educate our children and to acknowledge and develop their abilities and their potential
- teachers' low expectations of black children and their active encouragement to black children to have low expectations of themselves
- the massive evidence up and down the country of the schooling system producing 'happy illiterates' and blaming black parents for having too high aspirations
- a labour market, aided and abetted by the careers service, which operated on the assumption that schools will churn out black school leavers to do the filthiest and most menial jobs, with only a few 'high fliers' getting into high status employment
- the schooling system's insistence that education and

schooling would both reinforce British racism and give blacks the same raw deal to which it had subjected the white working class for generations

- the complete denial of black people's cultural heritage, and of the massive contribution to knowledge and to the development of modern societies that past and present generations of us have made

- the dismissive, disrespectful and often hostile treatment to which black parents were/are subjected by the schooling and education system as we attempt to stand up for our children and in defence of our education rights.

That racialization of underachievement and of low expectations went hand in hand, and became institutionalized side by side with the racialization of immigration, the racialization of various forms of crime, and the racialization of unemployment. Street crimes, a phenomenon much older than Robert Peel (the 'father' of modern policing), was racialized into muggings, and for 'mugging' read 'black youth'. That is how 'Sus' became inextricably linked with the activities of black youth and the criminalization of them by the police for suspicion of being about to commit a criminal offence.

Most black people, certainly those from the Caribbean, did not have to imagine an alternative education culture. They had lived within one or been the products of it. It was an education culture where it was commonplace for the children of illiterate peasant farmers or plantation labourers to win Island Scholarships and end up in institutions such as Oxbridge. It was an education culture in which teachers had high expectations of students and demanded that they disciplined themselves, take responsibility for their own learning, work hard and succeed. Those teachers laboured with commitment, dedication and love, especially when it came to the education of children from poor backgrounds, and in that they had the total cooperation and respect of parents and of the whole community.

The one thing that I and my parents' generation cannot believe (and the whole wretched situation does defy belief), is that the brain matter, the genetic material of people like us underwent some sort of inexplicable metamorphosis when we crossed the Atlantic, such that the predominant experience we have had in the British schooling system is of underachievement and failure. So much so that we are expected to believe that it is beyond the capacity of the schooling system to give us quality education. We now have the disturbing situation in which the academically successful, high achieving, working class, inner city British born black male of African Caribbean background is an increasingly rare species. He is much more to be found among the worrying statistics that gave rise to this particular study and are confirmed by it: Outcast England – How Schools Exclude Black Children.

This is 1994. In 1971, almost twenty-five years earlier, Bernard Coard alerted the education establishment to the other scandalous phenomenon I mentioned before, in a little book called: How the West Indian Child is Made Educationally Subnormal in the British School System. Outcast England now, no less than that book then, is a major indictment of the British schooling system. Then, as now, black parents have felt the need to take drastic measures to safeguard their children's education and ensure that they did not develop such an irrecoverable resistance to schooling and education as to risk damaging their life chances for good.

Those measures included:

- removing children from British schools and sending them to grandparents or other relatives in the Caribbean to complete their schooling, before returning for higher education in Britain
- finding places for children in private schools and making horrendous sacrifices to fund them
- paying up to £15 per hour for private lessons for children to compensate for the disruption in or poor quality of their schooling

And, so institutionalized is the racialization of underachievement that even OfSTED inspection teams approach their task with deeply ingrained expectations and biases. Let us take an example from one OfSTED inspection report. OfSTED carried out an inspection at Hornsey School for Girls in North London in March 1993. In the report that followed, they stated thus:

Hornsey School serves the whole of Haringey and also admits students from neighbouring boroughs. The intake represents the full range of ability and is rich in cultural and linguistic diversity. The largest groups are White British (27 per cent), Black British (13 per cent) and those of Bangladeshi heritage (11 per cent). Nearly 70 per cent of the students speak a language other than English at home. Over 60 languages are represented and while some 20 per cent of the girls know Bengali or Turkish, the other main languages are Arabic, Greek, Gujarati, Urdu and Yoruba. There is a range of religions represented in the school population, including several branches of Christianity, Islam, Hinduism and Sikhism.

Hornsey School for Girls is a very good school. Standards of work are high and students achieve good examination results in GCSE which compare favourably with national figures in spite of the untypical intake. *The quality of teaching is high; lessons are well planned and interesting; good use is made of resources and students work hard and respond well.*

Given everything else that that OfSTED inspection found out about the school, what on earth does 'in spite of the untypical intake' actually mean? Does it mean that, given the intake, one should automatically expect poor examination performance, poor quality teaching and learning, and evidence of students not working hard and not responding well? Would the same underlying assumptions have been made if perchance the students were fluent White French and German speakers whose parents for whatever reasons had relocated to North London in similar numbers?

By their extraordinary comment, the OfSTED team appears to be saying that the very positive attributes they identified at Hornsey School are typically to be found at a girl's school in Haywards Heath. According to their implicit model, Hornsey School should not be what it is, given its location and having as it does only 27% White British on its school roll.

To paraphrase the published title of this talk, 'Teaching for Excellence' is presumably not something OfSTED expects to find in a school on the outer ring of the inner city.

Creating an Alternative Education Culture

How are we in Hackney addressing the task of creating an alternative education culture? In Hackney, we repudiate the social determinism exemplified by that OfSTED statement. Rather, given the not dissimilar composition of our population, we see the challenge facing us as:

how to ensure that our schools cater for the individual and collective needs of their particular communities, acknowledging the attributes children bring, and building upon them in facilitating their learning

As I stated in my address to the annual conference of Hackney Education Managers in 1992:

I believe that LEAs, no less than schools, do have a right to exist as democratic providers of services and guarantors of people's educational entitlements. We need to rediscover our sense of common purpose and, with a clear vision and mission, work together to create a learning partnership, being attentive at all times to 'customer' requirements and 'customer' satisfaction.

Put simply, the LEA's vision is:

'To achieve high quality education for all, underpinned by principles of equality'. The mission of the LEA, i.e., its core business in this new dispensation is: 'to promote and support the provision of high quality education according to the needs, entitlements and aspirations of the people of Hackney, and to make every school a good school.

We, together need to be much more focused on quality and equality as we seek to build a learning infrastructure in the borough that is responsive to the disparate needs of all of Hackney's residents. We need to attend to establishing measurable objectives and deal with the practicalities of implementing the vision that we agree'.

In Hackney, educational underachievement ranks high on our list of equal opportunity issues. The educational entitlement of students of low ability, students with special educational needs, multilingual students, students without English as a first language, girls of whatever ethnic origin, working class students and black students generally, must always be of paramount concern to us. One obvious way of demonstrating that concern is to have in place appropriate systems for monitoring and evaluating the quality of teaching, the quality of learning, and the quality of educational outcomes. Not every four years, not just at 7, 11, 14 and 16, but as a continuous process in the education and schooling cycle. Teachers, particularly, must have ownership of those monitoring systems and they must be demonstrable to governors, students, parents, Advisers and Inspectors, or anyone else who might have an interest.

I would like to think that all our headteachers, especially in the secondary schools, are on task as far as that particular agenda is concerned. We in the education directorate have sought to plan with them, very carefully, ways in which they could be supported in this task, and especially in ensuring that they, and we, are constantly alert to the various barriers to students' achievement.

We have a number of hard indicators by which to assess our achievements since Hackney became a LEA. I have chosen just one to share with you, one which I believe would be of interest to this particular audience.

All Pupils	January Roll	% Entered for 1+ GCSE	% Gaining 1+ A-G	% Gaining 1+ A-C	% Gaining 5+ A-G	% Gaining 5+ A-C	% Gaining No Passes
1993	1,224	96.5	93.8	65.8	75.9	25.0	6.2
1992	1,318	87.6	85.1	56.3	68.1	20.9	14.9
1991	1,321	86.6	83.6	54.5	64.3	17.9	16.4
1990	1,351	81.1	77.3	46.9	58.2	14.1	22.7

Table 1: The performance of 15 year old pupils in GCSE examinations
Note: The table excludes the results of pupils in special schools.
[Source: 'GCSE Results 1993' – Research & Statistics Section, March 1994]

Table 1 shows the percentages of pupils entered for GCSE exams, achieving at least one pass, achieving 5 or more passes at grades A-C (higher grade passes) and achieving 5 or more passes at grades A-G. Comparative figures are given for the previous three years (1990, 1991, 1992). The table shows the progress made since Hackney took over responsibility for education from the Inner London Education Authority.

As the table shows, 1993 saw overall improvement at GCSE for the fourth consecutive year. Of particular note is the increase in the percentage of pupils achieving 5 or more GCSE passes – from 68.1% in 1992 to 75.9 % in 1993. It is encouraging to note the decrease in the percentage of pupils failing to gain any GCSE qualifications – only 6.2% in 1993 as compared to 22.7% in 1990.

Forging an Effective Partnership?

Where, then, does what we are doing in Hackney and what other colleagues are also doing in their schools or their LEAs, match up to what the Admissions Tutors from the Colleges represented here are doing?

If I could begin with some anecdotal evidence based on feedback from Hackney. We must accept that there is still a heavy overlay of mystique about Oxford as a University, and that students in the state system in urban areas view the cultural transformation that is necessary to be able to deal with Oxford as the metaphorical equivalent of crossing the Alps.

Very few students have an understanding of Oxford's heterogeneity and of the autonomous, some would say idiosyncratic, manner in which individual colleges with their devolved management operate. What most would-be students assume, however, is that it is a prerequisite of entry to, and progression at, Oxford that you give up a great deal of what makes you the person you are, with all your cultural rootedness, your inner city street cred, and the rest of it, thus, they suspect, making you a cultural outcast for all time. You have fears that your peers, siblings and other members of your family would see you as a toff or a snob, and would liken you to some of the products of Oxford that they see parading around the place, including some of the walking disasters in national government.

It is against that background that I wish to propose the following:

Demystifying 'Oxford' and its Admissions Procedures

a. There is an urgent need for inner city students, and inner city black students in particular, to be encouraged to see Oxford Colleges as places to which they are entitled to apply as they would think of applying, automatically, to other provincial universities, old and new.

b. There is an equally urgent need for Oxford Colleges to put an end to the mystique surrounding their admissions arrangements and practices, and especially to the individual idiosyncracies to be found in the admissions interview.

c. There needs to be a greater understanding on the part of Admissions Tutors' and Subject Tutors' of the dynamic within inner city schools and the overall circumstances surrounding any one student's decision to submit themselves for an interview at Oxford.

d. There needs to be a clear statement of the quality and extent of the support arrangements students could expect to access if they are given a place at Oxford.

In relation to a), I would propose a number of things:

i. There surely can be no better way of demystifying Oxford as a University to which inner city students could go than by having inner city black Oxford undergraduates or graduates share their experiences of being there with groups of school students. Opportunities should therefore be created for members of the Oxford Access Scheme to make programmed visits to schools and to host inner city black students at Oxford Colleges.

ii. An extension of that arrangement could then be a mentoring scheme where, once students and their form tutors determine that the student could successfully work towards the grades necessary for College entry, the student could be paired with an Oxford undergraduate mentor and work towards preparation for application and selection. I envisage that happening as early as Year 10.

iii. Oxford has a tradition of Open Days and those are usually very well attended. I suspect that most inner city black

students would find them enormously off-putting, not least
of all because of the preponderance of students from private
and independent schools who attend them.

iv. What monitoring systems are in place, for example, so that
any one College could satisfy itself that discrimination is not
taking place at the interview stage, especially through the
autonomous and seemingly idiosyncratic propensities and
practices of some interviewers? What basis is there for
comparisons within and between subject disciplines in
Colleges and across the University as a whole?

v. With approximately forty British born African-Caribbean
students out of a University population of some 15,000, what
evidence is there to assist you in explaining what is going on
here? Is it that black British students are being rejected in
proportion to the rate of rejection of applicants in all other
ethnic categories?

vi. Is it that those are the only ones who applied and you were
so delighted to see them that you took the lot?

vii.Do black students as a whole have a greater chance of being
accepted in some Colleges rather than others, or to Arts
subjects rather than Sciences?

viii. You appear to have no basis for answering these
questions.

ix. If, therefore, the University is supporting the initiative taken
by African, Caribbean and Asian undergraduates in 1991 to
establish the Oxford Access Scheme, and many of you as
Admissions Tutors give the Scheme your active support,
how can you and the black students be so sure that even as
you succeed in widening access, the system does not
continue operating with a rejection rate that cannot be
interrogated?

x. It appears to me that, individual College autonomy or not,
the issue of monitoring cannot be ducked. Autonomy need
not and should not mean the absence of accountability,
especially in an institution that places such great store on its
historical work in the area of rights and entitlements.

xi. Similarly, there needs to be a clear statement from each
College as to what it is looking for through the interview

process, and how it ensures that interviewers do not apply all sorts of stereotypes in dealing with inner city applicants.

xii. Colleges need to give due consideration, also, to the sort of student they are looking for and the assumptions they make as to whether an inner city school could give them that student, especially if they are black.

In relation to c., Understanding the Inner City school

i. The first thing to be said here is that there is a considerably greater degree of heterogeneity among inner city schools than there is even among Oxford Colleges. As we observed in our evidence to the House of Commons Select Committee on *Performance in City Schools*:

Not all families living in inner city areas are poor and not all poor children are at an educational disadvantage. Some inner city schools, by virtue of their location or their ability to pick and choose, admit a high proportion of the children most likely to succeed. Others do not. Again, some schools have a high turnover of pupils and some do not. Some have to cater for very diverse needs and some do not. Those schools which are coping with multiple demands and admit large numbers of pupils who, individually, suffer multiple disadvantages are the schools with the hardest job of all.

ii. In a. I made suggestions for involving undergraduates in helping school students understand Oxford and its system of devolved Colleges. I believe schools can help the Colleges understand inner city schooling and the quest for excellence.

iii. I envisage a Compact operating at two levels, i.e., a Compact between the school and the College, and a Compact between the College and the students at that school. The former will spell out what each respective partner would do in the way of Widening Access, (e.g., number of visits by Tutors and Heads of Department or Heads of Year; joint planning of Open days; feedback on admissions interviews, etc.). The College /Student Compact will operate on the model of the East London Compact of which Hackney was one of the pioneers. The individual College and the students, in conjunction with the subject teacher, would set and review

Compact goals, and the student would know that if those goals are met, s/he would be guaranteed an interview by that College, with the possibility (in a small number of cases) of being recommended to another College if they fail to gain entry to their first choice.

iv. Under that arrangement, the College could start working with students as early as Year 9, with the quantum of time devoted to the exercise increasing as the students approach Years 11, 12 and 13.

v. Schools could make other contributions, for example by way of the secondment of teachers to Oxford Colleges to act as Secondary Liaison Workers, liaising between the respective Colleges and inner city secondary schools. The secondment could be for anything from one term to one year depending on the funds the College had or had the capacity to attract. Preferably, this arrangement would be accompanied by some form of staff/career development for the teacher.

vi. Adopt a School
In order to facilitate the implementation of the proposals made in this section, I would recommend that each College adopt an inner city school. The school (its students, staff and community) will be encouraged to play a part in the life of the College in whatever ways are considered practicable and appropriate, and vice versa. This could be enormously valuable in breaking down cultural barriers, in giving achievement a high profile in the school, and in confirming on both sides the acknowledgement of inner city students' entitlement to pursue higher education studies at Oxford University. It will also underscore the entitlement of inner city teachers and headteachers to have their work taken seriously.

d. Student Support Arrangements
The University needs to consider whether, in the context of Widening Access, it needs to review the support arrangements currently in place through the central student counselling provision and the tutorial system. Given the specificity of the experiences black students are known to have on entering higher education and seeking to progress

within it, I would have thought that at the very least the University should see what the experiences of current black students are telling it in this regard, and decide on the basis of that how student support arrangements that are sensitive to black students' concerns might be put in place.

Celebrating Success

Earlier in my talk I argued that our alternative education culture must be predicated upon high expectations, expectations that can be seen as legitimate because the system produces ample evidence of those high expectations being fulfilled. That culture would see success as the norm and, within it, success would breed success. Schools celebrate students' achievements in a number of ways, including the formal presentation of their National Record of Achievement folders and the organizing of Prize-giving at annual speech days. I feel it is very important to celebrate the achievements of all those students attaining their compact goals and also those finishing at Oxford who entered via the Oxford Access Scheme.

Finally, I was asked a couple years ago to lead a seminar at the Borough of Manhattan Community College in which we addressed the question: Can we make schools work in communities that don't?

That is clearly the subject of not just one but many lectures. Suffice it to say here that we all have to ensure that we make inner city schools work. The consequences of the existing education culture are plain enough to see right now. If we don't actively commit ourselves to creating that alternative education culture, the consequences not just for those communities but for the society as a whole would be pretty dire.

Let me end by congratulating Robert Berkeley and all his colleagues in the Oxford Access Scheme for the work they have done over the last three years, against monumental odds, and for organizing this important conference. I would like to think that as a result of the successful work of the Scheme future generations of black Oxford graduates would consider themselves in your debt.

PARENTAL AND COMMUNITY INVOLVEMENT IN EDUCATION
Time to get the balance right
Commission for Racial Equality
1 June 2005

Foreign Is Not Best

Early in 2005, Trevor Phillips, Chair of the Commission for Racial Equality visited the East St Louis School District in Missouri and saw how the school administration and schools there were tackling the problem of underachievement among black school students, boys in particular. Phillips was especially impressed with the methods used to keep black boys focused on learning and to help them build upon their achievements. Foremost amongst those methods was the practice of teaching black boys in their own teaching groups, separate from girls since the school population was virtually all black.

On his return to Britain, Phillips intimated that a similar method of working with underachieving black boys might be adopted here. The media reported Phillips as proposing that black boys should be taught in segregated groups, thus sparking a massively irrelevant debate about segregated black schools or segregation within schools.

Throughout the last 4 decades, education and schooling, as well as that historical by-product, underachievement, have become increasingly racialized. It is that racialized discourse that the media fuelled in response to Phillips' enthusiasm for what he had seen in East St Louis. The fact that black supplementary schools and voluntary education projects had been working in similar ways with young students who *voluntarily attended* weekly sessions seemed not to matter to the media. Among those catered for in community schools were many of that vast number of black boys the mainstream schools permanently excluded. It is a measure of the marginalization of our efforts, by the schooling system itself, that no real attention has been paid to the many successful methods the supplementary schools have employed over the years, to build the self esteem and confidence of young black boys and help them become successful learners and socially competent adults.

Having been so grossly misrepresented in a bizarrely distorted debate, Phillips organized a seminar at the CRE on 1 June 2005, bringing together academics and non-government organizations with an involvement in the issue, to try and establish the factual situation and see what might work best for black school students in Britain, England in particular. What follows is the text of the presentation Gus John made at that seminar.

Where We Were Then

For at least the last 4 decades, black parents and communities have been actively concerned about:

- the quality of education on offer to black school students
- levels of educational attainment as between black boys and black girls, and as between black boys/girls and other ethnic groups, including white ethnics
- access to, and progression in, employment by black male school leavers in comparison to black female school leavers
- the rate of exclusion of black boys from school, and the correlation between that and levels of black male unemployment, and the percentage of black youths and adults in custodial institutions

Voluntary and community education projects, including the now well established Saturday and Supplementary Schools movement, have attempted since the late 1960s to make meaningful interventions in respect of those concerns. There are an estimated 1,500 supplementary and Saturday schools in England and Wales, some 300 of which are in London alone. Those schools and the parents, teaching staff, and community activists associated with them, have a record of intervention in relation to the four key concerns highlighted above, and more. Indeed, their activism and remedial, supplementary, and complementary education activities, pre-date by at least two decades any serious interest in these matters, let alone concerted action to deal with them on the part of the State.

The key issues in parental and community involvement in education, I suggest, are:

- What has been the result of those 40 years of community activism in response to our experience of the schooling and education system?
- How, in spite of that activity, has the condition of being black, young and particularly male in the schooling system led to so many casualties among two generations of British born black people?
- Why has the cumulative experience of the schooling and education system led to 'the abandonment of hope and the death of aspiration' for so many of our young people?
- Crucially, how can black parents and communities learn from the advances and failures of the past, and refocus our activities both in relation to our own responsibilities and in challenging what schools continue to do?

Time does not allow me to develop each of these key issues in any detail. Let me therefore make a few observations about the state we are in, and what we, as parents and communities, need to be doing about it.

Until comparatively recently, it was impossible to get mainstream schools to take seriously what black communities were doing about the quality of the schooling experience of black children. When we sought to make the school curriculum more relevant, and provide black children with an understanding of themselves, of the contribution to knowledge, and the humanizing of societies black people have made throughout history, we were roundly accused of political indoctrination and teaching black kids to hate whites. Well now, we couldn't have done too great a job there, for 55% of all African-Caribbean males and 35% of all Caribbean females in the UK have white partners. Those that have children are having to deal with a more insidious and visceral form of racism than that suffered by black individuals as part of black communities.

With royal and imperial British arrogance, the state schooling system refused to heed the messages that were coming forward from our interface in the community education projects with the same students they were writing off as unteachable or ill disciplined.

For decades, the 1960s to 1990s at least, successive governments operated structures which suggested that the problem lay with black people because of our immigrant status and our backward language and backward ways. Remember Section 11 of the 1966 Local Government Act? Section 11 funding gave way to Ethnic Minority Achievement Grants, followed by Ethnic Minority and Traveller Achievement Grants, and special funding programmes to deal with the deficits that black learners were presumed to have. Needless to say, those operating these highly questionable programmes were mainly black people themselves. We were and always are put in charge of our own assumed pathology, not unlike the colonial arrangements of yesteryear.

Sadly, however, the supplementary schools movement was not a mass movement of black people in education, nor did it give rise to one. While many individual parents got involved in the work of the schools and supported their and other children's learning, most were content in the knowledge that the supplementary school was limiting the damage the mainstream system was most likely to inflict upon their children, rather than being concerned about taking collective action to make the mainstream schools adopt approaches to teaching, learning, and curriculum, that would give all children a greater zest for learning and a chance to excel.

What is more, the issues that exercised black parents were not shared by the majority of white parents, let alone white teachers and teaching unions. For example, when some of us attempted to get the then Council for National Academic Awards, the precursor of the Qualifications and Curriculum Authority, to stipulate the knowledge, understanding, skills and core competences teacher graduates should have in order to teach in inner city schools with their growing numbers of black children, not only did we encounter resistance from the CNAA and the teacher training institutions, black parents on the whole felt that that was asking too much of teachers, and that our aim should be to get more black teachers in schools.

There was an automatic assumption that just by virtue of being black, a teacher would be able to deal with all the issues black students were bringing into the classroom from home, peer group and community, irrespective of the age of the teacher, their ideological position or whether they were progressive or downright reactionary. That assumption was also predicated on the suspect notion that black students would automatically welcome and respect a teacher simply because they were of African Caribbean or West African heritage. Grandparents and some first generation migrant parents might have had residual knowledge of the contours of the relationship between children and teachers, based on their own experience. The situation is clearly considerably more complex now, impacted as it is by sharp contradictions of class, image, professional versus marginal status, and all the rest of it.

As important, of course, is the fact that if black student teachers are subjected to the same training as white, with all the underpinning pedagogical values, the assumed ideological neutrality of the teaching and learning process etc., their training would not have addressed the central issue of the place their blackness has in the teaching and learning relationship, and in negotiating power relations within the school.

Where We Are Now

There is an increased level of self organized and self directed educational activity within our communities. However, unlike the 1960s to the 1980s, let's say, the focus of that activity is much less on issues of character building, black identity formation, the curriculum mainstream schooling ignores, the potential of black school students that is not being developed, etc., and much more on performance in relation to test and examination results.

For example, since the Labour Government in the last administration set aside just over £1m to support the supplementary schools, schools in receipt of that money are being routinely inspected by OfSTED to ensure that the quality of teaching and learning matches the Government's raising achievement agenda.

Yet, despite two full scale reviews of the National Curriculum, the Government is still requiring schools to deliver a curriculum that is essentially geared to preparation for life in a principally mono-racial and mono-cultural environment. In other words, despite the fact that in many urban centres black people number anything between 25% and 55% of the population overall, we are still not considered mainstream enough to have the curriculum reflect British society as it is, rather than how some would prefer it to be.

The State We're In

Meanwhile, the education project has become contaminated for far too many of our children. The malaise is indeed characterized by 'the abandonment of hope and self belief and the death of aspiration'. To put it even more bluntly, it is characterized by an implosion within our communities to the extent that the mainstream schooling agenda is a massive irrelevance for many black students, boys and girls, who are dealing with issues in their homes and communities that make what goes on in the average classroom sound like a catechism class.

The consequences of that for black communities, for the future of black people in the economy of this nation, for the nature and quality of black parenting and for social order generally are immense.

The Government's own report on Ethnic Minorities and the Labour Market (produced by the Strategy Unit in the Cabinet Office in 2004) identifies African Caribbean, Pakistani and Bangladeshi groups as having the lowest educational attainment and lowest occupational status. The report notes that African and Asian people make up 1 in 13 of the UK population and that over the past 20 years they have accounted for two-thirds of the growth of the total UK population.

Similarly, in the coming ten to twenty years, the British labour market will be dependent, increasingly, on the supply of labour from those communities. That knowledgeable and skilled labour force will not be available if the current pattern of underachievement, school exclusions and youth offending within African and Asian communities persists.

In 1998, for example, black school students aged 6-16 were twelve times more likely to be excluded than their white counterparts. That trend has continued, albeit the Government's targets for reducing school exclusions have led to a marginal decrease in the number of black students being excluded.

Sadly, and understandably in many respects, the State and our communities are much more focused on manifestations of black communities imploding, than upon the growing number of African heritage young men who are high achievers, who are faithful partners and exemplary fathers, and who occupy elevated positions in the professions. But, we should not forgot them.

We need to constantly remind ourselves that that profile is not an aberration, but in fact a true reflection of the range of capacities and of family organization in our communities, and all communities, here and elsewhere.

Parents and communities need to engage them in forums for young people to share experiences of surviving schooling and becoming high achievers, despite coming from the same social background and neighbourhoods, and being faced with the same challenges as those who are failed by the system.

There is a tendency among us to adopt a pharisaic attitude and celebrate the fact that our children are not like 'dem dutty bwoy dem, all ah dem so damn wicked and bad', as one frustrated parent put it to me recently, rather than giving thanks and saying: 'there but for fortune go mine'. We cannot consider ourselves or any of our offspring to be safe until we ensure all our boys are safe and do not represent some kind of grenade waiting to go off indiscriminately.

What Is To Be Done
So, where do we go from here?

First, we must acknowledge and mobilize widespread

support from within our communities and the wider society for the view that the whole schooling project is increasingly arse about face, not just for our children but for a growing number of children of all ethnicities. It is futile to keep on complaining about the lack of discipline and the anti-academic stance adopted by some black boys and girls.

Yes, there are girls who routinely see fit to plait one another's hair throughout a lesson, chatting amongst themselves as the teacher tries to deliver a carefully prepared lesson plan. And there are boys who spend the entire lesson messing with their mobile phones and honing their text language development skills.

Yes, there is an unacceptable level of bullying by black boys *and* girls of their peers who are bright, focused and are working to their potential.

What is clear is that such conduct is never a true reflection of the ability of those students, let alone of their capacity to cooperate and be focused learners. So, we need to deal with the issue of internalized negativity and the effects of the constant refrain that black students, boys in particular, do not achieve.

Second, we need to challenge the 'one size fits all' approach to the structuring of schooling that make such unrealistic and futile demands on some young people, however much Mr Blair might protest that his is 'not a one size fits all' formula.

It is perverse at worst and politically cynical at best to persist with a system that is patently producing massive casualties in every succeeding generation of Black British citizens. In order to do that, you must have decided that that section of the population is much more expendable than others, capable of bearing more collateral damage in peace time.

Third, if we accept that parents have a legal duty to ensure that their children attend school up to the age of 16, unless they opt to educate them themselves as more and more are now doing. If we accept that those children are entitled to an education and that the more dysfunctional their attitudes to their self management and to schooling, the more need they have for education for self development, then the question arises: why should their emotional, spiritual and self development needs not be met in school as part of the teaching and learning process?

Why can schools not be organized in such a manner that where children's needs require them to work in much smaller teaching and learning groups the school has the flexibility to facilitate that?

In the broad scale of things, given all the rhetoric about choice, about combating social exclusion and promoting community cohesion, what is wrong with class sizes of no more than 8 for some learning groups? And why should not those learning groups be of black boys specifically, or of Bangladeshi boys specifically, if their learning and developmental needs warrant it? Surely, the fact that few schools actually give themselves the space or pay students the respect to discover how and in what circumstances they learn, would imply that a deeper level of engagement might be necessary with students who stand in opposition to the regime of schooling or plainly derive very little from it, however regular their attendance.

Why can parents of school students with challenging behaviour at home and at school not join activity in the school that seeks to support the transition from disruptive and self destructive behaviour to becoming students who have purpose and for whom learning at their own pace is meaningful and enjoyable?

Part of that activity must of course be 'talk'. Students must be allowed to see conversations with teachers especially, as the norm. The student's right to be heard and to express an opinion in relation to issues affecting them, including the dynamics of schooling, is one that is not always respected. That single fact accounts for more of the aggravation that results in school exclusion than any other factor. The citizenship curriculum addresses itself to, among other things, the teaching of democracy. Pity it does not engage with the issue of how sensible it is to teach democracy in schools without democratizing schooling itself.

What might be the role of school in helping to support parents in their parenting role and thus empower them to be better partners in their children's learning?

Fourth, we need to support parents and young people in devising strategies for surviving schooling, acknowledging the fact that this or any other Government is not about to hurriedly reform the organization of schooling in the manner I suggest. On the contrary, Government appears to believe that you could legislate for respect and that by shouting 'zero tolerance' you actually frighten people into conformity.

And what about communities?

We need to acknowledge that seeking private solutions to these deep seated public ills that put our entire communities under threat is counterproductive in the long run. I may send my child to a private school, I might even pack him off to relatives in the Caribbean so he could hopefully do better in an entirely different education culture. I may send him to the supplementary school and thus give him extension classes for a very modest fee. But until we act collectively to tackle the appalling experiences so many young people have at home, in school, and in our communities, we run the risk of being in fear of our bright and successful children's lives.

As one very distressed parent in a mainly white suburb put it to me recently:

You make the sacrifice and move to places like this because of all the gun crime and horrendous things these black boys are getting up to, and then you find yourself face to face with some very nasty racists threatening you with all sorts. I suppose it's a case of who you would take your risks with, your own kind in the city or vicious racists who want to force you back into the inner city.

In summary, then, I am calling for collective action by black parents and communities:

- to find ways of discharging our own responsibilities and supporting one another to save our children and
- to apply pressure on the Government to ensure that so many of our children are not written off by schools but are facilitated to become confident learners and responsible social citizens, demanding and safeguarding their own rights and having due regard for the rights of others.

I am interim Chair of a national organization called PaSE, Parents and Students Empowerment. PaSE operates as a partnership of parents and young people, bringing together school and college students, and those not in education, training or employment from across the country:

- to debate the issues confronting them
- share experiences and strategies for positive engagement with school, community and society and
- to work towards the formation of a national organization of young people committed to working together to tackle those issues, share good practice and influence government policy at local and national levels.

PaSE has been working across the country in collaboration with the Communities Empowerment Network (CEN) and targeting young people, their parents/carers, learning mentors, counsellors and other significant others in the lives of those young people. Some of that work has involved case work in relation to school exclusions, strategies for avoiding conflict, and for focused, disciplined learning, as well as work concerning involvement in gangs and dealing with bullying by members of gangs.

I believe that that process of engagement which enables young people and parents to share experiences, discuss challenges, and work towards solutions is necessary across the country and we need to make full use of the new technology to network nationally and internationally.

3.0

SCHOOL EXCLUSION –
WASTEFUL, DESTRUCTIVE, DISCRIMINATORY

Introduction

For many, the exclusion had been a traumatic experience, which had led to a loss of dignity and self-respect and, for those in care, being excluded had been particularly distressing. However, this loss of self-worth was an immediate and temporary reaction. In the vast majority of cases, it was followed by the development of a resilient sense of self, aided by adopting a black identity that motivated them to disprove official expectations of them and instead seek to create their own aspirations informed by the positiveness of their identity. In spite of their experiences, they remained committed to gaining an education. (Wright, et al., 2005)

In September 2005, the Joseph Rowntree Foundation (JRF) published the report of a study it commissioned on the way African-Caribbean pupils overcome the effects of school exclusion and make the transition into adulthood. The study looked at the role of family, community and other agencies in supporting excluded young people and used the young people's own accounts to examine their exclusion and transition.

'Overcoming School Exclusions' (3.1) was written to provide an overview of the context in which the research was conducted, and to connect themes from the narratives of the young people in the research, and the community groups that supported them, with the wider struggle of black communities to tackle schools and Government about the wasteful, destructive and discriminatory process that is school exclusion.

The JRF report provides evidence from young people themselves to support claims that organizations such as CEN, PaSE, and community education projects have been making for some considerable time, based upon our advocacy work, and our efforts to support progressive teachers in schools who build relationships with young people and support them through crises in their learning and personal development.

Key themes emerging from the evidence in the report are that:

a. African-Caribbean pupils excluded from school are not disaffected learners who have no interest in schooling and education. On the contrary, they are mostly sure of their abilities and keep their motivation to learn, going on to excel when they receive support to overcome the trauma of exclusion and restore their self-esteem.

b. Some excluded pupils have good cause to harbour feelings of injustice and of being denied basic rights because of the way the situation leading to their exclusion was handled.

c. Pupils who are treated respectfully by teachers and who have a sense that teachers are willing to listen to them, have a much more positive experience of working problems out in school, or working towards a return to school after exclusion.

d. Parents who are concerned to work with the school to sort out problems often find that the school is uncooperative and hostile in its attitude towards them, and adversarial towards their child.

e. Provision of education otherwise than at school does not appear to be anyone's responsibility, and where it is provided within Pupil Referral Units, it is often not tailored to the needs or academic progress of the excluded pupil.

The testimonies of parents, and of community organizations and social networks are especially instructive, especially in the light of the proposals in the Government's White Paper. To date, parents of excluded pupils could depend upon their local education authority to find a place for their excluded child, even though that process could take over a year, depending on the number of schools that refuse to have the pupil. In the final analysis, the LEA had the power to direct a school to take the pupil. Individual schools will be self-governing and independent and will have autonomy over their admissions procedures. If schools decide that it is not in their best interest to take in an excluded pupil, the LEA could do nothing about it. Indeed, as many are already arguing, the Government cannot promote a policy of 'zero tolerance' and of giving schools freedom to deal with bad behaviour and discipline, while at the same time compelling schools to accept pupils whose behaviour has been judged elsewhere to be against the interests of other pupils and of teachers.

Given the fact that African-Caribbean pupils are still massively over-represented in school exclusion statistics, it is predictable that the children swirling around the system trying to find alternative places would be predominantly black. The local further education college could opt to take pupils aged 14 or over, but given the rate at which primary age children are being excluded, parents up and down the land have a right to be seriously concerned about the implications of this 'free for all'. This scenario is bound to put even more strain on single mothers who, in addition to having the responsibility to ensure that their children are 'properly supervised doing school work at home' during the first five days of their suspension, or risk being fined, would be anxiously trying to get an alternative school place for the child.

Single mothers are often doing more than one job and parenting more than one child, especially in those urban settings where schools exclude the most. They may also be having problems managing their child who is facing school exclusion. Children's indiscipline or poor behaviour at school is not always attributable to indifferent parenting or social incompetence and low educational aspirations on the part of their parents. Punishing parents financially and by throwing them into prison for not making sure their children attend school is a far cry from the rhetoric of social inclusion and 'building community cohesion' the Government trumpets on about.

The structure the Government is seeking to place around school provision is likely to test the capacity of many white working class and black parents to deal with independent state schools. As in other areas where we see a mismatch between what Government delivers and the assumptions we make about hard-won gains which we considered inviolable, such as the guarantee of a school place for your child in a school local to your community, the poor and those who cannot readily exercise choice and exploit opportunity are bound to suffer.

In October 2002, there was extensive media coverage of a school in Surrey, The Glyn Technology College, that had been instructed by an Independent Appeal Panel (IAP) to take back two boys who had been suspended for making telephone death threats to a teacher they disliked. The media set themselves up as judge and jury in this case, failing to report all the salient facts, impugning the integrity of the members of the IAP who had reached their decision after hearing all sides in the affair and deliberating for a day and a half. But, even more than the IAP, Gerry German, Director of CEN, was pilloried for representing the two boys and their parents at the IAP hearing and for influencing the panel's decision.

What is worse, no sooner had the Sun newspaper reported the IAP's decision and the fact that the teachers in the school were threatening not to teach the students if they were returned to the school, the then Secretary of State, Estelle Morris and her Minister, Stephen Twigg, became involved in the matter. In an unprecedented intervention, way outside her powers, Ms Morris stated that the boys should not be allowed to return to the school. That intervention isolated even more the boys and their parents who had used the appeals procedure put in place by Government and had simply and properly put their case to the IAP. It also encouraged the teaching unions in the view that they could decide whom they should teach and to whom they could refuse an education, irrespective of the decisions of a properly constituted IAP. Furthermore, it called into question the legitimacy of the IAP as a statutory body convened by Surrey LEA for purposes stipulated in law.

As if that were not bad enough, the media unleashed a vicious and defamatory attack upon Gerry German and upon CEN as a charitable organization in receipt of Lottery funding.

As Chair of CEN, and on behalf of our Management Committee and all the staff, I issued a statement to the media (3.2), setting out the issues the media should concern themselves with. Those included the irregular intervention of the Secretary of State; the need to preserve IAPs and their independence from schools', LEAs' and Government influence; and the danger to our liberal institutions and decision making structures, if a newspaper, in this case the *Daily Mail*, was able to trigger an investigation of CEN, its work and its application of its funds by a Government body such as The Community Fund.

Such was the extent of the distortion and misreporting of the facts and the sequence of events in the Glyn Technology case, that we at CEN decided it was necessary to tell our side of the story. And so, in October 2002, we published a detailed statement, 'Death Threat Boys, the School, CEN and the Secretary of State', charting the development of that debacle (3.3). Needless to say, the media more or less ignored all that CEN had to say about the matter. It was clear, however, that the matter of Estelle Morris' judgement in getting involved in the affair as she did, and undermining an IAP acting in accordance with her own guidelines was not entirely laid to rest.

Since then, the Government has both reviewed the membership of IAPs, weighting them much more heavily in favour of schools, and withdrawn the Guidelines governing the way schools exclude pupils (Circulars 10/99 and 11/99). They were replaced in January 2003 by 'Improving Behaviour and Attendance: Guidance on Exclusion from Schools and Pupil Referral Units'. This guidance has itself been revised and the Government has issued further 'Advice and Guidance to Schools and Local Authorities on Managing Pupil Behaviour and Attendance', advice and guidance which is likely to be rendered redundant by the proposals in the White Paper.

In November 2002, CEN represented a boy and his parents in a case of bullying by pupils and senior managers. Having been thrown to the ground and kicked and punched by a group of boys, this pupil then suffered further humiliation by a senior manager arriving at the scene asking him who gave him a fat lip, much to the amusement of his assailants. The school failed to assess the physical impact of the vicious and unprovoked attack on the boy, to the extent that his parents had to take him to the Accident & Emergency Unit at the local hospital when he arrived home. The matter was not properly investigated as the headteacher promised, and the school was less than cooperative with the parents who dealt with them reasonably and courteously throughout.

That case epitomizes the treatment that too many parents complain of in their dealings with schools, black parents in particular. The parents removed the boy from the school for his own safety. They learnt subsequently that the headteacher had also left the school.

The case raises important issues about parental access to experienced independent advocates as well as to specialists in education law. If the system as it has operated, at least since 1988 and the Education Reform Act, has given rise to a need for organizations such as CEN which barely touch the tip of the iceberg, it is difficult to imagine the need for advocacy, guidance and support, and legal representation parents will need after Mr Tony Blair's schooling revolution. The Schools Commissioner will not only need a huge body of staff to conduct the arbitration that once fell to LEAs, s/he would need to ensure that parents in communities across the land have access to such guidance and support services in order to safeguard their, and their children's, rights in the face of schools' unfettered freedom.

3.1

OVERCOMING SCHOOL EXCLUSIONS AND ACHIEVING SUCCESSFUL YOUTH TRANSITIONS WITHIN AFRICAN–CARIBBEAN COMMUNITIES

The Study in Context – An Overview
20 February 2001

Telling their story

A principal focus of the research was to give the young people a chance to tell us what happened when they were excluded, how they felt about it and the impact that being excluded had on their lives. Additionally, we wanted to know what the young people, their families and community organizations could tell us about what worked in reducing school exclusion and enabling inclusion, what insights might be provided with respect to community and family strategies.

Black young people in the schooling system have been subjected to much research and community and government intervention as we have observed throughout this report. Over the years they have been the subject of numerous conferences annually. Seldom, however, have they been involved in the proceedings of these conferences, either as presenters or participants.

The testimonies of the young people in our sample suggest that an overriding concern for them in their schooling experience was to be listened to and to have their point of view heard, if not respected. Significantly, the experience of the young people in school, and the quality of the relationship with teachers that in many instances triggered their exclusion, were in sharp contrast to their experience of engaging with those resources that constituted the social and cultural capital in their efforts to overcome school exclusions, and make the transition to adulthood (sympathetic teachers, significant others, alternative sites of education and schooling, family and friends).

It has long been the experience of voluntary education projects in the African Caribbean community that children who come to them, having been excluded by mainstream schools and thought to be unteachable or uncontrollable, form positive relationships with adults, develop a positive attitude to learning and become much more confident communicators, all of that leading to positive educational outcomes, an accelerated rate of self development and high levels of attainment. A key function for those projects, supplementary schools especially, has been to help those young people prepare for readmission to school, post-exclusion, by developing strategies for surviving schooling.

A recurring theme throughout the young people's narratives in this study is the sense of injustice they felt about the way they were excluded. That stemmed variously from not having been allowed to put their case, from a feeling that they were labelled and stereotyped to the extent that teachers were effecting outcomes that they themselves had anticipated as inevitable, or the experience of seeing their white peers involved in the same, or similar incidents, being allowed to stay in school or return after a fixed term of exclusion, while they were kept out of school or permanently excluded.

The importance of talk, of reasoning, and of respectful exchanges in teacher-pupil interaction is frequently overlooked. The notion that talk opens the way for conflicts to escalate or for unacceptable attitudes to gain verbal expression leading to loss of control on the teacher's part, is perhaps, one of the greatest barriers to child-centred approaches to behaviour management in schools. It is not unusual in the schooling system for teachers to spend 75% of their time talking at students and the other 25% listening to some of them and failing to see, hear or acknowledge the others. That 75% effectively constitutes listening time for students, and problems arise when instead of listening they distract one another, or engage in their own 'talk'.

If that is the pattern of teacher/student interaction in lessons across the timetable in any one day, the amount of time the student actually spends in meaningful interaction with teachers, interaction that enhances their communication skills and that allows the teacher to get a real sense of the learning that is taking place for them, or not, becomes pretty limited.

The young people, their parents, and significant others in their communities, all make reference to stereotypical attitudes, behaviours and expectations on the part of teachers, headteachers, governors and independent appeal panels. These attitudes, behaviours and expectations manifest in relation not only to pupils but also to their parents and, invariably, to their community advocates.

In addition to stereotypes about family circumstances, parents experience the schooling system as setting up a 'them and us' polarity with an accompanying subtext, namely, 'if you are not with us, you're against us'. An added dimension is introduced when a decision is taken to include a black governor among the members of a governors' discipline committee or an independent appeal panel. The sense of fairness and reassurance to the pupil and parents the system seeks to convey in so doing, is often in inverse proportion to the sense of injustice and irritation the pupil and parents feel when that panel upholds the decision of the school.

In a workshop at the London Schools and the Black Child Conference (2002) on *How the School System is Failing Black Boys*, many parents expressed the view that:

schools adopted such a 'them and us' attitude towards the home that they did not often consider the difficulties parents themselves have with rebellious and ill disciplined children whom they are not allowed to smack or punish physically. Rather than seeing the issue of the child's inability to manage his/her behaviour, anger and frustration as a problem both for the parents and the school, the assumption is made that the failure is with the parents. Consequently the school is unconcerned about the impact that excluding the child will have on already struggling and bewildered parents (John, 2003)

Commenting on what parents could do to help themselves and the school, other parents suggested that:

Parents could stop their children 'Back chatting' from an early age and teach them to listen and take their turn to speak. Parents should also listen to children and show them that they respect the child, their opinions and their right not to agree with everything a parent says or does. Unless these ways of communicating are taught, learnt and practised at home, schools would continue to see the way our children communicate with adults as 'challenging' behaviour

The experience of unjust treatment that many of the young people dwelt upon in their narrative overlaps with their experience of other institutions and interactions in society. Stereotypical attitudes and behaviours of the police, security guards, adults generally, ushers in cinemas, etc., combine with those of schooling agents to induce in young people negative attitudes not just to schooling and education, but also to figures in authority.

That continuity of their experience of the society as young black people and their experience of schooling makes schools an arena of resistance for many young people. The critical issue here is how parents and families then deal with that reality. The parents of many of the young people in the study were also products of the same schooling system. As some of them observed, they had had to learn hard lessons at the interface with schools, in the same way that their children are now doing. Their experiences did not automatically lead them to make assumptions about the school environment as safe, valuing of all, respecting of all, supportive and *in loco parentis*.

In loco parentis is interpreted mainly as schools being responsible for children's safety and discharging a duty of care towards them once parents have handed them over to their charge. Interpreted more broadly, however, it becomes a questionable notion when, clearly, schools have power to do with children what society does not typically expect parents to do. Parents are expected to work in support of children's self development; to help them inculcate values and self governing principles that make them sociable beings, fit for living in society without constant aggravation and stress; to seek help when necessary and, in the final resort, to ask for children's services to intervene and remove the child to a place where their assessed needs could be professionally addressed. They are not expected to eject the child from the home for repeated unacceptable behaviour, or to deny them proper care and nurture as a punishment for repeated wrong doings.

The emphasis that there has been on home/school liaison and on developing parent partnership with schools has tended to be on the school's terms. The school invariably informs parents as to what it is they are seeking to do with the young person or their group and seeks the help of parents in reinforcing that in their dealings with the child, whether it be in terms of punctuality, wearing school uniform, self management or academic work. Where well-adjusted parents in settled home circumstances work in partnership with schools, the model is advantageous to all. However, in stressful family situations where the child is causing major difficulties at school, and where the label of 'problem family' may already be applied, it is less likely that the parent(s) could successfully convince the school to work in partnership with them, conversely, and assist the young person in dealing with the behaviours which give the school cause to permanently exclude. They typically do not feel able to say from inside their end of the partnership: 'This is what we are trying to do, albeit it is taking some time. It will set us back massively if you insisted on this exclusion. Work with us to achieve this goal'.

Part of the reason for this is, as organizations such as the Communities Empowerment Network have found, that there is a tendency for schools and governors' discipline committees to see parents in such situations as being too indulgent and as colluding with children's unacceptable conduct. The scepticism with which certain submissions by parents are greeted, causes students and parents alike to have a lack of faith in the independence of the governors from the school managers' decisions. This is most evident when a parent assertively insists that: 'I know my child. I have taught him to be honest and tell me the truth from the time he was able to talk. I have absolutely no reason to doubt his version of the events'.

Too often, schools fail to see parents as genuinely requiring the school's help in working with the student, not only towards better self and behaviour management, but to give them reasons to trust adults and people in authority, and to experience the latter as acting fairly and justly.

The typical response to this sort of plea is that the school has the other children's progress to think about. But, the difficulties those parents have in seeking to make the school/parent partnership work is in trying to square that response with their belief that, as a young respondent in our study observed so poignantly:

I think no-one should be excluded from school ... everyone deserves an education; ... I don't care

Those parents whose own schooling experience mirrored that of their children could put up two forms of resistance. Resist by challenging the injustices, holding the school to account by having recourse to law if necessary, or by being prepared to go into the school, however frequently, in response to the petty aggravation that punctuates some children's daily school life.

On the other hand, they could resist by working with the child to develop strategies for coping with classroom situations; with teachers who talk much and listen too little, especially to children who are seen as disruptive; with their peers, whose conduct might be geared to triggering some familiar reaction from the young person; with their own propensity to irritation and anger.

As we have observed, black women constitute the majority of black people in further and higher education. Many of those would have effected successful transitions and transformations not just in spite of, but because of their schooling experience. Belief in self, the knowledge that their own survival, and that of their family, would most likely depend upon their earning capacity, and the sense of security they could give their children and, above all, their eagerness to demonstrate to those who had written them off that they could succeed, are all factors which enable them to engage their children in adopting strategies for surviving schooling. They could demonstrate that 'They proved them wrong'. If they could do it, then so could their children, with their constant support and guidance.

The frustration many of those parents have with schools and governing bodies is with their apparent reluctance to accept that schooling is but a stage in young people's development, emotional, cultural, spiritual as well as academic, and that development involves change. Therefore young people can, and do change. The capacity for and rate of change has a great deal to do with the nature of the change agents. What is it about the way this child experiences this institution and the people in it, that will make them inclined to see themselves as students, and the other people in the institution differently, and want to treat them differently?

Punishment as an End in Itself

The experience of many young people and parents alike is that the punishment is never enough for the 'crime'. Labelling and stigmatization follow excluded pupils, black males especially, in much the same way as a custodial sentence. In this sense the experiences of young black males excluded from school, sits along a spectrum with that of black male offenders seeking to reintegrate within society and access employment. Social exclusion becomes their reality, not least because of the assumptions and stereotypical expectations the society applies to them.

Exclusions have been presented in Government circulars as a last resort to be imposed when all other efforts have failed. The practice appears to be far from the truth. Schools seem to jump too quickly into punitive mode, and despite OfSTED advice that exclusions in excess of a couple of days are counterproductive, one still gets reports from pupils of excessive fixed term exclusions, where the punishment bears little relationship to the incident triggering the Head's decision to exclude for a fixed term.

Some permanent exclusions seem intended to set an example

to other pupils rather than be a natural consequence of the misdemeanour or offence.

If schools actually followed the advice given in Chapters 1 to 5 and in Chapter 7 of DfES Circular 10/99, there would probably be no need to exclude at all.

Crucially, this would also depend on the school's access to essential resources to cater for individual academic and social needs. The notion of 'personalized learning', in other words having an individualized education plan for students, is one that most schools readily accept. That implies a rejection of the opposite notion of 'one size fits all'. Different individuals or groups of children do often require different approaches to meeting their individual education needs in order to deliver their education entitlement as part of integrated mainstream schooling. That does not necessarily place them in the category of having special educational needs, nor does it mean that are to be labelled and stigmatized.

Staff development and training would need to be undertaken in relation to events that trigger exclusions if schools are to respond appropriately to the circular and its implications for personalized learning. There is little such training at present.

School Exclusion and the Creation of Educational Disadvantage

A concern expressed in this study, by young people and parents alike, about the educational disadvantage suffered by excluded children is about the lack of planned provision for their education while they are excluded.

At the same conference mentioned above, parents highlighted the failure of local education authorities to:

provide meaningful programmes of study for excluded students and to have regard for the organization of their time during school hours; and to find an alternative place for permanently excluded students (boys in particular).

That failure was described as 'a national attack on the future of our children'. Those parents detected 'a conspiracy to prevent children getting back into education once they'd been excluded':

It could take up to 6 weeks to get a decision from a school as to whether or not they would have an excluded student. If that school decides they do not want the student, parents have to repeat the whole process all over again. Meanwhile, the student becomes de-motivated and loses interest.

One parent at the conference put it very pointedly when she said:

Children are not stupid. They know those headteachers talk to one another and warn one another off. That is why it is a conspiracy. The LEA in that situation doesn't care less about the right of the child to have schooling. As far as they are concerned, he forfeited that right the moment he got permanently excluded.

The narratives of parents in this study point to the stress such situations generate in a family, and the consequent impact upon relationships within the home and wider family circle. Parents and other siblings become concerned about the lack of educational provision and about excluded students wandering around aimlessly all week, prone to temptation and ever in danger of being lured into criminal activity.

The Youth Justice Board is increasingly encouraging the use of restorative justice models not just in the work of organizations supporting young people in the community, but also in schools. This is based upon their clear assumption that it must be possible to engage young people in looking at their behaviour and aspects of their relationships which cause offence, allowing for the fact that they, too, might be experiencing the conduct of others around them, and particularly towards them, as equally problematic. They might also be dealing with trauma caused by other aspects of their living, at home and in community from which they cannot totally disengage in order to feel positive about themselves and focus on learning.

A major part of the problem as far as behaviours that lead to exclusions are concerned is the manner in which those situations are managed. The sense of injustice and resentment young people feel is often associated with the denial to them of opportunities to say how they experienced the situation, why they did what they did, whether they were even involved, or why it should not be automatically concluded that it is they that did it. The pressure to defuse the situation, regain control and assume a semblance of normality often means the individual dealing with the young person and their feelings is not the teacher or other adult principally involved, but whoever it is to whom the young person is sent out of the class. In such situations, it is the reported behaviour of the young person that is in focus, as distinct from that of the other individual(s) involved and the totality of the exchanges which led to the student being sent out in the first place.

Where a learning mentor, personal assistant or trusted teacher is the member of staff dealing with the young person, it is seldom the case that they would involve the class teacher in the discussion of the conflict. Teaching and related duties usually displace the time and space all parties might spend in dealing appropriately with the situation so that the young person feels they have been listened to, they had the opportunity to comment on the way the teacher handled the situation, or/and that they and the teacher had worked out a *modus operandi* for the future.

The Youth Justice Board's encouragement of the use of restorative justice models in schools, contrasts hugely with the increasing incidence of teachers' refusing to teach children being reintegrated into schools, following independent appeal panel decisions and receiving their union's backing on their stance. Indeed, at successive annual conferences in the recent past, teaching unions have called for the abolition of students' and parents' right to appeal against schools' decisions to permanently exclude. The irony in the fact that the most unionized body of employees, with a proud history of fighting to protect their terms and conditions of employment and exercising their right to withdraw their labour, is actively campaigning to get government to deny a fundamental right to students and parents has gone largely unremarked.

This is a classic case of two aspects of the Government's strategy to combat social exclusion coming into conflict with each other.

On the one hand, despite growing evidence of the link between exclusions and youth offending, evidence highlighted by the Youth Justice Board itself, the Government makes it easier for schools to exclude. Independent Appeal Panels (IAP) are established to hear appeals against school exclusions. They operate independently and overturn a minority of decisions (some 30%). Schools resist taking back children who the IAP says should return to school. Unions back their members in those schools and use their might and power to tell Government that it cannot expect them to raise standards and improve behaviour and discipline, while at the same time compelling them to teach children who they feel should be permanently excluded. The Government capitulates and, short of abandoning IAPs altogether as potentially a step too far, it loads the dice in favour of schools by altering the composition of the IAPS in a manner that is more likely to result in school decisions being upheld.

Meanwhile, Youth Justice Panels continue to deal with young people's involvement in youth offending while excluded from school, and the Youth Justice Board highlights concerns about the percentage of young people in young offender institutions excluded from school less than three years before offending. This, as much as anything else, has been the trigger for the Youth Justice Board's drive to promote the use of restorative justice models in schools.

Successful transitions

Reassuringly, many of the young people in this study were very clear about having been derailed and now working to get back on track. Some highlighted the fact that in order to alter their behaviour they needed to change their attitude. They were clear about their job and career aspirations. Above all, they saw their refusal to allow the label of 'excluded pupil' and all the school and societal expectations that go with that as being crucial to their capacity to go ahead and achieve their goals.

Exclusion, as we have shown, represents a 'critical moment' not just for the student but for entire families. It induces stress both in those excluded and in their families. It dents parental aspirations for children, it dents confidence in the system's capacity to treat young people as people with rights. It denies parents the opportunity for the proper exercise of power by denying them information about increasingly complex school processes.

Assumptions are made by schools, no less than by some Independent Appeals Panels, that most parents are aware of, and have access to, the circulars and amendments that govern the way schools should deal with exclusions. Acknowledging the complexity of this whole matter and of the workings of disciplinary committees, IAPs and the rest, legislation required local education authorities to appoint parent support or liaison officers to provide advice and guidance to parents, independently of the schools.

Local Management of Schools and the requirement that LEAs devolve most of their education budget to schools have meant that more and more schools buy back services from the LEA, especially personnel services. Many schools protest, therefore, when they perceive employees from the same LEA with which they trade, as 'working against them' on behalf of parents. The fact that they as schools have direct access to government circulars, so much so that they complain about the number of them they receive, they have direct access to LEA advice and services and could buy in other help, does not appear to many schools to be a situation that creates an imbalance.

School students are not organized as teachers and headteachers are, nor are parents. Many parents are having to look to law centres or to community organizations, such as those in this study, to even make sense of what the various steps are in the exclusions and appeal cycle. Yet, there is an expectation on the part of many schools that LEA parent support officers and exclusion coordinators should not act independently of them and of their relationship, contractual or otherwise, with the LEA.

We believe the above provides a useful context for situating and understanding the narratives of the contributors to this study. It is a context that points to the need to refocus on the links between school exclusion and social exclusion. It underscores, also, the need to see the exclusion of worrying numbers of young people of African Caribbean heritage not as a problem located within themselves but as the result of a complex set of school, home and community dynamics, that schools and government must acknowledge and seek to tackle systematically with the communities themselves.

This study points to the dynamism and functionality of the support networks available to excluded young black people, and their centrality to their success in overcoming school exclusions and making the transition to adulthood. There is an important category of excluded young adults from whom we have not heard, notably those in young offender institutions and in prison. For them, the 'critical moment' of exclusion led to, or contributed to, different pathways. They have their own story to tell.

The challenges facing Government are: to ensure that there is continuity of access to education and opportunities to make up for lost schooling in the provision that is made for them, giving their over-representative numbers; to take active steps to bring an end to the situation that results in more and more young people being sentenced by the courts to join them.

The challenges facing communities are

• To work to correct the massive power imbalance that exists between schools on the one hand and black and ethnic minority parents (African Caribbean in particular) on the other

• To support, safeguard and expand the community based services that are available to parents and students, such as the ones in this study that have played such a key role in supporting parents, and acting to ensure the delivery of children's right to education

• To help build independent organizations of parents and students that could act in their own interests and in support of the interest of teachers and schools, in seeking to change the structure and processes of schooling that are so evidently producing casualties within specific ethnic groups.

Unless the structures and processes of schooling are examined as part of the cause of pupil alienation and disaffection the situation can only get worse, despite the crisis management provision of learning mentors, counselling, referral to Youth Offending Teams and other agencies, as well as to community organizations.

The racialization of school exclusions has been a matter of grave concern to black communities since the late 1960s. Patterns of racial discrimination in school exclusions have been regularly exposed since the publication of the Formal Investigation by the regional CRE in Birmingham, and the Swann and Eggleston Reports in 1985. The field is still fertile for such discrimination to take place.

Tinkering with the system, amendments to the procedures and peripheral provision (through mentoring, counselling etc., no matter how well intended) will not change things for black pupils generally. Those who have been subjected to negative prejudice, destructive stereotyping and low expectations in the past will continue to suffer unless there are fundamental changes in schooling, a refocusing on children's education rights, and unless there is a halt to the present trend by government to make excluding pupils easier than keeping them in the mainstream.

CEN COMMUNITIES EMPOWERMENT NETWORK
The Glyn Technology exclusion affair and CEN

Since 11 October 2002, the media has focused on the role of CEN and its Director, Gerry German, in the decision of Surrey LEA's Independent Appeal Panel (IAP) to reinstate two permanently excluded pupils. Gerry German has been vilified, defamed and maligned for assisting the IAP in their consideration of all relevant factors in the case, including the background to the boys' irresponsible and hurtful actions.

CEN's involvement has been used, further, as ammunition to pillory the Community Fund and to force the Government to abolish the right of school students and their parents to have schools' decisions on exclusions independently assessed. This is something which certain teaching unions shamefully demanded at their annual conferences in two consecutive years.

The Communities Empowerment Network was established two and a half years ago to provide advice, support, counselling and representation, for people experiencing problems in education, principally. It also provides advocacy to people in employment, especially where adequate or no representation from trade unions is forthcoming.

CEN is governed by a Management Committee of some fourteen people, most of whom are parents with school age children and have considerable contacts with the schooling and education system.

Members of CEN's committee include a former director of education (now Visiting Professor of Education and member of the Home Secretary's Race Relations Forum), a former LEA councillor and Education Committee member, school governors, LEA education officers, solicitors, university lecturers, senior teachers, and a former college vice-principal.

CEN came into being in response to the over-representative number of black students being excluded from school across the country and the excessive number of those who end up in penal institutions as a consequence of school exclusion. Many members of the CEN management committee are and have been involved in voluntary education projects and the Supplementary Schools Movement. The five full time members of CEN staff are able to draw heavily upon the expertise of their committee members in matters of policy, working with students and parents, assisting schools in building effective home-school partnerships, engaging with schools in implementing preventative strategies, and in re-integrating excluded students.

These latter aspects of our work, on which we place no less importance than advocacy and representation, have hardly received a mention in all the reporting there has been about CEN's involvement in school exclusions.

Members of the management committee have trained as advocates and, depending on their particular circumstances, also represent students and parents at disciplinary committees and appeal hearings.

We make no apology for the fact that our success in having exclusion decisions overturned is higher than the national average. Our record in this respect is due not exclusively to the representational skills of Gerry German, but to the principles, knowledge of the Government's own guidance, and advocacy skills applied by all CEN staff. It is precisely those principles, skills and knowledge with which we seek to empower communities of students and parents through the training we provide.

We need to emphasize, therefore, that while Gerry German does a great number of appeal cases, he is not on some 'fanatical' frolic of his own.

Advocacy Not the Preserve of CEN

Contrary to what the media would have us believe, CEN is not the only organization that the scandalous practice of excluding thousands of students from school each year has stirred into action.

As early as 1975, the Black Parents Movement (BPM), operating in London, Manchester and Bradford, campaigned for *Independent Parents Power and Independent Students Power* as the *Key to Change in Education and Schooling*. The BPM argued then that the quality of in-school experiences, and of educational outcomes, for the majority of black and white working class students was such that they needed to act in their own interest, as did their parents, in much the same way that teachers, headteachers and support staff have trade unions and professional associations acting to safeguard and advance their interests.

The Inner London Education Authority (ILEA) had the best organized, most militant, and most influential teaching unions in the whole of Britain and they were responsible for many advances. Yet, when Margaret Thatcher abolished ILEA and the inner London boroughs assumed responsibility for providing education, the quality of what the majority of children were receiving was inexcusable. That fact was not uppermost in the concerns of the ILEA trade unions.

Government responses to the quality of educational outcomes have been to focus on school effectiveness, to set targets for raising standards, to do something about teacher and headteacher quality and to test every child that sits still for long enough. Power has been devolved from LEAs to schools under the guise of giving power to parents as if that is an unproblematic concept.

Governance of schools at local level is assumed to have nothing to do with class, race and ethnicity, occupation, experience of managing complex institutions, experience of confronting institutional practices that are pitted against oppressed minorities, and the rest.

The checks and balances necessary to support locally managed schools needs to include a network of independent students and parents organizations.

In the absence of those, and in the light of schools' and LEAs' practices on admissions, exclusions, and special educational needs there have emerged in practically all of the Greater London boroughs, LEA-funded organizations, and independent voluntary and community organizations dealing with students' and parents' experience of those practices. The former include: the *Parent Pupil Advocacy Scheme for Reducing School Exclusions* in Greenwich LEA, the *Elfreda Rathbone Advocacy Service* in Camden, the *Exclusions Parent Support Service* in Southwark, the *Parents Advice Centre* in Tower Hamlets and *KUFI Educational Services* in Brent.

Rather than being outraged at CEN's successes in representing parents/students, the media should be seeking to explain the fact that one third of all Independent Appeal hearings find in favour of the student. CEN, let alone Gerry German, has not been responsible for all those cases. Moreover, it would be perverse to suggest that the refusal of IAPs to uphold the schools' decisions in those cases has been due solely to the fact that schools are overstretched and cannot familiarize themselves with DfES Circular 10/99 in the manner the groups representing parents do.

Goodness was not made in schools

Is it not about time that we acknowledge that goodness was not made in schools, that headteachers could be capricious and unconcerned about natural justice, that many do deny students due process, and that it is not generally part of schools' management culture to listen to the story of the child and of how they experienced a particular event and the way in which the person in authority dealt with it?

One crucial point that all the reporting of the Glyn Technology School affair seems to have lost sight of, is the fact that Gerry German had no power to make the decision in that, or any of the other hearings he attended as a CEN advocate. That power rested with the Independent Panel. Indeed, in 11 of the 40 cases Gerry German dealt with in 2001, the IAP heard his pleadings and decided to uphold the governors' decision to exclude. In the Glyn School case, they deliberated for a day and a half, without the help of Gerry German. The panel included at least one person with experience of listening to evidence and adjudicating, a magistrate, and two former teachers. Is it being seriously suggested that Gerry German cast a spell over them and held them in his intellectual grasp for one and a half days?

What is frightening, and should concern the public in this whole affair, is not Gerry German, but the fact that it is widely assumed that by acting as they did those boys forfeited every right to due process and to have their situation looked at by a creation of the Government itself, an independent appeal panel. We have even heard it suggested that 'after what they did, no teacher anywhere should be expected to teach them, never mind teachers at that same school'.

It is tantamount to demanding that every person accused of child abduction and murder should be handed over to an irate and vengeful public for summary execution. No trial, no jury, no specialist reports, above all, no protection of the state, not anything ... just uncontrolled and unregulated fury.

The fact that the Secretary of State intervened at all, and in the manner that she did, thus fuelling the bigotry that characterized so much of the reporting of the affair, should cause us all even more concern.

In CEN's experience, it could take up to six weeks for a parent to be told whether an alternative school would accept a permanently excluded student. If the parent(s) are made to run the gauntlet of six schools, the student could be denied organized schooling for a whole school year, and many regrettably often are.

The Chairman of the Youth Justice Board, Lord Warner of Brockley, is on record as saying that the correlation between school exclusion and youth crime is becoming increasingly obvious and that schools might as well give such young people a ticket for future entry to a youth custody institution.

The Government's own School Community Officers, i.e., police dealing with truancy and offending behaviour in schools, are finding that in some parts of inner London, they are picking up more excluded students on the streets or in arcades than those playing truant. OfSTED has introduced criteria schools must meet for promoting inclusion and are retraining their inspectors so that schools could be inspected with regard to their work in this area.Furthermore, OfSTED has helpfully provided schools with empirical evidence of secondary and primary schools that don't exclude and the factors enabling them to avoid exclusions.

We believe that exclusion from school is much more than a transitory event in a student's life. Permanent exclusion, in particular, mars their chances in life and often sets them on a career path which is injurious to themselves and a threat to the community around them. As far as children, young people, and their parents are concerned, these are critical matters affecting their future survival as fully developed, responsible beings entitled to consideration, respect, equality of opportunity and non-discriminatory treatment.

Children have rights. Mercifully, those rights do not automatically disappear as a consequence of those children's failure to exercise the responsibilities that go with their rights, or this society would descend into sheer barbarism.

In the light of the Government's own concern about school exclusions and the disproportionate manner in which they impact upon black students and their communities, we believe that

- It is essential that Independent Appeal Panels remain and that their independence is not compromised
- Parents should be able to avail themselves of the services of experienced independent advocates of their choosing (including other parents trained for that purpose)
- The DfES and LEAs should fund the provision of such services and they should be seen as a LEA responsibility similar to SEN provision
- Members of Governing Body Discipline Committees, like members of LEA Independent Appeal Panels, should be obliged to undergo regular and proper up-to-date training in both the exclusions guidelines and procedures, and human rights/race relations legislation
- Governing Body clerks, like the clerks to Independent Appeal Panels, should have up-to-date legal experience and

the same training as members of governors discipline committees
- Membership of adjudicating bodies should include at least one person from the same ethnic group as the excluded student
- It should be obligatory for LEA Exclusions Officers to be present at Governing Body Discipline Committee and Independent Appeal Panel hearings. Representatives of the Discipline Committee should also be required to attend the IAP hearing
- Serious consideration needs to be given to establishing a nationwide school based Students Grievance Procedure whereby schools' failure to deal with complaints about, for example, bullying and mistreatment by any member of the school community may be independently adjudicated
- The DfES should reinstate its exclusions reduction programme, with even more radical targets
- With the OfSTED guidelines in place, all schools should aim to practice the Nil Exclusions policy operated by 25% of primary and 5% of secondary schools nationwide.

The Community Fund

The *Daily Mail* appears to have a massive problem with principles of equity and justice. It appears to want to establish 'in groups' and 'out groups' as far as the recipients of lottery funding are concerned. It says nothing, however, about the fact that those relegated to the confines of the 'out group' are amongst the biggest spenders on lottery tickets.

As a collective group across the country, should the parents of students excluded, or belonging to communities suffering disproportionate numbers of exclusion, be debarred from buying lottery tickets, or should they just not be eligible to benefit from lottery handouts?

If and when punters are given the right to state what cause they would like their money to go to, would the *Daily Mail* and the Culture Secretary compile a list of worthy causes that omits grassroots organizations campaigning against injustice and discrimination? What incipient totalitarianism are we being asked to sign on to here?

The Community Fund set certain criteria for disbursing its funds. CEN met those criteria. The Community Fund has satisfied itself that we are who we say we are, we do what we say we do, and as competently as we claim to do it. As far as our application for funding is concerned, therefore, that is what matters.If the *Daily Mail*, various Secretaries of State or anyone else who has pronounced in this debacle succeeds in getting the Community Fund to reconsider its position with regard to CEN, then we clearly are not dealing with an incipient totalitarian state but a badly camouflaged one.

3.3

DEATH THREAT BOYS, THE SCHOOL, CEN AND THE SECRETARY OF STATE
The other side of the story
October 2002

Much of what has appeared in the media up until now has been distorted and one-sided. CEN would like to set the record straight. Some of the media seem intent on discrediting CEN in order to get at the Community Fund.

The boys and their parents in the Glyn Technology School case apparently have no safeguards even under the procedures laid down by the Secretary of State for Education & Skills who now appears to have come out on the side of the teacher unions and against her own guidance in DfES Circular 10/99.

The boys and their parents were prepared to undergo the humiliation of being taught in isolation and did so for the two weeks of their return to school after reinstatement by the Surrey LEA Independent Appeal Panel until the Secretary of State stepped in with a directive that they should not return to school after she had seen only a distorted, one-sided article in the Sun newspaper. She would have been better advised to wait a little in order to read the comprehensive 16 page decision made by the Independent Appeal Panel

One family has been severely traumatized. Both families feel under pressure to accept transfer to another school where their sons will have to readjust to new teachers, new friends, and a new curriculum and examination syllabuses. Life has been difficult enough already without the added complications of a Secretary of State whose intervention is wholly one-sided and an inappropriate use of her powers.

CEN is contemplating making an application for judicial review involving both the school and the Secretary of State.

The pages that follow are divided into 3 parts:

a.   the facts behind the Death Threats case
b.   the bigger picture of school exclusions
c.   facts about CEN

The Death Threat Boys – The Other Side of the Story
The Facts of the Case

Two 15 year old boys were excluded from school for making threatening telephone calls to a teacher they disliked, because they felt he had treated them unfairly. He had found them in the school hall eating their sandwiches during lunch hour, and he had made them pick up litter every lunch hour for a week. He had spotted them with five others throwing stones after school at the canteen window, and just these two were excluded for three days each. They felt aggrieved and used their mobiles to indulge in what their parents, and CEN, clearly and bluntly stated to them was completely unacceptable behaviour.

There was a third boy who made similar calls with them. The three were initially excluded for ten days each. The parents of the two boys in this case asked to see the headteacher, but he refused outright to see any of them. In the meantime he allowed the aggrieved teacher to conduct the inquiry, along with another teacher, and he, the aggrieved teacher, played the leading role in interrogating the boys. One of the boys said he was quite intimidated when the teacher lost his temper and kicked a chair over while interrogating him. The Independent Appeal Panel found his involvement in the inquiry quite inappropriate.

The next time the families saw the headteacher was at the hour long governing body Discipline Committee hearing when the governors rubber-stamped his decision. However, the third boy was not permanently excluded despite also having made the telephone calls. The parents of the two boys saw this as quite inequitable. The Independent Appeal Panel also questioned the differential treatment.

The Independent Appeal Panel was wholly independent. It included two people with teaching experience, one of them a former school governor, and the third was entirely independent like them, but with a specialist knowledge of the locality. One of the three was a local Justice of the Peace. They were all trained in the exclusions procedures and the principles of natural justice. They were advised by an experienced fully qualified member of the authority's Legal Department.

A number of things emerged at the hearing

- It was significant that the aggrieved teacher stated in his evidence to the panel that once he knew the identity of the two boys, he knew that they constituted no danger to him or others.

- The headteacher admitted that he had had nothing to do with the inquiry, and that he had refused to see the parents and the boys before taking the decision to exclude.

- He also admitted that he had been very incensed when he had made his decision – which is contrary to the guidance given by the DfES Circular 10/99 stipulating that an exclusion decision should not be made *in the heat of the moment*.

- The boys had written a full apology to the aggrieved teacher, Mr Taverner, but had not received even an acknowledgement. They also undertook to make a public apology in front of the whole school with their parents present – that is quite a daunting experience for 16 year old boys.

The Independent Appeal Panel considered all the evidence and deliberated for one and a half days before making its decision. It issued a 16 page, 71 paragraph judgement and decided that the boys should be reinstated.

Upon receipt of the decision, Gerry German of the Communities Empowerment Network promptly wrote to the school and offered his services in assisting the school to facilitate the boys' reintegration into school life following their five months' absence from crucial formal education during their GCSE preparation.

The boys returned to school and were taught in isolation by a Supply Teacher. Work was supposed to be set and marked by the relevant teachers.

The boys had no social contact with anybody else. They

arrived in school after the other boys and left before them. They had their breaks at different times. They had to be off the premises at lunchtimes. They had to be accompanied to the toilets if they wished to use them.

It was a trying time for them and their parents. They felt humiliated but were patient about the inevitable penance they were expected to undergo. However, unlike adults facing the consequences of crimes or misdemeanours, they were somewhat confused by the appearance, in their case, of what seemed to be a life sentence to be spent in solitary confinement. At least, offending adults know the length of their sentence and the standards they have to meet to merit parole/release.

At this point CEN again intervened to ask about arrangements to ensure that they received their full entitlement to education. Gerry German also asked how long they were to remain in isolation, and what criteria they would have to satisfy in order to gain access to fulltime mainstream education.

He subsequently received a telephone call from the Deputy Head, Mr Webb, who wished to avail the school of the reintegration services CEN had offered. He asked if Gerry German would be prepared to meet him and the Head of Pastoral Services preceding a meeting with the Senior Management Team. Gerry agreed. He then asked if Gerry would be willing to meet the whole staff. Gerry agreed to that too, pointing out that the meeting might be fraught because of the deep feelings among some of them. It was clear that some of the teachers were professionally concerned about what was going on in relation to the boys' education.

The boys' parents had separate meetings with the headteacher when he assured them that he wanted both boys back in school, but that there were problems with some of his staff who objected to teaching them at all.

Subsequent to the school's request to meet Gerry German, agreed for Tuesday 15 October at 4 p.m., a thoroughly one-sided, distorted article appeared in the *Sun* newspaper. Nobody from the *Sun* contacted either the parents or CEN. Obviously there appeared to be at least one member of the school staff who objected to the possibility of the boys' reintegration into school life following a meeting between the school and CEN.

It was at this point that Estelle Morris and Stephen Twigg of the DfES intervened. They must only have read the *Sun* newspaper report. They obviously had had no time to read the 16 page, 71 paragraph decision of the Independent Appeal Panel. Ms Morris said that the boys should not be allowed to return to school – (there seems to be nobody in the upper echelons of the DfES who is on the side of children or their parents).

The whole situation then became murky and difficult to handle because of Estelle Morris' intervention, which was outside her powers anyway as defined by her own document *Social Inclusion: Pupil Support Circular 10/99* in Paragraph 54, which states categorically that *The Secretary of State has no power to consider complaints against the decisions of Independent Appeal Panels.* She seems also to have ignored Paragraph 49 which states *The decision of the panel is binding on the parent of the excluded pupil, the governing body and the local authority.* The boys and their parents accepted the decision. The local authority did too. Some of the staff at the school didn't. Nor did the Secretary of State who had issued the guidance in the first place.

CEN sees this as completely outside her powers and consequently a justification for an early application for judicial review linking her and the school. The parents feel that her intervention is encouraging the school, and others, to pressure and intimidate them to remove their children from the school.

It was not the parents or CEN who publicized the case. They feel that delicate matters of this kind should be dealt with privately and with cool heads. The only reason CEN and one of the parents have agreed to appear in the media is to attempt to set the record straight, especially in the interests of justice for pupils and their parents who otherwise have nobody on their side, unlike the teacher unions who have misguidedly used their muscle and their party connections to inflate prejudices and publicize their opinions.

School Exclusions – the Bigger Picture
25% of primary and 5% of secondary schools don't exclude pupils at all. Why can't others do the same?

Exclusions are patently *wasteful* – it costs at least twice as much to educate an excluded pupil; *destructive* – they have a traumatic effect on young people and their families as well as a negative spin-off on the schools themselves; and they are demonstrably *discriminatory* – black African Caribbean pupils are three to four times more likely to be excluded for fewer and less serious offences, and at a younger age than their white counterparts, and also less likely to get back into mainstream schooling.

In parts of some high-excluding boroughs they are still 15 to 16 times more likely to be excluded.

Children in care are eight times more likely to be excluded, a further blow to their battered self-esteem and their already bleak future prospects. There are other vulnerable groups such as Travellers and Refugees who are equally misunderstood and mistreated by a schooling system that is becoming increasingly splintered and exclusive.

Teachers are under pressure too from the oppressive league table system. But the ones who really suffer are the slower learners, the less confident, and those who have problems with relationships and with self discipline. Exclusion, unfortunately, seems an easy option for those in authority.

At its height some few years ago, permanent exclusions totalled over 13,000. Fixed term exclusions number some 100,000 annually. Truancies amounted to over one million. The Department for Education & Skills announced a one third exclusions reduction programme which had some success.

But even that was limited in its aims. If successful with those figures, we'd still have 667,000 truancies, 67,000 fixed term and some 9,000 permanent exclusions.

In Greater London alone in the academic year 2001/2 there were 199 primary school, 1197 secondary school and 52 special school permanent exclusions, and perhaps ten times that number of fixed term exclusions. A massive number of missed days, rejected students and lost opportunities.

During the same period, CEN did almost 800 fixed term and permanent exclusions cases, an average of 65 per month. It enjoyed a considerable degree of success in reinstating pupils at the excluding schools, perhaps more than any other organization.

However, its greatest success was in achieving a 100% reintegration rate, that is enabling pupils to learn from their experiences and settle down fully at the excluding or the new school, and make the appropriate academic and social progress. Boys and girls learned self-discipline and developed a sense of what behaviour was appropriate in different situations, even when they felt provoked.

It is interesting to look at absenteeism among pupils and teachers. During 2000/1 almost 9,500,000 half-days were missed through unauthorized absence from secondary schools in England, and over 5,300,000 from primary schools. Teachers are similarly stressed or disaffected, and their rate of authorized sick leave absence is at a rate 7 times greater than pupil truancy. We need to ask what makes schooling so uncongenial.

There are other serious problems:

- The cost of school fires has risen to 87 million pounds per year, up by 54% between 1999 and 2000. In England, approximately three schools are set on fire each day. So much for the Home Office's Arson Prevention Bureau set up in 1991.

- Admissions appeals almost doubled between 1995/6 and 1999/2000, to more than 60,000, just over 96 per 1000 admissions. Recent research by the London School of Economics exposes what a confusing labyrinth it is for most parents.

- The Special Educational Needs process is often just as slow, confusing, and distressing for parents and their children, despite the best intentions of Parent Partnerships set up to help them. Many children are still not properly provided for and several are still excluded partway through the statementing process that seeks to determine whether a child should be given a statement of their special educational needs

- A report by the Children's Rights Commissioner states that childhood poverty is higher, and childhood illness more acute in London. At least 100,000 five to sixteen year olds have mental health problems. They are entitled to education.

Crime among young people is rising but youngsters are more likely to be victims than perpetrators. In October 2001 there were 433 juveniles behind bars. How many of them were excluded from school?

- Inner London schools exclude at a rate twice the national average – most at risk are ethnic minorities (40%), and those with special educational needs (25%); SEN pupils range from 11% in Sutton to 34% in Islington.

- The highest excluding boroughs are Doncaster, Kensington & Chelsea, Leicester, Liverpool, Sandwell and Wandsworth. The lowest are Bournemouth, Calderdale, Cambridge, Knowsley, Middlesborough, and Poole. There are twelve urban authorities that exclude more than one in 500 pupils.

- Wandsworth excludes one in 300 compared with one in 10,000 in the much more deprived conurbation of Middlesborough. Are Wandsworth children really thirty times worse behaved than their counterparts in Middlesborough – or is it because there are more black pupils to be excluded in Wandsworth?

But what seems to excite the public schools and high status state schools? And what occupies broadcasting time and newspaper column inches? And what seems to get the wholehearted response of the Secretary of State? Oxbridge admissions and 'A' level papers! Surely those at risk of failure and rejection by the school system are equally deserving of time and interest.

CEN has just completed a survey of organizations in the Greater London area that provide representation services for the parents of excluded children. They cannot meet demand. CEN estimates from its careful enquiries that no more than 40% of excluded children could have been represented during the past academic year. It would appear then, that there are over 1,000 families in Greater London who could not have been represented at exclusion hearings. Unrepresented parents enter hearings, especially governing body hearings, like lambs to the slaughter. This contrasts sharply with what our system specifies for adults faced with disciplinary and legal proceedings.

Teacher unions and some other unenlightened persons are calling for the abolition of Independent Appeal Panels. These are the same people who insist on their rights to checks and balances, including appeals under grievance and disciplinary procedures. What makes them think that children who are far more vulnerable, and have no unions, should be less entitled to justice and fair procedures?

We ask again, who is on the side of the children and young people, especially those who are not seen as gifted high-flyers but as troublesome and underachieving? It is struggling organizations like CEN who do the work that we should be demanding from properly funded independent experienced representatives. We hope that the Community Fund will continue to keep its courage and integrity under the media and government onslaught.

The Communities Empowerment Network

This was set up with a grant from the then National Lottery Fund and its work came on stream in June 2000, under the direction of Gerry German working on an unpaid voluntary basis. Because of the rapidly increasing number of school exclusions, he works a 70/80 hour week and operates a telephone helpline from his home on a 24 hour, 7 day a week basis. His colleagues work for a pittance, but like him they are committed to justice and equality in education.

CEN provides advice, support, counselling, and representation for people experiencing problems in education and employment. By far the most casework has to do with the increasing problem of school exclusions. Some are to do with grievances, disciplinary hearings, and employment tribunals for teachers whose unions refuse to give them adequate representation, especially if they are black, the same unions who resist the reintegration of excluded pupils, again a huge number of them from the black communities.

CEN has a vision of education and schooling as inclusive, integrated, welcoming, and congenial for all children from whatever linguistic, cultural or religious background to enable them to realize their full potential and to enter adult life as confident, contributing, responsible, citizens of the United Kingdom, Europe and the world.

The other side of the coin is ensuring that all children are given adequate opportunities for positive personal development through courses such as those CEN has successfully piloted with challenging pupils at various schools in the Inner London area. This enhances their self-confidence, self-esteem and their capacity for mutual respect and empathy as well as academic and social progress.

CEN believes that nobody is irrecoverable. CEN believes in rehabilitation rather than rejection. CEN believes in discussion and negotiation, rather than confrontation and punishment. CEN believes in giving children, young people, and their parents a say in how their life-chances are ordered, their actions self-motivated, and their lives organized and fulfilled. The younger generation is the world's future, and it is up to all adults to set a good example for them to follow, they need to provide respect and consideration.

We hope that even at the present time, somehow, good sense will prevail and the DfES will start thinking about supporting the otherwise weak and vulnerable instead of just the big battalions. We trust that they will find a way to stop intimidating funding bodies and struggling organizations such as CEN.

Postscript

Gerry German has never claimed to support Osama Bin Laden in any way. What he did say to the Daily Mail reporter was that he was a pacifist who didn't believe that there was any justification for killing. He added however that he could well understand how people's experiences of oppression could lead to violence. His concern was to look at the antecedent and surrounding circumstances in order to find a way of dealing with anger and violence. Nor did he refer to the United States of America as a warmonger although he said that any consideration of violence in the world would have to be strictly contextualized in relation to the role of the superpowers, including the USA. When pupils are accused of violence or inappropriate behaviour of any kind, he adopts a similar kind of micro-enquiry to establish the underlying causes, in order to rehabilitate the perpetrator and resolve the conflict. It works.

3.4

CEN ADVOCACY IN SUPPORT OF STUDENTS AND PARENTS
The case of Paul Bright
Autumn Term 2002 – All names are changed

In my role as Chair of the Communities Empowerment Network, I found time to do a limited amount of advocacy work, mainly in cities and towns outside of London.

This case involved the son of one of our Management Committee members who shared CEN's concern over a period of time about the number and pattern of exclusions in the London boroughs that were high excluders, especially of black boys. She herself was suddenly faced with a situation involving her son for which she sought CEN's help. Such was the extent of our full time workers' and volunteers' casework involvement and the obviously damaging impact of his school experience on Paul, that CEN agreed that I should take the case on and provide advocacy support to the family.

The first letter below was written to Paul's headteacher, copied to the Chair of Governors of the school and to the Director of Education.

The Director sent a prompt reply, stating that he was having discussions with the Chair of Governors and would ensure that the matters complained about were properly dealt with. CEN later learnt that the headteacher was not best pleased with the letter I sent to the school and to the education director. Reports reaching CEN suggested that she felt she 'had been ambushed' in that I had not revealed at the meeting on 27 November 2002 that I had been a director of education.

Time and again, we at CEN witness schools treating ordinary

parents in the most disrespectful and dismissive manner. Some headteachers surround themselves with senior colleagues well versed in school and exclusion procedures, and often eager to provide parents with information about the school's assessment of the conduct of their children. Seldom do these encounters encompass a discussion of the child's academic progress or the positive relationships s/he has with adults and peers in the school. CEN is about empowerment of students and parents. We work on the premise that schools should treat all parents with respect and be prepared and willing to listen to them. Their willingness to do so should not depend upon the status or degree of knowledge of any individual attending in order to give the parent support and the confidence to present their own views. As far as I am concerned, therefore, it was enough for me to introduce myself by name, to say that I was from CEN and that I was there to support the parent.

Whatever the Director of Education did, the Bright family were able to inform CEN some weeks later that that headteacher had left Ravenscroft High School.

5 December 2002

Ms V Williamson
Headteacher
Ravenscroft High School
Elderbrook
London SE33 7DZ

Dear Ms Williamson

Re: PAUL BRIGHT – YEAR 7

On 8 November 2002, Mr & Mrs Bright, Paul's parents, wrote to you giving details of the treatment Paul had received at the hands of a group of students and members of your Senior Management Team at the school on 8 October 2002. You responded on 11 November 2002 stating that the matters they had raised were 'most serious' and you would 'therefore be carrying out a full and personal investigation'. You would not only 'speak with witnesses of the original events but also would be interviewing staff about their involvement' and would then notify the parents of your conclusions.

At the Bright's request, I accompanied Cynthia Bright as 'friend' at the meeting on 27 November at which you gave your response to their letter of 8 November. I have since received from the Brights a copy of your letter dated 3 December and which you had promised to write when we met.

The Bright family are extremely distressed at your response and have asked me to write to you to convey their views of your handling of this unfortunate affair.

Before I continue and in view of the recent publicity this organization which I Chair has received, let me tell you the capacity in which I am involved with the Bright family in this matter. I run a training and management consultancy as well as working as a Visiting Professor of Education, training graduates for the PGCE and helping to manage an Equality & Discrimination Centre in my Faculty. I was for over seven years a Director of Education and Leisure Services in London and I am a member of the Home Secretary's Race Relations Forum and Chair of its Agenda Group. In the latter capacity, I worked closely with Jack Straw and his civil servants on the amendment of the 1976 Race Relations Act.

The Communities Empowerment Network (CEN) was established two and a half years ago to provide advice, support, counselling and representation for people experiencing problems in education, principally. CEN also provides advocacy to people in employment, especially where adequate or any representation from trade unions is not forthcoming.

CEN is governed by a Management Committee of some sixteen people, most of whom are parents of school age children and have considerable contact with the schooling and education system in a number of capacities. They include, apart from myself:

- A former LEA councillor and Education Committee member
- A serving LEA councillor

- School governors
- LEA education officers
- Solicitors
- University lecturers
- Heads of Department and Senior Teachers
- A former College Vice Principal & Head of Equal Opportunities

The five full time members of CEN staff are able to draw heavily upon the expertise of their committee members in matters of policy, working with students and parents, assisting schools in building effective home/school partnerships and engaging with schools in implementing preventative strategies for working with students at risk of exclusion, as well as in re-integrating excluded students.

We place no less importance on these latter aspects of our work than we do on advocacy and representation because our primary aim is to keep children in school and focused on learning. Should you and your Governing Body wish to engage in discussions with us as to how we might assist you at Ravenscroft, we would be more than delighted to work with you.

Turning now to the matter of Paul Bright, I have to say that the family and I found your letter of 3 December 2002 equally as distressing as the manner in which you conducted the meeting on 27 November. Let me deal with that meeting first.

Paul's parents sent you a detailed and considered letter, giving you both Paul's and their accounts of events surrounding his unofficial and illegal exclusion from school and its aftermath. You indicated in response that you were personally going to investigate the matters they raised and get back to them. Their letter gave you clear pointers as to the issues to be addressed and the persons to be interviewed.

When we met with you on 27 November, however, it was evident that, despite the clear undertaking you gave in your letter of 11 November, you had not sought to get from some key individuals their accounts of what had happened and what they had personally witnessed. I would refer you to page 2 of the Bright's letter:

'What investigation had the school done to establish how the fight had come about and who the aggressors were?

Had the male teacher, who helped Paul off the floor, provided voluntarily or been asked to produce an incident report of the scene he had witnessed? Was any of the students present interviewed as to Paul's supposed role in the fracas?'

It was absurd and indeed quite disruptive for you, having failed to do so as part of your so-called investigation, to seek to get a written account of the incident from that teacher, some seven weeks later, while he was in the middle of teaching a lesson and while you carried on the meeting with us in your office.

You started that meeting by saying how you would on no account cover up for the malpractices of members of your staff and 'never have done'. You then launched into an impassioned recitation of a litany of Paul's wrongdoings, throwing in everything under the sun, including matters which were patently false, which you had not verified and which, even if they had been true, would not have justified the conduct of the two most senior members of staff complained against, namely, Mr Braveboy, your Deputy and Mr Sheen. I will return to what the family regards as the wilful misrepresentation of Paul's conduct presently.

You conceded a number of things during that meeting. You agreed that Mr Sheen had acted unprofessionally and had caused Paul unnecessary distress. In mitigation, you argued that both Mr Sheen and Mr Braveboy had been extremely angered by Paul's conduct. You did say, nevertheless, that you had disciplined Mr Sheen. When I asked you what that meant, you said you had given him a Verbal Warning and that that was recorded on his Personnel File.

You conceded, also, that the school had not taken any steps to satisfy itself that Paul had not suffered serious or potentially serious injury as a result of the kicking and punching he had received, and that he could have developed serious health problems at home later that same day.

So hell bent were you on demonizing Paul, however, that you

kept insisting that he it was who had turned off the lights and started the fight. First, you claimed that the male teacher in the ICT room had seen Paul switch the lights off and had said so; then you claimed that Mr Sheen was told so by other students present. You were insistent that this 'atrociously behaved boy' had brought his injury and suffering upon himself by starting the fracas outside the ICT classroom. Yet, you had clearly made no attempt during your 'investigation' to interview the teacher who had been in the ICT room and who had emerged only when he heard the fracas. You sought to get his version of events during our meeting only because you wished to verify, or perhaps disprove, what Mrs Bright was saying to you and had reported in great detail in the letter of 8 November.

Nor had you interviewed Ms Gomes or Mr Halstead, again despite the role they placed as narrated in Mrs Bright's letter of 8 November.

It was rather distressing for Cynthia Bright to hear some of the allegations you were making against her son, not least because, despite your obvious horror at the seriousness of them, neither she nor her husband had been notified of them and you could produce no documentary evidence that Paul had been punished for them.

You produced a report, purportedly from Ms Oswald, giving details of an incident in which Paul allegedly 'kicked, spat and swore at her in front of the whole class'. You were asked why it was that Paul had not been sent home for something so serious and why his parents had not been notified. You claimed that a letter had been sent home with Paul and you implied that his parents had not received it because Paul had intercepted it in order to hide his wrongdoing. Asked whether the school had imposed any sanctions, you said that Mr Braveboy, the Deputy Head, had excluded him.

That incident, according to Ms Oswald's record, took place on 3 October. What happened, as Paul and other boys present recalled it to us, was as follows:

Paul's school bag was thrown out of the classroom window by FS. Paul got up from his seat to inform Ms Oswald of that fact and to ask her permission to go and retrieve it. She would not listen and simply told him to go and sit down. He continued putting his hand up and to try and tell her what FS had done. She eventually turned to him and said: 'Right, that's it, Paul, out! Go to Mr Burrows' (Head of English). As he left, Ms Oswald shut the door behind him. FS who had caused Paul's interruptions remained in the class.

Paul went to retrieve his bag from outside before going to see Mr Burrows in the classroom next door to Ms Oswald's. When he went into Mr Burrows, Paul was asked for his homework diary. Mr Burrows looked at it and uttered:

'This is a mum who cares', adding that he would be speaking to her. Paul went from Mr Burrows' class to his next lesson, i.e., History.

Cynthia Bright collected Paul from school that afternoon and he told her what had happened. Mrs Bright actually went into the school and no one mentioned anything to her about the alleged objectionable conduct.

The next day, Friday 4 October, Cynthia Bright again went to collect Paul from school. The receptionist went to look for him and returned to tell Mrs Bright that he had left. She had also told Mr Burrows that Cynthia Bright had come to meet Paul and Mr Burrows came out to the reception area to see her. He invited her to follow him into a room to have a chat about Paul's work. They discussed the difficulties Paul had been having at Ravenscroft, for example, being late for lessons, not finding classrooms, not producing enough work in class during lessons, especially in Ms Oswald's English lessons.

Mr Burrows told Cynthia Bright that he himself had gone into Ms Oswald's class to observe the class. He suggested that one way to help Paul was to put him on report as a way of recording his work and his behaviour. Cynthia Bright asked Mr Burrows to look into the possibility of Paul being moved from Ms Oswald's class and he said he would see what he could do on the following Monday, 7 October.

Cynthia Bright spent up to an hour with Mr Burrows who even tried to obtain a copy of the letter regarding Parents Evening which was due to be held on 9 October, but could not find one. He suggested that Mrs Bright returned to the school on

Monday 7 October to get a copy of the letter from the school secretary. At no point during that whole period did Mr Burrows even intimate that Paul had been involved in something as serious as kicking, spitting at and swearing at a teacher in his English department.

Paul was in school on Friday 4 and Monday 7 October. He had not been excluded before then, despite the insinuation that he destroyed the letter of exclusion given him by Mr Braveboy, the Deputy Head. If the alleged incident occurred on 3 October and Paul attended school on 4 and 7 October, when was he supposed to have been out of school on account of exclusion?

My assessment of those allegations and the manner in which you, with a sense of outrage, confronted Paul's mother with them, is that in the light of the very serious issues the Bright family was raising in their letter to you, you decided to see what you could find to throw at Paul and make his mother feel that the school was bending over backwards to accommodate him, so disgraceful was his conduct. It was also a way of saying that, faced with such a boy, even people as experienced as Mr Sheen and Mr Braveboy would lose their temper.

What you seemed to fail to grasp is that when adults in authority conduct themselves as Mr Sheen and Mr Braveboy did, it gives the green light to students to do the same and plenty worse.

In this connection, we find it incredible that you failed to see what was wrong in Mr Sheen arriving at the scene of a fight and saying to the only person who appeared to be injured and the victim of the melee: 'who gave you a fat lip?' to the obvious derision of the very boys who had been involved in kicking and punching Paul?

In their letter of 8 November, the Brights provided the names of three boys who had been perpetrators of the assault on Paul. You made no mention at the meeting on 27 November of any steps you had taken to interview those boys and their parents. It was common knowledge, however, among them and their peers, that Paul was being kept at home. They were presumably free to continue their bullying and intimidating conduct.

It was one of those same boys, M, who attacked Paul on the

street earlier this week as Paul made his way home. M was violent, intimidating and insistent that Paul should fight him on the street. He snatched Paul's hat from his head, causing him to sustain a slight injury to his forehead in the process. We believe that had M been dealt with appropriately for his involvement in the 8 October attack on Paul, he would not have been so bold as to go outside school and behave in a manner that could have resulted in serious injury for one or other of them, if not got both of them arrested by the Police had Paul not shown total restraint.

In order to avoid any further bullying from or possible confrontation with M and his friends, Paul is now having to take a route home that gets him home at 5pm rather than 3.45pm.

There is clearly a bullying culture at Ravenscroft, amongst teachers and students alike. Part of that institutionalized bullying is the dismissive way in which you appear to have treated the matters raised by the Brights in their letter on 8 November. Your attitude appeared to have been that Paul was a foul-mouthed troublemaker and that whatever he tells his parents must be false. They should not therefore rely on accounts from their son and his peers about incidents in which they all had some involvement, even as onlookers.

That same lack of empathy with Paul's situation as a victim of bullying was epitomized by your attitude towards the boy at the meeting on 27 November. You never once inquired as to how he was, even when his mother described how they had to take him to (Accident & Emergency) the evening of the incident. You made no mention of his academic progress, either. When I sought to point out matters which I felt you as headteacher needed to attend to in the light of what the Brights had put in their letter to you, you somewhat arrogantly suggested that you did not need me to tell you how to do your job.

Yet, in the letter you sent to Paul's parents, you could not even bring yourself to apologize for the wholly inappropriate and unlawful conduct of your senior staff. What on earth could you mean when you say, for example, 'I appreciate, without prejudice, where you feel we might have let you down'. That is surely a euphemism for 'I am not admitting in writing to anything, not even to what I conceded and owned up to in front of you and your "friend" in my office'. No, your total focus is on Paul. No apology, either, for the fact that the school failed to provide him with the most basic medical attention but rather, continued to pile on the agony by treating him as Mr Sheen had done, aided and abetted by Mr Braveboy, while the child was still frightened and traumatiszed by the violence he had suffered outside the ICT room. So, why 'where you feel we might have let you down'? Why not 'I am sorry for the fact that less than half way through Paul's very first term in the school we have failed him and let you down so badly'. That, Ms Williamson, is the reality of the situation and as such an indictment of your school.

Mrs Bright told you on 27 November that as a result of the kicking Paul had received while curled up on the floor outside the ICT room, he now had to wear glasses because of damage to an optic nerve. Yet, you feel justified in writing to his parents about 'where you feel we *might* have let you down'.

Your letter was as disingenuous as was your attempt to paint for Cynthia Bright on 27 November a picture of an utterly horrible little boy whose behaviour was such as to cause your experienced senior managers to conduct themselves in ways that were untypical and wholly out of character.

Now that Paul has left your school, you have one less victim to blame. We at CEN, no less than his parents, would ask, however, that you ensure that none of your students continue to victimize, intimidate and physically harm Paul as he goes about his lawful business whenever and wherever he so chooses. We would support the Brights in whatever ways necessary to ensure that Ravenscroft students do not have Paul living in fear or run the family out of their area.

Moreover, we trust that you yourself would derive some learning from your wholly inappropriate management of this affair, including your cursory investigation. We would stress the need for you and *all* your staff at Ravenscroft to treat parents and your own students with due respect, acknowledging that they have a voice and one that requires to be heard, and that they also have protection under the provisions of the Human

Rights Act and the Race Relations Amendment Act 2000.

Yours, with sadness

Professor Gus John

Chair, the Communities Empowerment Network.

Cc:Mr Richard Littlemore – Chair of Governors
    Mr William Pryce – Director of Education, Elderbrook LEA

5 December 2002

Mr William Pryce
Director of Education
Elderbrook LEA
Education Directorate
High Street
Elderbrook
London SE 33 1LU

Dear Mr Pryce

PAUL BRIGHT AND RAVENSCROFT HIGH SCHOOL

I am aware that Mr and Mrs Bright sent you a copy of their letter
of 8 November to the Headteacher of Ravenscroft High School,
Ms V. Williamson. The family are very distressed at the letter
they received from Ms Williamson following a meeting at which
I represented them as 'friend' on 27 November and have
authorised CEN to write to the school on their behalf. I therefore
enclose for your attention a copy of that letter and my response.

Whilst I am fully aware of the limited role LEAs now have in the
affairs of schools, it seems to me that insofar as the experiences

of Paul and other students at Ravenscroft High, black boys in particular, amount to child protection issues, your LEA should be seeking to investigate what is going wrong at that school as a matter of urgency. Judging by the number and nature of the complaints coming to CEN from black parents at Ravenscroft, we rather fear that something quite appalling is waiting to happen there, which would inevitably cause some hapless parents a lot of grief and plunge the LEA into a crisis management situation, no doubt in the full glare of the media.

We would urge you, therefore, to use whatever residual powers you still have and intervene to ensure that the Governing Body of that school get a grip and take all necessary steps to prevent someone at or associated with the school getting very seriously hurt.

Yours sincerely

Professor Gus John   –   Chair of CEN

4.0

DEVELOPING BLACK TEACHERS AND SCHOOL MANAGERS

In 2004, the Institute of Education launched a leadership programme for black and ethnic minority staff. The programme goes under the banner of: Identity, Culture and Pedagogy – Black and Ethnic Minority Leaders for the twenty-first century, and is targeted at serving black teachers who are already in middle management positions and aspiring to become heads or deputies, and those who wish to become middle managers.

The programme is led by Rosemary Campbell, herself a former headteacher, LEA Adviser, and OfSTED inspector, and a dynamic and inspirational black educationalist.

Leaders and Managers in Black Skin – So what? (4.1) sought to raise a number of issues for participants in the introductory stage of that programme. What difference does being a black teacher make? What are the expectations schools and governing bodies have of black teachers? How sensitive are they to the racialized context in which such teachers operate and that shapes people's expectations of them? If teacher education and training continues to prepare white teachers and black for the classroom in a manner that eclipses consideration of the dynamics of 'race', gender, sexuality, etc., and does not engage with their racial identity, what then are black teachers expected to bring to their interactions with students, irrespective of whether those students are black or white? To what extent would their own schooling and education have helped those black teachers in being sufficiently confident in their black skin and in navigating the stormy seas of racism in schooling and society, so as to be able to deal with the challenges of being a black teacher in a racialized schooling and education system?

The majority of black teachers in today's schools are themselves products of the same schooling system they have joined. That helps to shape their expectations of students, black and white. In the mentoring I do and in the focus group sessions I have conducted with black teachers, they give vivid testimonies of the way their schooling experience has led them to have higher expectations of black students, including getting those students to take themselves more seriously, have high aspirations and work harder. That often brings them into conflict with their white colleagues, especially those who are quite happy to resign themselves to seeing those students coast along and operate below their potential. More troubling, however, is the aggravation black teachers endure at the hands of black parents, especially in primary schools, when they insist that children adopt positive attitudes to their own learning, work to their potential and develop competence in their social interactions. I have had the task of counselling black teachers and mediating conflict between them and black parents because those parents have verbally abused those teachers for 'demanding too much hard work' from their child.

Black teachers tell of white headteachers' lack of understanding of these issues and of a consequent lack of support, particularly when they as black teachers call into question the attitude of their white colleagues to the quality of black children's learning.

All of this raises concerns about the expectations schools, parents, and black communities have of black teachers. Crucially, it calls into question the responsibility those communities feel they have to support black teachers so that they could be effective in making a difference to the schooling experience of black children by virtue of being black teachers. The reality is that black teachers experience the schooling system, and black communities, as believing that there is something magical about being a 'black teacher', and that positive benefits accrue simply by having some more black faces around the staffroom. That leads, among other things, to a lack of sensitivity to the way black teachers are experiencing the regime of schooling and to the support needs that they might have.

What, then, does a black teacher do with all this when s/he becomes a headteacher? How do they go about building upon the best examples of leadership, sound management and relationship with students and parents they, hopefully, would have identified in the practice of their line managers and bring the added dimension and experience of their blackness to the headship function?

As part of its headship development programme, the Institute of Education organized a round table discussion for black middle managers aspiring to become headteachers. The 'Notes' that introduced that discussion (4.2) provided participants with a framework for examining not only the qualities and competences that make for effective leadership, but also the particular challenges they would face as black headteachers.

Does the National Association of Head Teachers, the Secondary Heads Association, the National Union of Teachers, or any trade union for that matter, have 'race' and the experiences of black headteachers and teachers sufficiently high on their agenda to provide leadership in tackling these systemic, professional and cultural issues? Teaching unions are clearly more comfortable dealing with individual cases of denial of workers' rights, and of discrimination or harassment, than engaging with strategies for dealing, holistically, with the range of issues identified above. We have yet to see, for example, teaching unions demonstrating that they share the African-Caribbean community's concern about the persistently high levels of exclusion of black boys and the growing number of them being excluded from primary schools and even from Pupil Referral Units. On the contrary, the greatest resistance to the black communities' attempts to keep more students in school, and provide them with support to overcome their behaviour and discipline problems, has come from the teaching unions themselves. They, too, have been clamouring the loudest to have the Government abolish the Independent Appeal Panels and the power of LEAs to make schools take back excluded students.

As in other professions that have been making strenuous efforts to recruit and retain more black staff in the last two decades, the police for example, the interests of the general membership of that profession, their operational culture and professional practice, are not always in alignment with that of their black membership. That is why it is both necessary and desirable for black staff within those professions to organize themselves independently.

In 1993, black teachers met in Bradford to discuss forming an Asian and African Teachers Association and invited me to present a keynote address and help give some direction to their efforts. *African, Caribbean and Asian Teachers in Hackney Education* (4.3) brought to black teachers in Hackney, a borough with some 67% black and ethnic minority students in its schools, the same message that had been shared with their counterparts in Bradford.

The presentation addressed questions to do with their identity as black teachers, what united them as a group, the purposes for which they wanted to form themselves into an association and the structure and method of organization most appropriate to those purposes.

Teachers in Bradford did form themselves into an Association, as did those in Hackney. The Hackney Association experienced severe growth pains, not least because of the lack of clarity amongst some of their members about the respective roles of the Association, of the local branch of the National Union of Teachers (NUT) to which many of them belonged, of the NUT itself and of tendencies within the Socialist Workers Party. Suffice it to say that some four years after leaving Hackney, I was still receiving requests for support from black teachers in Hackney whose rights and professionalism headteachers and governing bodies were signally failing to respect.

Among those teachers were several who had been recruited from Trinidad in 1990 when Hackney first became a local education authority, a period that coincided with a massive primary teacher shortage across Britain. They, like the rest of their group, have now been teaching in Hackney and other

London schools since September 1990. In November 1991, the UK Government introduced new immigration rules which impacted upon the status of those teachers as people holding two year work permits. By the time those work permits were due to be renewed, the teacher supply crisis had abated somewhat and the Department of Employment was insisting that Hackney Education provide evidence of failure to fill the posts occupied by those teachers with local teachers or with recruits from the European Community. The statement in 4.4 tells the story of the intervention that caused the government to change its mind and enable all the teachers recruited from Trinidad who so wished to continue helping to raise standards in Hackney schools.

4.1

IDENTITY, CULTURE AND PEDAGOGY
Black and ethnic minority leaders for the twenty-first century
25 February 2005

It has become fashionable, in the public and voluntary sectors particularly, for passionate pleas to be made for more black people to be represented in the workforce or/and in senior management positions and among decision makers in public institutions. Those pleas come as much from black and ethnic minority communities themselves as from the majority white leadership of those institutions. That has been and remains true for social work, teaching across the phases of education, policing, the armed forces, the prison service, the crown prosecution service, the judiciary, the health service and so on.

Recently, the Metropolitan Police, with the support of a rather capricious Home Secretary, have proposed the fast tracking of black police officers into senior ranks within the Force by means of positive discrimination, a practice which is quite properly forbidden under the provisions of the Race Relations Act 1976 and by the Amendment to that Act, the RRAA 2000.

At the recent London Schools and the Black Child conference, Mayor Ken Livingstone expressed his wish to see a massive increase in the number of black teachers in London schools. He was responding to the Education Commission's report on the performance of black children in the capital's schools.

It is interesting to note where all of this comes from. Our struggles in the 1960s, '70s and '80s targeted, among other things, the discriminatory practices of employers in the public and corporate sectors who were nonchalantly excluding black people from various forms of employment in a manner and with a consistency that defied all explanation except on grounds of race. Early arguments suggested that there were no black people sufficiently qualified, or that blacks simply did not have the confidence to apply for and perform successfully in those positions, or that one's duty as an employer was fulfilled once you had appointed a number of blacks relative to their percentage in the overall population, not of the geographical area in question, but of the country as a whole.

In my experience as someone who was actively engaged in those struggles, our fight was not for some crude numerical or statistical representation, but for equal rights to employment opportunities and to selection on the basis of criteria that were not arbitrarily biased and weighted against us. Ours was a struggle for basic human rights and to put an end to unlawful discrimination on the grounds of ethnic origin, usually coupled with our class background and the way we spoke.

Some of us became very passionate about the dubious notion of black people with certain attributes and in particular professional roles acting as 'role models' for others. I say 'dubious' because as far as I am concerned it simply bought in to the general perception of black people as deficient, not quite managing to make it in their own right and therefore needing to see those who 'break through' and get to sit at the table with the white man, as individuals to emulate. So, you shadow them to see how they managed to overcome the barriers, what they bring to their roles, how they manage to survive within the mainly white and sometimes hostile environment in which they find themselves. And, invariably, the sub text was/is: If I could do it as a black person and, more to the point, as a black person from the same social background as you, then so could you.

The focus, therefore, is principally on the individual and their presumed inability to access opportunities and be supported by an inclusive culture in which they are respected and valued. They are presumed to need to learn the ropes, to round off those rough edges, to socialize themselves into ways of thinking and behaviour that would make them more acceptable to employers. Thus has come about the racialization of processes that are organic to most communities, especially the ones from which black settlers in Britain originally came.

This phenomenon, not unlike the desire to see more black this, that and the other, begs a whole host of questions. I would highlight just five:

- What assumptions are being made about the factors that black staff have in common with black service users or mentees, apart from 'race' as a common signifier?
- What is the quality of the values and principles those mentors are bringing to their engagement with those to whom they act as 'role models'? What is the level of their consciousness and to what extent do they embrace a commitment to combating the discrimination and processes of exclusion that impact upon our communities?
- Does being black automatically confer upon staff in those situations a capacity to empathize with, understand or extend black service users or those whom they are mentoring?
- Does the common experience of being constituted a target group necessarily lead black staff to understand the meaning of that and the different dynamics involved in the response to that experience?
- How does the presence of a more representative number of black staff impact upon the organization, its culture and its structures and processes such that it is experienced by would-be black employees as being more inclusive and respecting of black people and their rights?

These questions and many more are generally avoided in the discourse about rectifying underrepresentation and increasing the number of black staff at all levels within organizations. These are all political questions which, too often, are reduced to ones of technical competence.

At the root of the problem is the manner in which structural, cultural, institutional, and personal manifestations of racism and discrimination are ignored, and the image and profile of black people which the system has itself constructed, with all the accompanying baggage, has become the focus of attention.

Speaking about baggage, it beggars belief that a service like the Police which is not exactly renowned for its treatment of black staff who are recruited and promoted on merit, however few in number, could actually contemplate increasing the number of such staff by a method of positive discrimination. One should hope that no self-respecting black person, however desperate, would allow themselves to be placed in any situation where they could be looked upon as gaining their position by grace and favour rather than by merit.

A number of issues arise from all this:

- Crucially, whose interest does it all serve?
- What difference does it make to the situation of the majority of the group such black staff are supposed to represent, if the training and professional socialization those black staff receive, the institutional culture of which they become a part, and the systems and processes they operate are identical to that of their white counterparts?
- What in particular are they assumed to bring to the service and especially to their interface with black service users by virtue of being black?
- How does the service identify those special qualities, promote them and allow them free expression in operational contexts?
- How does the service deal with those situations in which the 'additionality' of black identity translates into decision-making, use of discretion and methods of handling situations involving black people, which are diametrically opposed to the regime of the service and the common approach it expects all its staff to apply?
- And what support do those staff receive when the very communities they are supposed to 'represent' show their hostility towards them for daring to raise the expectations of and demand more effort from their children, if not from themselves?
- To what extent do those communities embrace the responsibility to struggle to ensure that such black staff could operate in the interests of all children, and black children in particular, without being picked off by managers of the service?

Let me turn now, more directly, to the implications of all that for black leaders and managers in schools. First, let me affirm the right of every black teacher to aspire to become a senior teacher, deputy head, headteacher, principal education psychologist, Her Majesty's Inspector of Schools, or the Secretary of State for Education. *I affirm your right, equally, to aspire to be any one of those things as a professional educator who happens to be black without feeling the need to take on the mantle of change agent and setting out to change the world simply because you are black.* I affirm your right, but that does not mean you will be able to exercise it.

I contend that so long as we live with racism in this society, so long as our existence as black people in all walks of life and in just about every interface with the society is mediated through the dynamic of 'race', so long as the schooling system continues to be anything but inclusive of black people in all our complexity and all our richness, we do not have the luxury of being professionals *who simply happen to be black.*

There is nothing 'simple' about being black in British society. There is no distinction between professional identity and practice, and personal identity and values when one is operating the schooling system, either as classroom assistant, teacher or headteacher, whoever your charges and your colleagues might be.

The context is given. The system defines the situation in a particular way and expects schools to operate broadly within that framework of understanding, and to operate its various forms of social engineering, whether it be Ethnic Minority & Traveller Achievement Grants or 'Aiming High' initiatives.

For the professional who happens to be black therefore, individual choice about the terms of engagement is effectively displaced by the range of expectations different constituencies have of you, irrespective of those you might have of yourself.

Governors might have certain expectations of you as a black school manager. Some of those expectations would be framed by various kinds of baggage which are not necessarily the result of perversity but of the cultural expectations there are of black people within a societal culture of racism. For one thing, we live in a society that automatically validates white people and that is still not accustomed to having black people occupy certain positions as a matter of routine. Black service users are not used to having black managers occupy such positions, either. Indeed, the experience some black parents have had of the British schooling system lead them to have high expectations of black school managers, not least in the direction of putting things right and doing their best by them, as parents, and by their children. Sadly, those expectations are not always matched by guaranteed engagement with and support for those black managers.

In terms of matters within the sphere of management of the black headteacher, there might be a reluctance on teachers' part to be expected to follow an agenda arising from the black headteacher's vision for the school and the steps s/he considers necessary in order to realize that vision. The vexed question of how to make the curriculum and teaching and learning truly inclusive and relevant, and how to monitor teaching quality and the delivery of that curriculum, might trigger potentially divisive debates about 'representation', the validation of knowledge and approaches to the National Curriculum.

Even more critical in this context would be the black manager's insistence that teachers should have higher expectations of themselves, and encourage similarly high expectations and career aspirations in their students, particularly when those students come from deprived backgrounds.

If, in relation to any or all of the above scenarios, the fact that the manager is black is not seen to make a difference, it would be very surprising indeed if that person were to manage to keep faith with themselves and their personal values, let alone with students and their parents.

Wearing or pretending to wear a 'white mask' while inhabiting a black skin under such conditions is a recipe for ontological dissonance and mental illness.

It would be clear by now that I believe that the blackness of black staff, especially leaders and managers, must be seen to make a difference. Try as we may, we would find it impossible to do our jobs while at the same time psychologically removing ourselves from the social, political and economic contexts that define us as black professionals and that mediate the realities of those round about us.

What then are the implications of that for us as black leaders and managers?:

- What is it that we are bringing from inside our being as black people, from deep within our spirituality and from inside the totality of our experience of the society and its relationship to the wider group to which we belong?

- Does my blackness and my experience of how the society relates to it induce me to articulate a set of values that act as my personal compass?

- Do I have a position on mediocrity as opposed to excellence?

- Do I have a position on exploitation and injustice?

- What am I prepared to collude with in order to save my own skin and earn the dubious 'acceptance' of the majority?

- Do I have a position on equity and the intrinsic worth of all human beings?

- What is it that motivates me to want to be a leader and a manager?

- What expectations do I believe others have of me, including family and friends? How do I maintain my own equilibrium and stay focused despite those often conflicting expectations?

- Despite the manner in which the majority group in the society might be predisposed to dealing with issues concerning black children from all their varied backgrounds, do I as a black person not have a responsibility to respect the traditions within Faith communities, especially from African and Asian backgrounds, which might account for the conduct and dispositions of certain African and Asian students?

- Do I as a black manager react in exactly the same way, or perhaps in an even more hostile manner than the majority community, in relation to certain practices and the expression of certain beliefs that are born of traditional African religion (as practised on the continent or as adapted in the Caribbean diaspora), or do such children and their parents have a legitimate expectation that as a black manager they could look to me for a greater degree of understanding, if not knowledge?

Inasmuch as I cannot separate my position as a manager in a school from the experience of black people in the society and the schooling system, irrespective of whether or not my school is all white, my approach to leadership must be one which reflects how I as a black person live my values and connect with my blackness.

In my role as a former Director of Education and Leisure Services in a multiethnic, multifaith, multiclass borough, I was sustained by my own core values and principles. Not surprisingly, they now form part of the Equal Opportunities Policy of the management consultancy of which I am the chief executive. They are as follows:

- I believe that everyone has a right to live with respect and dignity, and to study and work in an environment in which that right is upheld
- I believe that in any society, respect for oneself and for others grows by giving it practical expression in all aspects of daily living
- I am committed to confronting oppression on the grounds of race, gender, class, disability, sexual orientation, age, faith, and the exploitation of the weak and defenceless as a matter of duty and civic responsibility
- I affirm the Human Rights of all people and am committed to upholding those rights in all aspects of my dealings with the public
- I take the view that Human Rights and equality legislation provides minimum safeguards for the individual and especially for members of target groups. It does not by itself create a climate in which people are valued and their rights respected
- I believe that combating inequality and discrimination is part of the practice of building a Human Rights culture where Human Rights does not immediately conjure up prospects of litigation, but a culture that signals respect for

the dignity and worth of each person

- I encourage each person to see her or himself as enjoying the democratic space won through the struggles of those who went before us, and as having a democratic responsibility to safeguard hard-won rights, to protect the environment, and to act as an agent of change

- I take it as given that Britain is a multiethnic, multifaith society and that each organization, public, private or voluntary, should reflect that reality in its ethos, human resource policies and arrangements, service delivery and general working practices

- I am committed to eradicating unfair and discriminatory practices where these occur within my own sphere of operation or influence, and ensuring that I am not made to collude, unwittingly or otherwise, with such practices in any organization that secures my services

Where did these values and principles come from? What was I bringing as a black chief education officer to the thankless task of working to improve the quality of education outcomes for children and adults in Hackney?

Above all, I was bringing my spirituality. Nothing, but nothing, gave me the capacity to manage the challenges of working in that environment with people who were intent on making you as deranged and dysfunctional as some of them were, as my spirituality did.

As an African person, faithful to our traditions, I walked with the Orisa and with my Ascended Ancestors of Light. I humbled myself in the constant presence of the Creator and asked Him to give me strength, forbearance and wisdom. But I was also sustained by the struggles of my own parents and many others like them, including those with whom I joined in the struggle in the many decades before I landed in Hackney.

I was born in Concord in the parish of St John's, Grenada. I grew up with most of the adults around me, including my own parents, being functionally illiterate or semi-literate but with an array of life skills and capacities, technical knowledge, a system of values and beliefs, and a wealth of common sense that was far superior to any book knowledge and book sense. Theirs was a set of values that made you fit for living, struggling, resisting and surviving. The way they derived meaning from their experience of hardship, their experience of overcoming odds and transcending adverse circumstances, and of resolving conflict was just awesome.

I learnt through their proverbs and ancient philosophical sayings. I learnt above all that circumstances of birth and of economy and class had conspired to prevent them being numbered among the most intellectual and successful entrepreneurs and professionals in Grenada, the Caribbean region and the world. I breathed their passion for education and their belief in its capacity to empower my generation and future generations to better ourselves, to become effective agents of change and not be limited in our choices by the circumstances that constrained them. I learnt that poverty was not an excuse for poor standards and amoral conduct, but rather that we who were poor had more cause to build our self esteem, to walk in our integrity and to let no one consider us less than we are and have the capacity to be.

My primary schooling taught me that our teachers shared the same aspirations for us as our parents did. They had high expectations of us and demanded that we had the same high expectations of ourselves. The concept of special educational needs was virtually unknown at the time and consequently some teachers and pupils were insensitive, to the point of cruelty sometimes, to the needs of children with learning difficulties. You were either bright or a dunce. There was no room for dyslexia, aphasia or any other learning disability.

Despite that, even those with moderate or severe learning disabilities demonstrated their strengths. They could do great things with their hands and with their creative imagination, they learnt by helping adults do and in turn they themselves taught.

It was all part and parcel of the web and weave of surviving and helping your folks eke out an existence. But the system stratified, and those who were judged to be bright received greater endorsement and support from teachers and parents alike than those who were considered a dunce or not so bright.

Those who attended secondary school expected to work hard and gain decent qualifications. Each school could boast high achievers in their roll of honour. All around us were former students who had progressed and were effectively running the country and its institutions. Standing in front of us in classrooms were students of yesteryear who had sat in the same seats as us, had gained degrees in their subjects and had come back to teach, some more brilliant at teaching than others. Positive and inspiring individuals to emulate were everywhere to be seen and many of them were never bashful at reminding us that their origins were equally as humble and poverty stricken as ours.

All of that helped to shape my attitude to myself as an African male, my attitude to learning, my zest to motivate others to learn and unlock their own potential. It informed the nature and quality of my parenting and the attitude to schooling and education I encouraged in my own children and still encourage in all children. It gave me a distaste of mediocrity. The mantra which resounded around my home, in the yard and in the fields with my father, a peasant farmer, still wells up in my consciousness now:

If a thing is worth doing at all, it is worth doing well.

That applied as much to digging a hole to plant a banana tree as it did to writing an essay for homework. That mantra was handed down from generation to generation.

We come with our different foundations and formative experiences. Yours would be different from mine, although I suspect that what I am sharing would resonate with your folks if not with you directly. Wherever it comes from, whatever it derives from, however, my plea to you is to affirm your values and live them. Let there be no discontinuity between your personal philosophy for living and the principles you take to your professional practice. Therefore, make sure that your personal philosophy for living is a wholesome, progressive and liberating one.

I run a Masterclass on Leadership and Management,

sometimes as part of a double act with Rosemary Campbell, and it always causes a sudden rise in the temperature in the room when I project on to the screen my firm belief that:

'Effective managers come from being effective people' ... Not from reading an endless supply of manuals for effective management.

Needless to say the most challenging part of the whole day is what follows that, when participants work individually and then in groups to consider what constitutes an effective person.

Recently I came across a chapter in a book called *Innovative Education and Training for Care Professionals* (eds. Rachel Pierce and Jenny Weinstein). In his chapter on 'Selection and Retention of Social Work Students', Jeremy Weinstein (p. 137) observes that:

At the beginning of the century, social workers recruiting students were told "The best workers must be the best human beings, those whose conduct of their own lives is most nearly what we wish the conduct of all lives to be"', a quotation from H J Gow 1900. Weinstein goes on: 'Fifty years on, it was argued that a student selected to train should have the strongest "identification with the ideals and objectives of his profession as well as with the group he serves. He must have an unwavering conviction as to the worth of the ends of his work" ... More recent authors whose texts critique contemporary social work, remind us of just how lacking we now are in this sense of professional self-confidence. We retain few concepts of what the "best human being" might look like, or the "worth of social work", let alone how one might dovetail into the other.

The exacting standards that society clearly expected social workers to meet at the beginning of the last century have been relaxed somewhat. What is clearly established though, is the link between the personal and the professional, the individual and the institutional. I would suggest that the link is effectively how one articulates and affirms one's values and principles, and applies them in one's professional life and institutional roles.

It follows that knowing who you are, where you've come

from, how you come to be here at all and what you stand for becomes paramount. If none of that encompasses the fact that you are black and that that is at the very essence of your being, then you have a right to declare anonymity and make it clear that although you are imprisoned 'in the castle of (your) skin', you do not wish to be numbered amongst those black managers, purportedly representative of the communities they are serving, more of whom the system would like to see occupy senior positions.

As a leader and manager, one needs to have an understanding of the culture of institutions and what sustains that culture, a capacity to focus upon, and be sensitive to, the situation of 'the person' in institutional life, and to examine the relationship between the personal and the professional. Professionals shape institutional cultures and are, in turn, shaped and protected by them.

Some people choose certain professions because of their perception of the culture of the institution and the extent to which it provides them with the opportunity and the protection to induldge their prejudices and unacceptable conduct. (cf. police trainees in the 'Secret Policeman' BBC documentary – October 2003).

In a Radio 4 bulletin in May 2000, Mr David Hart, leader of one of the biggest teaching unions in the country, the National Association of Headteachers (NAHT), stated adamantly:

I categorically reject the idea that there is institutional racism in schools.

His vigorous disclaimer was being made in the context of OfSTED (the Office of Standards in Education) and ethnic monitoring.

Mr Hart gave no evidence to the contrary, no evidence to disprove the experiences of generations of black students, parents and teachers, including some of his very own black members. Their experience was being reconstructed and redefined simply by his say-so. The likes of me were expected to agree, the nation was being invited to agree, just because it was the authoritative Mr Hart, a white union leader, dismissing the very notion of institutional racism as it applies to schools.

That tendency to reconstruct target groups' experience of institutional and personal forms of discrimination and of structural barriers is perhaps one of the biggest challenges facing organizations with a huge majority of white managers and with black staff who cluster, in the main, at levels in the organization where they exercise neither influence nor power. In such situations they are often coerced into acquiescing in their own exploitation, their own stress-inducing denial of their reality, as the organization insists that it is other than the way members of target groups experience it.

We as black people have historically performed the function of interpreting this society to itself through the way we experience it, good, bad, and sometimes murderously ugly. Regrettably, however, the evidence has been building up over the years of the society refusing to see itself through the prism of our experience.

Despite the disturbing statistics of over-representation on all sorts of negative indicators (school underachievement, school exclusions, numbers in prison and youth custody, suicides, deaths in custody, etc), and underrepresentation on others (numbers in senior management, numbers in particular professions, numbers in elite Universities, etc), there is still a reluctance on the part of most employers to put appropriate mechanisms in place for consulting with black and ethnic minority stakeholders about the way they experience the organization and the corrective action that should result from that.

The challenge facing black managers in education, especially headteachers in inner city schools, is how to engage black students and parents, not just in dialogue but in partnership and joint working, in order to tackle some of these issues. White managers do what they have to do without any concern as to whether they might be seen to be favouring a particular group. We somehow seem to lack the professional confidence, principally because of the absence of societal and often peer validation, to do just that in relation to the situation confronting black students and parents. We look over our shoulders, we erect our own barriers and mental hurdles, we are reluctant to face down our critics.

My belief is that with or without the requirements of the Race Relations Amendment Act, the school continues be a legitimate site of struggle for black students and black employees, as are other organizations, until such time that institutional discrimination is eliminated, barriers are dismantled, imbalances are corrected, organizations stop seeing it as their duty to close ranks and provide cover for the racists and bullies in their midst, and black students and staff have their concerns addressed appropriately.

I am not implying that black staff and white staff, black staff and their predominantly white managers, should situate themselves on different sides of the imaginary barricades. Indeed, increasingly we need to form alliances with progressive white colleagues who refuse to validate what the system is doing to black children. I am arguing rather, that black managers have a choice:

- to help make racism look respectable and accommodate it in its institutional forms, thereby identifying themselves as part of the problem, or
- to acknowledge that new ways of working with black staff and black communities have got to be found, and that they need to demonstrate that they are centrally a part of the solution

Conclusion

It is part of our history in this society that systems, structures, policies and processes are systematically allowed to impact with dire consequences upon sections of the black population. Those responsible for operating these systems and policies tended, until comparatively recently, to ignore the efforts we ourselves were making within our communities to fix things and to grow awareness within mainstream institutions of alternative strategies we had found workable. Meanwhile, the 'quick fix' most organizations sought after was increasing the number of black staff and managers.

Inevitably, black staff exercising their right to pursue career opportunities and become managers must expect to manage the crisis, as so many others in the schooling system must do. Expectations placed upon them by black communities, however, are far greater, irrespective of whether or not those same Heads are having difficulty taking the staff body with them.

In addition to whatever efforts would-be black managers are making to hone their technical management skills, I believe that they must create opportunities to spend time debating the issues raised in this paper and to build quality circles as a medium for sharing good practice, professional skills and building greater awareness of the thorny issues of identity, culture and pedagogy.

In the year 2000, Vaclav Havel declared that:

Courage means going against majority opinion in the name of truth. I implore you to have the courage to challenge the consensus that keeps people in their comfort zones. Have the courage to challenge one another, especially when there is evidence of collusion with racism and institutional discrimination. Learn from one another and share your dazzling array of talents, skills and competences to the enrichment and professional development of one another.

Anais Nin observed that:

Life shrinks or expands in proportion to one's courage.

Let me say, finally, that the time has come to resurrect the defunct Caribbean Teachers Association. Time has moved rapidly on since its demise and so have the issues facing black staff and students in the schooling system.

Take it upon yourselves, therefore, to build a National Movement of Black Teachers and empower yourselves to deal with the crisis facing black teachers, students, and parents, not least by becoming a national force for the Government and the schooling system to reckon with. Begin, at least, with the former cohorts of staff who have been part of this programme. You already have the basis of such an organization and I am totally convinced that, given what I know to be black teachers' needs out there, your numbers will grow rapidly.

You do not need Ken Livingstone, Lee Jasper or the Secretary of State for Education to set an agenda for you. The agenda is becoming longer and more urgent year after year. What is necessary is to decide what you would prioritize and the principles and method of organization you would adopt to take forward that agenda. And as you go forward as a truly *Independent* Organization, make sure that you do not become anyone's political pawn or the vehicle by which they advance their political ambitions, irrespective of the amount of money they want to throw at you.

Above all, let no one, not even your own over cautious 'self', render you less than you are or less than you know you have the capacity to be, individually or collectively.

I wish you strength, energy, courage and success in all your endeavours.

4.2

INSTITUTE OF EDUCATION
HEADSHIP DEVELOPMENT PROGRAMME:
Developing black managers
July 2005

Notes for Round Table Discussion

Our discussion will focus around some key themes, as follows:

- The critical importance of quality leadership in securing equality of opportunity and equality of outcomes in education for *all* students.
- The values and principles that make for that quality of leadership.
- The institutional and professional barriers and hindrances to be overcome.
- The leadership imperative for black and ethnic minority headteachers as far as tackling the historical and systemic pattern of underachievement of particular ethnic groups (including poor working class whites) is concerned.
- The importance of being clear about what of yourself and your grounding (or not) in the struggle for *an educational entitlement for all* you would be bringing to the headship function.
- The potential barriers and challenges you would face, and the opportunities you might create for pursuing the equality and diversity agenda, guided/inspired by a commitment to social justice and by unfailing hope.

These provide a framework for examining your and your managers' current practice and the way you would use the *additionality of your blackness* and your experience of being a member of a target group to inform your approach to headship.

The Leadership Challenge

- The Vision: Education, Equality, Excellence
- Confidence to stand in your own skin and not be hindered in your purpose by the expectations different constituencies have of 'a black headteacher'
- Clarity and personal conviction about the *entitlement* all students have and the responsibility of the school to deliver it
- Clarity about the background to inner city schooling and the expectations the school community and the wider community would have of you as a black headteacher
- Capacity to unite the whole school (teachers, students, parents, external partners) behind your vision and your project
- Capacity to ensure accountability from those you lead and manage for discharging individual and collective responsibility for maintaining high standards at all times
- Capacity to put in place a learning infrastructure that supports the Vision
- Confidence to cultivate and use mechanisms for your own support

Aim for Excellence and Be the Best

The Leadership/Management Imperative

a. Knowledge and Understanding of Operational Context

- Understanding the structural bases and origins of the challenges in urban education as situated in the dynamics of class, gender, ethnicity, race, and religion
- Understanding the racialization of educational disadvantage, underachievement and school exclusions
- Understanding the link between children's self development, underpinned by the acquisition and application of sound values and self management skills, and their academic development
- Understanding diversity in urban education as characterized by class and socio-economic background (first and foremost), by race and ethnicity, by language, and by religion/faith

- Situating Government initiatives and expectations against the background of the above

b. Realizing the Vision

- Forging an effective partnership of *trust* with students, parents and teachers and with external partners (communities, business partners, other childrens' and young peoples' services)
- Ensuring that transparency, respect, fairness and consistency are the hallmark of that relationship
- Establishing a 'contract' with students, parents, and teachers to reflect that relationship and to jointly pursue the shared vision
- Ensuring that the entire school community knows that teacher expectations, and students' high expectations of themselves (by way of performance and purposeful self management), and of their teachers, are among your top priorities for action
- Establishing very clearly for everyone concerned the way you link those priorities with your priority to personally keep under review the quality of teaching, of learning and of educational outcomes
- Ensuring that middle managers take ownership of those priorities and pursue them in discharging their own responsibilities in a manner that is measurable
- Encouraging a culture in which all staff put their practice up for scrutiny within a process that is developmental, supportive and rigorous
- Ensuring that 'talk' is a central plank of that contract ('Talking oneself into understanding' – Bullock, 1974) and that opportunities are built in for students (especially) to share and be listened to as a matter of routine, and especially in situations of conflict
- Providing students with the opportunity to comment in a formal and ordered manner on the quality of teaching and of their learning
- Dealing routinely with contestations about issues of quality, accountability, equality, fairness, the pace of change, and the

extent to which staff are embracing change
- Making sure that teachers and all adults in the school model, by their own behaviour and by giving expression to their own sound values, the behaviours and attitudes they expect students (and their parents) to exhibit. This means encouraging a culture of respect, an abhorrence of bullying behaviour, and a commitment to minimizing conflict

c. Curriculum, Teaching, Learning and Assessment
- Paying due regard to the requirements of the Race Relations (Amendment) Act 2000 and their implications for the key race-equality-relevant functions of curriculum planning/ development, teaching, learning and assessment
- Ensuring that curriculum planning and delivery has regard to the multiethnic, multiclass, multilingual, multifaith profile of the school and of the society
- Putting in place, and keeping under constant review, key measures for raising standards of achievement:
- It is well known that unsatisfactory standards are generally related to staffing turbulence, poor classroom management, a poor match of tasks to the range of ability in the class, low teacher expectations and a limited range of teaching and learning styles, all correlated with poor student motivation
- Therefore, undertake a rigorous analysis of 'setting and streaming' practices and of test and examination performance by ethnicity and gender across subjects, and adopt strategies aimed at raising the achievement of all groups of students, including those who are the most able
- Address the issue of unsatisfactory teaching with a focus on classroom practice as a key aspect of monitoring and evaluation
- Encourage developmental activities among both teachers and students to improve the range of teaching and learning styles, with special emphasis on increasing challenge and high expectation in teaching, and on the part of students, and encouraging effective learning
- Adopt rigorous practices for eliminating stereotyping and discrimination in setting and streaming, and for the

evaluation of entry levels and results in GCSE examinations

- Ensure there is a strong and consistent focus on children's special educational needs, and a capacity for early identification, intervention, and for providing support as necessary
- Ensure that there is in place a language policy across the curriculum that is fit for purpose and that can assist students in gaining confidence in their oral and writing skills, and in their ability to contribute confidently to discussion and debate
- Review curriculum structure in the context of the length of the school day, the requirements of the National Curriculum, and the school's curriculum initiatives that relate to its particular student profile
- Pay particular attention to the organization and content of the library, and to the use of computer-assisted learning, in relation to the school's use of the curriculum in pursuing its equality objectives and in supporting learning
- Put in place and sustain procedures and daily routines that support positive attitudes to attendance and punctuality amongst students, and which win parental support in applying those
- Develop the role of middle managers with particular emphasis on planning, monitoring, and evaluation within their areas of responsibility, and ensure that they are supported in that role

Keeping Faith with Communities

It is essential that the community of students, parents, teachers, and external partners are made aware of your vision, how you intend to deliver it and what their role is in working in partnership with you to deliver it. It is also essential that they know how to hold you to account and that they do not see your governing body as acting as a bulwark against them in protection of you and the school.

A school and its effective performance is a team effort and requires all partners to take collective responsibility for ensuring the highest standards are maintained. The leadership challenge is how to forge relationships such that that responsibility is actively embraced and people spend their time working with you towards a common goal, rather than putting obstacles in your way and draining your energy as you struggle to overcome them.

Stay focused, cultivate your inner strength and keep it topped up. You will need every ounce of it.

DEVELOPING BLACK MANAGERS
A forum for building on strengths and eliminating weaknesses
7 October 1993

In October 1993, I was invited by the Director of Education in Bradford to deliver a keynote address to an audience of 100-plus Asian and African-Caribbean Teachers who were meeting to consider among other things, the formation of an Asian and African-Caribbean Teachers Association.

The paper that follows is the full text of my address to that meeting.

In the 90-minute discussion following my address, it became evident that each and every black teacher and education officer in that meeting could identify with some aspect of the central thesis in the paper, and they actually gave chapter and verse of their experience, past and current.

By far the most important messages emerging from the meeting were the following:

a. that Local Management of Schools had made it more necessary than before for black teachers to share their experiences and to develop a collective voice. Therefore, a forum for effective networking was considered to be especially necessary.

b. that governors' practices, both in respect of serving teachers and those seeking employment, were giving increasing cause for concern, and that the LEA needed to play a crucial role in ensuring that equal opportunities for black teachers in gaining employment and for promotion were not being denied for whatever reasons.

c. that a significant number of Section 11 teachers in Bradford
     were black, and strategies needed to be devised for ensuring
     that they were kept within the service as Section 11 funding
     was cut by central government.

Those who attended the meeting have since established the
Bradford Asian and African-Caribbean Teachers
Association.

On returning to Hackney, I shared my experience of working
with those colleagues in Bradford with a number of black
teachers in Hackney, and it was their wish that I make the text
of my address available for discussion in Hackney.

ASIAN AND AFRICAN-CARIBBEAN TEACHERS IN BRADFORD EDUCATION BUILDING ON STRENGTHS, ELIMINATING WEAKNESSES – A DEVELOPMENTAL PERSPECTIVE

Introduction

It gives me enormous pleasure to be back in Bradford again, and
especially to be engaging in discussion with you about the
importance of networking and working in solidarity with one
another.

I am no stranger to this city, having lectured in Social Policy
and Applied Social Studies in the university here during the late
1970s, and contributed over the years to teacher education
programmes at the former Margaret McMillan College. I was a
member of the George Lindo Campaign here between 1978 and
1980, and have been involved as a co-organizer of and
contributor to the annual (now biennial) International Bookfair
of Radical Black and 3rd World Books.

I bring to this discussion my experience as a teacher-trainer,
an external examiner, a teacher counselor, and, as a director of
education, someone who spends a good deal of time visiting
classrooms and encouraging teachers to concentrate upon the
quality of teaching, the quality of learning, and the quality of
educational outcomes, all of which are critical determinants of
the extent to which schools are delivering to students their
educational entitlement.

In January 1990, during the nationwide primary teacher crisis,

I went with a black (Barbadian) Senior Primary Inspector and recruited some 45 teachers in Trinidad to teach in Hackney schools. Those teachers had an average of no less than 18 years teaching experience, and some had taught for upwards of 25 years. The experience of placing and supporting them in Hackney schools is a very lengthy and very instructive story in itself, and I will be drawing upon some of that experience in sharing insights with you at this session.

The Process

The purpose of today's meeting could be encompassed by six key questions:

i.   Who are you?

ii.   Why have you come?

iii.   What do you want from this session?

iv.   What are you bringing to it?

v.   What do you want to happen after today?

vi.   What are you personally committing yourself to do in order to make it happen?

Let me hazard a couple of answers. You have come: because you are an Asian or African-Caribbean teacher who is keen to see an association established and a series of networking arrangements put in place to provide you and others like you with support, and to enable the collectivity of black teachers in Bradford to find strength in unity, and to exercise power on the basis of numerical strength.

You are bringing: yourself as you are, with your personal life history, ethnic, cultural and social class background, your experience as a classroom teacher and a member of a school community, experience as a learner, experience as a black person in the role of a teacher, manager, parent, partner, member of a professional association, member of a union, member of a community organization, member of various societies.

As a parent, you may well have concerns about your children's schooling and the quality of their educational attainment. As a teacher, you may have similar concerns about the educational achievement of the students in your and other

Bradford schools. As a black teacher, black parents in your school or in the wider community may well have certain expectations of you as far as correcting historical injustices and imbalances are concerned. Others may feel that they have a right to expect you to stand up for traditional values and take up a position in respect of what they deem to be the widespread occurrence of rampant secularism in the Bradford education system.

As a teacher or, what is more, in some cases, teacher-manager, students or other colleagues may expect you to perform at a mediocre level, or to tolerate poor standards and a lack of professional accountability, often in the name of black solidarity.

An important part of the process, therefore, is defining clearly what it is you want to achieve and, consequently, what is the best formation to enable you to achieve it.

Options

a. One limited but achievable goal is to aim for a loose structure, a federated structure of individual cellular networks where people are self selecting, each network develops its own dynamic and 'modus operandi', coming together as a collectivity once or twice per year. This is the 'minimum risk' option. Alliances are formed and alliances are broken, individuals retain their autonomy and move on when they feel the network has outlived its usefulness in respect of their needs.

b. A series of open meetings timed for a specific day of the month when teachers meet and share experiences, compare notes, give support to one another, and move on again until the next time. A refinement of that model is for a number of teachers to seek, through the Professional Development Centre or otherwise, to arrange for a speaker to lead a discussion at each of those meetings, and follow up the discussion with refreshments and general socializing.

c. The model which I suspect commends itself most and which is nevertheless the most difficult to sustain is that of a formally constituted 'Association'.

Options a. and b. are pretty much self-explanatory, and there is any number of variations on those themes. Option c., however, is the one which has been tried and tested in other parts of the country for many a year, and in too many cases failed to withstand the test of time.

Whatever model you choose, it is instructive to examine some of the pitfalls those who went before you failed to avoid.

Some Basic Assumptions and Some False Premises
'Blackness' as a unifying concept.

I would suggest that the most difficult task facing the group at the outset is to answer the question 'who are you?' collectively, in order to arrive at some shared understanding and forge a common identity.

Identifying the factors that unite the group, one can highlight:

a.   being a teacher
b.   being black (Asian, African/African-Caribbean)
c.   working in the same LEA
d.   susceptibility to racist treatment and to racial attack
e.   willingness to explore the possibility of working together as a collective

I would suggest that beyond that, the group is unable to go forward until a series of conversations have taken place and there are some negotiated understandings.

Taking each of the unifying factors in turn, one has to assume that:

a. Being a teacher is a 'catch-all'
Among you there will be confident, experienced teachers; less foot-sure and more inexperienced teachers; teachers who are curriculum leaders in their chosen specializations; others who are good at classroom management and those who are poor; teachers who find staffroom cultures oppressive and who endure staffroom interactions with a degree of suffering and stress; others who can and do cut through the pretense and hypocrisy and confront people's rudeness and racism; teachers who have a healthy track record of collaboration with students and their parents, and those who don't.

None of this makes any one person who elects to come and be part of the group as a result of an open invitation any less or more worthy than the other person. It could determine to a large extent, however, those who emerge as the people taking part or being nominated for leadership roles in the association, and those who demonstrate certain diffidence in terms of active and sustained involvement.

b. Being Black (Asian, African/African-Caribbean)

Being black is similarly not, in itself, a guarantee of anything. It is certainly not an index of political awareness, ideological progressiveness, willingness to empathize with and struggle against class and racial oppression of other blacks, willingness to be identified with black struggle or even fight back against one's own oppressors. Neither is it a guarantee against sexism, backwardness, reactionism, conservatism, and the propensity to heap oppression upon other blacks, especially women.

Above all, it is not a guarantee against individualism, greed and self-interest, nor, conversely, is it a guarantee of support and solidarity.

There is always a tendency in some circles, both black and white, to express amazement at the acts of oppression perpetuated by black individuals or black nation states against other blacks, e.g., communal violence in India, political repression in Kenya or Jamaica, so-called 'black on black' crime in Chicago, Moss Side, or Cross Roads.

This is based on the utterly false premise that members of an oppressed group cannot, should not, or would not themselves take on the mantle of the oppressor. By that logic, black people in or out of the South African armed forces should not want to collaborate with the apartheid regime. Blacks in Britain should not want to join the police force and immigration service. You and I should not have to suffer the indignity of being stopped in the Customs Hall at Heathrow Airport nine out of ten times by a black customs officer, no doubt trying desperately to demonstrate to his white counterparts that he is not going soft on the blacks, but rather going decidedly soft in the head. Women of any ethnic grouping should not have to suffer tears, pain and hardship, while their male partners hook up with other women sometimes without looking back at their fatherless children.

Clearly, from the beginning of history, oppression has been an ever-present part of the human condition. The fact that oppression became racialized at particular stages in history does not mean that racially oppressed groups have themselves lost the predisposition to oppress.

c. Working in the same LEA

Time was when that would have been a simple and straightforward concept. There were county schools, voluntary aided schools, and independent fee paying schools with or without assisted places. To these have been added grant maintained schools, city technology colleges and locally managed schools. The regulatory powers of LEAs have been steadily eroded, and teachers are now increasingly at the mercy of governing bodies, headteachers and principals acting as virtual company directors or chief executives, with very little standing between them, the teachers, and the due process of law.

d. Susceptibility to racist treatment and racial attack

This is perhaps the single most unifying factor. Existing as we do within a culture of racism where an East Indian teacher just arrived from Trinidad who has never set foot on the Indian subcontinent is viciously attacked and called a 'stinking paki'; where every Sri Lankan, Malaysian, Goan and Guyanese Indian is 'a stinking paki'; where every Ghanaian or Nigerian is a suspected illegal immigrant, and where every African-Caribbean is potentially a 'yardie' on crack cocaine; the one thing that unites us, irrespective of the image we have of ourselves or of how much we want to identify with one another, is the certainty that if we found ourselves in the wrong place at the wrong time, we are likely to become the victim of a racial attack or some form of racial abuse.

As teachers, we are frequently called upon to deal with the victims of such attacks and to devise strategies for supporting them as well as for combating the violence being perpetrated against them.

With the resurgence of fascism in the society, and with an estimated 150,000 such attacks being perpetrated against black people every year, this single issue has to be high on the agenda of every group of black people coming together, especially teachers.

e. Willingness to explore the possibility of coming together as a collective

That 'willingness' is assumed or inferred.

Curiosity takes people to pretty strange places, even on wet and damp October evenings in Bradford. For many of you, I suspect that the willingness to stick a toe in the water is tempered by questions such as:

- Does this really have a chance of leading to anything?
- What's all this business of an Asian and African-Caribbean Teachers Association? Who are they trying to kid? Those Asians are in the majority anyway and we would simply be dancing to their tune.
- Why should it take the LEA to bring us together? Whose initiative is this anyway? Why couldn't we do it ourselves?
- What is the hidden agenda? How independent of Bradford Education can this group really be? Would the LEA's support run out when, from our combined strength, we start to turn the heat on them?

These are all good, healthy questions that I would expect any conscious and self-respecting group of black people to raise, and a mature organization like Bradford Education to be prepared to enter into dialogue around. I suspect, however, that for the majority of you, there would be a range of other concerns, as follows:

Given what is taking place in education just now, and the way black, antiracist, multicultural, multifaith issues in schooling and education are steadily eclipsed; given also the fact that governing bodies are doing their own staff recruitment and selection, appraisal is on the agenda, performance related pay is on the agenda, and black multilingual children in Bradford are being blamed for depressing the LEA's scores in the government's league tables, we have to reclaim and use our voice as black teachers and parents in Bradford.

The 'Association' Model

Why have an Association?

The above reasons are as good as any for deciding to form an 'Association'. And if you were to have a series of conversations about the issues raised in my testing of the commonsensical assumptions one might make as to what unites you, a number of experiences would be shared, positions adopted, and insights gained which would render the exercise in itself immensely valuable.

Opportunities

Additionally, I would suggest that a properly constituted, democratically organized and, above all, democratically run Association could provide timely opportunities for:

- self and professional development
- creating a powerful learning environment to support one another
- a constant dialogue on education standards
- examining ways of interrogating the quality of teaching, the quality of learning and the barriers to high quality educational outcomes for black and working class students
- influencing LEA and school policies
- networking, especially on the issues of the content and delivery of the National Curriculum, and the school's own curriculum
- co-counseling and joint evaluation
- building a powerful coalition between black teachers, black students and black parents
- intervening in national education debates, especially as Bradford is often seen and used so much as a laboratory
- relaxation and recreation
- creating a forum for testing out new ideas
- mutual and inter-group solidarity.

Requirements

To ensure the growth of a successful Association, one that meets and surpasses the aspirations of its members, and to avoid the fate that has befallen many others along the way, close attention

must be paid to the following:
- Principles and Method of Organization
- Democratic Structure
- Democratic Process
- Democratic Accountability
- Financial Probity
- Discipline
- Reliability
- Dependability
- Credibility as an organization
- Promotion of high standards in teaching no less than in the affairs of the organization
- Preparedness of individual members to take risks, to fail, and to be helped
- Confidentiality
- The need to progressively create a safe and supportive environment where people could feel able to share and not be exposed and violated in the process
- Collective responsibility for the usefulness and success of the Association
- Willingness on the part of each member to commit time to building the Association and making it work for them and for others
- The need to register and discuss criticisms and issues in open, free and democratic debate, and to rectify wrongs
- Collective agreement at the outset about membership and associate membership in the 'principles and method' document. Would educational psychologists and educational social workers be entitled to join, for example?

Barriers

If the above requirements are to be met and opportunities grasped, the following barriers would need to be removed:
- Self denigration and self doubt
- 'It won't last because black people never agree on anything'
- The 'somebody else's responsibility' syndrome
- 'I think it's a brilliant idea but I really don't have the time to devote to it'

- Unwillingness to take risks and reveal imperfections:
- 'I can't trust these people and I certainly won't want to share my anxieties and my faults with them'
- The potential for oligarchies to form and manipulate the democratic process
- Male attitudes to women holding office, or women demanding that men talk less so that their voices could be heard.

Rationale for Adopting the 'Association' Model

I would suspect that most black teachers in Bradford are in one or other of the teaching trade unions. I suspect it is also accurate to assume that those unions do not necessarily represent the interests of their black members always, nor do they necessarily safeguard their rights, rights which are often not violated in ways which contravene standard employment practices or collective agreements, but are trodden upon as part of the daily, niggling and insidious manifestations of racism in the society.

An Association of Black Teachers (Asian and African/ Caribbean) can act as a forum for addressing many of the professional concerns of teachers in terms of their employment, as well as providing support for teachers who, as parents, have concerns about their children's education.

A formally organized body, with the authority to represent members' interests and influence decision-making in respect of the education of black students is clearly desirable, if not absolutely necessary in a city with a population such as Bradford has.

The Black Person's (Professional) Burden

My experience as an education manager in a position to assess the capabilities and the performance of white managers and of white front line staff, and to see how black staff perform at all levels and are treated within majority white situations, confirms to me that we live in a society which validates white people automatically, and which is forever requiring black people to prove themselves.

Excellence in performance and integrity in the conduct of

professional and social affairs on the part of whites are seen as confirmation or fulfillment of society's normal expectations. In the case of blacks they are seen as a cause for celebration and amazement. Conversely, mediocrity, incompetence, bungling, a lack of commitment or sheer laziness on the part of whites are seen as part of the flotsam and jetsam of daily life, irritating perhaps but not extraordinary or characteristic.

In the case of blacks, they are seen as characteristic, as conforming to expectations, and as virtually inevitable if not ingrained.

The form of validation on the one hand and pathologizing on the other runs deep in the psyche and cultural consciousness of the nation, and invariably determines the quality of the experience we as black people have in our day to day work and our day to day living.

Some of us are considerably better at challenging those forms of racism and confounding white people's expectations than others. All of us have got to find ways of sharing experiences and discussing strategies for coping in such situations.

Schools are artificially constructed environments for staff no less than for students. They could be happy places in which to work, learn and teach, and they can also be hellishly alienating and miserable places. Either condition is very often clearly reflected in the culture and ethos of the school, and especially in the culture of the staffroom.

Black staff in particular suffer the alienation of those environments daily and usually with few, if any, support networks. The networking that an association can facilitate could go a long way to easing the pressure that many black teachers face, and providing the context within which strategies for confronting such situations could be shared.

Very little is written about the school as a learning environment from the teacher's viewpoint, and even less about the staffroom cultures and the experiences of black staff within them. When the Macdonald Inquiry Panel investigated the circumstances surrounding the racist murder of 13 year-old Ahmed Ullah in Burnage High School in South Manchester in 1986, black teachers at the school had some chilling stories to tell. The Burnage Report is well worth reading if only to gain some insight into the experiences of black teachers at the school, the different perceptions and expectations black students had of them as compared to white teachers, and the relationship between those black teachers and the parents of their black students.

There is an urgent need for black teachers and black managers in schools to reflect upon, discuss, and write considerably more about those experiences, both in order to interpret those institutions to themselves by holding a mirror up to them, and to provide insights and support to other black teachers in similar situations.

The power of the case-study, of the ethnographic account, of the success story, cannot be underestimated, nor is there anything to be lost by coming clean about those situations in which black teachers who needed to be told to get their act together are allowed to go on repeating the same mistakes, and compromising children's life chances, simply because white managers couldn't care less, or are petrified about being accused of racism.

Apart from the fact that we should seek to be professionally accountable to one another, we owe it to those joining us in the profession, and indeed to black parents and to the students whom we teach, to reflect upon our practice and seek to remove those institutional barriers.

At a time when school based teacher training is high on the agenda, without schools being required to provide a shred of evidence of their track record in dealing with these issues, it is important that the black teachers collectively claim that agenda and engage school managers and other staff in addressing them. This, I suggest, is our historical responsibility towards new (and often younger) black recruits joining the service. If we do not construe it as such, then we are effectively proclaiming that our blackness is purely coincidental, that it does not matter if we remain atomized, that the fittest amongst us will always survive, and that it is of no consequence if some of us go to the wall.

This brings me to my next, very crucial point. A fundamental difference between black teachers and white teachers is that for black teachers, the school with all its structural arrangements becomes a site of struggle against racism in much the same way that the community outside the school is. The experience of racism within the society generally is replicated within schools in a wide variety of ways, in approaches to the curriculum and its content, in attitudes of students, staff, and parents, in the negative expectations people have of black staff on the one hand, and on the other, institutional confidence in their ability to deal with the 'difficult' black students and 'awkward' black parents.

While not many black teachers would disagree with those assertions, it is nevertheless the case that too few of us identify fully with the struggles facing our communities, or consider our own struggle in our work places as being on a continuum with theirs.

Wearing another hat, as a founder member of the Black Parents Movement and its Chairperson in Manchester for a number of years, I would like to restate the position we propounded in 1975 when we argued that we saw: *Independent Parents Power and Independent Students Power as the key to change in education and schooling.*

I continue to affirm the right of parents to organize as parents independently of teachers. I similarly affirm students' right to organize as students independently of parents and teachers. And it goes without saying that I believe, absolutely, in the right of black teachers to organize independently of white teachers, and of students and parents.

Having said that, many of us are parents as well as teachers and, as parents, we should use every available opportunity to work with existing parents groups or to form new groups with parents from our children's schools or with those who are parents of our children's friends.

I believe that a Black Teachers Association has a particular role to play in supporting black parents' organizations and in encouraging and assisting the development of black students' organizations.

Increasingly, there is need for organized parents groups to

seek to work with schools and to make governing bodies accountable for what goes on in those schools. Given the extended powers and responsibilities that governors now have, it is vital that we do not take the view that the need for democratic accountability is discharged simply by the presence of parents on the governing body of the school.

Conclusion

As black teachers you are seeking to determine whether and how you might work together in what is arguably the most critical period in the history of the post-war black presence in Britain.

The relationship between Education, Economy and Society is being reconstructed weekly, with major consequences for schools and for classroom teachers. Keeping students motivated when they are more and more aware of the growing numbers of school leavers among the long term unemployed, and the number of skilled and underemployed black people there are in the economy, is a massively difficult task, as I suspect is also true of keeping teachers highly motivated.

The resurgence of fascism and the year on year increase in the number of racist attacks and racist murders give an urgency to the need for networking and for having a collective basis for intervening in those situations and dealing with their effects on school communities.

The growth of communalism and religious fundamentalism on the one hand, and the increasing eagerness of certain black groups to use the 'opt out' provisions in the Education Acts to create particular types of schools, would require teachers especially, and our communities more generally, to declare publicly where we stand on such issues.

I do not believe that any single one of the many issues raised in this paper could be ignored by any teacher, and certainly not by black teachers with a genuine concern about the persistence of racial oppression and social injustice in the society.

You may think that I have set out too broad and all-embracing an agenda for you, and that all you can really deal with is a forum in which you can come and unwind, have a good moan, rap a while, recharge the batteries and go off again till the next time.

The decision as to the type of forum you want is entirely in your hands. All I would advise is that you consider carefully what would be most appropriate to the conditions and circumstances in which you exist now, and those you are more than likely to face in the future.

There is an enormous amount of talent and a huge reservoir of experience among you, and you must collectively find ways of using that to build on your strengths, eliminate your weaknesses, and grow into a force to be reckoned with in this city if not in the country.

I wish you lots of creative energy, and every success.

4.4

THREATENED DEPORTATION OF TWENTY-FIVE TEACHERS FROM TRINIDAD AND THE CASE FOR THEIR RETENTION IN HACKNEY'S SCHOOLS

30 July 1993

Statement of Gus John, Director of Education, London Borough of Hackney

To: The Home Secretary, the Secretary of State for Education and the Secretary of State for Employment

A. Background: Facing a Teacher Supply Crisis

1. I took up post as Director of Education in Hackney in March 1989, having worked as an Assistant Education Officer in the Inner London Education Authority (ILEA)

2. From March 1989 to 1 April 1990 I led a team of people in preparing the borough for the transfer of education from ILEA. We needed to address two critical concerns:

   a. How to devise an education structure appropriate to the task of raising standards and enhancing achievement in Hackney schools, and

   b. What to do about the primary teacher shortage that was already at crisis point in the borough and that was having a disastrous effect on the quality of teaching and learning in the schools in general, but in primary schools in particular.

3. In his Annual Report (1988-89), Her Majesty's Senior Chief Inspector of Schools stated:

There are complex and worsening problems of teacher supply. They are to do with demography, recruitment problems in some parts of the country, and actual shortages of certain kinds of expertise and skill ...

The majority of schools have sufficient teachers to put before classes. That cannot be said of some schools in parts of Greater London. Here, vacancies are covered by a variety of expedients; temporary redeployment, the use of instructors, advisory and supply teachers or Section 11 teachers. In some parts of Inner London such measures have been used to such an extent that pupils' learning, relationships within schools, and inservice training have all been damaged. For some groups of pupils a succession of stop-gap teachers have put paid to continuity and coherence in their curricula and assessments. One Inner London borough already employing in its primary schools 86 probationary teachers and 60 overseas teachers (including some unqualified), was also covering 140 permanent and 30 temporary vacancies at the beginning of the autumn term 1989 of which 50 could no longer be covered by the end of the term. In its primary schools there were 17 acting heads. A further 14 had been in post for less than two years and six were due to resign at the end of 1989. While the Inner London picture is an extreme one, elsewhere in the country the shortfalls are becoming more evident as available expedients are increasingly use. (DES, 1989)

4. A former ILEA inspector observed that during his five years as a primary school inspector in Hackney, he dealt with primary schools where in the course of one academic year certain pupils had had up to 9 different teachers and in the case of one class, 14 teachers. He concluded at the time that the rapid teacher turnover 'could hardly be said to be working in the best interest of pupils and their education. It certainly does not guarantee stability or quality and makes a nonsense of the government's talk about improving standards'.

5. Hackney has a population of some 186,000 residents of whom an estimated 32% are black (African-Caribbean and Asian). Some 65% to 70% of the school population are from

black and other ethnic groupings. The social demography of Hackney is frequently a cause of public comment, and featured highly in teachers' decisions about whether or not to seek employment in Hackney.

6. Between March and December 1989 I held discussions with Her Majesty's Inspectorate (HMI) regarding their perspectives on education in Hackney. Responsibility for running education was to transfer to the Inner London boroughs from the ILEA on 1 April 1990. HMI highlighted a number of concerns, not least of all about the quality of primary teaching in Hackney, the lack of stability in the workforce, and the effects on children of having to be taught by unqualified teachers and a constant flow of supply teachers.

7. Those concerns were further underscored in two HMI reports in 1990, one in January on Hackney Free and Parochial School (secondary) and the other in July, highlighting issues of concern in schooling in Hackney generally. Both reports made for very disturbing reading, and Hackney LEA was required to provide the then Secretary of State for Education with an Action Plan designed to address the issues of concern raised by HMI.

8. Top of the list of our thirteen point Action Programme was 'the Recruitment and Retention of Teachers'. For one full year I provided regular reports to the Secretary of State on Hackney LEA's progress in stabilizing the staffing situation in our schools.

B. Corrective Action

1. Through the initiative of the Senior Primary Inspector in Hackney (ILEA Division 4), the ILEA agreed an arrangement with the Barbados Ministry of Education whereby twelve Barbadian teachers were seconded to the ILEA to work in Hackney schools for a period of two years. Those teachers arrived in August 1989 and started induction and training for teaching in the classroom in the 1989-90 academic year.

2. Hackney LEA committed itself to assuming responsibility for those teachers, their pastoral support and their eventual

return to Barbados on the abolition of the ILEA.

3. In December 1989 the Hackney Education Committee approved my recommendation that a body of teachers should be recruited from Trinidad and Tobago. In January and February 1990, I led a team of officers and recruited just over forty teachers in Trinidad. They had been displaced by their government's cut in public spending as a consequence of conditionalities imposed by the International Monetary Fund and the World Bank as part of a 'structural adjustment' package.

4. All of those teachers had completed the two year teacher training course, one year school-based training, and had an average of fifteen years teaching experience in the classroom. They had all been subject to formal appraisal on a regular basis during those fifteen years.

5. The majority of the group arrived in June 1990 and began teaching in September 1990.

6. In view of the fact that the DES required those teachers to have done all three years of their training in a college or university, the Trinidad teachers were placed on a Licensed Teacher Scheme in order to gain qualified teacher status (QTS). Registration for QTS and the granting of the Licence was on condition that each licence holder had teaching responsibility for a specific class for the duration of the licence. The scheme was run by the LEA in conjunction with the Polytechnic (now University) of North London.

7. Once the first tranche of teachers had received confirmation of QTS from the Department for Education, the Council, having already notified the Home Office of its intention to appeal against their decision not to renew the teachers' work permits, sent the QTS certificates with letters of appeal. The Department of Employment and the Home Office then proceeded to issue some work permit extensions and to endorse the teachers' passports accordingly. Some were given two years extension, others four years. In some cases a wife would be given four years and her husband two, or vice versa. No explanation has been provided and none appears to be forthcoming as to the reasons for that differentiation,

especially as all the teachers with QTS satisfy identical criteria.

8. Another tranche of teachers who needed to acquire 'O' level Maths in order to qualify for the Licensed Teachers Scheme were allocated classes like the rest, but were required to study for the mathematics examination in a programme devised by Hackney College and agreed with the Department of Education and Science. They consequently joined the Licensed Teacher Scheme later than the rest and are due to complete between September 1993 and March 1994.

9. The teachers were all given permanent contracts with Hackney subject to the renewal of their work permits. I went to great pains to make that absolutely clear in my briefings with the teachers in Trinidad and in their letter of employment. The relevant paragraph of their letter of employment reads as follows:

The offer of employment will be for permanent status with the Authority, but subject to renewal of your work permit, and permission to enter the United Kingdom being renewed at whatever interval as determined by the United Kingdom government. Failure to obtain the necessary clearance will necessitate our terminating your employment

Each teacher recruited received this letter in Trinidad in February 1990, signed and returned it.

C. 'Catch 22'

1. Some twenty-five Trinidad teachers are facing deportation as a direct result of problems encountered in having their work permits renewed.

2. In January 1990 when we interviewed the teachers in Trinidad, it was possible for them to gain Qualified Teacher Status after one year. However, by the time Hackney applied for licences for them to join the Licensed Teacher Scheme, the DES required them to complete two years licensed teacher training before they could be given QTS. Most of the teachers

were thereby placed in a 'no win' situation. The lack of synchrony between the duration of the two year work permit and the beginning and end of the two year Licensed Teacher Scheme meant that, for the majority, the work permit expired before they completed the scheme and were thus eligible for QTS. In the case of those starting the scheme late, the problem was further compounded.

3. It was in recognition of this fact that we took proactive steps to deal with the anticipated problem. In 1990, shortly after the arrival of the teachers from Trinidad, my colleague, Paul Cave spoke to Mrs Thompson at the Department of Employment to ascertain the possibility of extending the work permits on expiry of the existing two year period. He outlined to Mrs Thompson that a number of the teachers would need to pursue a course of study for Mathematics/ English or both, in order to follow the Licensed Teacher Scheme, which would lead to the award of Qualified Teacher Status. Mrs Thompson stated that it was a possibility that at the time of expiry individuals who still had not completed the scheme may be granted a temporary right to remain until such time that the course was completed, at which point their individual cases would be reviewed further.

It became more and more apparent, however, that some individuals would have difficulty obtaining a work permit extension after the implementation of the new Immigration regulation enforced in November 1991, as the Home Office and Department of Employment became aware of the growing number of teachers within the United Kingdom who were in the market for full time permanent teaching posts.

As part of the new regulations the Home Office introduced a change in the new type of work permits available, as follows:

a. Trainee Work Experience scheme (TWES)

These work permits are valid for a period of two years, to enable individuals to follow specific training courses, or gain relevant experience which would be put to use on returning to their country of origin.

These permits are not renewable, and in the case of the Trinidadian teachers retrospectively applicable.

b. Main Scheme Work Permits

This is the type of work permit which all Trinidadian teachers received in 1990. The main scheme permit requires the individual to have gained qualified teacher status and be employed in a post which cannot be filled from within the United Kingdom, or the European Economic Community (EEC).

Given the type of permit originally issued to the teachers this was the type of permit for which we were advised to apply.

4. In November 1990 I spoke to Kelvin English in the Department for Education seeking his assistance in extricating ourselves from the 'Catch 22' situation the teachers had found themselves in. I followed up that conversation with a letter which Kelvin English passed to John Adams to deal with. John Adams sought to address the work permit issue but gave no indication in his letter as to whether or not the DFE was minded to facilitate the LEA in the manner I outlined to Kelvin English in my letter of 30 November.

5. Since then, I have had no success in getting the DfE to authorize the teachers who are still on the Licensed Scheme in order that they could satisfy the qualification requirement of the Department of Employment. Moreover, as the letter of 15 July 1993 from the Department of Employment indicates, that department has hardened its position and is effectively giving the green light to the immigration and police authorities to deport those teachers for whom we have not yet secured work permit extensions.

6. One such teacher has had a letter requiring her to leave the country forthwith or face a hefty fine, imprisonment and deportation.

7. The unequivocal position outlined in Deborah McCormack's letter effectively means that twenty-five teachers, all of whom have licences which expire between 31 August and 31 March, and all of whom are committed classroom teachers

who, as a condition of the Licence, would have been in their school for at least two years, now face expulsion from the country.

D. Fallen Angels of Mercy

1. As I observed in my letter to Mrs Girvan in the Home Office's Immigration and Nationality Department, when I and my Senior Primary Inspector recruited those teachers from Trinidad in 1990, we had no basis on which to assume that the chronic primary teacher shortage would not continue to bedevil LEAs and schools for some years to come. We targeted experienced teachers with a track record of success because we were conscious of the ground to be made up in Hackney schools. The teachers uprooted themselves and their families (in many cases, mother and father are both teachers) and made a commitment to working to improve education standards and enhance pupils' achievement in Hackney. HMI highlighted a number of concerns in 1989 and repeatedly in 1990 in respect of the quality of primary teaching in Hackney, the lack of stability in the workforce, and the discontinuity in children's learning regimes. OfSTED subsequently scrutinized HMI's files and designated fifteen Hackney schools (thirteen of them primary) as being 'at risk'. Having inspected a number of those schools in the current academic year, OfSTED has taken the majority of them off the 'at risk' register.

2. This welcome improvement has been due in no small measure to the success Hackney LEA has had in stabilizing its teaching workforce, and in attending to the quality of teaching and learning in its schools. The contribution of the Trinidad teachers to that success is unquestionable.

3. Having exploited the considerable teaching skills and experience of those teachers in our two years of crisis, and having granted licences to teach and prepare them for Qualified Teacher Status, it is surely not in the interests of improving inner-city education to throw them out of the country just as they are on the point of satisfying the conditions for QTS and consolidating the significant

contribution they have made to the improvement of primary education in Hackney.

4. The consequences of such action in my view are much too horrendous to contemplate. Schools which have got stable staffing and fully expect this rare and happy situation to continue would find themselves in chaos as highly respected teachers are forcibly removed from their communities.

5. Children and their parents who have expectations of a permanent teacher teaching their class in September and for the next academic year, could suddenly find that the school is without an experienced class teacher.

6. By virtue of being highly competent teachers with, in some cases, up to twenty-eight years teaching experience, the Trinidad teachers are mature people with families. Their own children are in primary and secondary education in Hackney schools. Many are due to take GCSE next Spring and some are in their final 'A' level year.

7. Having been uprooted from their homes in Trinidad and had their schooling disrupted for no other reason than that their parents were recruited to come and teach in Hackney in a time of crisis, those children now face the prospect of being uprooted again, this time to face an even more uncertain future, and at the cost of their education.

8. Some spouses who were not themselves teachers gave up their jobs to come here with their teacher wives/husbands. Deportation or enforced removal will render both jobless as well as jeopardizing their children's life chances.

9. The contribution those teachers have made to raising educational standards and enhancing students' achievement in primary and secondary education in Hackney is beyond dispute.

10. At a time when the Secretary of State for Education is placing a premium on school-based Initial Teacher Training, Hackney LEA considers it an enormous asset to have teachers of such proven experience in its schools. Schools already acknowledge the significant contribution the teachers make to the development of good classroom practice among other younger and less experienced staff.

11. The governors, staff, students and parents at all our schools in which the Trinidad teachers are deployed are all united in their desire to see the respective teachers continue at their school, and are in some confusion at the prospect that their work permits would not be extended.

12. While the supply of primary teachers is no longer a recruitment issue as such, it is still very much a retention issue in boroughs such as ours. The teachers from Trinidad made a commitment to working in Hackney education in 1990, and uprooted themselves to come here to do just that. Their commitment is now stronger than ever because they have seen the value of the contribution they make.

13. At a time when OfSTED is targeting a significant number of primary schools in Hackney as giving cause for concern, when we are seeking to build further upon our achievements since becoming a LEA, and are introducing a number of additional strategies for raising standards and enhancing achievement in our schools, we simply cannot afford to lose some of the most competent and experienced teachers in the borough, especially after we invested so much resource in recruiting and training them in the last three years.

14. I believe that this country has a moral obligation to those teachers as it clearly saw no problem in issuing them with work permits and giving them leave to bring their dependents here in our moments of desperate need. It is morally unacceptable and decidedly inhumane to turf them out now that the country is able to recruit teachers locally, thus imposing upon them the status of 'gastarbeiter' (guest workers).

15. As for giving proof of our efforts to recruit from the EEC, I find it a trifle absurd that Hackney LEA should be required to terminate the contracts of twenty-five black, African-Caribbean teachers all of whom teach in schools with 50% or more African Caribbean students, in order to seek to recruit from among EEC nationals who, more likely than not, would have little understanding of, or empathy with, the predominantly black, multiracial Hackney community, its children and their parents.

16. The Trinidad teachers are role models in several respects. First, in terms of their professional status as examples to black and white children; second, the fact that they bring to their teaching a wide repertoire of teaching methods, including an advanced ability to teach the 3Rs and to integrate didactic methods with the now more commonplace facilitative teaching. Third, they bring and utilize their experience of involving parents in their children's education and in working in concert with the educational objectives of the school.

17. For all of those reasons, I believe that logic demands that the requirement that Hackney LEA shows proof of failing to recruit from within the UK and the EEC be waived, and that every effort is made to renew the work permits of the teachers and put an end to their distress, so that they could continue to be singleminded about the task they were brought here to do, i.e., to use their considerable skills in improving primary education in Hackney.

18. I appeal to Ministers in the Department for Education, in the Department of Employment and in the Home Office to intervene in this situation to effect a positive outcome and above all to recognize that the initiative I took in 1990, in the most proactive manner, was entirely in keeping with what the Secretary of State for Education later demanded of Hackney Council.

19. Finally, as Director of Education and the officer leading the team that recruited the teachers in Trinidad, and as the chief officer answerable to the parents of Hackney, I feel a deep sense of responsibility for the outcome of this matter.

20. For the sake of the children of Hackney and the integrity of the teachers and their families, I most strongly urge that the Deborah McCormack letter be put on hold, and that urgent steps are taken to provide work permits for the teachers.

Gus John
Director of Education
30 July 1993

Afterword

This statement led to a series of discussions between civil servants in the three departments. Finally, Viscount Ullswater responded on behalf of the Secretary of State for Employment and invited personnel in the Education Directorate to go and meet with civil servants in the Overseas Labour division of his ministry in Sheffield.

At that meeting, the file of each of the twenty-five teachers was reviewed and a time scale agreed for enabling each to meet the requirements so that their work permit could be renewed. For all but three people the process was relatively straightforward. The others were given time to complete their QTS preparation and within months all were granted work permits. One year later, all the Trinidad teachers applied for and were granted leave to remain permanently by virtue of their length of stay and their employment since 1990.

Some headteachers, believing that the teachers could not avoid deportation had advertised their posts and were inviting candidates for interview. The Education Directorate was able to intervene and reverse those actions, confident that we were not going to allow the teachers to be fined, imprisoned or deported.

While some have been promoted and have headships and deputy headships in other LEAs, some 50% of the teachers are continuing to raise standards in Hackney schools.

THE LETTER

Alex Pascall

Me De'ar Grace
Me reach ah England, me live ah London.
Me get ah work, cleaning muck.
De Bank funny, but me save little money.
Me goin' buy a house, without cat or mouse.
Me go ah night school, as a golden rule,
To learn 'bout the nation and colonisation.
The cold ah bite, from me left to me right.
The place full ah darkness, and plenty fastness.
Me miss the sun and all the fun.
Me miss you cooking and Knockabouting.
You sweet embrace, gosh! ah miss you Grace;
the fresh tittiri and lambi stew,
with chive and thyme, yes du, du.
The calypso and the Julie mango,
the moonlight walk and de ole talk.
In a year or two, me goin' send for you
Grace du, du, darling whatever you do –
Never forget, I love you
Tell everybody me send how-de-do,
Sweet sugar plum may God Bless you.
Yours forever and ever and ever.
Please drop me a line to say all is fine.
Your Love
    DEVINE

CARIBBEAN LANGUAGES IN BRITISH SCHOOLS

Introduction

The notion of 'Caribbean languages' is strange to many, including people of Caribbean heritage. For one thing, the very word 'Caribbean' conjures up images of the English speaking Caribbean. The French, Spanish, and Dutch speaking Caribbean is typically much more remote in people's consciousness. For another, current and former inhabitants of the English speaking Caribbean are thought to be just that, English speaking. So why Caribbean 'languages' in British schools with a predominance of Caribbean heritage students from the English speaking Caribbean?

How many Jamaicans or Barbadians, for example, regard the language they use as a national language in its own right, just like French or Dutch? This subject was hotly debated in the period (1960s and 1970s) when black children arriving in Britain to join their parents or carers were being assessed by education authorities before being placed in bands and streams in schools. The tests applied in these assessments were found to be biased on a number of grounds, including culture and language. Education psychologists and Child Guidance officers, no less than teachers, demonstrated a level of ignorance of the countries from which Caribbean children came and the languages of the region which could have been second only to that of the average resident in the United States of America. And as if that were not bad enough, the only characterization they could find for the language and speech patterns of the children they were assessing was that they were particularly bad examples of 'broken English'.

When asked what the English those people might speak in its unbroken form would sound like, the answer invariably came that the speakers of 'broken English' did not know that themselves, because they clearly had never spoken it and showed no signs of being able to. Despite that reasoning, such 'professionals' who had the power and authority to condemn children to a fairly predictable future by labelling them as educationally subnormal, stubbornly refused to acknowledge that they were dealing with Caribbean speakers of languages other than English, French, Spanish, etc., languages constructed around English but distinctly different from the form of English that is standard and intelligible to listeners and readers worldwide, precisely because it is 'standard'.

What is extraordinary is that it is only racial stereotyping and English chauvinism that could have prevented those very 'professionals' from looking in their own backyard and seeing the same phenomenon at work. That was the burden of my contribution to the special symposium on 'Strategies and Action for Black and Ethnic Minority Education' organized by the International Bookfair of Radical Black and Third World Books at Camden Town Hall in 1988.

In sharing 'A Perspective on Caribbean Languages in British Schools' (5.1), I was able to draw heavily upon work I had done over some fifteen years with black children in Oxford, London, Leicester, and Birmingham, who had arrived from the Caribbean to join parents and carers, and with the schools to which they had been admitted. Of equal relevance was the work I did on behalf of the Inner London Education Authority at the Centre for Urban Educational Studies at Aberdeen Park, Islington, in the middle to late 1970s, where I sought to enhance teachers' understanding of these issues and assist with a critical examination of their classroom practice and their interface with Caribbean children and their parents.

The paper argues for an appreciation of how 'language' and class featured in debates about schooling and education in

Britain prior to the arrival of post-war black settlers, as a prerequisite to understanding how the schooling system greeted the arrival of children of the predominantly peasant and labouring classes from the former colonies of the Caribbean.

In the late 1970s and throughout the 1980s in Adult Education in Manchester, London and elsewhere, adult learners from the islands of the Caribbean, then long resident in Britain, were assisted in owning their language(s) and using them as a bridge towards more confident written and oral communication in standard English. In the last seven years or so, the National Institute of Adult Continuing Education has built upon that work, especially with the strong leadership provided by a former education officer, Alyson Malach. Also building latterly upon that groundbreaking work has been Jamaica 2K, a body of people working in adult and further education who have joined forces with adult education workers and academics in Jamaica for collaborative work on giving the Jamaican language a higher profile in schooling and education, in public life, and in the delivery of services, especially here in Britain.

'Related Language Issues in the UK Today' (5.2) was presented at a Jamaica 2K conference on Valuing Caribbean Languages. The paper asks some key questions about the status of Caribbean languages, both as conferred by its users and as recognized, or not, by schooling and education. Is the continuance of those languages dependent solely on the oral tradition and, if so, how sustainable are they? Can they survive as living languages, especially in the Caribbean diaspora?

'Language, Identity and Social Transformation' (5.3) is the unabridged version of a paper delivered at a Jamaica 2K conference in Birmingham the following year. That conference launched in the UK a book by Dr Pauline Christie, *Language in Jamaica*, in which she explores the relationship between Jamaican Creole and standard English over the centuries, with each language undergoing development and transformation in its own right.

'Language, Identity and Social Transformation' addresses four main themes:

1. Caribbean languages in schooling and education

2. Caribbean languages in the identity formation of British born children of African heritage and the relevance of that for their learning and self development

3. Caribbean languages as the first language of adults in their interface with social institutions and with other language groups in the society

4. The possible influence on the British situation of the way Jamaica resolves the national language issue and especially the place of Jamaican Creole in formal education in Jamaica

The paper argues that compared to other speakers of languages other than English within Britain's black and ethnic minority communities (Chinese, Bangladeshi, Pakistani, Indian, Turkish, Somali, etc.), speakers of Caribbean languages have been given little systematic support in appreciating their mother tongue and using it as a lever for learning English and accessing the curriculum.

Some black parents are themselves ambivalent about the value of preserving the language they themselves speak, in that they give schools clear signals that they want their children to be good communicators in the language 'that would help them get on', even though they themselves know no other language than the one they don't want their children to speak and the schools to validate.

The relationship between language, identity, self esteem, and self confidence is explored as are the implications of that relationship for learning and for educational outcomes.

INTERNATIONAL BOOKFAIR OF RADICAL AND THIRD WORLD BOOKS
A perspective on Caribbean languages in British schools
Camden Town Hall 1988

Introduction

The first thing I want to say is that I am talking about the black language issue in education and I am going to address myself principally to the issue of Caribbean language, but I am also going to do it from a practical point of view. I want to approach it from the point of view of someone who has been involved in education as student, parent, and teacher and has been trying to make sense of this complex issue in its historical, social and political context.

So, I want to start off by reminding all of us of the context in which this Caribbean language issue in British education assumes the importance that it has, and to do so I want to take you back to the key debates in British education in the 1950s and 1960s. I think it is important that we remember what those debates were so that we can contextualize the current discussion on Caribbean language and the wider issue of black people in British education.

In Britain in the 1950s and 1960s, the principal debate was about education and social class. But part of that debate was about education, language, and social class, and particularly white working class people's access to schooling and education, and performance in the schooling system. Let me remind you of some of the voluminous documents, books, research reports, and government circulars that were circulating during that period. There were things such as:

Social Class and Educational Opportunity – 1957
The Robbins Report – 1963
The Newsam Report – 1963
The Home and the School – 1964
Education and the Working Class – 1966
The Plowden Report – 1967
Social Relations in a Secondary School – 1967
Social Class, Language and Education – 1968

These are but some of the endless reports and books about social class and education in Britain.

My reason for making that point at the start of this talk is to emphasize that when mass black migration into this country started in the middle 1950s, the question of education and schooling was already set in a particular mould. So, we didn't arrive here and then everything was suddenly different because of our presence. There was an existing context and range of matters that were bothering the political authorities in Britain as far as public education was concerned. The most pressing of these as the country sought to expand state education in the post-war period was: why is it that working class children do not achieve in the school system? That was the key to all those reports. And, just as they have done with the black population, a good deal of the research tended to suggest that there was something not quite right with the white working class families and children themselves.

I am arguing that we need to be aware of that background if we are to understand how and why the issue of blacks in British schooling came to have the particular profile that it has. Unless we engage with the debate about social class and education, rather than focusing solely on 'race' in the schooling system, we will fail to understand the process by which underachievement came to be racialized, in much the same way that immigration and crime have been racialized.

We should have expected the preexisting debate about social class and education to have some effect on the presence of black people in the schooling and education system, or else it would have been like saying: We are outside of that debate, we come from a completely different educational tradition, we are not like other people and, therefore, we could expect the system to deliver to us what it has signally failed to deliver to generations of white working class people. If those earlier research reports show that working class children do not get equality in education, we should therefore expect that black working class children, carrying the added burden of racism, would have an even harder struggle. But, we must always remember that it is not a completely different struggle.

As I stated earlier, part of that debate was about language and social class in education and schooling. That debate has got buried as education policymakers and practitioners deal with the language issue as it relates to black people in the schooling system. However, the 'language and social class in education' debate was about white working class people in education and the failure of the schooling and education system to deal with white working class language issues. Yet, people have a tendency to ignore that white working class language issue and just concentrate on black languages, particularly those of people from the sub-continent.

I am making this point for another reason. Black children in the schooling system who were born and brought up in Britain are not just bringing, in this case, Caribbean languages with them from their families and their heritage. They are also increasingly part of the working class language heritage in Britain, concentrated as they are in urban centres mainly, the largest population group of all being in the thirty-two London boroughs. Any discussion we have about the issue of black language in British education must therefore take into account the fact that language is dynamic, there is a certain fluidity to it, and so we can expect that language forms among white working class people would change, similarly, as a consequence of their interactions with Britain's black population.

In terms of the aspirations of people in the education system, the key thing is obviously succeeding at school and getting qualifications, getting a job and so on, but one of the often neglected factors in aiming at this is the power situation which exists on language. The power situation on language is that if you want to be successful in virtually any course in an educational institution in Britain, you are expected to reproduce, in writing, one particular language form. That particular language form is called Standard English.

Now, although that is undoubtedly the case, a very large number of parents don't really understand this crucial fact, i.e., that it is a particular type of language. It is 'standard' in the sense that whether you are from the West Midlands, Essex, or Newcastle, in your written communication you are expected to conform to standard forms of grammar, syntax, punctuation, etc., however vast or limited your vocabulary. It is not just a question of 'proper' or 'correct' writing or speech. It is a specific linguistic form which has great social, political, economic, and educational power in this country, albeit it is not the majority language of Britain but one that is imposed upon everybody else in society as a route to educational qualifications, a measure of educational success, an indicator of social class, and the rest of it.

If you look at the language map of the British Isles, you find that in every region of Britain the working class population clearly has its own language, whether they are situated in conurbations such as London, Glasgow, Tyneside or the West Midlands. The working class population of all those areas have very specific language forms of their own, which are vastly different from the language of power in the society, i.e., Standard English.

So, I want to flag that up because one of the key problems for black parents in this schooling system is having high educational aspirations and an expectation of educational success for their children without attending to the question of language and how the child negotiates the language of home and community with that required for educational success in school, college, and University. In this sense, language is as much a matter for us as it is for people from the Indian sub-continent.

How has this difficulty or problem come about?

I think there are two sides to it. One side of it is what the schooling system does to us. But, the other side of it is what we allow them to do to us and what we ourselves perpetuate. I don't think there can be any meaningful discussion about forming organizations, struggling collectively, building independent organizations unless we have a perspective on both those aspects of the problem.

We must look at what they do to us, in this case in schooling and education, to deny us opportunities and the full use of our abilities, but we must also look at what we ourselves do that hampers our progress. I shall return presently to the specific case of language in schooling and education.

If we are talking about the mass of the population that migrated here from the Caribbean, we are talking about a population who have had a historical experience of fierce conflict and persistent struggle with British colonizers and with the British colonial state. A historical struggle starting with the slave trade, continuing with the slave plantation societies in the Caribbean region, continuing with the plantation economies of the colonial era, continuing with the postcolonial legacy of education, trade, etc., right up to post-war migration to Britain and the struggle for our rightful place in this society, free from racial terror and from being pushed on to the margins of the society.

Throughout all those phases of our history there has been conflict, but those phases have also been characterized by continuous language development, with all the usual variations within and between languages in the region. The result of that is that there is awkwardness and difficulty on both sides of the debate about language development in the Caribbean. So, although you can say that the whites have been racist towards black people and their languages, sidelining them, denying them of origin, worth and substance, it is also the case that a lot of black people coming out of that historical experience have also been very negative and sometimes downright pejorative about their own language, particularly in the context of schooling and education. We ourselves have down-pressed our languages by actively robbing them of valid expression and of the validation that is conferred, typically, by the literary gatekeepers and intelligentsia in the society.

There are various theories about the evolution and

development of Caribbean languages in the various nation states. What is beyond dispute is the fact that the languages that have developed in the region cannot be separated from our own origins:

- where we came from
- how we came to be in the region
- what we came with
- what we met
- whom we met
- what we created in our attempts to understand and communicate with one another
- whom we interacted with, learnt from, were influenced by, and influenced
- who conquered and plundered and superimposed their language, culture, and religion

In the process of becoming Caribbean people, therefore, our language drove our development and took shape as an integral part of that development. In other words, we cannot separate our language from our identity, our spirituality, our folklore, our medicine, our music, our cuisine, any more than we can separate language from the words and phrases we use in it.

The colonizers and slave traders attempted to separate the indigenous peoples of the Caribbean (whom they did not entirely obliterate) from their language in much the same way that they did the Africans who were forcibly transported to the region. But the Africans managed to perform an immensely creative feat. They took what they could retain of the most prominent African languages, what they were forced to acquire from European languages (French, Spanish, English, Dutch) and created new language forms.

Whether we are from former Francophone colonial territories such as Haiti, St Lucia and Dominica, or from Anglophone territories such as Jamaica, Trinidad and Grenada, it is those language forms through which our being gains expression in this country, and which impacts upon, and are impacted, by the languages we encounter in the communities we inhabit.

The challenge for us in our communities, therefore, is to ensure that the language forms our children own and through which they express their realities are not used as a basis for determining their level of intelligence, their educational potential or the professions to which they should aspire. There is as much need for open discussion of the Caribbean language issue in schools and LEAs as there is within our communities. If we fail to engage in such a debate and find ways of charting the interventions we must make, our children will continue to be penalized for the content and manner of their written and oral expression. As of now, we have no way of assessing the extent to which our children are being demotivated and turned off learning because of teachers' and their own parents' negative attitudes to their written and oral expression.

Speaking for myself, I have always regretted the fact that my parents and the elders in my village actively thwarted my attempts to learn the French creole their generation spoke. They made plain their desire to have us learn 'proper' French and speak 'good English'. So much so, that unlike people of my and later generations in St Lucia and Dominica, we in Grenada have lost our French creole. The French and Spanish we learnt in our schools in Grenada, and throughout the Caribbean, have for most of us remained 'dead' classical languages, not least because few opportunities presented themselves or were created for us to use them and keep them alive as modern European languages. Some of us created those opportunities for ourselves here in Europe. Conversely, however, many young speakers of French creole are so far removed from the source in St Lucia and Dominica that they now fear that what is, in many cases, the only additional language they have, will disappear in the next generation.

For all of those reasons, I am arguing for a focus on Caribbean languages in schools and in our communities, at least as part of the seemingly endless debate about the issue of black underachievement in the British schooling system.

5.2

VALUING CARIBBEAN LANGUAGES
Related language issues in the UK today

South Bank University, London
30 January 2003

Preamble:

It gives me enormous pleasure to be part of this hugely important conference and of the work that Jamaica 2K is doing to address critical issues in language use and abuse, development and marginalization, growth and transformation, as it relates to Caribbean peoples at home and in the second diaspora.

I congratulate the National Institute of Adult Continuing Education (NIACE) for their vision in engaging with this agenda and South Bank University for their foresight and commitment in continuing their focus on language and empowerment, not least by enabling the consolidation and growth of the work of the London Language and Literacy Unit, a Unit which for over two decades has done such pioneering work in London, radiating outwards as far afield as Tobago, Grenada, Trinidad, and Jamaica.

I once worked in the Inner London Education Authority as Assistant Education Officer and Head of Community Education. The ILEA, through the expertise of some visionary people, not least in the Language and Literacy Unit (Roxy Harris), and in the African-Caribbean Education Resource Centre (Len Garrison) did more than most other LEAs to acknowledge Caribbean languages, to engage with Caribbean languages in transition, and in development, and to unleash the potential of language to empower people and confirm their identity. It is fitting, therefore, that the new home of the Language and Literacy Unit should also host the first of this important series of conferences.

What I want to do in this paper is raise some issues relating to language development and use among Caribbean heritage people in Britain today, and in the process say something about language and identity, and language as a tool of empowerment, especially for people whom societies do not routinely validate, whether because of the dynamics of class and caste, as in Jamaica and other English, French, and Spanish speaking Caribbean countries, or of 'race' and class, as in Britain, France, Germany and elsewhere in Europe.

Context

Who, then, are we talking about when we focus on Valuing Caribbean Languages in the British context?

Essentially, we are talking about Caribbean settlers and their descendants, all of whom are carriers of the languages that characterize the societies from which they came; and all of whom are a living testimony to the dynamism of language and its capacity to shape, reshape and blend; its capacity to reinvent itself as a consequence of a combination of economic, social, cultural, and political factors.

That is evident in cultural activism, in writing, in oracy, in music, in comedy, in theatre within our communities, but evident above all in the rich variety of speech patterns and especially in what might broadly be called 'street rap' or 'black talk' among young black british.

It is important that we isolate certain key issues in this transitional and transformational phase of Caribbean languages in Britain and its implications for language and learning across all ages and all phases of education. What are some of these?:

a. Migration

The first generation of Caribbean migrants were both monolingual and bilingual. Some indeed were multilingual. The extent to which they were bilingual would have depended upon their economic status and the schooling and education they had received. Crucially and commensurately, it would have depended upon the level of functional literacy in the country from which they came. For example, people from Trinidad would be more likely to be bilingual than those from Jamaica, not only because the Jamaican language is more distinctive in structure and composition, but because more people in Trinidad, of any class, would have had more opportunity to develop the capacity to move between Trinidad creole and standard English than was the case in Jamaica. The same would be true of people from St Lucia and Dominica, both of which preserved and developed a French creole, unlike St Vincent and Grenada where the functioning language was English.

At the interface with British society, this became a crucial factor for the following reason. In the Caribbean, your capacity to use both registers depending upon context, i.e., the situation you were in, who you were speaking or writing to, whether it was formal or informal discourse, etc., was determined largely by socio-economic status, class, education, and upbringing. That enabled you, empowered you indeed, to treat monolingual speakers, those who couldn't speak 'the Queen's English' as inferior to you.

They were expected to be deferential in your presence, especially if you were in a position to offer them work or grant them a favour; to know instinctively that you were superior to them, and to know that when you felt like it you would break into French patois or Jamaican creole to abuse them and put them down, make them feel small, put them back in their box.

In the UK, however, the fact that you could twirl the Queen's English did not cut any British ice. The very fact that you sounded Jamaican or St Lucian, bilingual or not, made you stupid, especially if you were Jamaican. Indeed, because Jamaicans were the largest group among 'the West Indians', the average British person saw all 'West Indians' as Jamaicans.

Suddenly, therefore, monolinguals and bilinguals found they had one thing in common. They were all black, unwelcome, did not belong, to be tolerated at best, and segregated at worst. In other words, in a society that was structurally and culturally hostile to black people, intonation, let alone difference in language, was considered yet another justification for exclusion and discrimination. Spare a thought then for the children of the first generation Caribbean migrants who went into British schools with the only language they had. But before I develop this theme and move on to my next main point, let me make an observation about intonation and accent.

I have always puzzled as to why every black person on British television sounds as if they have been sent to school to unlearn accents, to have it drummed out of them. I used to think it was because the BBC and Independent Television insisted on a uniform, sanitized, English broadcaster's speak. But then I heard Kirsty Wark and John Cole and Eamon Andrews and Jim Naughtie and I thought, wait a minute, I love that sound, that mellifluous Celtic sound. But whatever happened to the equally melodious Trinidadian sing-song of Trevor Macdonald? Why can't black broadcasters sound like black broadcasters of Trinidadian heritage, Jamaican heritage, Grenadian heritage? How marvellous it used to be to hear the uncompromising Alex Pascall on BBC Radio London's *Black Londoners* magazine programme. Here was a most effective communicator in 'the Queen's English', adding richness to the sounds on the airwaves by being his distinctive Caribbean/Grenadian self.

But, I digress.

b. Settlement and Language in Transition

The extent to which a people shape and affirm their identity in any society and become a confident, self-respecting people is the extent to which their language is developed, intrinsically respected, and is the medium through which they externalize their very being. Mess about with that and you undermine their self esteem, their sense of personal and group identity and their capacity to appreciate other languages.

I am no Professor of Linguistics, but I believe that this is so fundamental, throughout history we find examples of the suppressed language of suppressed peoples becoming a powerful language of protest and of resistance.

Anyone who knows the history of the evolution of reggae in Jamaican society, or of Kaiso and Soca in Trinidadian and

Grenadian society, or of the Orisa tradition and culture in
Grenada, Carriacou and Trinidad (including the Yoruba chants,
drumming and rituals of the so-called Shango Baptists) would
connect with this.

Moreover, those powerful languages of protest and resistance
give birth to other language forms and language arts. Examine,
for example, the relationship between the language of reggae
and dub poetry, between those and so-called street talk, what I
prefer to call 'black rap', and the relationship between that black
rap or black talk and the rap movement in Britain. It is worth
noting at this time that whatever influences there might have
been from Black America and there have been many (from
Blues, Gospel, Rap and Hip Hop), it is important that we situate
'Rap' in Britain and similar language art forms in our
communities very much within the history of migration and
settlement that I am dealing with ever so cursorily in this paper.

In Britain, as in Jamaica, even teachers of modern European
languages who genuinely subscribe to the belief that a person's
first language plays a key role in their learning and acquisition
of a second language, conveniently set that aside when they are
faced with black speakers of a Caribbean language. And while
in some respects that might be excused when dealing with
Caribbean heritage children from other islands, it has a
devastating effect upon the learning and educational attainment
of Jamaican children.

Those of us who struggled against the schooling system in this
country in the early period of settlement, the 1960s to the late
1970s, know the part played by that single phenomenon in the
banishment of scandalous numbers of black children into
schools for the educationally subnormal.

The marginalization and denigration of the Jamaican
language and of other Caribbean languages by schools and by
education policies and structures had a number of effects. I
believe it affected fundamentally black children's self esteem,
their sense of being valued and their capacity to give fully of
themselves as learners. Learners of any age are not empty
vessels into which stuff organized by others is poured. Learners
are sharers, sharers from whom the best teachers also learn. If

the medium in which you think, speak, give expression to your deepest feelings and in which you have your very being is rendered invalid, then you, also, are being invalidated. That is even before we begin to deal with the structural issues to do with learning what is presented as the superior language, and the basis upon which such learning could best take place.

No one in this audience needs reminding, however, that not every community of speakers of other languages was treated with such disdain. It was accepted from the outset, however reluctantly, even by those who insisted that 'they should all speak English and forget about this mother tongue nonsense', that South Asian communities had a first language or many languages other than English. It was equally accepted that provision needed to be made for them to learn English as an additional or foreign language.

The more progressive teachers encouraged mother tongue classes, arguing quite rightly that the more Bengali, Pakistani, Indian, Chinese children appreciated the language they were naturally acquiring in their homes by being taught them properly, the easier would be their learning of English.

One wonders whether, had the British colonial education system and a succession of Jamaican governments after Independence acknowledged Jamaican creole as a bona fide 'language of the nation', and formally engaged with its phonology, morphology and graphology, as well as its lexicology and its syntax, the Jamaican education system and the British schooling system, would still be failing so many working class black children of Jamaican heritage.

Some may say that that is looking backwards and we must now look forward, especially as to quote one local government official I heard recently:

We should be encouraging these British born black children to look towards Europe and identify with things European, because that is where their future lies. It does not help to be constantly pointing them back to the Caribbean.

And I thought to myself, you white people seem totally

incapable of seeing the world through the prism of other people's experience. You should try taking groups of these young black British to continental Europe, as I used to do when Director of Education in Hackney, and see how warmly you are welcomed at the ports of entry and on the streets of Paris, Brussels, and Hanover, and how enthusiastic British immigration officials are to have you back when you return to British ports of entry.

Cultures of oppression generate cultures of resistance. In schools, part of the culture of resistance developed by black school students was/is the use of the language that the school does not acknowledge. I am Chair of the Communities Empowerment Network, an organization that does a great deal of work with excluded black students. I cannot count the number of exclusions that have come to our notice, the trigger for which has been the response of teachers to black boys and girls reacting to not being allowed to state their case by resorting to creoles, black talk, call it what you will, which teachers do not understand but feel intuitively that, whatever it was that the student uttered, it wasn't meant to be nice. That then leads to more contestations and then full blown conflict, with both sides refusing to back down. It is what I call the 'Stop and Search' syndrome, school style. And as on the street with the police, it is the black youths that lose. They get excluded, not the teachers.

The main point I wish to emphasize here is that while there are now three new generations of descendants of black settlers here in the UK, there is still no sign and there will not be any sign of the fulfilment of the oft-stated expectation Government and educators had in the 1960s and 1970s, i.e., that once the immigrants' children are born here, go to our schools, learn to speak proper English and adopt our ways, we will have overcome all the problems we now associate with their presence as newcomers. That's like wiping a genetic slate clean.

Language reinvents and reshapes itself. The Jamaican creole that my children who share Jamaican and Grenadian heritage speak is not as rich as that which their Jamaican mother speaks. It has very distinctive features to it, but it is influenced by other language forms which have never been part of their mother's experience.

On the other hand, their generation continues to write and perform poetry, lyrics and short stories in Jamaican creole, the language in which they express their strongest emotions, especially frustration and anger. However accomplished they are as communicators in that other register, the one I am using to address you now, that remains an integral part of their reality.

The question then is, how can the schooling and education system in all four phases: early years, primary, secondary and tertiary, learn from that past and factor in the issue of Caribbean languages in their various measures to tackle the persistent underachievement of black students in the British school system?

Whether in Jamaica, St Lucia, Dominica, Barbados, or England, language remains critical to the formation and maintenance of group identity. Through it, people exercise a great deal of authority and power.

But, as I have observed above, using language to exercise power is also the privilege of the powerless. It spawns new waves of radical and revolutionary writers, poets, comedians, playwrights, lyricists, rap artists. It is the very substance of the politics of protest.

Conclusion

So, where now for the UK?

I believe that before we insist that the education system takes these matters on board as fundamental issues in the education of black school students and of adult learners in communities, colleges and universities, we as black communities must demonstrate that we ourselves take them deadly seriously.

Right now, much is happening, but much is happening almost by default. For generations, the Chinese communities of Britain, the South Asian communities of Britain, have run their Saturday schools, mother tongue classes and the rest. The preservation of their languages and the role of language in art, culture, religion, and commerce remain a key preoccupation of theirs. More recent communities, comparatively speaking, e.g., Nigerians and Ghanaians, organize similarly.

We, hardy Caribbean souls, leave everything to chance, to find its own way in the general order, or dismantling, of things. I believe there is a crying need for an informed debate about these issues amongst ourselves, and I would like to think that this series of conferences can be the beginning of that debate.

Let me leave you with some questions for that debate and for us to consider today:

- Do Caribbean languages have any place in the black British education and artistic movement?
- Do they have any place in the British schooling system?
- Indeed, what are they? How do you recognize them when you see or hear them?
- Do bright young black British want anything to do with them?
- Do they help us to understand ourselves and our history and, if so, how?
- If they and their development are such an important part of our history, how can our academics and teachers do more to produce formalized versions of them?
- Is their continuance dependent solely on the oral tradition and, if so, how diluted are they likely to become?
- Can they survive as living languages, especially in the Caribbean diaspora?

These questions and all that I said before them are only a few of the issues we need to address in relation to this hugely important matter. I trust we would all feel able to contribute to the debate from inside our very own experience, because for each of us language plays and has played a very critical role in the shaping of our world of knowledge, our self-development, self-expression and understanding, as well as our capacity to understand and appreciate the world of others.

Thank you for being so attentive.

5.3

LANGUAGE, IDENTITY AND SOCIAL TRANSFORMATION

Jamaica 2K Conference, Birmingham
26 March 2004

Preamble

I want to thank Jamaica 2K for the invitation to address this important conference today. I consider it a tremendous privilege to be sharing this platform with Dr Pauline Christie to whom I feel we owe a great debt of gratitude for her lifelong work and especially for this hugely important book, 'Language in Jamaica'.

I read the book non-stop over a period of three hours, noting key passages as I went along and marveling at just how readable and accessible the book is. Dr Christie has managed to let us all in on what is often either a highly intricate conversation among academics, or an uninformed rant by people in the media about an issue of mind-bending complexity.

I want to begin this presentation with two quotations: the first is by Niyi Osundare, a long time Professor of English at the University of Ibadan in Nigeria:

When two languages meet, they kiss and quarrel. They achieve a tacit understanding on the common grounds of similarity and convergence, then negotiate, often through strident rivalry and self-preserving altercations, their areas of dissimilarity and divergence ... Yoruba and English. I do not only write in these two languages. I also live in them. I am close enough to hear their amorous chuckles and bitter bickerings. Poetry comes more naturally to me in Yoruba: the words dance to the drum of the heart; the lines pluck their beat from the rhythm of the mind. Mediating all this in English is a problem which has long become a challenge. (my emphasis)   (Osundare, 2000)

The second is Edward Kamau Brathwaite, another Professor of English and, like Osundare, a distinguished poet, writer, and literary critic:

Now I'd like to describe for you some of the characteristics of our nation language. First of all, it is from, as I've said, an oral tradition. The poetry, the culture itself, exists not in a dictionary but in the tradition of the spoken word. It is based as much on sound as it is on song. That is to say, the noise that it makes is part of the meaning, and if you ignore the noise (or what you would think of as noise, shall I say) then you lose part of the meaning.

When it is written, you lose the sound of the noise, and therefore you lose part of the meaning. Which is, again, why I have to have a tape recorder for this presentation. I want you to get the sound of it, rather than the sight of it.   (Brathwaite, 1984)

I want to make a link between Osundare's living in Yoruba and English and Brathwaite's assertion that if you ignore the noise of nation language, you lose part of the meaning.

In 'Language in Jamaica', Dr Christie places literacy and the orality of creoles or patois in their proper historical context, reminding us that English is not the native language of Jamaicans. Indeed, creole was constructed in the very process of forging a Jamaican identity and cannot now be separated from it. That process is not completed and will never be as long as human beings interact and communicate with one another, absorbing influences from home and abroad, transcending their own circumstances and negotiating power relations based on class, access to education, lifestyles, patterns of employment and all the rest of it.

Language is dynamic, and that is as true for creoles as it is for Yoruba, Swahili, or English, or French, and standard European languages. Dr Christie has very helpfully charted for us the retentions and adaptations, the derivations and deviations, the inventions and additions that have accompanied the 'kiss and quarrel' between Jamaican creole and standard English over the centuries, with each language undergoing development and transformation in its own right. As Dr Christie notes:

All languages are subject to change over time and space.

The teaching of English, and teaching in English, that Africans in Jamaica were subjected to was not matched by the teaching of African languages, let alone teaching in African languages. The assumption that by superimposing a new language you would displace people's formative language, the language in which they learnt to construct their world and share their innermost feelings, the language they must negotiate in order to communicate with their ancestors, their deities, and with one another was bizarre, even for imperialists with their unmatchable arrogance.

My task today is to establish the connections between the issues Dr Christie addresses in her book and the dilemmas confronting us here in the second African diaspora. If you have not yet read the book, do so this weekend while these thoughts I am sharing with you are still near the front of your mind.

I want to consider briefly four main themes:

1. Caribbean languages in schooling and education
2. Caribbean languages in the identity formation of British born children of African heritage, and the relevance of that for learning and self development
3. Caribbean languages as the first language of adults in their interface with social institutions, and with other language groups in the society
4. The possible influence on the British situation of the way Jamaica finally resolves the national language issue, and especially the place of Jamaican creole in formal education

Caribbean languages in schooling and education

A major concern to education practitioners like myself over the last four decades has been the insistence on the part of education policy makers and providers, from nursery schools to Universities, that the languages spoken by Caribbean people and their descendants are simply differing versions of broken or bad English, with varying levels of desecration of 'the language of the Crown' and the symbol of British influence across the world.

In this respect, as in many others some of which I will mention, British attitudes to the creoles and patios of Caribbean people in Britain were simply a more extreme and ill-informed version of that which was prevalent within and across most of the Caribbean countries themselves. Contrast that with British attitudes to speakers of languages other than English from other backgrounds (e.g.: Chinese, Bangladeshi, Pakistani, Indian, Turkish and more recently Somali). Local education authorities encouraged and funded the development of community provision to teach the mother tongue to children in those groups. Teachers were and are actively encouraged to see those children's first language and their acquisition of proficiency in that language as pivotal to their learning of English as an additional language and their access to the curriculum. Their mother tongue was readily acknowledged and vested with worth and importance for their sense of well being and self confidence. It was widely acknowledged that if children were simply allowed to straddle both languages, lacking confidence and proficiency in either, there would be major consequences for their identity formation and their capacity to perform to the best of their ability.

Prior to becoming the Director of Education and Leisure Services in Hackney in 1989, I worked with the Inner London Education Authority in the late 1980s as Assistant Education Officer and Head of Community Education. In that capacity, I had responsibility for grants to voluntary organizations. The ILEA funded a plethora of mother tongue teaching projects across London and actively encouraged their growth. Polish, Chinese, Greek, Turkish, Bangladeshi, Gujarati, and other community based projects received sustained funding for the promotion of 'mother tongue' teaching. It also funded black supplementary schools that were focused as much on identity building as on tackling academic underachievement of black children in mainstream schools. Few of those schools, however, had the acquisition and preservation of 'nation'/mother tongue languages as their primary focus

Despite the large and growing number of speakers of Caribbean languages across the ILEA, Jamaican heritage children in particular, no attempt was made to formally validate those languages which, at best, were considered to be 'dialects' or, at worst, corruptions of standard English that had become part and parcel of popular usage over time.

But, as they say, charity begins at home. If we as a people were ambivalent about the provenance and centrality of our own languages, if we were hotly disputing whether or not what we spoke and, increasingly, wrote as part of our cultural and artistic expression could properly be called 'languages', what messages were we sending out to the education system about how it should regard the languages our children presented in school and college?

In a social and political system that had a tendency to stereotype us massively as a matter of course, it was to be expected that that situation would lead to us being seen as the problem, no less than the manner of our speaking and writing.

That is despite the fact that throughout the 1970s, people like me ran classes at the ILEA Centre for Urban Educational Studies at Aberdeen Park in Islington, in which we helped white teachers and black to come to an understanding of the origins, basis, and structure of the languages spoken by Caribbean children in London's schools. We were assisted in that by the work of a number of people whose historical contribution must be noted. New Beacon Books, the first black publishing house in Britain reproduced *The Theory and Practice of Creole Grammar* by John Jacob Thomas. That publication, in 1969, marked the 100th anniversary of the first publication of the book.

Then there was the ground-breaking work of Louise Bennett (Miss Lou), a cultural activist, teacher, poet, performer, who dedicated her life to reclaiming and validating the Jamaican language and helping the speakers of the language, and everyone else, to understand its roots and structure and its spiritual connectedness with the very core and essence of the people of Jamaica.

Frederic Cassidy and Robert Le Page researched the language and its usage over many years and were able to identify the African retentions in the language, retentions that could be identified in all other aspects of the lives of the Jamaican people, from spirituality to culture, religion, medicine, agriculture, cuisine, and economic activity. Cassidy and Le Page first published their influential book *A Dictionary of Jamaican English* in 1967.

The late Andrew Salkey, and Kamau Brathwaite built upon that body of knowledge, making their own significant contribution to our understanding of 'nation language' and of the 'voice' in our expression of our fullest selves. Salkey was a mentor to the young Linton Kwesi Johnson who has since done more than most through his own poetry, recordings, and writings to demonstrate not only the authenticity of Jamaican creole as a language in its own right, but also the fact that Jamaicans, like most other Caribbean people are bilingual speakers, often moving between two registers with consummate ease, moving between Jamaican creole and standard English.

I need hardly remind this audience of the scandalous practice of shunting masses of black children into schools for the educationally subnormal, principally because of language issues and the assumptions that were made about children's potential performance because of their speaking and writing. When their frustration with the way they were being treated, including teachers' refusal or incapacity to help them make the transition from their first language to the language of the classroom, led to certain inappropriate behaviours, that simply helped to confirm teachers' views of those children as unteachable or as having varying degrees of learning difficulties, from moderate to excessive.

Despite all the theory about how children learn, about differentiation (popularly known as 'personalized learning' these days), about mixed ability grouping and much else besides, the fact still remains that teachers spend 75% of their time on average talking at children. The other 25% is spent either not listening to them, not actually seeing some of them, or hearing and responding to but a few of them. Given that scenario, the possibility of the average teacher understanding how children actually learn is in my view very remote.

What I do know is that the tendency to attribute poor educational performance among Caribbean heritage children to the way they speak, and the influence of their speech on their writing skills, has taken on a new lease of life. Schools have begun to focus to a much greater extent recently on the assumed link between underachievement and the use of what is variously called 'patois', 'dialect', 'black talk', 'street talk', and 'slang'. The Government's 'Aiming High' initiative, intended to help raise the achievement of Caribbean heritage children, is leading more and more schools to target their language as well as their dress and other aspects of their life style. There appears to be very little evidence, however, of the schooling system (or, indeed, those children and their parents themselves) acknowledging the need to assist Caribbean heritage children in making the transition from their spoken language to standard English, validating the former and using it as a lever to support the development of the latter.

Some schools go as far as prohibiting the use of Caribbean languages, Jamaican creole especially, while children are in school. This in my view is nothing short of oppressive and is potentially deeply damaging. In terms of theories of teaching and learning, that practice seems particularly absurd as the best speakers of other languages are people who are confident in their own language and take the self confidence that that engenders to the learning of the other language(s). If children are being told 'your language is rubbish, it is getting in the way of your progress, it helps us and the society stereotype you as unsophisticated and unable to communicate in a manner acceptable to the majority of the society, it prevents you from learning to speak and write proper English, so suppress it and don't let me hear it or see you write it', it is questionable how they could then be expected to be the confident learners and achievers the schools are seeking to produce.

The 1974 Bullock report argued the case for talk as a teaching and learning strategy, i.e., the encouragement of talk between teacher and students and among groups of students. Bullock used the phrase:

Talking oneself into understanding

'Talk' in the context of teaching and learning has many advantages. It allows students to engage, using the language that they feel most comfortable with to demonstrate their levels of understanding, to express their views, share their emotions, etc. It also allows the teacher and their peers to help them develop strategies of mediation between the students' first language/mother tongue and standard English, especially as, for many students, creole or patois remains the principal means of communication in their home and among their peers.

Teachers have access to an increasing range of material written in the first language of Caribbean students that could help those students develop an awareness of the language in its written form and of being bilingual if not multilingual. We have all come across Caribbean students who regard themselves as bilingual, with high level skills in French, German, Spanish, and even Russian, but who would not consider the creole they speak as one more language in their repertoire. Such students in my view must be encouraged to be ambassadors for the validation of our languages and their formal and informal usage.

Moreover, rather than focusing solely on Caribbean children, their language base and home backgrounds, the schooling system should examine the skills teachers bring to the task of facilitating the learning of such children so as to help develop in them rounded communication skills in speech, writing, and the use of information and communication technology. An abiding problem for the schooling system, however, is the fact that many teachers themselves have been poorly served by their own schooling in respect of writing and speaking skills.

Teachers (including Caribbean heritage teachers) often argue that no two speakers and writers of Jamaican, Trinidad or Dominican creole could agree on the precise spelling of certain commonly used words and phrases and, therefore, it is difficult to standardize usage and find enough common elements in terms of structure, vocabulary, and syntax to constitute a language. While it is undoubtedly the case that Caribbean creoles have developed and been sustained much more through the medium of a rich oral tradition than through texts and the formal teaching of the language, the fact remains that generation after generation has preserved a language with identifiable characteristics and agreed usage, a language in which children become socialized, and through which they identify themselves and the language group to which they belong.

Caribbean languages, identity formation and self-development and learning

In the briefing document for the Mayor of London's Commission on African and Asian Heritage, Naseem Khan writes as follows:

A sense of heritage – who we are and where we have come from – gives us all a sense of identity. It contributes to a feeling of value and self-respect: for individuals and for a society too. It empowers, creates respect and unites. One-sided versions of heritage that focus on only a few selected aspects impoverish us all.

Language is crucial to black students' understanding of their African heritage and of the role of the first and succeeding diaspora in the formation of the creoles they now speak. This is important if only because Caribbean languages in Britain in the post-war period have borrowed extensively from one another. Theatre and music no less than electronic media have propelled that mix in myriad ways, from the international reach of the resistance language of reggae and of the Rastafarian movement, to soca and kaiso, to rap and hip-hop, to 'house' and 'garage', and to the work of people such as Alex Pascall, Abdul Malik Decoteau, Merle Collins, Paul Keens-Douglas, the late Mikey Smith, Linton Kwesi Johnson, Errol Lloyd, Benjamin Zephaniah, John Agard, Grace Nichols, and Marc Matthews, CLR James, Sam Selvon, Andrew Salkey, David Dabydeen among others.

Caribbean people in Britain are still being defined in terms of 'race' some sixty years after the beginning of mass migration from the Caribbean to the UK. Terms such as 'ethnic minority' have replaced 'second generation' and 'third generation immigrant'. 'Britishness' is therefore seen as having to do principally with whiteness. Everybody else is an 'ethnic minority', British born and bred or not. And one distinguishing feature of their ethnic minority status is that of language.

I find it galling to hear statistics reeling off the tongues of commentators that pointedly juxtapose the high levels of achievement of 'ethnic minority' students that joined the schooling system comparatively recently 'with no knowledge of English' with the relative underachievement of Caribbean boys and girls born in Britain. While there are other factors that go to explain these differentials, I believe the system here continues to miss the point with regard to the status of black children in the British education system.

Dr Christie reminds us of a fact that this education system has acknowledged for a very long time, hence its support for the languages of other ethnic groups, i.e., that:

Children learn best in the language with which they are familiar.

The symbiotic relationship between having your language valued, and commensurately having worth and respect given to the group who are carriers of that language, and from whom you learn it as your first language, and developing a positive self image and a confidence in your communication cannot be underestimated.

For one thing, it gives you the confidence with which to approach other languages, including standard English, and to take responsibility for your own learning. This is as true for speakers of Yoruba, Hausa, Ashanti, and the other West African languages that are the first language of a growing number of children in London's schools, as it has been for the children from the Indian sub-continent, China, Hong Kong, and elsewhere whose mother tongue the ILEA and Greater London LEAs sought to help them acquire.

Caribbean languages as the first language of adults in their interface with social institutions and with other language groups in the society

The importance of acknowledging that Caribbean people speak languages other than English, but that have a resemblance to English, is perhaps best illustrated in the conversations that groups of speakers of the same language have amongst themselves, and the difficulties many experience when they attempt to communicate in formal settings such as with doctors and dentists, civil servants, post office workers, people in the criminal justice system and in further education.

Serious misunderstandings frequently occur which could easily lead to life threatening situations, especially where doctors are involved. Caribbean adults who communicate in creole, whether derived from English or French, have more difficulty, generally, in switching from their first language to standard English than their British born children and grandchildren. This is especially the case in situations where people are anxious or agitated. Even speakers who are fluent in standard English have a tendency to reach for the creole when they are agitated.

It is for that reason that in the 1970s the British police took steps to equip their officers and staff with 'pocket guides' to assist them in their dealings with Jamaicans as the largest Caribbean language group in Britain's black population. Imagine the scenario. A police officer proclaims with the full authority of the law:

You are not obliged to say anything, but anything you do say will be taken down and may be used in evidence against you

The reaction of some people would be: You're going to give me a ticket anyway, so why don't you just get on with it and let me go about my business. For others, however, especially if they are already none too pleased about being stopped, or about not being listened to, the reaction could be to rattle off some Jamaican/Barbadian/Trinidadian creole which the police officer could make neither head nor tail of.

Sitting as a freelance journalist in magistrates' courts up and down the land, I found it hilarious to hear the police relay to the court what black defendants, Jamaican and Barbadian especially, were alleged to have said. To say that the police were creative in their recording of Caribbean language use in their interface with black communities would be an understatement.

Nowhere is this exemplified more than in the case of the late George Lindo, a Jamaican worker in Bradford, West Yorkshire, who was arrested in 1977 for holding up a betting shop at knifepoint. Lindo was charged, convicted and given a five year jail sentence. His conviction was secured on the basis of an alleged confession he made to the police on interrogation. Lindo argued his innocence from the outset and was emphatic that the confession was extracted under duress. He appealed against his conviction and sentence and set out to prove that the police record of his 'confession' was a complete fabrication. Lindo was fluent in his use of Jamaican creole and made no secret of the fact that while he could make himself understood in standard English, that was not the language in which he was most proficient. He certainly did not switch between the two with any ease.

Working at the University of Bradford at the time, I was a member of the 'Bradford Black Collective', sister organization of the London-based 'Race Today Collective', and the convener of the Black Parents Movement, Manchester. Against the background of the work I had been doing with Teachers Centres in the ILEA, I offered to do an analysis of the 'confession' the police had used in Court as being a verbatim record of what George Lindo had told them.

Using the University's facilities, I got George Lindo to read, to write, and to engage in a conversation with me. I then analysed his language use, his choice of vocabulary, turns of phrase and the grammatical patterns in his writing and speech. A similar analysis was done of the 'confession' the police had written and got him to sign. The discrepancies between the two were so great and so fundamental that serious questions needed to be asked about the so-called confession itself, the manner in which it was extracted, and the circumstances that led to George Lindo signing it.

Come the appeal, Lindo's barrister was able to demonstrate that the police evidence was bogus and that George Lindo had been framed as he had claimed from the very beginning. Lindo was duly acquitted, having already spent eighteen months in Armley Gaol. He later received compensation from the Crown for wrongful arrest and false imprisonment.

It would clearly be ridiculous to ask speakers of English as a second language, such as George Lindo, to abandon their first language. Similarly, it is iniquitous to encourage their children and grandchildren to see them as backward and stupid because they do not communicate in standard English. But that is precisely what the schooling system is in danger of doing when schools insist that children should abandon the language they acquire in the home because, to quote one secondary school headteacher, 'it gets in the way of them learning to speak and write *properly*'.

That headteacher was concerned, also, that Caribbean heritage students were 'increasingly using their brand of talk to exclude teachers and to engage in unhelpful encounters with their peers'. That school identified their language both as a language of protest and resistance, and as a reflection of their 'backwardness and lack of ambition'. In the headteacher's words: 'if we are to motivate them to higher levels of achievement, we must get them to abandon that way of speaking and to understand that it is against their educational interest to continue to communicate in that way. What is worse is that many of them write as they speak and therefore their written work is appalling'.

The 'problem' with the language, therefore, is that it is seen as having no legitimacy in itself, but rather as a tool of resistance, bolstering the 'attitude' that Caribbean heritage learners, boys especially, are thought to have. As such, it must be outlawed in the same way as their trainers, their hooded jackets and their baseball caps.

Adult Education services in most large cities with a significant black population have recognized the language strengths of black adult learners since the early 1970s and, in the 1980s particularly, developed a number of projects to celebrate

Caribbean languages and language speakers, and to aid their acquisition of skills in written and spoken standard English. Caribbean language and literacy projects in the ILEA and in Manchester did some pioneering work in this area, as did the National Institute of Adult Continuing Education more recently.

Some of that work has served to restore worth and esteem to speakers of Caribbean languages, not least by enabling them to share that vast repository of knowledge the older generations have as a consequence of their 'life experience with Britain', both in the Caribbean and here in the UK. The projects validated them as writers, and as teachers and instructors, and validated the language(s) in which they communicated. They had the confidence to teach other adults, to share their knowledge with school children in their classes, and to write their stories. Above all, they had the thrill of seeing themselves in print.

The schooling system has been much less creative and respectful. Worse yet, some schools came to believe that there was no point in developing the 'literacy hour' and trying to push up standards in literacy in primary and secondary schooling if children were 'being encouraged to speak badly and to write as badly as they speak'. Some schools used the home languages of Caribbean heritage children imaginatively and helped develop confident bilingual learners, especially through the medium of poetry and creative writing. Others have combined that with music making, through rap, hip hop and song writing. In the main, however, the schooling system both at local authority and national level, has failed to deal with the issue of language and Caribbean heritage learners.

Schools are always eager to point out that, notwithstanding the above arguments, 'our black parents support the stance of the school as they want their children to be effective communicators and to hold their own in any profession in this country. They don't want them to be limited in their choices because all they know is how to speak patois and the language of the street'.

As a Director of Education, I received letters from irate black parents who took great offence at the pieces of creative writing some of their children brought home in which creole was used liberally. Those parents demanded to know what I was going to do about it, because that is not what they were sending their children to school for. They wanted them to be taught proper English. Invariably and ironically, those letters were written very confidently in the sort of Jamaican creole that would have made headteachers cringe, albeit it was the only language available to those parents. Alas, the parents writing them failed to see the irony of that.

All of this, in my view, is an indication of the fact that there has not been a mature debate of this thorny issue either within our own communities or in education circles. As a result, not only are many Caribbean heritage children being penalized and judged wrongly for the way they speak and write, black parents are themselves so frustrated by the persistent levels of underachievement amongst Caribbean heritage children that they themselves are buying in to the theory that the very language they themselves speak and have taught their children is contributing to that underachievement.

This has enormous implications for the future of Caribbean languages in Britain, especially if schools succeed, aided and abetted by black parents, in getting Caribbean heritage children to abandon the language they were hearing even before they learnt to speak.

Statistics show that for every child born of two Caribbean parents, there is one born of a union between a Caribbean parent and a white parent. This means that some children of dual (Caribbean/English) heritage would be lucky if one of their parents is able not just to speak a Caribbean language but to make the link between that language and their origins in the Caribbean, in Africa and (in the case of Caribbean Indians) the Indian sub-continent.

Should it be a condition of claiming Britishness that the very roots of one's being, the language of your ancestors that shapes your thought processes, that links you spiritually with your people and with your past, that remains the 'nation language' of the people in the places from which your forebears migrated, should it be a condition of claiming Britishness that that language is obliterated altogether? Should British born black children, dual heritage or not, be encouraged to see their black grandparents as backward and un-educated because of the way they communicate?

To deny people their language is to deny them their history and 'a people without a knowledge of their history are a people without roots'. It is in the interest of older Caribbean people to find ways of keeping Caribbean languages alive and of sustaining and validating them in a manner that makes for the personal and cultural rootedness of their offspring and of future generations. That means that we must all, young and old alike, engage the Government and the schooling system in a meaningful debate about the damage that has been done over the years and continues to be done through the neglect of Caribbean languages and the very denial of their existence except as 'bad English' .

The possible influence on the British situation of the way Jamaica finally resolves the national language issue and especially the place of Jamaican creole in formal education

Over the last three decades, there has been a debate in Caribbean countries about what has been variously called 'the national language question', the 'formalization of creole', 'creole in the school curriculum', 'nation language as the official language', etc. Indeed, the work of academics and socio-linguists such as Professor Hubert Devonish and Dr Pauline Christie in Caribbean countries with English and French derived creoles has helped to focus the attention of governments on the key question of language in the Caribbean, past, present and future.

The question of the place of Jamaican creole in formal education in Jamaica is currently exercising that nation, and the way in which it is finally resolved is likely to have an impact on the decisions that other Caribbean countries make.

Notably, there is much less debate about the issue of Caribbean languages in educational circles in the UK currently than there was twenty years ago, although the link being established between black underachievement in schooling and the use of Caribbean languages makes such a debate more necessary now. I believe, however, that inasmuch as the influence of Jamaican creole in the UK as in the USA is considerably greater than that of the languages of the other Caribbean nations, the status of that language and of other Caribbean languages in the UK will be seriously enhanced by the decision Jamaica makes about the role of 'nation language' in the life of that nation.

Conclusion

I welcome the fact that the issue of Caribbean languages is back on the agenda in such a focused way and that conferences such as these by Jamaica 2K are being organized once again.

Many of us have wrestled with these issues in schools, colleges, community education, and higher education for decades. If I have a fear it is that new groups of migrant settlers will make sure their issues are addressed by the State and would take care of their business to the obvious advantage of their children, while we continue to be seen as congenitally unable, and as the 'almost' people. Almost making it in the schooling system, … but not quite. With languages that almost qualify for recognition as languages, first second or third, … but not quite. With languages that are almost validated in print and could be included in the national curriculum and in examination syllabuses, … but not quite.

Meanwhile, our young people continue to be ungrounded, uprooted from their history and the language and customs of their people, estranged from their spiritual selves and, increasingly, falling for anything and anyone because they stand for nothing. We render ourselves weak and valueless; we invite the disrespect of a cynical and manipulative system and we risk displacing future generations from any connectedness with their past by not attending to these issues in a serious and concerted manner, making alliances with progressive people of any ethnicity as our struggle demands.

For those reasons, I want to welcome Dr Christie once again and thank her for the insights and direction she and other colleagues, such as Professor Hubert Devonish, continue to provide to us on this side of the water.

I trust that all here will find the conference a stimulating learning experience and will each commit to the action that is necessary in our own cause, in our communities, and in relation to Government, after this conference.

6.0

INTERCULTURAL LEARNING, THE KNOWLEDGE ECONOMY AND DEMOCRATIC CITIZENSHIP

Introduction

Further and Higher Education institutions across the British Isles are recruiting international students in unprecedented numbers, especially from China, and in an increasingly competitive market. Coincidentally, many of those students find themselves the subject of equality and diversity programmes that have domestic students as their primary focus. There is as yet little evidence that the presence of that sizeable body of international students, predominantly from Asia, Africa, the Middle East and Europe, gives rise to programmes of intercultural learning. Indeed, focus group discussions with such students across a number of Universities have revealed that what they desire, more than anything else, is to be left alone to get on with the business for which they came and for which they pay so handsomely.

Promoting international and intercultural education remains high on the agenda of a number of bodies. Papers in this section were presented at the request of a couple such organizations, namely, the Council on International Educational Exchange (CIEE) and the Institute for International Cooperation of the German Adult Education Association (IIZ/DW). Founded in the United States in 1947, CIEE was set up to restore student exchange after World War II and give students educational experiences abroad. The 1988 CIEE report, *Educating for Global Competence: The Report of the Advisory Council for International*

Educational Exchange, made four recommendations, one of which was:

Special efforts should be made to identify and encourage both students from underrepresented academic and social groups and students with leadership ability, to incorporate study abroad in their academic programs, and to do so in a greater range of subjects.   (CIEE, 1991)

That recommendation underscored the growing concern in higher education in the United States about 'how to deal with diversity issues'. CIEE's 1990 report, *A National Mandate for Education Abroad: Getting On With the Task*, stated:

Efforts to expand the number of undergraduates who study abroad must address the lack of diversity among them. Traditionally, American study abroad students have come from affluent, middle or upper class, white, professional families rather than the broad spectrum of American society.   (CIEE, 1991)

In November 1990, CIEE held its 43rd International Conference on Educational Exchange, *Black Students and Overseas Programs: Broadening the Base of Participation*, in Charleston, South Carolina.

'International Comparative Approaches to the Problems of Underrepresented Groups'[1] (6.1) examines the issue of underrepresentation from several perspectives, including the low participation of black students in educational exchange programs, their absence on high level courses in higher education and the somewhat insulated experience such students have in their host institutions which, typically, are themselves disengaged from the black and ethnic minority communities round about them.

The considerable experience the higher education sector has of educational exchange over many decades should prepare it for a more effective and meaningful engagement with international students. It would seem, however, that inasmuch as that experience did not encompass some of the issues to do with building a genuinely inclusive curriculum and seeing the overseas students as having a contribution to make to that, and the intersection of such students and their interests with those of black and ethnic minority domestic students, those issues remain a challenge when it comes to responding appropriately to the needs of that growing population of international students.

In 1998, the new Blair Government took up the Presidency of the European Union. In keeping with its prioritizing of 'education, education, education', the Government organized a pan-European conference in Manchester in May of that year, entitled, *The Learning Age: Towards a Europe of Knowledge*. The Government launched its Green Paper, *The Learning Age – A Renaissance for a New Britain* at that conference and invited responses to it.

'The Learning Age – Towards a Europe of knowledge' (6.2) sought to provide a critique not just of the Green Paper but of the range of assumptions upon which the Government's vision of a 'Europe of Knowledge' was built. The paper highlights the absence of a perspective on 'race' in Government policy, and on racism as a dynamic factor in the processes of social exclusion that many black people in the society experience. It calls for a definition of the rights of disadvantaged and marginalized groups, and signposts the historical role of lifelong learning in opening up opportunities and combating social exclusion for such groups. It points to a wider purpose for learning and education than simply equipping people with skills for the workplace and for individual advancement. It suggests, rather, that part of the 'knowledge' we need in the new Europe is the knowledge and understanding of the roots and the persistence of racial and social injustice in society, and of the tools with which we could combat both, acting individually and collectively.

The paper argues for European programmes to fund support groups and campaigns in black communities in Britain and continental Europe that are targeted against neo-fascist activities and racial murders. It calls for a focus on the educational needs of offenders in prisons and young offender institutions, and for transition programmes in communities to assist with their rehabilitation, skills development, and re-entry into the labour market. The paper invites the Government to acknowledge the role of formal, non-formal, and informal adult education in the rapid expansion of social movements and trade union basic education in the previous five decades.

Reaction to the paper was as positive as it was negative. There were at the conference various attempts to 'shoot the messenger' for being decidedly 'off message'. Some delegates expressed the view that 'having just emerged from under the heavy yoke of Thatcherism', the message in the paper was being delivered in the wrong place, at the wrong time and to the wrong people. Suffice it to say that eight years of Blair Government have not diminished my enthusiasm for the message. The message, after all, was aimed not only at Tessa Blackstone, David Blunkett, Kim Howells and other members of the Blair administration present. It was also aimed at the French, the Belgians, the Germans, and all those other Europeans in attendance, who were failing to come to terms with their black settler populations in much the same way that Britain was. It was not a case, therefore, of choosing to wash Britain's dirty linen in public. Rather, it was reminding that audience that as 'we are all Europeans now', in the same way that at the level of nation states they could be having these conversations, those settler communities confronting racism, xenophobia and marginalization in the European Union had a right to be facilitated to collectivize their struggles, share knowledge, influence the way Government treats them, and use education as a force for liberation.

The Council of Europe established its Project on Education for Democratic Citizenship in the 1990s. It established 'sites of citizenship' in the various member states, facilitating the organization of communities and the development and practice of the skills and capacities necessary for citizenship participation.

'Citizenship Participation: New Skills and Capacities' (6.3) sought to clarify for participants in the Project and community activists in 'sites of citizenship' what the practice of citizenship might mean in countries where the rights and privileges that accompany the legal definition of 'citizen' are denied to sections of the population, as well as in countries that do not grant the status of 'citizen' to those or/and other sections of their population. The paper argues that the re-ordering of power in communities and the goal of mobilizing diverse communities of interest to work together for common ends, require the development of a range of tools for analysis and for practice. It concludes that empowering the individual to develop his/her full capacity to act in a self-directing way and to take collective action with others is at the heart of the process of managing a democratic culture.

In June 2005, the National Institute of Adult Continuing Education (NIACE), hosted a symposium in collaboration with Network Intercultural Learning in Europe (NILE), bringing together adult education practitioners and academics from across the UK and continental Europe,. 'The NILE Symposium – Intercultural learning and adult education'[2] (6.4) set out to answer the question: what is lifelong learning for, and what in the context of the new Europe is the function of intercultural learning. It explores notions of intercultural and of multicultural approaches to learning and argues that intercultural learning should have as much of a focus on intra-cultural learning within and across cultures within individual nation states themselves, as on cultures between states.

The paper warns against divorcing 'culture' from politics, and from the struggle for rights and for equality and social justice. It argues against a fixed and essentialist view of culture and of adult education practice which reinforces that view. It points to the need for adult education to make full use of advances in new technology and empower people across nation states to make their own media, link their cultural and educational activities, create their own cultural industries, and build independent social and cultural movements.

1. First appeared in CIEE (1991) Black Students and Overseas Programs: Broadening the Base of Participation, CiEE, New York
2. First appeared in Beate Schmidt-Behlau. ed. (2005) Adult Education Embracing Diversity II – Developing Strategies for Mainstreaming Intercultural Learning Based on Needs and Experiences, Institute for Internal Cooperation of the German Adult Education Association

6.1

INTERNATIONAL COMPARATIVE APPROACHES TO THE PROBLEMS OF UNDERREPRESENTED GROUPS

Charleston, South Carolina
7-9 November 1990

I wish to bring to this discussion my experience as a student in the Caribbean and in Britain, as a teacher and lecturer who for many years endeavored to influence the content and delivery of curriculum, and institutional approaches to 'foreign', or 'overseas' students, and as the chairman of a black parents movement campaigning for black education rights.

In this brief presentation, I will attempt to do three things:
1. To examine briefly the issue of underrepresentation
2. To focus on the organization of programmes and their orientation
3. To indicate what the role of underrepresented groups might be in relation to international education

It might be something of an understatement to suggest that the educational environment, internationally, is extremely volatile right now, and in some countries it has been so for the last decade. It is significant, for example, if local polls are to be believed, that in a large number of states in yesterday's elections in this country, education ranked higher in voters' concerns than did the Persian Gulf Crisis or the US budget deficit.

The volatility of the international economic situation, and debates about the relationship between education and the national economy, as well as recent events in world politics, have a direct bearing on the issues of international education and the participation of underrepresented groups.

Black Students and Overseas Programmes

In the first place there is the issue of how certain nations in the developing world and their history and politics are represented not just in and through the media, but also in the popular consciousness of the nation states of the West. The economies and social and political systems of these nations are invariably projected as inferior or deficient, no less than are their literary and cultural traditions, and their religious practices.

I consider it to be one of life's supreme ironies that a nation such as the United States of America which has appropriated to itself the task of policing the world, is so intensely parochial and provincial that its people do not, on the whole, establish a relationship between its internal policy and its global strategy. At the most basic level, the majority of the people on whose behalf that policing function is supposedly taking place, have not an earthly clue about where the countries are that are being thus policed, let alone about the ordinary citizens of those places, their economy, their hopes, or their aspirations.

With the prospect of a war in the Persian Gulf, attention is focused in a serious way for the first time since the Vietnam War on the issue of blacks in the United States armed forces, why they are represented in such large numbers, and why that section of the American population time and again takes such a high casualty toll in these external conflicts. People of the African diaspora in the United States suffer a variety of forms of human rights violations, an implosion of violence within their communities, and levels of poverty and degradation that amount to the total brutalization of the human spirit. Underrepresentation, underachievement, and barriers to access serve as powerful incentives to join the armed forces. It has become the most open manifestation of the so-called open society. It unites, under the wings of the eagle, a body of people who are often called upon to go in and 'kick the butt' of folk who are often struggling to put an end to the very marginalization and dehumanization from which they themselves sought to escape by joining the US Armed Forces.

As a Grenadian, being in South Carolina has a particular poignancy for me both because of its history in the making of the African diaspora, and because I am still trying to get my head around the spectacle of black Americans dropping from the sky via the 82nd Airborne Battalion to kill indiscriminately my loved ones under the guise of coming to rescue and protect. It was from these very shores that they left for the invasion of Grenada in October 1983.

In the second place, there is the issue of the growing population of students in Europe and North America who are refugees or asylum seekers, and who are having to adjust to educational systems which demonstrate very little if any understanding of their political realities and their support needs, and which see them as beholden consumers of curriculum rather than potential contributors to curriculum.

The Council on International Educational Exchange is clearly committed to addressing the issue of underrepresentation in respect both of regions that are poorly represented, and of disciplines that do not participate on an international scale.

Underrepresentation

I wish to examine the issue of underrepresentation directly in the context of Britain and continental Europe, and to do so from three interlocking perspectives:

1. the underrepresentation of certain groups within the country itself in its higher education programmes, and of certain curricula in schools, colleges and universities
2. the marginalization of the black presence and of the struggles waged by black people in an attempt to correct that underrepresentation and to interpret the British educational system to itself
3. the underrepresentation of black groups in educational exchange programmes both as participants going abroad, and as groups whose marginalization is further reinforced by not having what they do taken into account in educational programmes arranged by host countries for participating visitors

In Britain it is still the case that the overwhelming majority of black students in higher education institutions are from overseas. There is a direct correlation between that phenomenon and the low number of British students staying on into further education beyond the age of 16, as well as the abiding problem of massive underachievement of British-born black students, especially those of African, African-Caribbean, and Bangladeshi parentage.

The consequences of this for the levels of motivation of black children entering and progressing through the schooling system, for the lack of participation of the underachieving groups in the local and national economy, or participation at predictably low levels, are matters that urgently need a higher profile on the local and international education agenda. So, too, is the overrepresentation of those groups in the alternative economy of drugs and prostitution, and in the custodial institutions of the state.

There are in Britain, and across continental Europe, communities of underrepresented groups serving commercial and industrial centres in much the same way that the South African townships serve Johannesburg and Pretoria. The suggestion that we all in the UK should be issued with identity cards in the new Europe, such as 'aliens' now carry in France, completes the South African analogy in a manner which black people, at least, consider politically suicidal.

In Britain, as elsewhere, education is and needs to remain high on the agenda of those marginalized and displaced groups. So much so that our communities, African and Asian, develop our own community-based institutions, supplementary schools operating on weekdays and weekends, Saturday schools, summer schools, and full time education projects.

In response to the underrepresentation at the level of curriculum, we have developed bookstores and publishing houses, creative writing workshops, and opportunities for those of us who have been through the formal education system, including higher education, and come out the other end without forgetting where we started – and without forgetting those who have not yet arrived at the starting post – to give and to share, and to build our communities. We encourage schools and higher education institutions to acquire books and other learning resources from our bookstores and our education projects and to use them in the curriculum. Above all we seek to influence the way the curriculum is constructed and its content organized.

Fundamental to the question of race and education, or even of multicultural education, is the issue of epistemology. Hegemonic approaches to the construction of knowledge and the development of ideas have been at the very core of the debate on race in education, and on Eurocentric approaches to knowledge and to learning. Who legitimizes and validates, who includes as acceptable and authentic, and who excludes as peripheral, primitive, or worthless? The epistemological question is for me more paramount an issue in international education than the readily acceptable and much less problematic goal of promoting international understanding.

A related issue is that of mainstream education versus the rest, and the interests that are served by the organization of mainstream education by the various nation states across the world. In each nation state, the mainstream represents the views, the values, the predispositions and the cultural supremacist assumptions of the minority dominant class. The majority, i.e., the workers and labourers, peasants, and the millions of functionally illiterate people are seen as having the role of consumers of the mainstream product, with only a marginal contribution to be made from inside their own experience.

In the context of the United States, stalwarts like W.E.B DuBois, Booker T. Washington, Fredrick Douglass, Fannie Lou Hamer, Harriet Tubman, and more recently people such as Richard Wright, Ralph Ellison, and numerous others have sought to deal with the epistemological question and the issue of hegemony. Against that historical backdrop and the growth of the black studies movement in the United States and in Britain, campaigns have developed around the notion of a curriculum of inclusion.

In Britain, despite the considerable shifts in focus that have come about in the last two decades as a result of projects around multicultural and antiracist education, there is nevertheless a massive detachment from, and ignorance of, the history of the post-war black presence in Britain on the part of young black people themselves. Our political advances, our political defeats, our influence on the whole political economy of race in Britain, and our impact on the very character of the society are matters about which young black people going through the British education system (let alone white ones) are predominantly ignorant.

This is remarkable not because it is a matter of choice in curriculum terms, but because the displacement of that awareness effectively handicaps the very people who need to continue struggling to assert their fundamental rights and civic entitlements in the face of structural and institutional forms of racism within the society.

If education and schooling is preparing them for citizenship and for life, if education and training is preparing them for a place in the economic reconstruction of Britain, then surely they have as much, if not more, to gain from an understanding of their continuity with that history, and with those struggles, than from much of what passes for curriculum in their everyday schooling experience.

This brings me to the second of my three aspects of underrepresentation: the marginalization of the black presence and of the struggles waged by black people in British society in the last five decades. The Educational Reform Act of 1988, by far the most comprehensive review of British education since the 1944 Education Act, failed completely to address the issue of race. It was not just an omission. It was a deliberate dismissal of some twenty-five years of organized activity by black communities and progressive white teachers, local councils, academics, etc., on the issue of race in education and schooling. That self-organization, linked to disturbing inner city revolts and the panic those insurrections engendered, has given rise to a number of policies and programmes in education that are geared to social control and managing the crisis in the inner cities rather than to ensuring access, progression and desirable outcomes to all those underrepresented black people with the same entitlement to education as anyone else.

How was it possible for Secretary of State for Education,

Kenneth Baker, and his eminent body of advisors to hijack and render null and void that mature movement in education around the issue of racial equality and social justice, without LEAs, the National Curriculum Council, and a range of other quasi-governmental organizations insisting on keeping the issue on their political and policy agenda? Could it be because the quest for racial equality and social justice in the context of education, its administration, and service delivery was, and is seen as, a somewhat peripheral and diversionary pastime of those sufficiently misled or subversive to pursue it – in other words – a suspect and marginalized concern about primarily marginalized if not suspect people?

For me, educational opportunities in the 1990s mean educational opportunities in Britain as well as in Europe in the 1990s. This raises the issue of identity not in the xenophobic way that Nicholas Ridley, Margaret Thatcher, and the self-proclaiming procurators of 'our national sovereignty' have posed it, but in the spectre that Norman Tebbit conjures up by asking us to apply the cricket test. In other words, who are 'we the British?'. What is the concept of britishness that resides in the popular consciousness and in the minds of education policy makers and practitioners? When will the concept of 'Britishness equals whiteness', equals Christianity, equals born in South Africa, Australia, New Zealand and Zimbabwe of expatriate white British grandparents and great grandparents ... when will that concept cease to determine people's entitlement to civic, educational and political opportunities in the society?

Providing educational opportunities in the 1990s, therefore, needs to be approached in the context of the underrepresentation of black groups in higher education within the European states, and of certain curricula in schools, colleges, and universities. Similarly, it needs to address the way such groups are further marginalized by not having what they do and the history they make taken into account in educational agendas drawn up by the various nation states.

This brings me to the question of the organization of programmes and their orientation. If there is one area in which there is reinforcement of the dominant views of the world from the point of view of that minority I described earlier, it is in the organization and orientation of programmes of international education. I want to share with you a couple of examples.

In Britain in the 1960s and 1970s there was a widely held view that in order to understand the problems black minorities posed to the society, one needed to go to the country of origin of those minorities. The British Home Office via the Community Relations Commission and, since 1976, the Commission for Racial Equality, provided bursaries for people to do just that. As a result, staff from police training colleges, chief officers of police themselves, senior social workers, local government administrators – all white – donned their safari suits and picked up their bursaries to go and study the natives in their natural habitat.

The majority of Caribbean people in Britain knew no island or country but their own before emigrating to Britain, and they had certainly never been to the Indian sub-continent. The majority of African people and people from the sub-continent had never been to the Caribbean. Yet it was virtually impossible for Caribbean people or Asian and African people to get their hands on those bursaries, for one simple reason: blacks were testing the tolerance levels of whites in the society and bucking the apparatus of the state. In order to effect better control, one needed to understand what made them tick at home, and how the various state apparatuses back home dealt with them. It was not about understanding cultures any more than it was about enabling those cultures to better influence and impact upon white British cultural and institutional life. It took years of hard work for those communities and activists such as myself to get the focus shifted from the 'blaming the victim' preoccupations that William Ryan wrote about, to the more logical interrogation of the effects of structural oppression, on the axis of class and race, on the minority peoples whose conduct the state sought to explain by studying the cultures from which they came.

My second example relates to the issue of international education exchange among higher education students, secondary school students, and youth groups in community education provision. As far as the higher education students are concerned the issue is somewhat more complex and I shall deal with it if there is time at the end. With regard to the youth groups and school students, I wish to make three main points.

Firstly, I wish to address the notion of 'One Caribbean'. People of my persuasion are constantly seeking to stress the unity of the West Indies, even though language, water, and political systems divide us. The English-speaking, French-speaking, Dutch-speaking, and Spanish-speaking West Indies, from Jamaica to Cuba, and Guadeloupe to Surinam, are to us One Caribbean with one common heritage and common experience of colonialism and imperialism. As we Caribbean people seek to locate ourselves in that historical sweep and engage in educational pursuits within those territories, we find little enthusiasm for the exchange programmes we submit for funding.

Even if we were to give those holding the purse strings the benefit of the doubt and argue that France, Spain, Holland and other European countries are geographically much closer to us, and in any event, with 1992 looming we now have even more reason to look to continental Europe rather than to the West Indies, we still run into major problems. The cost to the student of international educational exchange often means that poor families cannot facilitate their children to sign up for such exchanges. Unless, therefore, the educational institution finds the means to enable poorer students to travel abroad, under-representation of certain groups takes place at this level also.

Institutions from which students come are not usually able to influence the study programmes or pastoral arrangements in the host country. Invariably, the institutions to which students travel abroad, especially in Europe, could have as many under-represented groups in the local community as there are at the students' home institutions. Support mechanisms or opportunities for cultural familiarization with the local underrepresented groups and their educational or social concerns could often be lacking. The student could therefore have an experience as an exchange student within the social confines of the host institution without gaining any real sense of the level of marginalization or of the strength of the local underrepresented groups.

In the European context, there are the added issues of xenophobia, racism, fascism, and the extent to which the treatment that is meted out similarly to black or ethnic minority communities is actually, or potentially, meted out to the student. There exists in Europe a culture of racism which underpins the violation of black people's fundamental human rights. Combating that culture and interrogating the extent to which their own institutional practices both feed off it and contribute to it, is seldom on the agenda of those educational institutions participating in international educational exchange.

Finally, to my third main point: How can underrepresented groups work more closely with educators and institutions to bring about desired outcomes as far as international education is concerned? Underrepresented groups both within educational institutions and within communities need to address relentlessly the issue of barriers to access, the adequacy or otherwise of student support services, and underrepresentation at the level of curriculum. The combined strength of underrepresented groups inside and outside the institutions must ensure that international education means more than just pursuing the same education programmes in a different geographical and educational environment. Students from underrepresented groups need to ensure that those arranging international exchanges from within their institutions ask the host institutions to take account of the issues raised above, and to give a clear indication of:

a) where it stands on those issues and what institutional practices it has developed in relation to them,

b) how the students will be facilitated in using their experiences and dealing with those issues from the viewpoint of a member of an underrepresented group

Education for Liberation?

In summary, I am arguing that we need to have an internal focus on the issue of underrepresentation in relation to who has access to education and at what levels, the extent to which the curriculum, pastoral arrangements and student support services take account of underrepresented groups and, more generally, the historical contribution of underrepresented peoples and nations to the development of knowledge across all disciplines. I am arguing for a genuine curriculum of inclusion which by its very existence poses a challenge to cultural supremacist values whether or not they originate in racism, ethnocentrism, or Eurocentrism, and has within it and its pedagogy the potential for a dynamic education for liberation.

THE LEARNING AGE
Towards a Europe of knowledge
Manchester
17-19 May 1998

I welcome the opportunity to make a presentation at this prestigious conference and particularly to share some thoughts on the subject of the role of Lifelong Learning in promoting active citizenship in civil society and work.

I do not intend to say much about the need for Lifelong Learning. All the speakers yesterday dealt with that in some detail. More than that, as a learner and community education activist ever since I attended my local village primary school, I regard Lifelong Learning not just as 'the best thing since sliced bread' but by far the best thing before and since the microchip. For one thing, Lifelong Learning sustained many societies for centuries, and to this day continues to regulate social mores and social arrangements, and to act as a transmitter of cultural norms and traditions within such societies. Many such societies would need to make massive leaps ahead in time before the delights of the new technology could have any relevance to them.

Baroness Blackstone and indeed Secretary of State Blunkett told us yesterday that they would like our deliberations here to provide some informed reactions to, as well as suggestions which could improve upon, the Green Paper: *The Learning Age – a renaissance for a new Britain*. I trust that some of what I have to say will qualify in that respect.

Let me begin with what the Secretary of State has to say about Learning and Citizenship in his foreword to the Green Paper:

As well as securing our economic future, learning has a wider contribution. It helps make ours a civilized society, develops the spiritual side of our lives and promotes active citizenship. Learning enables people to play a full part in their community. ...

There are many ways in which we can all take advantage of new opportunities:

- *as citizens we can balance the rights we can expect from the state, with the responsibilities of individuals for their own future, sharing the gains and the investment needed.*

Learning supports active citizenship and democracy, giving men and women the capacity to provide leadership in their communities.

The Learning Age (pp. 7-8)

On the face of it, there is not one thing in the Green Paper with which most responsible citizens could be expected to have major disagreements. For this responsible citizen, however, far too many taken-for-granted assumptions are made, too many questions begged, and there is a fundamental flaw in the approach the Green Paper takes.

We are given a vision of the Britain and the Europe the Government wishes to build towards the first decade of the new millennium. A number of key policy initiatives are indicated and partnership arrangements adumbrated as a means to realizing that vision. However, apart from highlighting some major deficits that affect if not determine the quality of Britain's economic performance and its position in the world economic league, deficits which are also barriers to employability and competitiveness, threats to social order and that reflect the inability of a large sector of the population to exploit 'the market', the Green Paper appears to presuppose that our starting point is a society that is largely homogenous.

Acknowledgment is given to the social and even the racial disadvantages experienced by sections of the society, especially with regard to access to learning opportunities and low attainment at the end of formal schooling. But despite all the taken-for-granted statements about active citizenship, not one reference is made to racism, to racial discrimination, to xenophobia, to homophobia, to ageism.

Paul Belanger, (of the UNESCO Institute for Education, Hamburg) to his eternal credit, was the only one of the speakers at yesterday's opening plenary to use the 'R' word, when he provided us with that useful reminder that 'racism cannot be dealt with just by forbidding it'.

Were I not at this conference today, I would be at the Elephant & Castle in South London observing the proceedings of the Stephen Lawrence Judicial Inquiry, the first ever Public Judicial Inquiry into a racist murder in Britain.

Stephen Lawrence was in every sense middle England's 'ideal type' of young Briton. An 18 year old 'A' level student, extremely bright, highly motivated, high achiever, ambitious, confident, sociable, socially committed and involved, and very well liked. An 'ideal type' in every sense bar one: he was a young black male. One black male too many as far as the six white males who stabbed him to death were concerned. Stephen was the third victim of a racial murder in the London Borough of Greenwich. The other two were also young black males from well adjusted home backgrounds and with aspirations that matched the high expectations of their families.

And even as I speak, there is another investigation going on, into the death in police custody of thirty-eight year old father of two, Christopher Alder, in Hull in the North of England, a black male and a former paratrooper. Five police officers have been suspended from duty following that death, one more added to the dozens of deaths of black people, predominantly males, in police custody.

I am saying all of this in order to stress that unless we own the society we have now, in all its ugliness, and examine the implications of its present state for the vision, the very laudable vision the Government has; unless we do that, with courage, with humility, and in the interest of Truth, the future we face won't be the future we want, irrespective of the vast potential of Lifelong Learning.

Promoting Active Citizenship and Social Inclusion in Civil Society and Work, therefore, requires a definition of the rights as well as the responsibilities of those groups who, typically, constitute the marginalized and disadvantaged within the society; it also requires a realistic view of their position within the economy. Those groups include: the functionally illiterate (an illiteracy invariably compounded by computer illiteracy), the unwaged, the long term unemployed, school students in the country's worst schools, mentally ill people in communities, young offenders, women on benefit and looking after children or other dependants at home, workers repeatedly displaced from the job market despite several programmes of re-training, black people facing discrimination in various areas of social and institutional life.

Active Citizenship and a truly participatory democracy that involves the nation and not just the few, must be predicated upon the affirmation and the safeguarding of rights and entitlements, and not just exhortations about civic responsibility. Only thus does one create a culture in which all citizens could reasonably be expected to entertain a notion of 'the common good' and of their responsibility to work in support and furtherance of it.   (John, 1998)

The problem with 'learning' when it becomes uncoupled from that increasingly esoteric activity called 'education' is that it reinforces the notion of individualized pursuits for individual gain. And the more learning is facilitated by arrangements such as 'learning accounts' and individual bank accounts, the greater is the tendency to regard the end purpose of it all as having to do with individual advancement and achievement, rather than with notions of interdependence and colective action for change.

If we have a particular focus upon those who don't just 'grow up on the margins', to use Frank Coffield's very evocative description, but who permanently exist on the margins, then, surely, we must take account of the group identities they project, the sense of group oppression they convey as their reality, and not reconstruct that into their existence as individuals with assumed deficits located deep within them.

Let me put my cards on the table as an old fashioned learner and education facilitator, and share the view of education that has informed my practice over many decades:

Education is for the whole community and should be accessible to the community from the cradle to the grave.

Education functions as much to provide the individual achievement of academic and technical competence as it does to provide a collective basis for change in communities and in society. As such, individual achievement of academic excellence is not an end in itself but must be tempered with a sense of social responsibility and social interdependence.

Education is for skilling people for the workplace no more than it is for developing in people the social skills and competence to take control of their own lives and to function as responsible social citizens, demanding and safeguarding their own rights, and having due regard to and respect for the rights of others.

Unequal opportunities, based on unequal resources and unequal chances, constrains individuals and communities no less than neighbourhoods or boroughs.

In a liberal democratic society, the concept of interdependence, the acknowledgment of the fact that wealth and material resources are unequally distributed, and the notion of collective responsibility for the sick, weak, the poor, the unemployed, and the homeless should all go hand in hand.

Among other things, education and schooling should be about assisting students, and adults more generally, in understanding the roots and the persistence of racial and social injustice in society, and providing them with the individual and collective tools with which to combat both.   (John, 1990)

Now, I would like to think that Tony Blair, David Blunkett and Tessa Blackstone once signed on to a similar education agenda. I have absolutely no reason to believe that they no longer subscribe to it, except that I do not hear too many references to 'rights', let alone equal rights and certainly not to the notion of learning as providing people with the 'collective tools' with which to combat social and racial injustice.

This is certainly not meant to be a cheap jibe. I affirm that those leaders of the nation once subscribed to my model because of the history of the Labour Movement in this country and its illustrious and historical contribution to the struggle for education rights and for the expansion of education among working class people and among women in the society.

It is a history that accords with Connell's view of the link between education and social justice:

Education has a fundamental connection with the idea of human emancipation, though it is constantly in danger of being captured by other interests. In a society disfigured by class exploitation, sexual and racial oppression, and in chronic danger of war and environmental destruction, the only education worth the name is one that forms people capable of taking part in their own liberation. The business of the school is not propaganda. It is equipping people with the knowledge and skills and concepts relevant to remaking a dangerous and disordered world. In the basic sense, the process of education and the process of liberation are the same. They are aspects of the painful growth of the human species' collective wisdom and self-control ... It is plain that the forces opposed to that growth here and on the world scale are not only powerful but have become increasingly militant. In such circumstances, education becomes a risky enterprise. Teachers too have to decide whose side they are on.

RWD Connell (et al), *Making the Difference* (1983)

Remember the years after 1926 and especially after 1940?
Remember Edward Thompson, Raymond Williams, F R Leavis, Karl Mannheim, Richard Hoggart, and more recently and significantly for women, Sheila Rowbotham?

Whatever happened to *The Making of the English Working Class*? Whatever happened to the role of the Workers Education Association in empowering that 'lumpen' reserve army who were regarded as not needing education because factories needed their brawn and not their brain?

Whatever happened to all those wonderful things that led us to embrace the late Paulo Freire and to cherish the legacy he left us?

What acknowledgment is given to the role of formal, non-formal, and informal adult education in the rapid expansion of social movements and of trade union basic education in the last five decades?

What is the relevance of that to the unprecedented large number of women Members of Parliament in Mr Blair's Government?

[By the way, anyone interested in an analysis of that crucially important period in British social history to which I have just alluded would find it useful to read Tom Steele's excellent essay, 'Marginal Occupations: Education, Cultural Studies and Social Renewal', in the *Scottish Journal of Adult and Continuing Education*, 4.1:1997]

Mrs Margaret Thatcher once declared with an air of arrogant invincibility that "There is no such thing as society'.

Mr John Major once asked us to believe that as far as our preoccupation with 'class' was concerned, fourteen years (then) of Conservative rule had produced the 'one nation' state. To continue to be exercised by concerns about 'class', therefore, was to act as Luddites in the newly constructed Britain.

I would like to think that *The Learning Age* could be constructed on more reliable foundations than that.

I intend to devote the rest of this talk to the challenges and opportunities that are implicit in the promotion of active citizenship, democracy, and social inclusion. But before I do that, let us be clear what it is we are up against. In an important essay in the reader: *Teaching for Diversity and Social Justice*, Hardiman and Jackson observe as follows:

Oppression is not simply an ideology or set of beliefs that assert one group's superiority over another, nor is it random violence, harassment or discrimination toward members of the target groups. A condition of oppression exists when the following key elements are in place:

- *The agent group has the power to define and name reality and determine what is 'normal', 'real', or 'correct'.*
- *Harassment, discrimination, exploitation, marginalisation, and other forms of differential and unequal treatment are institutionalised and systematic. These acts often do not require the conscious thought or effort of individual members of the agent group but are rather part of business as usual that become*

embedded in social structures over time.

- *Psychological colonisation of the target group occurs through socialising the oppressed to internalise their oppressed condition and collude with the oppressor's ideology and social system. This is what Freire refers to as the oppressed playing 'host' to the oppressor.*
- *The target group's culture, language, and history is misrepresented, discounted, or eradicated and the dominant group's culture is imposed.*

(Rita Hardiman and Bailey Jackson, 1997)

Clearly, Lifelong Learning by itself cannot promote active citizenship and social inclusion in Britain and across Europe. It would help the process, however, if we provide answers to the following questions:

- Who are 'we the British', 'we the French', 'we the Belgians', 'we the Germans'?
- How do I promote social inclusion in a Britain where Britishness is stubbornly equated with whiteness?
- How do I deal with my schizophrenia when I wave my Union Flag to greet the Monarch as she opens a new civic building in my city in the morning and then have to literally run for my life as I am chased by white racists wearing the Union Flag in the night?
- How does Lifelong Learning assist me in promoting active citizenship and social inclusion when my children at school are subjected to a curriculum which panders to monoculturalism and fails to project pluralism let alone antiracism?
- In our vision of a 'Europe of Knowledge', who decides which brands of 'knowledge' are 'legitimate' and which are not? Can we seriously duck this epistemological question in the light of the glaring evidence of structured marginalization of the products of black people's cultural creativity, of non-Christian faiths, of black literature and history, of the thirty-five years of the black education movement in this country?
- Would the European Social Fund (ESF) contemplate the use of its £1.3 billion Objective 3 programme funding to promote

the sharing of skills between, for example, the Stephen Lawrence Family Support Group and families from the Maghreb mobilizing around the racist murders of their children in Lille and Lyon, or Turkish families in Brussels and Antwerp? If not, why not?

- Given the fact that the struggles among black communities in this country over the last fifty years has resulted in some significant shifts in the society's attitude to discharging its responsibility to black people, albeit not as visibly as it has in relation to the Women's Movement, why should ESF programmes not link us in Britain with communities like us in continental Europe so that we could engage in some education for liberation in the style of Paulo Freire?

- Would that not be a wonderful way to share knowledge and skills, genuinely build a 'Europe of Knowledge' and in the words of Paul Belanger, 'democratize democracy'?

I stress this because it is my firm belief that whatever else Lifelong Learning gives them, marginalized communities would require those collective skills more and more as we move into the next millennium.

I do not believe we can dismiss out of hand the prognostications of Jeremy Rifkin and see his 'End of Work' scenario only as a spectre of gloom and defeatism. I believe that it is a mistake to lead this nation, or the rest of Europe for that matter, to believe that the good times are there to be had if only we could grasp the learning opportunities and pull ourselves up by our own bootstraps. Apart from the fact that some of us ain't got no boots to start with, the market is forever setting more and more stringent criteria for employability, and it is therefore safe to assume that many of those in the Lifelong Learning target group won't catch up in their lifetime.

It seems to me that we need to face up to the inevitability of the reorganization of working life and of our attitudes to work and leisure in the next millennium; a reorganization that would usher in a shorter working day, shorter working week, shorter working life, and more time for learning, more time for collective action for change in communities, and at work; and more time for rest, recreation and cultural creativity.

I have no difficulty constructing a Lifelong Learning agenda within that scenario, redefining 'leisure' and establishing a functional link between learning, leisure, cultural creativity and cultural expression.

Let me make two final points.

First, it is generally agreed that three principal agents of socialization and of social control operate in society: the family, the school, and work; and indeed the Lifelong Learning Agenda is directed at each. I want to suggest that we include a fourth, i.e., prison or custodial/penal institutions.

In paragraph 3.26 of the Green Paper, a somewhat tentative reference is made to 'adult offenders', the only such reference I could find:

Education and Training will form a fuller part of the new constructive regimes in prison, to which the Government attaches great importance.   (p. 40)

I well recall that as Head of Community Education in the Inner London Education Authority, with responsibility for the five Inner London prisons, we provided a comprehensive education and training programme through the respective Adult Education Institutes. Changes in prison regimes and in the allocation of budgets have led to a steady reduction in education provision in custodial institutions.

Given the stigma attached to being in prison and the unattractiveness of ex-offenders to employers, the Government should make a commitment to funding an expanded education programme in prisons and youth custody institutions, ringfencing that funding, and encouraging at the same time the development at community level of 'transition' projects that could support ex-offenders to pursue personal development plans and in seeking employment or work placements. This is especially necessary for ex-offenders who gained little from full-time education and are from lower socio-economic backgrounds.

In view of the massive over-representation of black people (male and female) in the prison population, especially those aged between 18 and 30, and in view of the double discrimination they face after parole, on grounds of race and because of their status as ex-offenders, the risk of recidivism and of continuing social exclusion among that sector of the population must give increasing cause for concern.

My second and final point is basically to re-emphasize the link between social inclusion and social justice. I will let the following quotes make the point for me:

Injustice anywhere is a threat to justice everywhere.
Martin Luther King Jr

A nation that presides over or condones the denial of basic rights and entitlements to any individual or any section of itself, puts at risk its own fundamental rights and entitlements.
Gus John

They are happy who are at peace with themselves.
To begin with oneself but not to end with oneself;
To start with oneself, but not to aim at oneself;
To comprehend oneself, but not to be preoccupied with oneself.
Martin Buber

To comprehend oneself, but not to be preoccupied with oneself......

If we genuinely wish to build a 'Europe of Knowledge' in the new millennium, a competitive Europe with an employable and informed workforce, we need to comprehend a few things:

• The egalitarian principles presupposed by a societal concern about social exclusion do not rest well with the notion of a Europe full of knowledge and of skilled people, all jostling in 'the market' and trying to gain a 'competitive advantage' over everyone else.

• The structural bases of the marginalization and social exclusion of the range of groups I listed above cannot be eradicated simply by building a 'learning society' and boosting the individual's competence, confidence and self esteem. However much information and learning enable individuals to gain an understanding of the dynamics and roots of sexism, ageism, racism, homophobia, and the rest, the disadvantages suffered by people experiencing these forms of oppression are not caused solely, or primarily, by the actions of the individual 'learner'.

- The heterogeneity of Britain and of Europe is no evidence of genuinely plural societies. Black British settlers of more than fifty years standing are still classified as 'ethnic minorities'. The ethnic majority of Europe, whom the likes of the National Front, the Vlaams Bloc, Column 88, and similar neo-fascist organizations purport to represent, are being told very loudly that they should not even have to 'compete' with that 'alien' presence.

- The discourse around 'competitiveness' would appear to postulate that it is possible to appeal to all of Britain or all of Europe to 'make us more competitive' in the global economy by each individual taking responsibility for their own skills preparation, while, at home, opportunities just to be themselves let alone to compete are being denied to large sections of the population.

- Economic globalization is not just about the reorganization of capital and the restructuring of markets on a world scale, in response to, or facilitated by, the new technology. It is also about the relocation of people on a global scale and the reorganization of societies. It is about the emergence of new national identities, a process so inevitable that it cannot be neutralized by Europe's xenophobic 'preoccupation' with itself.

- That relocation of the peoples of the world means that the multiethnic population of Europe cannot have a view of European competitiveness vis à vis the rest of the world as something which they have a patriotic duty to generate, on the grounds that 'we are all Europeans now'. A huge proportion of Europe's black and other ethnic minority population continue to carry financial and other responsibilities for their dependants in the rest of the world. Where, for example, should European citizens who once were citizens of the Windward Islands of the Caribbean stand on the question of European 'competitiveness' when it comes to Tariffs and Trade agreements in respect to the banana industry? Would we be called upon to pass the 'banana test' in much the same way that the former British parliamentarian, Norman Tebbit, required us to pass the 'cricket test' and declare our loyalty as proof of our britishness?

- In order to combat functional illiteracy and promote active citizenship and democratic participation, a number of countries in the so-called 'developing' world have instituted a Campaign for Popular Education (CPE). The underlying assumptions in most if not all of those programmes (Brazil, Costa Rica, Chile, Jamaica, Grenada, Guinea Bissau) have been that:

    all people in the society operate their lives with a certain level of social and technical competence

    all people engage in learning and in teaching at some point each day of their lives – small village communities as well as large urban slums manage to maintain a level of social cohesion despite the high rates of functional illiteracy in the local population

    given the range of skills people employ in managing their lives and their communities, especially in very straitened and chaotic circumstances, and the repository of knowledge that they could all be expected to have, learners could also be teachers, and vice versa.

Consequently, it is not unusual to find such campaigns employing the slogan 'Each one, teach one'.

I have no doubt that the delegates at the *Fifth International Conference on Adult Education* (Hamburg, July 1997), had those basic principles very much in mind when they drew up the Hamburg Declaration on Adult Learning. The Declaration is pretty silent on racism, racial discrimination and xenophobia, preferring to deal with 'cultural diversity':

The challenges of the twenty-first century require the creativity and competence of citizens of all ages in alleviating poverty ... consolidating democratic processes, strengthening and protecting human rights, promoting a culture of peace, encouraging active citizenship, strengthening the role of civil society, ensuring gender equality and equity, enhancing the empowerment of women, recognizing cultural diversity (including the use of language, and promoting justice and equality for minorities and indigenous peoples) and a new partnership between state and civil society

Significantly, 'Promoting justice and equality for minorities and indigenous peoples' is placed in parenthesis, as a function of 'recognizing cultural diversity'. That said, the Hamburg Conference nevertheless committed itself to:

Linking literacy to the social, cultural and economic development aspirations of learners:
- *by emphasizsing the importance of literacy for human rights, participatory citizenship, social, political and economic equity, and cultural identity*
- *by encouraging the creative uses of literacy*
- *by replacing the narrow vision of literacy by learning that meets social, economic and political needs and gives expression to a new form of citizenship*
- *by integrating literacy and other forms of learning and basic skills into all appropriate development projects, particularly those related to health and the environment, and by encouraging grassroots organizations and social movements to promote their own learning and development initiatives*
- *by launching the Paulo Freire African Decade on Literacy for All beginning in 1998 in order to create literate societies responsive to the different cultural traditions. To that end, special funds should be created by both public and private sources.*

Hamburg Declaration on Adult Learning, UNESCO, Hamburg

Unlike the Declaration, the Green Paper curiously avoids any reference to human rights, to political and economic equity, to grassroots organizations and to social movements, issues which were central to the concerns and the agenda of the British Labour Movement as it took its course on the wings of a workers education and adult learning campaign.

Let us hope that while we welcome the Government's ambitious agenda for ushering in *'the Learning Age'*, all those individuals, organizations, and social movements that were empowered by, or facilitated others in their self-empowerment through, adult education, community education and all the varied forms of non-formal and informal education, would assist the Government in anchoring *the Learning Age* on much firmer foundations by helping it draw upon the rich history of adult learning in these islands.

I want to leave you with the following words:

We, the peoples of the world are involved in a new quality of witness to interactions between art, music, dance, language, thought, the theatrical into theatre. Through direct live international television, computers, video and the Internet we are witness to the incessant interconnections between ourselves, between politics and economics, the inevitable transculturation between religions, nationalities, ethnicities and cultures.

Visions of change, survival and advancement are marred by doubts, uncertainties and hopelessness about the future; by inhuman cruelties, inequalities, bigotry, sexism, racism, and ethnic cleansing. Still many mountains to climb, still many barbarities to be confronted; the struggle to transform promise into reality. But the indomitable capacity of the human spirit to confront oppression and to make and remake change marches forward and onward.

John La Rose, 'Call to the 12th International Book Fair of Radical Black and Third World Books', London (1995)

You have been most patient. Thank you for your attention.

6.3

CITIZEN PARTICIPATION
New skills and capacities

Lillehammer, Norway
October 1998

Education for democratic citizenship is fundamentally a process, a dialectical process. It is a process that places individuals in a new relationship with themselves as actors, agents in the struggle for change. It provides people with a more informed sense of self in relation to the social world and of their power to influence how the social world impacts upon them and their communities.

Education for democratic citizenship presupposes the empowerment of people through the development of the social skills and competence to take control of their own lives and to function as responsible social citizens, demanding and safeguarding their own rights and having due regard to, and respect for, the rights of others.

In a paper on 'Promoting Active Citizenship and Social Inclusion in Civil Society and Work' in May this year, I observed that:

Active citizenship and a truly participatory democracy that involves the nation and not just a few, must be predicated upon the affirmation and the safeguarding of rights and entitlements, and not just exhortations about civic responsibility. Only thus does one create a culture in which all citizens could reasonably be expected to entertain a notion of 'the common good' and of their responsibility to work in support and furtherance of it.

Clearly, this raises a whole series of questions in the European context. The term 'citizen', especially when it is linked to notions of nationality and civic entitlements means completely different things in different European States and for different categories of people in Europe. The discourse on Education for Democratic Citizenship appears to be comfortable with an unrestricted definition that sees citizens as people residing in a country irrespective of whether or not a nation state confers on them the status of immigrant, alien, 'auslander', 'gastarbiter', migrant worker, asylum seeker, political refugee, Count, Duchess or Lord. It is legitimate, therefore, to pose the question: new skills and capacities in relation to what aspirations, goals and objectives, and for whom?

Democratizing Democracy

Democratizing democracy is perhaps the most obvious and relevant goal of Education for Democratic Participation. It presupposes the involvement of the powerless, of those denied a voice, of those structurally located and kept on the margins of the society, of those otherwise excluded from the democratic process in:

- democratizing political representation
- democratizing access to information and knowledge
- democratizing schooling
- redefining the values that underpin education and schooling
- combating the marginalization of ethnic minority communities, their cultures, language, faith, and their contribution to the re-shaping of national identities
- making central and local government more responsive to the deeply entrenched inequalities of wealth, gender, access to education and employment, opportunity to influence decision-making processes, opportunity to have cultural creativity validated and cultural products exposed and celebrated, access to quality health care and health education
- developing strategies for cooperating with others and resolving conflicts by non-violent means
- making connections between their own struggles and social movements and those of others nationally and

internationally
- building their own institutions (economic, social, cultural, religious) and interfacing with those of the dominant culture.

The complex, interactive and dynamic relationship between the social world, citizenship, and political, economic, and educational procedures and practices is effectively what determines the skills and capacities needed for citizenship participation.

The 'Sites of Citizenship' are already throwing up or generating a whole battery of skills and capacities necessary for the practice of democratic culture. As people come together with an explicit desire to make a difference, they discover in themselves and in one another skills and capacities they never knew they possessed. The process of change is accelerated as that new confidence motivates them to take on bigger and bolder challenges.

The re-ordering of power in communities, including the power to direct and redirect financial and material resources, the challenge to the technocratic approach to service planning and delivery that central government and municipalities usually adopt, and the goal of mobilizing diverse communities of interest to work together for common ends, require the following skills and capacities:

Tools for Analysis
- The capacity to project and articulate the realities of a given situation from inside the experience of the groups principally affected (the young, school students, the unemployed, those without access to public information or to transport in rural areas, gypsies, refugees, young offenders)
- The capacity to structurally locate processes of exclusion and to identify the protection (or lack of it) that groups have under the law
- The capacity to describe and analyze the strengths and shortcomings of existing arrangements as they affect the community or group (Health & Social Services, Education & Training, policing of communities, action against drug and

alcohol abuse, labour market survey data and the incidence
of skills shortages among specific groups are key examples.)
- The ability to make connections between one's own situation
  and agenda for change, and that of other
  communities/projects confronting similar issues
- The capacity to devise principles and methods of
  organization and information exchange which are
  themselves empowering
- The capacity to extract meanings and insights from the
  group's, or community's, self-directed activity, including an
  understanding of why some starting assumptions may have
  been wrong and why some strategies worked and others did
  not
- The capacity to chart/evaluate the learning that is generated
  through the group's activities and to package it so it could be
  utilized to refine the group's own activities or that of others
- The capacity to understand the source of conflict and to
  resolve conflict within and between groups, especially where
  the communities of interest assert rights that conflict with
  the entitlement of others (school exclusion/expulsion of
  students, the treatment of young offenders in the community
  rather than in penal institution would be examples here)
- The capacity to build effective partnerships and contribute to
  multi-agency approaches to community development and
  problem solving
- The capacity to demonstrate how society's structures,
  institutions, and cultural norms, lead to the social exclusion
  of specific groups and must be challenged as part of any
  effort to combat discrimination
- Similarly, the capacity to challenge and deconstruct
  accepted, commonsensical definitions of 'normality'
- The capacity to demonstrate the dynamism and immanence
  of culture, and that people create and recreate their cultures
  and identities; but that 'the common good' is promoted
  through an understanding and practice of interdependence
  and interconnectedness
- The capacity to motivate others to believe in themselves and
  in their individual ability to make a difference, and to act

collectively to bring about change
- The capacity to monitor and challenge media reporting which routinely reinforces negative stereotypes of certain groups of people in society (young people, young black people, women, the homeless, the unemployed, recipients of state benefit, etc.)
- The capacity to develop effective models of communication and participation

Tools for Practice
- Communication skills (language, new technologies, using the media, public and private meetings, rallies)
- Organization skills (organizing meetings, lobbies, public information campaigns)
- Problem solving skills
- Negotiating skills
- Motivational skills
- Persuasion skills
- Record-keeping skills
- Information storing & retrieving skills
- Self-management skills
- Project management skills
- Ability to be flexible
- Ability to be creative

Clearly, this rough and ready list of Tools for Analysis and Tools for Practice is in no way meant to be exhaustive.

Challenges and Dilemmas
1. Given the differential status and access to education and political influence of the diverse communities in Europe, how, concretely, are Sites of Citizenship applying notions of democratic social change?
2. Education reforms in most European countries have relegated school students to the status of consumers of products or services organized by others. How can Education for Democratic Participation provide pedagogies and a 'curriculum of inclusion' as a lever for the democratizing of schooling?

3. How can the 'praxis' exemplified by the Sites of Citizenship be best evaluated and disseminated such that models of social action for social change could be accessible to the most marginalized groups in the society?

4. How can educational structures and processes be encouraged to develop communities of learning in which 'self-contained' schooling ceases to have the pre-eminence it has long enjoyed? How should communities of learning be constructed organically, such that Europe's children of the millennium could be better prepared to manage the next century without racial conflicts, ethnic cleansing and the multiplication of excluded groups in European societies?

5. Partnerships, increasingly in the form of Multi-Agency Panels, are being constructed to provide a formalized approach to working together to tackle social ills such as crime, racial attacks, juvenile delinquency, drug and alcohol abuse, school dropouts, etc. How can we ensure that multi-agency approaches do not shroud inaction and a refusal to confront their own practices on the part of the individual agencies themselves? How can such partnership arrangements avoid creating 'talking shops' but rather become powerful catalysts for 'action for change'?

Conclusion

The critical issue in democratizing democracy is in recognizing that individuals experience their living holistically. Empowering the individual to develop his/her full capacity to act in a self-directing way and to take collective action with others is at the heart of the process of managing a democratic culture.

6.4

THE NILE SYMPOSIUM
Intercultural learning and adult education
Liverpool
30 June 2005

This symposium is being held at a crucial stage in the European project. We meet at a time when:

- Europe is agonizing about the collapse of the European Constitution and the implications of that for the future of the European Union
- The G8 leaders are meeting to discuss, among other things, world poverty, global climate change, global population shifts and the relationship between the rich nations of the world and the desire of people from the poorer nations of the world to relocate and improve their life chances in those rich countries
- The British Government's insistence on introducing identity cards such as no nation has seen before, not even the security conscious United States of America, as a measure against terrorism and against illegal immigration and the attempts of economic migrants to reach these shores
- European states and the USA are increasingly preoccupied with China and its rate of economic growth and social transformation
- Asylum seekers continue to mar social relations in the nation states of Europe
- The policies of the Far Right are gaining popularity among the British electorate. The British National Party (BNP) stood 119 candidates in the general election of May 2005 winning 192,750 votes, 60,990 of them in the Yorkshire and

Humberside region alone as compared to 3,245 in the same
region in the 2001 General Elections

- 55% of all African-Caribbean males and 35 % of all
Caribbean females in the UK have white partners. Those that
have children are having to deal with a more insidious and
visceral form of racism than that suffered by black individuals as part of black communities. The experience of dual
heritage children in the schooling system is now as great a
source of concern as that of African-Caribbean children.

- The report on *Ethnic Minorities and the Labour Market*
(produced by the Strategy Unit in the Cabinet Office in 2004)
identifies African-Caribbean, Somali, Pakistani, and Bengali
groups as having the lowest educational attainment and
lowest occupational status. The report notes that African and
Asian people make up 1 in 13 of the UK population and that
over the past twenty years they have accounted for two-
thirds of the growth of the total UK population.

- Similarly, in the coming ten to twenty years, the British
labour market will be dependent, increasingly, on the supply
of labour from those communities. That knowledgeable and
skilled labour force will not be available if the current pattern
of underachievement, school exclusions and youth offending
within African and Asian communities persists. Indeed, if
current trends continue it is more than likely that the British
labour market will look to meet its labour supply needs from
the member states of the expanded European Union than
from its own black British population. We may well be
experiencing the inexorable growth of a British born, British
schooled black underclass, operating on the margins of the
society.

Those inter-related, macro issues raise fundamental questions
about taken-for-granted constructions of national identity, the
homogeneous nation state, racial and ethnic identity,
democratic citizenship, commonly shared values, social
inclusion, multiculturalism and intercultural relations.

They also raise the question: what is life long learning for, and
what in the context of the new Europe is the function of
intercultural learning?

Intercultural Learning

Ever since multiculturalism as a concept and an approach to teaching and learning came under scrutiny, in Britain at least, thus giving rise to antiracism as ideology and practice, there has been a tendency to substitute the term 'intercultural', for multicultural and to use both interchangeably.

In the European context, intercultural learning has too often had common undertones with multicultural learning, insofar as cultural and linguistic differences were seen as central, especially when linked to ethnicity and 'race'. Like multiculturalism, it eschewed considerations of class, and material issues to do with disadvantage, unequal access to opportunity, and to power, and social inequalities generally.

Intercultural learning should be about, first and foremost, learning about the mix of cultures within the nation state, the heterogeneous cultures based on the way people organize their working lives, occupational groups, wealth, urbanity and rurality, folklore, cultural creativity and the differential use of leisure, the knowledge-based economy and social class. No nation can approach the culture of another sensitively and with understanding and respect, unless it first understands its own cultural tapestry and that there is never one unified and undifferentiated 'culture', despite the number of national icons with which the majority of the populace identify.

In order for the white majority in Britain to fully appreciate the cultures of its ethnic minorities, it must first have a sense of its own cultural roots, its own social history and the way that that history spawned a variety of cultural forms (from sport, to music, to art, to cuisine, to volunteering, to social manners, to the differential use of leisure time). An appreciation of that provides a deeper self understanding and a fuller understanding of how systems of oppression, of marginalization, and of validation and privilege, and the struggles to which they have given rise have created the political space for democratic expression and for the exercise of hard won rights.

Armed with that understanding, white people in Britain, for example, stand a better chance of:

- engaging with the experiences and aspirations of minorities
- appreciating the extent to which their respective histories as majority and minority, colonizers and colonized, are intertwined
- understanding that culture does not exist separately from the economic and other structures that govern how people make their livelihood and form their social relations
- not divorcing 'culture' from politics and from the struggle for rights and for equality and social justice
- understanding that culture is not politically neutral
- seeing the cultures of ethnic minorities as more deeply meaningful than simple or even elaborate exotica.

In Post War Europe, twinning arrangements between municipalities in different nation states have done a great deal to foster understanding and knowledge, and to break down barriers and deep seated prejudices. As a Chief Officer in local government in the late 1980s until the middle 1990s, I had cause to arrange some exciting education exchange visits between my borough and far away places such as Turkey, Poland, Israel and Russia as well as France and Germany.

Those visits involved both school students and adults actively engaged in formal learning. What interested me about the visits, however, was that the country visited would invariably project itself and its culture as homogeneous. In the British context, multicultural learning was, and is, still very much projected as learning that has due regard to the culture and cultural products of Britain's multiethnic communities. The failure to see culture as heterogeneous and that therefore multiculturalism in Britain pre-dated the arrival of black migrants from Africa, Asia and the Caribbean is matched by a tendency on the part of the countries visited to project a common national identity and a commonly shared set of values. That is reflected at its most banal in the gifts that are exchanged, icons by which the nation state is presumed to be identifiable and with which all of its people are assumed to proudly identify.

The unequal distribution of wealth and material resources, the inequality of access to opportunity and to outcomes in education and employment, the social exclusion that is often experienced by people in rural communities and by the long term unemployed, the multiple and shifting identities of young people, particularly those of migrant populations, are seldom identified as factors that make for a certain cultural fluidity. On the contrary, one is treated to a fixed and essentialist view of culture and therefore to examples of adult education practice which reinforce that view.

One major challenge for intercultural learning is whether or not it has the capacity to engage the schooling and adult population in any one country in a discovery of its many cultures, situated on an axis of class, economic activity or inactivity, a sense of belonging to and being valued by the society, access to power and to opportunity, religion and faith, and above all, the axis of the dynamic interweaving of cultural preferences, at one and the same time from aspects of one's own culture and from that of other cultures.

Returning to my anecdote about European twinning arrangements for a moment, I could not help pointing out to my colleagues in education in Britain that I could see no logic in taking groups of young people from London's inner cities all the way to Haifa in Israel and Krakow and Chelmo in Poland in order to experience other cultures and enhance their education, when the people of Ascot, Sunningdale and Windsor might as well be living in Haifa and Krakow for all the understanding they have of them and their sense of identity. Similarly, adults from Gottingen and Hann Munden in Lower Saxony had a most fruitful learning experience in East London with its rich kaleidoscope of cultures and ethnicities, but I who lived in London knew much more about and had more regular interaction with the African-Germans in Berlin, Hamburg and Hanover than they ever did or would.

For centuries, capital moved around the globe at will, but apart from slavery and forced labour, the population of nation states tended to stay very much at home. Globalization and the revolution in international travel have given rise to the movement of populations on a vast scale, and a refocusing of identities, allied to the need to revisit notions of ethnicity and nationalism. The irony is, however, that the more the movement of populations require nation states in Europe to engage with ethnically diverse groups, the less inclined they are to see themselves as 'ethnic'. The discourse deals almost exclusively with 'ethnic minorities', with little or no reference to the ethnic majority and the extent of the fluidity of its own ethnicity.

55% of all African-Caribbean males and 35 % of all Caribbean females in the UK have white partners. Those couples and their children are having to deal with a more insidious and visceral form of racism than that suffered by black individuals as part of black communities. The ethnic majority is therefore ill at ease with itself and is fearful of its changing identities.

Another challenge for intercultural learning is that the dominant discourse in relation to learning 'per se' posits it as an individual activity. It offers the individual, especially those of working class/lower socio-economic background, the opportunity to rise above, if not escape from, their group identity and from the wider set of relationships that shape and determine how they see themselves.

In the globalized world we live in, and given the changed social landscape in Europe, intercultural learning must decide what its project is and what its vision of a shared society and a shared and commonly owned future is.

We in the Gus John Partnership set out our vision of that society in our Equal Opportunities Policy. It is a vision of a society in which:

* it is acknowledged that in a liberal democratic society, the concept of interdependence, the acknowledgement of the fact that wealth and material resources are unequally distributed, and the notion of collective responsibility for the weak, the sick, the poor, the unemployed and the homeless should all go hand in hand
* it is uncontested that everyone has a right to live with respect and dignity and to study and work in an environment in which that right is upheld
* respect for oneself and for others grows by giving it practical expression in all aspects of daily living
* oppression on the grounds of race, gender, class, disability, sexual orientation, age, faith, and the exploitation of the

weak and defenceless are confronted as a matter of duty and civic responsibility
- the notion of an individual's worthlessness has no place
- the human rights of all people are affirmed and safeguarded and there is a commitment in civic society and evidence of the State commitment in all its dealings with its citizenry
- each person is actively encouraged to see her/himself as enjoying the democratic space won through the struggles of those who went before and as having a democratic responsibility to safeguard hard-won rights, to protect the environment and act as an agent of change
- it is accepted as given that Britain is a multiethnic, multifaith society and that each organization, public, private or voluntary, should reflect that reality in its ethos, human resource policies and arrangements, service delivery and general working practices

As a service supplier, we in GJP are committed to eradicating unfair and discriminatory practices where these occur within our sphere of operation or influence and ensuring that we are not made to collude, unwittingly or otherwise, with such practices within the organizations that buy our services.

RWD Connell established the link between education and social justice as follows:

Education has a fundamental connection with the idea of human emancipation, though it is constantly in danger of being captured by other interests. In a society disfigured by class exploitation, sexual and racial oppression, and in chronic danger of war and environmental destruction, the only education worth the name is one that forms people capable of taking part in their own liberation.

The business of the school is not propaganda. It is equipping people with the knowledge and skills and concepts relevant to remaking a dangerous and disordered world. In the basic sense, the process of education and the process of liberation are the same. They are aspects of the painful growth of the human species' collective wisdom and self-control ...

It is plain that the forces opposed to that growth here and on the world scale are not only powerful but have become increasingly militant.

In such circumstances, education becomes a risky enterprise. Teachers too have to decide whose side they are on.

(Connell RWD et al., 1983)

I am arguing, therefore, for an agenda for intercultural learning that can empower individuals to:

- learn about the multiplicity of cultures that surround them, especially those not defined by 'race', language and religion
- understand the basis and the persistence of poverty and social exclusion and of discrimination and unequal treatment that are part of the cultural mix in their nation state
- be clear about the basis of their own cultural, ethnic and national identity and of how that identity is shifting
- be at ease with the answer to the question: who are we the British? Who are we the French? Who are we the Germans? and with the fact that the answer must be inclusive of other ethnicities
- see themselves as agents of change and architects of the new European order based upon social justice, the defence of the rights of minorities and the affirmation of the right of children of the ethnic majority not to inherit a nation and a Europe characterized by racism and xenophobia
- engage with social movements within and between the nation states of Europe and in other parts of the world.

To that end, adult education should position itself to make the fullest use of the rapidly developing digital technology and be part of the iPod, Podcasting generation, thus empowering people across nation states to make their own media, link their cultural and educational activities, create their own cultural industries and build independent social and cultural movements.

The technology has the capacity to enable adult education to forge the links between education, intercultural learning and human emancipation, with the not unwelcome by-product of growing a generation of adults who have much less of a phobia about the new technology than the dwindling majority of the current one.

Intercultural learning has huge liberating potential and can do for Europe what adult education did and continues to do for workers and peasants in the world of Paulo Friere and other visionary facilitators of people's learning and self discovery.

But, in order for it to do so, we must ourselves liberate intercultural learning from its very narrow confines and exploit its potential to mutual understanding and good relations between cultural groups in the same nation state, in order to encourage learning about and meaningful exchanges with other nations and their cultures.

The expanded and expanding European Community and the new identities to which the movement and meshing of populations is giving rise surely make this not only a desirable goal but a most urgent task.

7.0

UNDERSTANDING 'THE ENEMY' WITHIN

Introduction

In the summer of 2001, Britain experienced a wave of civil unrest in three areas of Northern England such as the country had not seen since the early 1980s. In May 2001, civil unrest erupted in Oldham and continued over a number of days. Violence erupted in Burnley on 23 June with clashes between Asian and white groups and escalated for a further two days as a result of attacks by whites on Asian taxi drivers. Events in Bradford the following month fulfilled the worst fears of the civic leaders in that City.

There are some instructive comparisons to be made between the two periods of serious civil unrest, separated by some twenty years. The first and obvious point to be noted is that many of the young people involved in the 2001 disturbances were not born in 1981 or would have been too young to store in their memory the detail and political significance of those events. The second is that whereas in 1981 the protesters were predominantly African and the protests in areas inhabited mainly by Africans, in the summer of 2001 the unrest was centred in Northern towns and involved predominantly Asian youths.

In those Northern towns, the dominant features in the unrest were tensions between Asian and white communities, and the activities of neo-fascist organizations such as the National Front and the British National Party within those white communities, and in opposition to the spatial location and forms of social, religious, and economic organization within the Asian communities. No commonalities here when compared to the causes of the uprisings in 1981.

As in 1981, the Government commissioned reports on the disturbances in Oldham (from Mr David Ritchie), and Burnley (from Lord Clarke), Bradford Vision had already appointed Lord Ouseley to report on race and community affairs in the City, a report that was being prepared for presentation to its sponsors even as the civil unrest erupted. Fundamental differences between the triggers for the events in 1981 and those in 2001 are reflected in these reports. Common to all three were concerns about communities divided along racial, faith, and cultural lines; 'disillusionment' among Asian youths; and white communities' belief that Asians command too many resources at their expense; Asian youths' feelings of abandonment and a denial of opportunity, faith schools, and majority Asian schools effectively constituting 'segregated' schooling; the need for 'programmes to unite communities and end racial hatred'. With the exception of young people's feeling of abandonment and lack of opportunity, none of the other features was present in the events of 1981.

Another key and disturbing feature that distinguishes the two sets of events is the reference to 'Asian gangs' in the civil unrest of 2001. Criminality associated with 'gang' activity is identified either as triggering the disturbances or fuelling them once they began. Ironically, the State once popularized the view that West Indians were rebellious and out of control, causing problems for the police, while Asians with their more disciplined family background and strong cultural boundaries were considerably more law abiding and docile.

The language describing the activities of Asians on the streets of Oldham, Burnley, and Bradford is now identical to that used to describe African young people's activities during the disturbances in 1981 and in Birmingham in 1985. Terms such as: 'simple thuggery', 'mindless violence', 'criminal minority', 'orgy of violence', 'anti-police violence', 'criminal acts perpetrated by a relatively small number of people', were commonly used in relation to both sets of events.

Another disturbing feature in the 2001 events was the far more overt and active presence of the National Front and the British National Party. The BNP took 16% of the vote in Oldham in the 2001 General Election and were not sparing in their claim to be the only people standing up for the white people of Oldham, who, according to them, are being dispossessed of their birthright by Asians. For their part, the National Front once again sees 'repatriation' as the solution to the trouble and violence in Oldham. In Burnley, the BNP describes its strategy as defusing tension by offering political alternatives to disgruntled whites by enabling them to elect more BNP councillors to Burnley Council and by physically separating the communities.

Mindful of all of the above, Sydney Roper, then Director of Queen Mary and Westfield (QMW) Public Policy Seminars, organized a seminar in December 2001 on *Delivering Effective Race Equality and Community Cohesion – Learning the Lessons from Summer 2001*. The seminar topic provoked a great deal of interest from people in local and central government, the police, race equality councils, education and community organizations across the country. The issue I was asked to address at that seminar was: 'What has Gone Wrong in Race Equality in Britain's Towns and Cities' – How can we Undo this and Build for the Future? (7.1)

The Race Relations Act 1976 was amended and became the Race Relations (Amendment) Act in 2000. Public bodies as defined by the Act were required to put in place a Race Equality Policy (or Scheme) by end May 2002 in England, Wales and Northern Ireland and by November 2002 in Scotland. The frenzy that ensued in response to that requirement was such that no one would have thought that those same bodies had been equally required to abide by the provisions of the 1976 Act. Indeed, successive Governments whose own commitment to eliminating race discrimination and promoting race equality remained questionable, adopted such a 'light touch' approach to holding the public and corporate sectors to account for complying with the 1976 Act that they gave tacit encouragement to the flaunting of it. Typically, therefore, employers and service providers busied themselves in relation to the stipulations of the Act only when they were taking steps to avoid complaints to the Industrial Tribunal, or in defending themselves against such complaints.

In 2002, QMW organized a seminar on *Effectively Implementing the Race Relations Amendment Act – Ensuring Genuine Equality Across the Public Sector*. At that seminar I was asked to provide some reflections on: 'Will the New Act Really Make a Difference? – Challenges, opportunities and pitfalls' (7.2). The paper points to the limits of an approach that simply complies with the requirements of the legislation and argues for a commitment to building a culture of equity and social justice. It makes the point that you can only 'promote good relations between people of different racial groups' if you first accept that those groups are not homogenous and that there are dynamics within, as well as between, them that create divisions and conflict. Above all, it makes the crucial point that since 'whiteness' is racially constructed, race equality must mean fairness and justice for whites no less than for blacks.

Even as the Race Relations Amendment Bill was being drafted, black staff in the Home Office were organizing themselves into a staff network to share experiences, provide support to one another, and work in partnership with Civil Service managers, to ensure that in its service delivery and employment practices, the Home Office put its own policies and guidelines into practice.

Jack Straw, as Home Secretary, had set up the Stephen Lawrence Inquiry and committed the Home Office and other arms of Government to implementing its recommendations. He had also established the Race Relations Forum to assist him and Tony Blair in 'placing race equality at the heart of Government'. Straw and David Omand, then Permanent Secretary at the Home Office, gave active support to Trevor Hall, former Home Office Race Adviser, in establishing The Network and facilitating its development.

In 2004, I delivered the feature address to the Fourth Annual General Meeting of The Network on: 'Managing Equality Issues

Together to Combat Discrimination and Promote Social Justice' (7.3). The issues addressed in that presentation included: why have a black staff network? How can black staff best mobilize themselves to influence the strategic management of the service? What is the role of the Home Office in enabling The Network to exert such influence and what measures might it take to tackle institutional discrimination? What are the limitations of training in this context? What should The Network and other such black staff associations do in order to make partnership working meaningful and effective?

The Citizens Advice Bureau, in the light of the Race Relations (Amendment) Act and the growing number of racist incidents across the country, committed itself to a series of actions to promote race equality and combat discrimination. In 2002, it launched its Race Equality Action Guide and *Bridging Communities*, a set of strategies for dealing with racial harassment and for promoting community cohesion. The theme of their annual conference in 2002 was 'Bridging Communities'.

In the keynote address to that conference: 'Confronting Divisions and Promoting Community Cohesion' (7.4), I explored issues to do with: divisions in society caused by social exclusion and how those militate against building community cohesion; the role of legislation in supporting the struggle against oppression; the role the CAB could play in supporting communities to monitor the implementation of the RRAA 2000, and the need for the CAB to guard against incorporation into structures and partnerships, at local and regional levels, that marginalize communities and their power to influence decision making.

As part of their celebration of Black History Month, Kingston Racial Equality Council and Kingston University host *The Cesar Picton Lecture*. The Cesar Picton Lectures celebrate the contribution and impact made by black and ethnic minority people to the life of Kingston and the UK as a whole. The organizers provide the following background information on Cesar Picton:

He was brought to Kingston in 1761 from the Coast of Senegal, West Africa, at the age of six as a gift to Sir John Philipps. He became Lady Philipps' protégé, receiving an education whilst working as a servant in the Philipps' household. When Lady Philipps died in 1788, she left £100 to Cesar who spent his legacy on renting a coach house and stables in High Street, Kingston, known today as Picton House. Giving himself the name 'Picton' (after the Philipps' home, Picton Castle, in Wales), Cesar set himself up as a coal merchant. By 1795, at the age of 40, Cesar was a much respected businessman having made enough money to buy another property, including a wharf and a malthouse. In February 1816 he moved to Thames Ditton where he bought a property for the then huge sum of £4,000. He is described in the deeds as a 'gentleman'. Cesar died in 1836 at the age of 81. He was buried on 16 June in All Saints' Church, Kingston.

I was asked to deliver the 2004 Cesar Picton Lecture and called it: 'No Island is an Island' (7.5). The lecture points to our increasing interdependence, however much we might seem insulated from one another both as nation states and as individuals or groups within them. Even the remotest island these days is not entirely unaffected by what others do in less idyllic parts of the globe. The 'race' question in Britain, therefore, is not just about whether or not black people have a declared allegiance to the State and to the values we are all presumed to share. It is also about how people, black and white, position themselves in relation to populations in other parts of the world and the forces that impact upon the lives of those populations. The 'race' question in Britain is therefore as much about white people's attitudes towards political and economic refugees, towards black and ethnic minority asylum seekers or towards white South Africans, Zimbabweans or Australians. It is as much about the extremism of the National Front and the British National Party as it is about the religious extremism and the 'acts of terror in the name of Islam' that the Government is seeking to eliminate.

The lecture critiques the Government's notion of 'a shared vision across diverse communities' and a 'shared understanding of human rights and values'. 'Extremism' and 'support for acts of terrorism' are posited by Government as threats residing within black and principally Muslim communities. Neo-fascist organizations in Britain have unleashed terror on black and ethnic minority communities for six decades. Their members, or people who subscribe to their extremist views, seek to gain entry to professions and services where they have the authority to indulge their hatred and deny black and ethnic minority people their human rights. There has never been a debate in Britain about the effects of their extremism and support for terror on 'our vision of a successfully integrated society' or on the task of 'building community cohesion'. Indeed, as we have observed, such neo-fascist organizations, without being required to swear allegiance to anything or anyone, put themselves up for election in defence of the rights of the white section of the community against black and ethnic minority communities.

When do racist murders become terrorist acts? When do neo-fascist organizations and their sympathizers begin to warrant the same degree of anti-terrorism surveillance as communities that are now considered suitable candidates for such surveillance?

The lecture notes that the Government can no more manufacture 'community cohesion' by extracting a pledge of good citizenship from those seeking British nationality, than it could separate those people from their concerns about Britain's role in the world and in the seemingly intractable conflicts across the globe that it appears to ignore or in which it is complicit. It argues the need to nurture visions of change among black young people and encourage in them the belief in their capacity to continue to transform the society, as well as the need to assist all people in Britain to embrace the values that make us fit for living in, and for building and managing a fair and just society.

Lest it be thought that by expressing the views put forward here and in the lecture I am condoning, celebrating or glorifying terrorism, let me comment for a moment on the title of this section of the book. There has been much obfuscation around the issue of whether, by claiming to 'understand' why people destroy their communities, as in Oldham, Burnley and Bradford, or engage in acts of terror, one is therefore 'condoning' such acts. For me, understanding 'the enemy within' is about taking a broader view of the social and political context of people's beliefs, convictions and justification for their chosen actions, however much I might feel that those beliefs and the actions that flow from them are abhorrent. It is only thus that I am able to avoid self righteous moralizing and ask myself: Are there conditions that spawn and nurture such beliefs and convictions? How complicit am I in the perpetuation of those conditions? How might I engage with those who hold those beliefs and convictions such that a dialogue could take place about causes, effects and cures?

It is for that reason the lecture stresses the need to ensure that the nation does not put the rights and liberties of us all at risk by denying rights and liberties to any other nation, or any section of itself.

7.1

WHAT HAS GONE WRONG IN RACE EQUALITY IN BRITAIN'S TOWNS AND CITIES?

London
20 December 2001

Introduction

I have a 'life experience with Britain' that spans the last fifty-six years, thirty-seven of which constitute my life experience with Britain in Britain, i.e., since 1964. That experience encompasses involvement in community and public life from being: the education secretary of the Oxford Committee for Racial Integration in the middle to late 1960s; the co-author of three books in the early 1970s, *Race in the Inner City* (1970), *Because they're Black* (1971), and *Police Power and Black People* (1972); a member of the Campaign Against Racial Discrimination (CARD) in the late 1960s and of the Council of the Institute of Race Relations in the early 1970s; author of the report *In the Service of Black Youth – a Study of the Political Culture of Youth and Community Work with Black People in English Cities* (1981); chair of the Moss Side Defence Committee (1981/82) following the inner city uprisings in Moss Side in 1981; co-author of the Burnage Report on the racist murder of thirteen year old Ahmed Iqbal Ullah at Burnage High School in South Manchester in September 1986; to becoming Director of Education and Leisure Services in Hackney; an independent consultant and Visiting Professor of Education at the University of Strathclyde since 1997; and a member of the Home Secretary's Race Relations Forum since 1998.

I have been able to read Lord Herman Ouseley's report on Bradford, Mr David Ritchie's report on Oldham, and Lord

Clarke's report on Burnley in preparation for this seminar. However, I read them against the background of a series of earlier reports, notably William Daniels' Political and Economic Planning report on race discrimination in Britain; the report of the Campaign Against Racial Discrimination that influenced so directly and empirically the drafting of the 1968 Race Relations Act, the precursor to the 1976 Race Relations Act; the late EJB (Jim) Rose's report 'Colour and Citizenship'; a host of annual reports of the Community Relations Commission and its successor the Commission for Racial Equality; volumes of Runnymede Trust Bulletins; of the radical journals Race Today and Race and Class; the Scarman Report following the Brixton uprisings in 1981; the Hytner Report following the Moss Side disturbances later that same year; the volumes of Hansard that recorded Mrs Margaret Thatcher's, Mr William Whitelaw's and Mr Michael Heseltine's pronouncements following the wave of uprisings across the country in 1981 (from St Paul's in Bristol to Newcastle in the North East); and more recently the Lawrence Inquiry report; and various reports from the Government's own Social Exclusion Unit.

I am telling you all this not because I believe you are remotely interested in how old I am, or because I want you to try and understand my deep feeling of *déjà vu*, but because I wish to make one very obvious point. The existential reality of what took place in these Northern cities earlier this year cannot be divorced from its historical and contemporary political and structural context.

Yes, the 1981 events that rocked this nation to its core and triggered the development of militarized policing such as Britain had never seen before occurred twenty years ago. Yes, they involved and were led by predominantly young people of African-Caribbean heritage with a surprising number of disillusioned and abused whites who took the opportunity to vent their own frustrations about the way they, too, were maltreated by the police, and about the unjust social system that had regulated their lives for generations. But, by seeing these uprisings, principally, as criminality and thuggery of the sort that the nation had come to expect of 'these young blacks' who refused to get on their bikes and cycle through the 'steel barriers' erected at key milestones along the route; by contrasting the rebelliousness and alleged lack of parental control of African-Caribbean youths with the apparent docility and social compliance of Asian youths, the Government of the day no less than the British media was missing the point completely.

Between 1973 and 1977, I conducted a study of youth policy and the organization of youth and community work amongst Caribbean and Asian young people in sixteen cities and towns in Britain. The 'rebellious West Indian'/'docile and conformist Asian' dichotomy was very much in vogue then and led the state and its institutions to have a set of false expectations of young Asians. In the aftermath of the battle between black youths and the police at the Notting Hill Carnival in 1976, for example, commentators played that dichotomy for all it was worth. The editorial in the 'West Indian World', 3 September 1976, noted:

Those youngsters' behaviour was in complete opposition to many of those who spent weeks of their time devoting their artistic talent in brightening up (Ladbroke) Grove for the Carnival ...

Black community leaders who thought it their duty to intervene in quelling the riot were shown little respect for their efforts. They were sworn at and abused like children and their credibility as respected leaders of the black community will no doubt be questioned.

Robert Govender, editor of the Caribbean Weekly Post, went much further:

But while the state has a lot to answer for, so too have West Indian parents. The Asians have in contrast maintained a strong family discipline and motivated their children in the direction of material success.

But West Indian parents for the main part have lost control over their children who have fallen into the hands of nihilistic merchants of rhetoric who seem to believe that a lot of fancy words about revolution can bring about a Utopia.

Caribbean heritage youths were saying loudly and clearly: we are not going to be pushed around by the police and by teachers any more. We are not going to accept 'shit work' and suffer the kind of humiliating treatment to which our parents and grandparents were subjected. We have rights and we want opportunities to discharge our responsibilities. Asian youths were not saying anything different. They shouted loudly and clearly: 'Come what may, we're here to stay'. Don't treat us as appendages to our parents whom you expect to return to their homeland sooner rather than later, taking us with them. You, the society, the schooling and education system, the police and criminal justice system, local politicians and service providers, employers, sporting organizations and the rest ... you will have to come to terms with us.

The fact is that no one listened. Rather, central Government no less than Councils up and down the land got hung up on identifying and manipulating or being manipulated by so-called community leaders. Typically, those community leaders were all male, and were endorsed and had powers vested in them by Councils which prided themselves on their various initiatives in defence of women's rights, including the setting up of Women's Units. When organized Asian women's groups sought to make their voices heard, often in opposition to the designs of those same leaders and gatekeepers, Councils capitulated to the demands of the men, signalling to the women by implication, at least, that they bowed to the authority of those men who insisted that the women should neither be seen nor heard.

Young people were not credited with the power or capacity to think for themselves, to articulate their own aspirations and define ways in which they would want to influence the way decisions were made about their lives and their future. Last year, Kathleen Raley, a former student newspaper adviser at Brookings Harbour High School in the USA, had cause to say that:

People don't understand why students are acting out, why they are violent. We don't give them any non-violent options to express themselves and they have a lot to say.

As early as 1937, Jawarharlal Nehru, former Prime Minister of India warned that:

Life experience has taught us that it is dangerous to suppress opinions and ideas; it has further taught us that it is foolish to imagine that we can do so.

Schools deal with a captive audience of compulsory school age children every single day. A good number of those students then progress on to post-16 education provision. But, how many schools and colleges, however large their African-Caribbean or Asian student population, are able to tell Mr Blunkett or the odd Council Leader what those youths think about their condition as young and black in Bradford, Oldham, Southall, Harlesden or anywhere else, let alone what they are minded to do about it? Similarly, how many schools and colleges know where their white students stand on the issue of their own identity as white young people and the way they experience their black and ethnic minority peers?

I am not proposing that it is the business of schools and colleges to provide intelligence to the state on the basis of which it could plan low intensity counter insurgency operations. I am simply making the point that schools are notorious for their 'structured omission' of issues to do with equity, fairness, justice, and especially the way their student population experience their social world.

In addition to the issue of the over-dependency on 'community leaders', a notion incidentally that has no currency when it comes to dealing with the ethnic majority of whatever class, the reports on last summer's events highlight a number of other key factors. Before I deal with some of them, permit me to note that I have lived in this country for over thirty-seven years and have conducted research, taught or otherwise worked in many parts of the British Isles. Never have I heard anyone say to working class whites, residents of discrete communities in urban or rural areas, or to middle class suburban dwellers: 'Take me to your leader!'. I dare say that any community police officer, council worker or social researcher who had the audacity to make such a request would soon be considered deeply suspicious if not eligible for the nearest mental asylum. No, trading in that notion of 'leadership' is, I suggest, the employment of former colonial structures to manage the postwar ethnic colonies of Britain.

In my view, one could turn the title of this presentation on its head and ask not 'what has gone wrong in race equality in Britain's towns and cities', but *what has ever been right with race equality in Britain's towns and cities*. Because, you see, the question posed for me to address rather makes the assumption that at some time in the past, recent or otherwise, something was right with it.

As Malcolm X famously said:

True peace is not the absence of conflict….
It is the presence of justice.
Therefore, we can conclude:
No justice, no peace!

And as recent events have so tragically demonstrated, in the words of Martin Luther King:

Injustice anywhere is a threat to justice everywhere.

It is an indisputable fact of history that cultures of oppression, repression, and the denial of fundamental rights generate cultures of resistance. Some movements of resistance do not themselves respect the fundamental rights and liberties of the oppressors.

So, why was 'race equality in Britain' never right?
Some headline issues:

- The assumption that you had ethnic minorities but no ethnic majority.
- That the unacknowledged ethnic majority was homogenous and undifferentiated and could be counterposed to the

ethnic minorities as an equally undifferentiated mass.

Take, for example, Mr David Blunkett's assertion on Radio 4 in May 2000, when he was Secretary of State for Education and Employment:

I've made it clear several times that as well as teaching about religions across the world, we should be teaching about our own culture.

Who is this 'we' of whom Mr Blunkett speaks? How inclusive is it? Does teaching about 'our own culture' apply to those black teachers and headteachers in the increasing number of mainly black schools in Britain, including those all-Asian schools in Bradford, Burnley, and Oldham? What are they here expected to define as 'our own culture'? How homogenous is this 'our own culture' that we, white British (let's face it) 'should be teaching'? Was it not Mrs Margaret Thatcher in an earlier era who suggested that *our own culture was in danger of being 'swamped' by these ethnic minorities and generally alien types and therefore corrective measures needed to be put in place*?

Some more headline issues:

- The assumption that class interests and other differentiating factors were not as evident within ethnic minority populations as among the ethnic majority.
- The assumption that women of whatever faith within the ethnic minority populations would be insulated from the movement to end gender subordination and oppression that has evolved and been led by women over many generations within the ethnic majority population and that has radically altered the pattern of social relations in the society as a whole.
- The assumption, moreover, that Asian women in Britain would be ignorant of and opposed to the self-organized movement of women in the Indian subcontinent and elsewhere in Asia, against practices such as forced marriages, dowry punishment, honour killings and similar violations of the human rights of women.
- The assumption that the interests of Asian women would

necessarily be antithetical to those of other ethnic minority women and of ethnic majority women in the women's movement in Britain generally.

- The assumption that you could adopt 'one-size-fits-all' solutions to the complex problems facing multiethnic, multilayered communities with all their historical oppressions, hyphenated identities, social and economic characteristics, spheres of influence, and the rest.

- The assumption that culture is static and that the cultural traditions and preferences of the ethnic minority communities are fixed in aspic, with the power to socialize, insulate and contain their young within these seemingly unchanging traditions for all time; the assumption, moreover, that the cultural traditions, preferences and practices of people within faith communities, Muslims in particular, necessarily emanate from the tenets and practices of the faith and are consensual and unproblematic.

- The assumption that the notion of 'cultural diversity' is meaningful only when you are juxtaposing cultures of the 'ethnic minorities' with that of the undifferentiated ethnic majority.

- The failure to understand that there is diversity both within individual ethnic minority communities, between them and other ethnic minority communities, as well as between them and the ethnic majority in all its diversity.

- That it is possible for common interests to bind certain sections of ethnic minority communities with some sections of the majority ethnic population rather more than with the rest of both those populations.

- The fact that local authorities up and down the land roundly ignored their responsibilities under Section 71 of the Race Relations Act 1976, proving that whenever governments seek to bring about change by advocating self regulation, the rights of marginalized communities and of historically excluded groups are always made subordinate to the vested interests of the majority and those who represent and protect them.

- The failure to understand that although 'class' has very

rarely been included as a factor in equal opportunity policy making and programmes, promoting equal opportunity and combating social exclusion apply equally to white working class communities as to ethnic minority communities.

This is something my colleagues and I were at pains to point out to the nation and to central and local government in particular in our report of the Macdonald Inquiry into the racist murder of Ahmed Iqbal Ullah at Burnage High School in South Manchester in September 1986. The book *Murder in the Playground* is worth revisiting in the present context because it contains many important lessons which the Councils in Oldham, Burnley and Bradford have failed to heed, as have so many others up and down the country:

- The need to concentrate as much on the cultural heritage and 'roots' of white working class people and on antecedents of the identity formation of white working class males as on that of ethnic minority communities.

- The lunacy of funding regimes or social engineering programmes that were competitive and that separated 'racial disadvantage' from social and economic deprivation of the worst kind, thereby setting up conflicts between dispossessed whites caught up in a cycle of deprivation and hopelessness, and blacks on whom they saw 'special treatment' being conferred.

- A confusion about 'equity' and 'sameness'. As Pat Mitchell, commenting on the equal opportunity debate in the United States put it:
  Somewhere in the struggle for equality, 'equal' got confused with 'same', but the evidence has mounted that 'different' has nothing to do with 'equal', as long as there is equality of access.

- The danger that the statutory duty placed upon public bodies by the Race Relations (Amendment) Act 2000 to promote race equality and eliminate unlawful discrimination would result yet again in programmes targeted at ethnic minority communities without a strategic approach to eliminating the cycle of dispossession and social exclusion in which so many white working class communities are trapped. 'Community cohesion' has got to be seen in that context.

- The lack of regulation of the private sector, given the critical role commercial estate agents and landlords have played over the years in urban gate-keeping and encouraging 'white flight' and the ghettoization of black and white communities alike.
- The failure of the Government so far, to define in a manner that is meaningful to local authorities and the partnerships they are leading, what precisely is meant by 'community cohesion'.

While it is a more sophisticated concept than the flaccid notion of 'community relations', it nevertheless is a problematic concept in that it appears to focus upon inter-ethnic mixing and spatial ownership rather than on the structural factors that militate against black people and white people in certain communities up and down the land being able to live peaceably with one another.

It is worth remembering at this point that the focus on the fact that there are all-Asian or mainly Asian communities in these boroughs as a negative and undesirable phenomenon is itself deeply racist. I know of no black or Asian household that physically expelled the white residents of the home they now occupy. I know of no Asian corner shop, convenience store or off-licence owner who hounded, firebombed or racially harassed the former white owners of those businesses out of their premises.

White flight cannot be laid at the door of the African, African-Caribbean or Asian residents of our inner city areas. Moreover, I heard no protests from local councillors, central Government or the media when whites were deserting their new found and most unwelcome black and Asian neighbours in droves.

Where was the concern about 'community cohesion' and inter-racial living then? Why does no one object when whites flee to all white neighbourhoods to escape the blacks and worship at the altar of their property value?

Why should a school with 90% or even a 100% black or Asian students be considered problematic and undesirable when that is considered 'normal' in the case of whites in the majority of schools in the country? What is more, the Government allows those who take the ultimate step of removing themselves from the state system altogether, to do their own thing as far as curriculum and communal values are concerned, so they don't even have to concern themselves with the fact, the shape, the composition, or the future of multiethnic Britain.

William James, a psychologist and philosopher at the beginning of the last century said:

A great many people think they are thinking when they are merely rearranging their prejudices.

In my view, this aptly describes the reaction from Government and the debate that has ensued in the media and elsewhere in the wake of the events in those Northern towns and cities. The focus has been on language, on religion, on the infamous Tebbit 'cricket test', oaths of allegiance, and much else besides.

Britain is full of segregated communities and of majority ethnic people who took a conscious decision to move as far away from the blacks as possible. They saw that as their incontrovertible right. Many others stayed precisely because they did not wish to have their children brought up in a white ghetto somewhere but wanted them to benefit educationally, culturally, and spiritually from the dynamism, creativity and humaneness of the multiethnic communities they continue to inhabit.

Sadly, however, too many Councils not to mention central Government, have failed them by their cynicism, lack of vision, lack of direction, incapacity to listen and to hear even when they are listening, and refusal to dismantle some shibboleths and sacred cows.

It is to the latter that I now wish to turn for the rest of this presentation.

Valuing Diversity?

I said earlier that there is as much diversity within ethnic minority communities as between them and the majority ethnic community. Local government particularly has failed to comprehend this basic fact and has consequently rendered certain sections of ethnic minority communities much more vulnerable.

Why is the assumption made that British women, who happen to be of Asian heritage and Muslim, do not have the same concern about the abuse of their human rights as white English women do? Why should local councils come to a 'settlement' with the 'leaders' of the local Islamic Council and deny Muslim women the right to represent themselves and make their voices heard in respect of the oppression they suffer generally, and at the hands of their menfolk in particular?

Why should a British girl, a high flyer at school, self confident and sophisticated, not expect the protection of the state when she is whisked away to Pakistan under false pretences and married off at age fourteen or less, returning to England with her first child at fifteen, only to be left with in-laws while her husband goes off to work abroad. In his absence, she is repeatedly raped by his father, her father-in-law, and by brothers-in-law. Her husband refuses to protest his father's and siblings' abuse of her and she feels totally trapped and suicidal. She eventually runs away and ends up in a refuge for women escaping domestic violence. This makes her a prey for 'bounty hunters', many of whom receive instructions to impose the ultimate punishment, if necessary, for the shame that is brought on the family.

'Shame' not because of the barbaric violation of that young woman's fundamental human rights, not because of the indelible scars and self abhorrence she is left with, to the extent that she indulges in constant self-mutilation, but because she dared to remove herself from that hellish situation and behave in ways contrary to what those men consider to be appropriate for 'their' Muslim women.

Why is it that when at the beginning of the 1980s I, and the Black Parents Movement in Manchester, launched a massive campaign against the threatened deportation of three Asian women, former brides from Pakistan, all of whom had deserted their families because of similar sorts of abuse, only to have their husbands report them to the immigration authorities ...

why is it that I was in fear of my life because of the physical threats and daily intimidation from males within the Asian community? Why did Manchester City Council not take a more robust stand – or any stand at all – in support of those women and of our right and that of the Asian Youth Movement to defend their right to stay in this country, and not be booted out because they refused to be subjected to that daily violation of their human rights?

It has been put to me by some Muslims, young and old, in Northern towns, that the 'preoccupation' with marital issues and practices within Muslim communities is as Islamophobic as the peddling of stereotypes in respect of African-Caribbean family organization is racist.

But, who is making the distinction between the legitimate opposition to the practices I have just described, opposition to the public burning of books at the height of the Salman Rushdie affair, the Fatwa itself and the millions of pounds it cost the taxpayer to provide security for Salman ... who is making the distinction between all of that and Islamophobia? Who is ensuring that cries of Islamophobia do not become a smokescreen for the continuation of such horrendous practices?

I make no comment on the merits or demerits of the Satanic Verses except to say that as a former student of Theology and Ancient History, I agree with George Bernard Shaw that:

All great truths begin as blasphemies.

What evidence is there that those who have a legitimate concern about Islamophobia are actively engaged in confronting those practices within Muslim communities and taking a stand, publicly, against them? Where is the evidence of their concern for the fact that the majority of women's refuges within ethnic minority communities are populated by Asian women fleeing domestic violence and forced marriages, or of the fact that their lives are potentially more at risk when they do manage to escape the brutal captivity in which they are held in the name of 'traditional family customs', or of what their oppressors conveniently attribute to 'Holy Scriptures'?

Our innate instinct for freedom alerts us, naturally, women no less than men, Muslims no less than Christians, to repel invasion of our liberty by others and by the evil-minded rulers and gatekeepers who support them and legitimize their actions.

Councils up and down the land should ask themselves, therefore, why it is that in all the years they have been negotiating with and giving a voice to 'community leaders' in the Asian community, those leaders have invariably if not exclusively been male. Those same Councils have equal opportunities policies, 'zero tolerance' policies on domestic violence, and the rest. But, somehow, they appear to have concluded that only the men speak English, only they know their way around the Council and its systems, and what's more that they have an inalienable right to speak for Asian women of whatever faith and of whatever age, in respect of any and all issues.

In the year 2000, Vaclav Havel declared that:

Courage means going against majority opinion in the name of truth.

Those Councils that seek to regulate if not control affairs within the Asian communities by engaging with these often self appointed colonial gatekeepers would do well to remember that, and consequently, to develop the political will to put in place democratic systems of access to power, influence and decision-making by women, by youths, and other marginalized groups within those communities.

We have a duty to defend the right of Pakistani, Bangladeshi, Iraqi, Palestinian men, women and children, and all others who happen to be Muslim, to go about their daily business, including collective acts of worship, without being targeted by malevolent folk of any ethnicity simply because they are Muslim.

What certain communities have been experiencing since September 11 and the subsequent pursuit of the Taliban and Bin Laden is identical to what Muslim communities (and individuals mistakenly identified as Muslim) experienced during the Gulf War and the pursuit of Saddam Hussein. Every Muslim is assumed by some, to be fundamentalist, a supporter of Bin Laden, committed to the domination of the world by the forces of Islam. For that very reason, children were taunted and physically attacked, Asian businesses targeted, and Mosques desecrated during the Gulf War, because some people believed that all Muslims must necessarily identify with the Iraqi invasion of Kuwait and the exploits of Saddam Hussein. In order to stop themselves, their families or their premises becoming targets of anti-Muslim attacks, many Asian shop owners (Muslim and non-Muslim) took to flying the Union Flag outside their premises to show their allegiance to Britain and their support for 'Operation Desert Storm'.

We need to be seen to take as firm a stand in defence of the rights of women and of children from emotional and physical violation within Muslim communities themselves, as we do in opposition to Islamophobia in all its various manifestations. Above all, we need to ensure that fear of being branded Islamophobic does not deter us from affirming those rights and acting with the progressive forces within Islam itself to safeguard them and give support to the vulnerable and to the excluded.

Finally, in terms of building for the future, I want to suggest that:

- We reinforce the notion that there is only ONE 'race'
- We promote the notion of 'whiteness' as ethnicity and as racially constructed
- We attend to the very urgent issue of identity formation within, and the need to raise the aspirations of, white working class communities, far too many of which are characterized by 'the abandonment of hope and the death of aspiration'
- We devise tangible programmes whereby Asian, African-Caribbean and white communities could plan the use of space and territory, and the organization and use of services, in an organic rather than a contrived and artificial manner
- Local Strategic Partnerships, the Regional Development Agency, the Government Offices in the regions, the Learning

and Skills Council and local authorities should all be required to establish their own youth 'parliament', and Asian and black women's 'parliament', and to demonstrate that their budget driven policy-and-strategic-planning incorporates the agenda agreed by those parliaments, however that agenda is prioritized

- Proper and effective guidance and support is given to those groupings, not least with regard to access to information and to adopting principles and methods of organization, in order to maximize the effectiveness of their work
- Due attention should be given to the effects of the 'democratic deficit' and the increasing privatization of services on the capacity to demand accountability and provide robust and sustained leadership of the agenda to effect the changes that are urgently needed
- The Government should simplify the multivariate requirements placed on local authorities (regeneration strategy, community plan, community cohesion strategy, social inclusion strategy, learning and skills strategy, strategy for implementing the CRE's Code of Practice on the statutory duty to promote race equality)
- Above all, every possible step should be taken to stop projecting British Asians as a 'race' apart, or as Muslims, irrespective of their faith or their atheism, as if that were the only defining factor in their identity. My work amongst young Asians in England and Scotland would suggest that those who are Muslim define themselves as British (English or Scottish) young people of Pakistani, Bangladeshi (or other) heritage who profess the Islamic faith.

It is when their aspirations and cultural and religious preferences are considered mainstream and 'normal' that they would see the society and its institutions as being ready to accept their self-definition rather than placing them forever on the margins and conferring upon them an alien identity.

The legacy of Empire is still very much with us, not least in the cultural supremacist assumptions of huge swathes of British society, and it is a legacy that haunts 'Great Britain'. It is a legacy, moreover, that makes it imperative that, for the future of this society, a future that is commonly owned and commonly shared, we all understand the difference between immigration, nationality, citizenship, and 'race' relations and place them in their proper perspective. For, 'come what may', not only ... we're here to stay', multiethnic Britain is here to stay, and therefore it has a need to take collective responsibility for every single part of itself and for the protection of every community within itself.

WILL THE NEW RACE RELATIONS ACT REALLY MAKE A DIFFERENCE?
Challenges, opportunities and pitfalls
London
10 July 2002

I have been involved in the struggle for racial equality and social justice in Britain since 1964. As a member of the Campaign Against Racial Discrimination (CARD) in the late 1960s, I worked with many others to gather evidence of racial discrimination in employment, housing, and access to public services. The political struggle waged by CARD made a significant contribution to the decision of the then Government to introduce the 1968 Race Relations Act.

In 1971, I wrote *Race in the Inner City* for the Runnymede Trust, followed by a Penguin publication *Because They're Black* which I co authored with Derek Humphry, then of the *Sunday Times*. The following year, we published a book called *Police Power and Black People*, and if you want to understand the origins of the situation the Stephen Lawrence Inquiry considered, you only have to revisit that book, if you could find it. Because, being in a state of total denial and feeling affronted that the great British police could be written about in such terms, the State colluded with the police to prevent the book being marketed. Consequently, thousands of copies were pulped.

Those were the days when some of us were much clearer as to the State we were in, a state in which we needed to be seen to be taking a stand in defence of rights and in affirmation of our desire to be allowed to operate as full citizens, wanting no less for Britain than the ethnic majority itself. A majority that never regarded itself as 'ethnic', in a country where, then as now, whiteness was not thought to be racially constructed. White people were not ethnic anything, neither majority nor minority. Ethnicity came with the ethnics, they carried it in their pigment, in their food, in their clothes, in their music, in their art, in their social graces, or their assumed lack of them. But they also carried it in their 'preposterous demands' to be given the right to impact upon if not displace British culture and British national identity, all the things that make us quintessentially British, the right to criticize our institutions and to join dissidents who insist in forcing the pace of change other than through the ballot box.

So, having been at the barricades for nearly four decades, do I really believe the Amended Act will make a difference? The short answer is that it has to and we all have a responsibility to make sure that it does.

Recent events have surely demonstrated what I have long argued, i.e., that no nation, no group of nations, should preside over or give tacit consent to the denial of rights and basic entitlements to any section of itself, or any group of people across the globe, without putting its own rights and entitlements at risk. Securing the borders does not by itself create safe havens. The enemy is very seldom at the gates. The enemy is more often to be found within, systemic and structured, programmed to create casualties on a cyclical basis.

So, why I am telling you all this so early on a Monday morning when we should be having a futuristic conversation about improving race relations in our country?

I take you back there because I believe if we fail to question some basic and erroneous assumptions, we risk repeating the mistakes of the past and sealing in inequalities under the guise of promoting equality.

A few quick observations in order to situate the debate, I leave it up to you to identify among them challenges, opportunities, pitfalls or just plain headaches:

- Social inclusion is effectively about promoting inclusion in a grossly unequal society.
- Promoting race equality is essentially about delivering minimum entitlements to black and ethnic minority people

in a society that routinely excludes target groups, and is structured in a way that accepts inequality as a given.

- By virtue of these patterns of exclusion and marginalization, all those public services and authorities that roundly ignored the duty that was no less explicit in the 1976 Race Relations Act, are now scrambling to develop the expertise to deliver what has been made obligatory.

- Most managers and decision makers in those services are white, many with a preference for touchy feely notions such as valuing diversity or building cohesive communities, rather than for the more upfront and urgent task of combating racism, including their own. In order to assist them in the mad scramble, caused no less than by the Government itself, to have meaningful and coherent schemes in place, they are having recourse to some decidedly dodgy 'experts' who themselves demonstrate precious little evidence of ever having confronted their own racism.The question begged by the 'duty to promote that', quite rightly, has been laid upon all public authorities is where and how are leaders and managers in organizations that dismissed the 1976 Act as being of peripheral concern to them, suddenly expected to develop the capacity to lead the agenda to promote race equality and eliminate unlawful discrimination?

- The amended Act, like all the other equality legislation, enshrines minimum requirements. It does not by itself create an environment or a workplace culture in which members of targeted groups are valued intrinsically and are provided with opportunities to be themselves, like the majority who are considered to be the 'norm'.

- The Act is in danger of making assumptions not unlike the valuing diversity lobby. Concepts such as valuing diversity, building cohesive communities and promoting good relations between people of different racial groups are ones which are so endearing and noble that no well meaning citizen is expected to have problems with them. Well, this socially adjusted and wellmeaning citizen finds them decidedly problematic. For one thing, they set up polar opposites. For another, they make the assumption that homogeneity exists at every pole. The problem we as blacks have is that, for centuries, the British Isles failed to celebrate its internal diversity. Its history is about attempts to subjugate people, pathologize difference and validate and lend legitimacy only to that which it could control and dominate. Despite an institution as powerful as the Monarchy, the United Kingdom was not so united after all. Liberation and devolution movements, language preservation movements and working class social movements, all gnawed at the consensual image that Great Britain projected to itself and to the world.

- The Welsh child that was made to wear a collar of shame for speaking Welsh, the Liverpudlian or Geordie that was discriminated against in employment for having 'that accent' and the young school leavers whose life chances were thwarted by virtue of living on the wrong side of the railway line all had tales to tell about those notions of a shared British identity and British culture.

Yet, those who maltreated and discriminated against them for generations, are suddenly expecting them to show how British and tolerant they are by welcoming the blacks and the refugees and asylum seekers with open arms and respecting their cultures, their 'alien' beliefs and their exotic backgrounds.

Time was when people genuinely believed the saying

Charity begins at home.

I happen to believe it still. If I do not love myself, if I internalize definitions of myself as worthless, if I am socialized into always apologizing for myself, for how I speak, for what I eat, for where I live, for my existence on the margins of society. If I spend my life trying to live up to someone else's notion of how I ought to be, then I am hardly likely to be open and generous towards others whom I perceive to be more favoured than I am, whose demands for the same things as me appear to be met with more concerted effort to deliver and to please than are my demands.

Whether in Oldham, Burnley, or Bradford, building cohesive

communities requires structural efforts to deliver social justice, as well as promoting race equality. And if, like me, you believe that whiteness is racially constructed, then race equality must mean fairness and justice for whites no less than for blacks. Those policies and practices, therefore, that have tended to project white, British National Front supporters as ferret-eyed racists who are totally beyond the pale, are in my view an exercise in off-loading and abnegation of responsibility for sustaining the conditions in which such citizens are moulded.

Any citizenship curriculum that fails to deal with these harsh realities, but rams young people and would be citizens full of unctuous pap, is destined to further underpin racism in the society.

So, I am arguing for a redefinition of race equality, I am asking for a reclassification (forgive the pun) of equal opportunities. In addition to 'race', gender, disability, sexual orientation, age, special educational needs ... let us also have 'class' and economic exclusion.

I am arguing for a redefinition of 'diversity' and of 'difference', such that Britain comes to understand, and learns to deal with, respect and validate the difference that makes it such a dynamic and vibrant society even after you leave the blacks and the 'ethnics' out of the equation. I am arguing for the dawn of commonsense and the eclipse of cynicism in the corridors of the Home Office, such that it becomes transparently obvious that you cannot have a Race Relations Amendment Act promoting race equality and eliminating unlawful discrimination on the one hand, and at the same time make it necessary for genuine refugees and asylum seekers to commit a criminal offence before they can even merit consideration for refugee status in this country. You cannot bait would-be racists on the one hand and boast an agenda to promote race equality and combat social exclusion on the other.

The 'Secure Borders, Safe Haven' fallacy is but a parody of the much vaunted 'without integration, immigration controls would be inexcusable ... without immigration controls, integration would be impossible'. There were those, of course, who genuinely believed that, its proponent Mr Roy Hattersley among them. The fact that that represented a process of racializing immigration, and that the immigrants being controlled were predominantly black, did not seem to matter.

Having said all that, I am all for empowering black and ethnic minority people and progressive whites to use the legislation for all it is worth, to hold institutions to account in respect of their duty to promote equity and understand and operationalize the relationship between racial equality and social justice.

There is but one 'race', the human race. It is just that some of us remain stubbornly visible, and even when others take extraordinary steps to enhance their visibility (whether through baking in the sun or lying under artificial sun lamps), it not only wears off, but they never ever become imprisoned in the castle of their skin.

7.3

MANAGING EQUALITY ISSUES TOGETHER TO COMBAT DISCRIMINATION AND PROMOTE SOCIAL JUSTICE

13 January 2004

I salute Danny Lafayette, Chair of the Network, and members of the National Executive Committee, past, present, and future. I commend the work you have done and are doing to develop the Network and to make a difference to the working lives and professional experience of black staff in the Home Office.

I welcome the opportunity to address this august gathering and particularly to focus on the role of Government, as one of the biggest firms in the country, with the capacity to lead by example and showcase good practice in employment and service delivery.

The last time I talked about an 'august' gathering, it was to a large group of staff who had been given a three line whip to attend a training programme which the more polite amongst them likened to 'dipping sheep'. Those who took pride in flaunting their racism and flying the flag for 'the silent majority' referred to the training in rather more colourful terms which cannot be repeated in this company. I knew I was in for some free and frank exchanges when some smart ass declared in booming voice: 'You're at the wrong conference, mate. We're in November, not August'. Needless to say, I was to discover in the course of that very long day that the gathering was not so august after all.

I know I am in much better company today and I am sure you would continue to be very august, however free and frank an exchange we will have.

The title of this talk is a trifle ambiguous: 'Managing Equality Issues Together to Combat Discrimination and Promote Social Justice'. I should explain that it is not my intention here to endorse Government proposals for a single equality commission.

By 'managing equality issues together', I mean the task facing Government as employer and you as its black employees in making race equality a reality and eliminating the institutional and cultural barriers that you face as black employees; black employees who have identities that are defined not just by 'race' and ethnicity but by that range of other factors which are often dealt with as if they are not inclusive of black people: disability, age, faith, gender, sexual orientation and class.

I therefore want to share some thoughts about the challenges, the opportunities and the pitfalls of your joint project, now that you are nearing your fifth birthday, and examine some of the implications of those for your future structures and relationships.

I hardly need to present the statistics to this audience, but it is worth reminding ourselves that:

Black people constitute 34% of Home Office staff
3% of staff of Senior Civil Service grade
1 Director (Special Adviser on Race Equality, etc)
The resident ethnic minority population in the UK is said to be roughly 7.1% of the total population.

ONS figures suggest that it is the fastest growing section of the overall population (an estimated 15 times faster than whites), with an increase of one million between the 1991 and 2001 censuses.

That demographic reality would suggest that the British labour market would need to depend increasingly upon workers from black and ethnic minority backgrounds in order to sustain the British economy and the capacity of local and central government and other public bodies to function properly.

What then are the issues confronting Government as 'the firm' and you as black employees in the post-Lawrence context and in the context of implementing the Race Relations (Amendment) Act 2000?

- Diversity in organizations is a fact of life.
- People come from a variety of class, educational, economic, cultural, and ethnic backgrounds. They are of different faiths and none. They are also male and female; some are transgender. The majority will be able bodied, young and old, and some will have disabilities.
- All of the various groups represented in the organization will see one another in different ways. Those 'ways of seeing' are influenced by the way the society treats the particular group to which they belong, relative to others who are defined as of more or less worth.
- Society's definitions are often reflected in structural, cultural, institutional, and personal forms of discrimination which become part of normal conduct and of the prevailing culture within organizations.
- Part of the collective experience of black people in this society is of the society automatically validating white people, including those that discriminate and harass, while explicitly or at least subconsciously expecting black people to prove themselves before they can be accepted as competent, 'able to fit in', worthy to be included, deserving of trust, deserving of equal treatment.
- It is for that reason that equality legislation becomes necessary. Legislation provides safeguards for groups rendered vulnerable by discriminatory conduct and systems of oppression in the society.
- Equality legislation enshrines minimum requirements for the protection of members of target groups. It does not by itself create an environment in which members of target groups are valued intrinsically and have their fundamental rights respected. Indeed, as the response to the 1976 Race Relations Act has taught us, public and private sector organizations invariably feel it is enough to simply ensure that they are operating just within the law.
- Equality legislation assists organizations in securing coercive

compliance, at the very least, and ensuring that people's attitudes do not get translated into behaviours and actions that discriminate against or obstruct the performance of members of target groups.

- It means that far from leaving things to chance, or having progress depend upon the disposition of individuals, managing equality requires the leaders and managers, as well as those they manage, to demonstrate what proactive steps they are taking to promote equity, combat discrimination and value diversity.
- It allows for built-in accountability and measurable outcomes. It allows for the appraisal of performance in meeting equality objectives as a key measure of management competence and of organizational performance.
- It upholds the right of everyone to live with dignity and to study, work and enjoy their leisure in an environment in which that right is respected.
- Crucially, it sends out a strong message to would be employees, customers, partners, and collaborators as to the kind of organization they are dealing with and what they could expect from it.
- It sends out a message to would be managers as to the commitment, leadership, and management capacity they would be expected to bring to their new roles.
- In an increasingly competitive market, that must surely be good for business.

One major challenge facing the Civil Service as employer no less than you as black employees is the tendency to deal in polar opposites and to assume that each group is somehow undifferentiated. To this day, the race and diversity discourse still fails to refer to the 'ethnic majority'.

Whiteness is not considered to be racially constructed. White people are not presumed to be ethnic anything, they just are. They are like fish and chips. There is nothing ethnic about them, not like curry and kebabs. The rich seam of cultural diversity is thought to exist only among the ethnic minorities.

Drill down into white society as you may, you are not expected to identify a rich cultural diversity that is born not just of aesthetic preference but of the relationship between labour and capital, regionalism and nationalism, elitism and subservience, and for example, the huge difference in wealth, amount of leisure time, and how that leisure is used that there is between lairds and crofters.

We as black people have historically performed the function of interpreting this society to itself through the way we experience it, good, bad, and sometimes murderously ugly. Regrettably, however, the evidence has been building up over the years of the society refusing to see itself through the prism of our experience. Despite the disturbing statistics of over-representation on all sorts of negative indicators (school underachievement, school exclusions, numbers in prison and youth custody, suicides, deaths in custody, etc) and under-representation on others (numbers in senior management, numbers in particular professions, numbers in elite Universities, etc), there is still a reluctance on the part of most employers to put appropriate mechanisms in place for consulting with black and ethnic minority stakeholders about the way they experience the organization, and the corrective action that should result from that.

As far as Government as 'the firm' is concerned, I applaud the fact that in just about every major professional area there is now an association of black staff: Police, Crown Prosecutors, Probation Officers, Prison Officers, to name but a few. I do not have the information, but I suspect that the extent to which those black staff groups are empowered and facilitated to influence the strategic management of their service and to audit organizational performance on the race equality agenda varies enormously.

This raises a number of crucial questions which doubtlessly exercise the minds of rank and file members of such associations no less than their national executive bodies. One perennial question is how can we, as black staff associations, get all our members and all the potential beneficiaries of our efforts who exercise their choice not to be members, how can we get them to work collectively such that we have both the information and the power to influence the strategic management of the service?

Often the assumption is made that class interests, ideological differences and other such factors are not as evident within and between ethnic minority populations as among the ethnic majority.

It is an indisputable fact of history that cultures of oppression, repression, and the denial of fundamental rights generate cultures of resistance. It is also a historical fact that some movements of resistance do not themselves respect the fundamental rights and liberties of the oppressors and those who are seen as identifying with them.

Hence the late Dr Martin Luther King's sobering reminder that:

Injustice anywhere is a threat to justice everywhere.

The existence of associations such as the Network could be seen as part and parcel of the history of resistance to oppression, discrimination, marginalization, and exclusion, that is an integral part of our history as a people in this society. Such a notion would no doubt add to the unease of certain members of the Network and other such associations who may not wish to be identified with any boat-rocking or overt talk about challenge, let alone resistance. That is to be expected. Indeed, that is part of the diversity that characterizes the workplace and those black staff associations themselves.

The fact remains however, that with or without the requirements of the Race Relations Amendment Act, the 'firm' continues be a legitimate site of struggle for black employees, as are other organizations, until such time that institutional discrimination is eliminated, barriers are dismantled, imbalances are corrected, organizations stop seeing it as their duty to close ranks and provide cover for the racists and bullies in their midst, and every meritorious school leaver and university graduate could have a legitimate expectation that they could join the Civil Service and become whatever and whoever they wish, preferably before they reach the age of fifty-five.

I am not implying that black staff and white staff, black staff and their predominantly white managers, should situate themselves on different sides of the imaginary barricades. It does mean, though:

For the employer

- Acknowledging the right of black staff to use the Network and similar black staff groupings to register issues and concerns with a legitimate expectation of being listened to, counselled and guided, even if it later leads to a referral to the formal structures, procedures, and post holders with responsibility for dealing with the particular matter.

- Acknowledging that the operational and social culture of the organization and of its human resource management might still be such that having to revert to the immediate use of standard procedures could be itself a traumatizing experience for certain black members of staff.

- Ensuring that opportunities are created for black staff associations to influence decision making, policy and performance review, and strategic management.

- Facilitating such associations by ensuring that their infrastructure is such as to enable them to meet the needs of their members and work in partnership with management and other collaborators.

- Having a focus, with such associations, on the support and development needs of black staff in geographically isolated areas where there is no available black support, or where they are isolated members of mainly white teams, teams invariably made up of individuals who feel they have nothing to learn from the black member of staff, not even about themselves and the way they handle issues of race.

- Ensuring black staff representation on committees, working groups, etc., that have a remit for monitoring performance on race equality issues, including monitoring racist incidents and complaints, and how those are dealt with and reported upon.

- As well as enabling Government to fulfil its duties, black staff are 'representative' of their communities that are often the target of government initiatives from education to social welfare to criminal justice and 'community cohesion'. Such staff networks representing as they do a broad cross section of ethnic minority communities should be enabled to provide focus group feedback on matters that impact upon them in their dual roles as civil servants, and black and ethnic minority communities.

- Ensuring that managers are made accountable for leading the race equality agenda, for the way they manage black staff and for seeing that white staff do not capriciously constrain black staff, if only by the validation that being white and in the majority gives them.

- A major problem in large, mainly white organizations is white managers' incompetence at managing black staff. That, more than any other reason, is what causes them to be paraded in front of the Employment Tribunal. By far the worst scenario is where there is persistent failure to manage black staff for fear of being called 'racist'. Every single employee has a right to know how well or how badly they are performing and to be developed through routine line management supervision as well as formal staff development programmes. A failure to manage situations involving black staff is a failure to develop those staff and to deal with situations, and with people, that might well be hindering them from performing to the best of their ability.

- Creating a climate in which whistle blowing is encouraged and bigotry and racism do not go unchallenged because of the protection the system affords to those who use power and authority to discriminate, harass and bully. Where such conduct provides justifiable reasons for bringing race complaints, it is usually the black staff member who is seen as the problem. The organization then goes to all lengths to avoid being judged to be racist, including paying out undisclosed sums in pre-trial settlement of the matter whilst leaving the offenders in place, or worse still, rewarding them with promotion. Meanwhile, as in one unresolved case that has its origins in events dating back to 1987, the aggrieved individual is sent home on 'gardening leave' for a period long enough to enable them to supply the entire Sainsbury's chain with organic vegetables. That black staff member has been on gardening leave for two and a half (now almost five) years. No one in the Home Office appears to be overly concerned about the effect this bizarre state of affairs is having on her career and her capacity to continue to believe in her skills.

- Ensuring that the unprecedented amount of training on race and diversity issues that has been provided since Lawrence does not simply result in staff and their managers being more informed and sophisticated in their discourse about, and treatment of, race matters. Rather, ensuring that it is having a measurable effect on people's behaviour, management practice and quality of decision making.
- Ensuring that evidence of the application of the training received forms part of professional development review and other staff appraisal systems.
- Accepting that training has serious limitations and that, as they say, the proof of the pudding is in the eating.

William James, a psychologist and philosopher at the beginning of the last century noted that:

A great many people think they are thinking when they are merely rearranging their prejudices.

Ironically, the RRAA 2000 is giving rise to a great deal of prejudice rearranging as organizations put their staff through training on implementing the Act. In my own experience, some organizations are so determined that their staff should not be taken out of their comfort zones that they insist on scrutinizing the training approach and every bit of training material to be used with them. This is especially true of academic institutions, where those who validate, parcel up and transmit knowledge are considered to be above having any need to examine the effect that being socialized into and within a culture of racism might have had on them, let alone the extent to which they might be implicated in institutional racism.

A famous education guru of mine reminded the world of the need for personal commitment and embracing of responsibility as much as two centuries ago. His observation is also a sober reminder of the limitations of training, especially in relation to issues such as combating oppression and bringing about behavioural change:

Whatever does not spring from a man's free choice, or is only the result of instruction and guidance, does not enter into his very being, but remains alien to his true nature. (Wilhelm Humboldt, 1765-1835)

That is why the human equivalent of 'dipping sheep' is of questionable value.

That is why we cannot come truculently to training but need to be ready and willing to turn ourselves inside out and develop the capacity to perceive 'the other', the 'deviation from our assumed norm', from inside their world rather than from the safety of our world, a world which we prefer not to have to understand ourselves or to open up to scrutiny by others.

I have heard attempts to dismiss the claims made by police officers who had been through probationer training, that Doreen and Neville Lawrence were just a 'f...ing pair of scroungers' and the Macpherson Inquiry was a 'f...ing kick in the bollocks for every white man' as the ranting of a few psychos whom the undercover journalist, Mark Daly, did us a service by unmasking.

My suspicion is that there is a percentage of people who, far from just rearranging long held prejudices, have those prejudices reinforced by certain forms of training before they rearrange them, using the content of the training itself as their justification.

For the Network and other Black Staff Associations, it means:
- Making a commitment to work together for change in your common interests and in the interest of all those who will come after you and in relation to whom you are trailblazers.
- Understanding, especially the young and bushy-tailed among you, that we do inherit the political space to organize and make a difference created through the struggles of, and the risks taken by, those who went before us.

- Identifying what it is that unites you and what it is that threatens your cohesiveness and your capacity to be strong and powerful; building upon the former and working collectively to eliminate the latter.

- Understanding the power imbalance and the power dynamics that operate within your networks and between the managers of the Civil Service and yourselves.

- Spending time dealing with issues of serious concern to yourselves and to the service, rather than wasting time and energy on inconsequential matters. One such red herring is to do with the relationship those who self-ascribe as 'ethnically ambiguous' should have with your group. Leave it alone! Life is too short. If such folk have difficulties deciding who they really are, the average racist, ferret-eyed or benign, would soon show them that they have no such difficulty.

- Demonstrating the most open and democratic forms of decision making and of governance of your affairs; encouraging open debate in an atmosphere of mutual respect.

- Being clear about how you wish to structure the partnership with your employer and what it is you are bringing to that partnership.

- Being bold and assertive in your statement of your reality, ensuring that your claims are based on sound evidence.

- Using the resources you are given wisely, to the advantage of your members and of the service, and being openly accountable for your choice of priorities.

- Ensuring that, acting as a staff association, you have the authority to challenge employment practices and workplace harassment and bullying on behalf of your members, without fear for your own jobs or career progression.

- Creating a climate in which your members could share matters in the full confidence that they would be pursued when appropriate, again without fear of repercussion or subtle forms of victimization.

- Not allowing your fear about what the system might do to you, your mortgage or your car loan to lead you to collude with blatant injustice, undermine the efforts of your colleagues in the Network, or/and lead others to feel that they could take liberties with you as wilfully as they might.

- Understanding that in this connection, it is possible for common interests to bind certain sections of ethnic minority communities with some sections of the majority ethnic population rather more than with the rest of both those populations.

- Giving serious consideration to the formation of a National Federation of Black Staff Associations, through which a critical mass of influential black people could make an impact upon what remains a highly conservative organization, Government, that has itself only recently begun to address issues of institutional racism seriously. Indeed, it still prefers policies and programmes on promoting diversity rather than combating discrimination and promoting equity and social justice.

Conclusion

The fact that public bodies up and down the land roundly ignored their responsibilities under Section 71 of the Race Relations Act 1976, is evidence that whenever governments seek to bring about change by advocating self regulation, the rights of marginalized communities and of historically excluded groups are always made subordinate to the vested interests of the majority and those who represent them. For that reason, I particularly welcome the Race Relations Amendment Act.

Many organizations are still adopting an 'I will do as I please' approach to implementing the Specific and General Duties of the Act. Some of those feel secure in the belief that the CRE and the various inspection regimes would never have enough resources to search them out and call them to account.

There is a danger that the statutory duty the Act places upon public bodies to promote race equality and eliminate unlawful discrimination would result yet again in programmes targeted specifically at ethnic minority communities, especially in terms of recruitment, retention and progression, without appreciating that the major task is in ensuring that white managers and the structures and systems they operate do not continue to exclude, to marginalize and discriminate against black people.

In the year 2000, Vaclav Havel declared that:

Courage means going against majority opinion in the name of truth.

I implore you to have the courage to challenge the consensus that keeps people in their comfort zones.

Have the courage to challenge one another, especially when there is evidence of collusion with racism and institutional discrimination.

Through your collective efforts, ensure that you help build a climate in the Civil Service in which it is possible to register what is causing you hurt and to work with managers in getting something done about it, without being branded, labelled and thwarted in your career ambitions. Learn from one another and share your dazzling array of talents, skills and competences to the enrichment and professional development of one another.

The legacy of Empire is still very much with us and it is a ghoulish legacy that haunts 'Great Britain'. It is a legacy, moreover, that makes it imperative that, for the future of this society, a future that is commonly owned and commonly shared, we all understand the difference between valuing diversity and combating racism, between raising people's awareness of 'race' and making sure that they do not routinely deny black people the opportunity to shape, transform and manage the society, together. Only thus will we ensure that we work, together, to make the future we face the future we want for ourselves, our children and our children's children.

Above all, let no one, not even your own over cautious 'self', render you less than you are or less than you know you have the capacity to be.

I wish you strength, energy, renewed courage and success in all your endeavours in the next twelve months.

7.4

BRIDGING COMMUNITIES
Confronting divisions and promoting community cohesion

1 October 2002

Preamble

I am pleased to be able to join you at your annual conference to share some thoughts about this crucially important agenda you have set yourselves.

Some weeks ago, I joined colleagues in Bradford for the launch of your race equality action guide and found those proceedings particularly stimulating.

Last year you passed a motion to unite against racial harassment and produced this extremely useful guide, *Bridging Communities*, to inform your activities and help order your priorities in this crucial area. You are looking in some depth this year at how successful you have been, and can be, in acting as effective agents of change in communities by combating social exclusion and promoting community cohesion.

Social Inclusion, Its Challenges and Pitfalls

The CAB has a history of promoting equality and celebrating diversity of which you can be proud. Yours has been an inclusive service, acting as the first port of call for people who are automatically expected to know how to navigate a path through an increasingly complex system but cannot do so; you are seen as the 'last chance café' by those who get worn down by the system and denied their basic rights and entitlements, or even as a substitute for and cheaper option than legal advocates by those who do know how to work the system.

Long before government adopted the language of social inclusion and placed it on their policy agenda, therefore, CAB have of necessity been confronting the many manifestations of social exclusion, including gender oppression, race discrimination and racial harassment, homophobia, the humiliation, stigmatizing and exploitation of the poor and unemployed, and of ex-offenders, the denial of consumers' rights and much else besides.

I have called this talk 'Confronting Divisions and Promoting Community Cohesion' because I wish to emphasize the fact that 'bridging communities' is not about promoting harmonious community relations.

Our commitment to promoting social inclusion must be informed by the realization that 'Social inclusion is essentially about inclusion in a grossly unequal society'. Those inequalities amount to and are often manifestations of racial oppression, gender subordination, homophobia, age oppression, class oppression, economic exploitation, cultural marginalization, disability discrimination, and denial of access to computer literacy and the world of information technology.

We combat social exclusion and seek to promote social inclusion in a grossly unequal society. There is a growing tendency to define social exclusion mainly on the index of class, income and individual and family pathology. It is increasingly obvious, however, that the marginalization of entire communities and ethnic groups in the population, irrespective of their income or the social stratum in which their occupation places them, is one of the most intractable forms of social exclusion. That is why racism is so pernicious. That is why everyone in the society needs to demonstrate their abhorrence of racial harassment and racial attacks. That is why we all have a responsibility to protest vehemently when the State itself defines and projects certain groups in the society in a manner that renders them vulnerable to discriminatory practices and, worse yet, to racial and xenophobic attacks. Refugees and asylum seekers are a particular case in point. Travellers and gypsies do not receive as much attention in social policy, legislation or the popular consciousness, let alone in the media, but our treatment of them remains the acid test of just how humane and civilized our society actually is.

Thankfully, we operate now within a legislative context defined by the Human Rights Act, the Race Relations Amendment Act, Article 13, the Sex Discrimination Act and the Special Educational Needs and Disability Act. We need to remind ourselves that it was not always so, and that that legislation came about not because the State was persuaded of the need to protect by law the fundamental rights and entitlements of its citizens, but because communities of like-minded people struggled to confront the divisions and dismantle the structures that encouraged and validated those forms of oppression and exclusion.

I am Chair of an organization called the Communities Empowerment Network (CEN). We provide advocacy training and help empower ordinary parents and students to act in their own interest as far as the appalling number of school exclusions among black students (boys in particular) is concerned. We encounter evidence of the crudest and most pernicious forms of stereotyping and bullying on the part of teachers and headteachers. We see disturbing evidence of some young people living up to particular stereotypes and acting 'in role', so to speak.

What alarms us most, however, is the fact that few parents, even black and ethnic minority parents themselves, are willing to confront those often illegal practices by schools which so mar the lives and life chances of such a huge number of young people.

The tendency is to see them as disruptive, injurious to the educational advancement of other children, causing problems for the schools that are desperately trying to push up standards, and therefore not worthy to have their rights protected.

We witness that phenomenon, also, in our communities ravaged by gun wars and trying to come to terms with the senseless deaths, sometimes weekly, of our young men. The vigilance with which black communities used to monitor police operational practices among youths, and protest about malpractices and the abuse of police power, has given way to indifference at best and, at worst, a tendency to see all black young males as deserving of the treatment they receive at the hands of the police. Anything else is seen as trying to obstruct the police in their attempts to rid the community of this murderous menace.

I want to suggest to you that, whether it be in relation to school exclusions, young black men in Moss Side, Harlesden, Brixton, or St Paul's, or refugees and asylum seekers, we have a responsibility to ensure that no group is classified as an 'out group' to whom basic rights and entitlements, and the protection of the law could routinely be denied. The CAB, historically, has been the one agency which people view as sufficiently independent of the apparatus of the central and local State to stand up for justice and for the safeguarding of rights.

The Race Relations Amendment Act 2000 and the requirement placed on public bodies to publish race equality policies or schemes to show how they will fulfil their statutory obligations under the Act, provide a crucial opportunity for CAB to work with local communities and monitor the implementation of such schemes. Patterns of exclusion abound at local and regional levels, in spite of neighbourhood renewal, local strategic partnerships, regional development agencies, and the rest. Evidence suggests that even when the most deserving communities are being denied access to geographically based funding or Single Regeneration Budget support because they do not have the infrastructure to satisfy the convoluted requirements of these funding regimes, it is often the CAB that intervenes and brokers their access to such funding, either by itself or in conjunction with the race equality council or/and the local council for voluntary service.

Government initiatives such as local strategic partnerships promise much but are often constructed upon the same people and processes that have secured the marginalization of black and other communities over time. However much CAB develop working relationships with them, therefore, it is essential that you do not become incorporated and that the most dispossessed, the least empowered and those change agents in local communities seeking to forge meaningful alliances could continue to see you as champions, safeguarding rights, demanding that the least amongst us be treated with due respect and ensuring that all that it is within your power to do is done to restore human dignity and self respect to those whom our culture, structures and policies so routinely deny self-worth and dignity.

I wish you a successful conference and much energy and endurance as you take forward this important agenda.

NO ISLAND IS AN ISLAND
Cesar Picton Lecture 2004

I wish to thank the Kingston Racial Equality Council and Kingston University for inviting me to present this lecture. It is especially fitting that I am making this presentation during Black History Month.

I decided to call this lecture 'No island is an island' because: I want to talk about common struggles, shared identities, bitter harvests and an inescapable interdependence. I want to suggest that we ignore black history at our peril, because you cannot be European and deny or falsify black history without misrepresenting your own history and falsifying your own identity.

Above all, I want to suggest that black history assists us in understanding the role black people have played and fulfil contemporaneously in humanizing British society. I want to ask you to beware of 'Born again' antiracists in Government and public life, with all their rhetoric about 'community cohesion' and cuddly concepts such as 'diversity' and 'cultural awareness'.

I will argue that such notions, usually undefined, simply serve to cement injustices and the structural omission of the dynamics of discrimination, marginalization and hegemonic domination by those who set the agenda. And in case you are wondering, I promise you that I won't keep you here until midnight.

First, though, a bit about myself. I was born in a tiny village in the island of Grenada, an island which hurricane Ivan battered beyond recognition at the beginning of September this year. My forebears were born in West Africa and borne forcibly to the Caribbean. Such was the process of displacing their true identity, that not even the rich oral tradition that survived in the diaspora could connect us with the original names of my slave ancestors. What I do know is that my maternal grandmother was part of the large Louison family and that old man Louison was a highly educated freed slave, a French creole who enjoyed a certain status in the island.

My maternal grandfather and his parents migrated to Grenada from Barbados and carried the name Hinds. My paternal grandfather somehow came by the name John. My father was called Wilfred John and I could never understand how these old people who spoke French patois and practised the traditional Yoruba religion in the Ifa tradition came to have such strange un-African names. For, nothing about them was European.

For my part, I was christened Gregory Eldon John. I could live with Gregory but absolutely hated Eldon and my loathing for the name had nothing to do with what I understand to be its Welsh origins. Thus, when in 1964 I joined the Dominican Order and became a Blackfriar in name and complexion, I chose the religious name 'Augustine' because I just loved that colourful character, Augustine of Hippo, him of the *City of God* and the *Confessions* and all that. So, in one fell swoop I had appropriated the names of three Saints: Augustine, Gregory, and John and I promise you that I am more saintly than the lot of them put together. The name 'Augustine', therefore, reconnected me to Africa but by the most bizarre of routes.

Cesar Picton was brought to England from the West African coast of Senegal as a boy in 1761. I suppose he would be the sort of character you see depicted in portraiture of the period, adoringly looking at the mistress of the home, or being publicly displayed as a symbol of the social standing of their owner. His house slave equivalents in the Americas were invariably given a more sinister function, typically to help 'massa' subjugate the field slaves. I suspect that Cesar Picton would have been given the surname Philipps before he adopted the name 'Picton'.

I was very close to my maternal grandfather. He was an inveterate peasant farmer and the best cook I have ever known. As a child I used to love going with him to the lands where he would work and cook simultaneously. He caused me much distress though, because whenever he ate his eyes ran water non-stop and he would be forever blowing his nose. When I asked him 'Papa, why are you crying?', he would say: 'It's OK. Just eat your food'. If I asked him for some of his food, he would say: 'If I give you some you will cry like me'. That fellow had a capacity to eat hot peppers and raw onions which was totally inhuman and, by rights, should have corroded his insides. Yet, he lived to the ripe old age of 98, forever sucking on his little white clay pipe. He soaked his tobacco in overproof rum.

One Christmas when all the adults were frantically cooking, baking, and curing meat, I took some of that tobacco and the pipe and went up into a tree to try and discover what joys my grandparents got from smoking pipe. After choking the first few times I learnt to inhale, and got so high after a very short while that I promptly fell out of the tree and broke my arm. I was totally panic stricken, not because of my injury but because I knew I had to go and tell my mother and face her wrath.

Well, as I predicted, my mother was none too pleased. She was fretting about my waywardness and the inconvenience of having to get transport to take me ten miles to the hospital and wait an age for me to be seen to, at a time when Christmas was just round the corner. As for me, my head felt as if I was about to die, never mind my damaged arm which, thankfully, was anaesthetized by the tobacco and rum.

My folks were either functionally illiterate, or barely semi-literate, and that meant that they listened to the radio non-stop. They gathered wherever there was a radio to listen to the BBC World Service and, less frequently, the Voice of America. I'll never forget the excitement in our home when my mother arrived from market with a brand new Phillips radio which was given pride of place on its own stand in the drawing room. The programmes I recall my folks listening to and discussing most were current affairs programmes and cricket commentaries, and they would get equally passionate about both. What the schools failed to teach us, therefore, we learnt at the feet of our elders in the yard or on the veranda with the radio in the background.

Thus it was that I learnt about the labour struggles in the West Indies, for 'bread, freedom and justice', I learnt about the British war ships that came at the behest of the Governor General who could always be depended upon to summon help from the British armed forces in defence of the landowners, the plantocrats and those who had appropriated the natural resources of the West Indian islands. I learnt about Jomo Kenyatta, Tom Mboya and the Mau Mau in Kenya. I learnt about George Padmore and the others who had organized the 5th Pan African Congress in Manchester in 1945. I learnt about Nkrumah and the struggle for the independence of the Gold Coast. I learnt about the Bandung Conference in 1955 when Africans and Asians in the anti-colonial movements got together to chart an agenda for Asia as they had done for Africa and the West Indies in Manchester in 1945.

I learnt about Mahatma Gandhi and the British Raj. I learnt about partition. I learnt about the caste system and working class movements in India. I learnt about the Indians in Trinidad and British Guiana who were brought there as part of the settlement of the colonialists on the slave labour issue.

I learnt about Fidel Castro and the Bay of Pigs. I learnt about Nikita Kruschev and the role of the Soviet Union *vis à vis* the USA in the geopolitics of the Third World.

I learnt about the hope and false promise of the West Indies Federation. I learnt about the push and pull factors of Caribbean migration to Britain. I learnt about the ANC and the trial of Nelson Mandela and Walter Sisulu. I learnt about the duplicity of the British Government *vis à vis* the Republic of South Africa and its apartheid system. I learnt about Ian Smith, Joshua Nkomo and Robert Mugabe. I learnt about Menachem Begin and the Palestinians.

I learnt about the Algerian Resistance Movement and the pivotal role of Frantz Fanon, the intellectual, political strategist and psychiatrist. I learnt about Ahmed Ben Bella and Houari Boumedienne. I learnt about Patrice Lumumba in the Congo and Moise Tshombe in Katanga. I well remember the widespread anxiety and fear that gripped little Grenada when Lumumba was illegally arrested in 1960 and then murdered in 1961. The anger and grief expressed could not have been more pronounced if he had been a Grenadian head of state. Indeed, when two decades later Maurice Bishop, then Prime Minister and Head of the People's Revolutionary Government in Grenada, was put under house arrest, later to be murdered along with most of his Cabinet, I could not help recalling the feelings I had all that time ago when reports reached us about Lumumba's murder.

I was not yet sixteen years old. Yet, for me, the discourse and sense of outrage among those functionally illiterate villagers about most of those events I have mentioned provided me with a level of understanding of imperialism and colonialism to which my schooling at Presentation College in St George's, organized and delivered by Irish Presentation Brothers from Cork, in Dublin, added but little.

I say all of that in order to underscore the point that, as my elder, friend and mentor, John La Rose, reminds us so poignantly:

We did not come alive in Britain.

Some of us as black people may have been born here, our parents may have made this country our home, but we did not come alive in Britain.

Thousands of us came from the West Indies before the *Windrush*. We were involved in international workers' struggles and in the struggle for the independence of Britain's far flung colonies in Asia, Africa and the West Indies, like George Padmore, CLR James and Amy Jacques Garvey. We came as Island Scholars to Oxford University, Edinburgh University, Cambridge University, London University, like the late Dr Eric Williams, the late Lord David Pitt, the late Dame Hilda Bynoe (sister of Baroness Ros Howells), and others too numerous to mention. We came as seamen, engineers, nurses, and of course as patriotic citizens of Britain to assist 'the War effort' in 1914 and again in 1939. To their credit, the Imperial War Museum in London has rightly organized an exhibition of black people in the First and Second World Wars.

We came before the *Windrush* and joined thousands more like us who had been part of British life for generations, Cesar Picton included.

We did not come alive in Britain because we had a life experience with Britain that made us the African, Caribbean and Asian people that we are. Our history is interwoven with Britain's history in the same way that Britain's future is inescapably bound up with our future, regardless of those who believe they could preserve *Little England* and keep Britain and all its institutions white.

We did not come alive in Britain.

The educational aspirations of the *Windrush* generation back home were matched by an education culture which induced high self esteem and in which high levels of educational achievement were seen as the norm. In that education culture, your potential was not judged by your race, your sex or your class. Your parents did not have to live in a certain area for you to go to a good school and succeed. Illiterate peasant farmers were the proud parents and grandparents of doctors, airline pilots, lawyers and High Court judges.

Parents who couldn't read and write and who spent their lives growing yams and minding cows had ambitions for their children to become doctors, lawyers, airline pilots, chief education officers, and more. Their children came to have those same high aspirations for themselves, and their teachers and the entire education system matched and extended those expectations. Nobody dared say to those parents that they had 'unrealistic aspirations' for their children or 'unrealistic expectations' of the schooling system. We came here from such an education culture and were treated as if our brains had been forcibly removed on the *Windrush* and hurled into the ocean. Suddenly, we were all imbeciles. Our children were assumed to be educationally subnormal, our teachers incapable of teaching white children, our parents too backward to understand the British schooling system.

But the problem was that we understood it only too well. We had been products of the British colonial schooling system and had refined it for our purpose, as part of our life experience with Britain, long before the Windrush. We knew what we were capable of and we sought to remain true to ourselves. We did not whinge and wallow in the victim status imposed upon us by British society and the British state.

We made history. We transcended our circumstances and sought to transform ourselves. We built our institutions, black publishing houses and bookshops: New Beacon, Bogle L'Ouverture, and more recently Karia and Karnak. We developed a supplementary school movement and created opportunities for our children to learn that *we did not come alive in Britain* and to repair the damage the British schooling system was doing to them. We created a movement in Black Theatre and in popular culture. We established businesses and struggled to establish and sustain an economic base in the society. We designed and patented things.

No one took our efforts seriously then, any more than they are being taken seriously now. The Blair Government lately discovered home study centres, Saturday schools, Easter colleges, etc., and have been peddling them all over the place like some brand new invention. Yet, no acknowledgment is given by government to the thirty-five years of the black supplementary education movement we built in this country and the pioneering work it has done through Saturday schools, home work centres, vacation 'colleges', etc., with successive generations of black children.

Our supplementary schools are still struggling and having their practice contested by mainstream schooling. As a result of lobbying by a number of black organizations, the Government set aside a measly £1.5m to support the work of supplementary schools. Now, as a consequence of receiving such funding, supplementary schools are undergoing inspections from Ofsted. Yet, mainstream schooling persists with its structured silences about the black contribution to the post-war development of Britain and the accompanying, massive contribution to British social history, let alone the sort of history I have drawn upon earlier in this talk. What is worse, underachievement has been racialized, and school exclusions have been racialized, in much the same way that immigration control and tackling street crimes were racialized.

The dream black parents had of an education system that was superior to that in their poor homelands back there, and that would generate even more successes than they had been used to, quickly turned into a nightmare. To escape that nightmare, a growing number of black parents have been buying private education for their children or sending them back to the Caribbean or to Africa for their education and to escape what they see as a negative youth culture. Negative, because it is seen as manifesting too many of the characteristics parents associate with failure, and as conforming to the society's negative stereotypes of black people. Negative, because whereas in the 1960s through to the middle 1990s black communities had cause to organize against racist murders and deaths in custody, the late 1990s have seen us preoccupied with murders and maiming of black young people by other black young people, predominantly male.

Some of us buy into a discourse about so-called 'black on black' gun crime, stabbings, etc. When some two weeks ago, the BBC screened a Panorama programme on the epidemic of knife related murders and near deaths across the country, I was intrigued to find that all the assailants and victims in that film were white. Certain cities have a history of violent confrontation involving white males, and white women defending themselves against battering by white men in domestic violence situations. (The city where I work for part of my week, Glasgow, is a particular case in point). But, never have I heard or seen that phenomenon described as 'white on white' crime.

Ever since the early 1960s, these islands have held an unwarranted focus upon us as blacks to the extent that British society has failed to see and understand itself through the prism of our experience. That experience has a great deal to teach the society about itself, especially the things which it continues to stubbornly deny about itself. It should not require the savage murder of an Ahmed Iqbal Ullah or Stephen Lawrence for the country to see itself reflected in the mirror in all its ugliness. Nor can it give vent to repulsiveness and disassociation by projecting their murderers as unreconstructed, ferret eyed racists who are not as moral as the rest of us and who do not subscribe to the same shared values.

If I have a frustration with the discourse about 'race' and community relations in these islands, it is that people fail to see, or knowingly contrive sometimes to ignore, the connection between things.

We, in the Caribbean at least, may have had dreams and expectations based upon how we had been told Britain was. For example, to prevent us becoming even more restive and rebellious than we were, the British colonial education system did not teach us anything about British labour history and the struggles of the white working class in Britain, any more than they taught that history to white working class children in British schools. On the contrary, Britain busied itself with trying to subvert our attempts to rid ourselves of the yoke of colonialism, resorting to military force to put down organized workers' struggles repeatedly and, in many of our countries, often with the active connivance of neo-colonialist governments who were ever so keen to occupy the positions the colonizers had vacated.

In his book *The Future in the Present*, CLR James (1977) quotes a letter Leonard Lyle, President of Tate and Lyle Limited, wrote in the *Times* on 10 May 1939:

I cannot believe that I was unsound in stating that the West Indian labourer does not even remotely resemble the English labourer.

James writes:

Tate and Lyle, as everyone who buys sugar should know, make a fortune every year by selling to the British workers sugar grown by Jamaican workers. They must keep these two divided at all costs. Hence, with that solemn shamelessness so characteristic of British capitalism, Mr Lyle discovers that the West Indies labourer does not remotely resemble the English labourer. The real trouble is, of course, that he resembles the English labourer too much for Mr Capitalist Lyle.

I used the above quotes in the report of a study of the political culture of youth and community work with black people in English cities (John, 1981) in order to illustrate the following point:

The black working-class who came to Britain are normally pictured by the English as benighted workers and peasants wielding hoes and cutlasses and being as dumb as the asses they rode. The archives in the British Museum and at the Foreign and Commonwealth Office tell otherwise. That working-class, from whatever land mass they came, experienced and waged the most bitter struggles against British and international capitalism, and were often defeated only by the guns and intrigues of the British. Whitehall had control of the working class at home and abroad, all in the service of the British economy. The potential was always there for massive movements of labour whenever the economy required it. Those who were in control, however, took great pains to ensure that those different sections of the working-class they controlled around the globe had little notion of their interrelatedness.

In this article first published in 1983, James is calling on the British workers in their unions to 'press for full democratic rights for the West Indian workers':

Tate and Lyle are planning to open factories in Jamaica. They want to take advantage of labour which has not the right as yet to protect itself. Thus black is used against white and Leonard Lyle seeks to poison the mind of the British worker against the West Indian worker.

(James, op.cit)

The period immediately prior to the World War II saw throughout the Caribbean area many strikes and uprisings of the kind which prompted Lyle's profound observation. Military force on the part of the British and the United States could always be expected, as was to be more and more the case after the war (in Guyana, in Grenada, in Trinidad, in Jamaica, etc.)

Commenting on that period, Stephenson Nicholson, in a letter to 'Race Today' (1974) observes:

The working-class movement in the Caribbean particularly after the Second World War, sought 'the advice of the British TUC', thereby digging its own grave. The nationalist movement of the same period pinned its hope on the support of the Labour Party in Britain who ensured its continued dependence on capitalist development.

... George Woodcock of the British TUC warned Guyanese in the 1950s that it was dangerous to twin trade unionism and politics. Woodstock's task, it appears then, was to break this link, to ensure the rise of the middle-classes and the entrenchment of capitalist exploitation. (John, 1981)

Nor, more to the point, did that colonial education tell us how alive and well and rosy pink racism in Britain was. I came upon it in all its ugliness in a very personal way that is exemplified by two related incidents, both in the late 1960s. The first is hearing some commotion outside my parents' home in Acton, West London early one morning, and seeing my father hurrying into the house covered in blood. We started screaming fearing he had been stabbed.

In fact he had been set upon by a group of skinheads on his way from his night shift as a janitor, and was being beaten about the body with chains and clubs. He had the quick wittedness to grab a recently delivered pint of milk from someone's doorway, break it and cut off the ear of one of his assailants, at which point the others took off dragging their howling mate with them. Some ten years earlier, of course, another Caribbean worker, Kelso Cochrane, had been murdered in a situation almost identical to that in which my father found himself.

The second is when the Acton police who had a notorious record of harassing black youths in the area arrested my younger brother and took him to Acton police station. At some point, an officer defecated in a standard lavatory bowl and then he and one of his mates took my brother and stuck his head face down into that same toilet bowl before flushing it. Some hours later, my brother was released without charge and returned home smelling fruity and totally traumatized. I determined that that was such a barbaric act by those who were supposed to be protecting the public that I was intent on revenge. I devised an elaborate scheme to firebomb that police station and take out whoever happened to be in it at the time. But even as I armed myself with enough kit to destroy half of Acton, my Higher Self told me that those who carried out that barbaric act might not even be on duty when I struck. Did I really want to live with the fact that I had denied wives or husbands and children their loved ones simply through my indiscriminating and unjust judgement that they were guilty by association, even if I had made up my mind to forego my freedom? That is the closest I have ever been to earning the title of what in today's political lexicon would be called 'a terrorist'. Interestingly and conversely, those barbaric police officers would still be considered 'rotten apples' today, racist perhaps and contaminating, but most untypical of the barrel as a whole.

Be that as it may, my entire family have had to endure the consequences of that single racist act, the traumatic stress of which affected my brother visibly throughout his life and led to a life style which undoubtedly contributed to his premature accidental death at the age of forty-nine.

Throughout the centuries, black people have struggled against a culture of racism in British society and its institutions. There have been personal acts of resistance, often costing black people their lives. There have been riots at various points at the beginning of and throughout the decades of the twentieth century, for example, in London, Cardiff, Bristol, Birmingham, Manchester and Liverpool. Those uprisings typically involved people of African heritage defending themselves against racist violence, or/and what they experienced as the institutions of the State yielding space to racists to spread fear and insecurity among black communities.

Up until the Southall demonstration and the death of Blair Peach in the middle 1980s, street disturbances involving people from the Indian sub-continent had been largely if not exclusively around labour disputes (the Imperial Typewriter dispute in Leicester, the Mansfield Hosiery dispute, the Grunwick dispute). Recently, however, uprisings in Asian communities have involved defence against neo-fascist organizations and racist aggravation, protests against styles of policing, etc.

It would appear that every time such events occur, the State has a standard reaction:

a. act as though it is the first time and as if there is no basis for the disturbance, except criminality
b. reach for more and more militaristic policing methods
c. set up an inquiry, preferably led by some worthy and not so in-touch member of the establishment

For the rest of this talk, I want to comment upon this phenomenon and make some observations as to where all of this leaves us.

First, forgive me for repeating a truism. To parody a famous saying, *no island is an island sufficient unto itself* and insulated from events and realities in other parts of the world. We certainly do not need globalization to remind us of that basic fact. During the period of my youth about which I said certain things earlier, the British colonial system went to great lengths to separate the struggles and aspirations of workers in the Caribbean from those of white workers here in Britain, albeit the livelihood of the latter depended upon the raw materials and the wealth generated by people like my folks. For their part, white British workers' solidarity with the international working class was not robust enough to withstand the pernicious effects of the culture of racism into which they had been socialized and of which they were very much a part. For one thing, they were certainly not falling over themselves to welcome into the British working class movement their 'brothers and sisters' from the withering, postcolonial economies of the Caribbean.

That culture of racism was so entrenched that it militated and continues to militate against the forging of a society in Britain where Britishness does not continue to equate with whiteness and where whiteness itself is seen as racially constructed; in other words that elusive 'ethnic majority' about which one seldom hears.

I have been associated with Southall since 1964. My relatives live there. I have been associated with Leicester City since 1968, fast becoming the only city in Britain where the black population exceeds the white population. I studied and worked there. I have been associated with the City of Bradford since 1977. I lectured in Social Policy and Applied Social Studies at the University there and was an active member of the George Lindo Campaign which Linton Kwesi Johnson has immortalized in one of his earlier albums. All of those were very different places then, with a totally different mix of population.

In the middle 1960s, a prospective parliamentary candidate in Smethwick, West Midlands, proclaimed with true British indignation: 'If you want a nigger for a neighbour, vote Labour'. Well, voting or not, his rallying cry about the undesirability of black neighbours appears to have struck a chord across the nation. The phenomenon of 'white flight' took on a momentum with consequences to which successive governments turned a blind eye for decades. Moreover, local councils themselves indulged in housing allocation procedures which compounded the problem. Communities such as those I have mentioned thus became artificially segregated, with whites finding newer pastures, not so 'contaminated' by blacks with all the structural consequences for property value, especially house prices, and blacks finding security and comfort in numbers.

No government talked about 'community cohesion' then. No one challenged the right of white British to pack up and go whenever and wherever they wished, leaving their black neighbours in surroundings which estate agents then told white prospective buyers were not desirable and which, too often, local councils themselves neglected. And so, inexorably, some parts of this society of 'shared values' (as the Home Office would have it) became all black in the same way that vast swathes of the British Isles continue to be all white, with no one distressing themselves about the non-cohesive consequences of that for multiethnic Britain.

The Home Office's recent consultation document: *Strength in Diversity: towards a community cohesion and race equality strategy* is one of the most problematic policy documents I have seen.

Apart from repeated references to 'a shared vision across diverse communities', the Government does not define what it means by 'diversity' and 'community cohesion', nor does it say why community cohesion is necessary only in terms of the growing numerical and political strength of black communities.

Indeed, the Government has popularized the notion of community cohesion as a desirable goal principally as a result of the deep fissures that were seen to exist in multiethnic communities in the North/North West of England.

Strength in Diversity states:

In many areas, the diversity within and between communities has been a source of rich cultural interactions, but in other areas segregation has led to fear and conflict, which has been exacerbated by political extremists *who capitalize on insecurities to promote their own narrow objectives.*

Structural inequalities and the legacy of discrimination have resulted in whole groups that are effectively left behind, with young people failing to share in the opportunities that should be available to all, which in turn fuels their disengagement from mainstream society and creates pathways to extremism.   (p. 5, para 1.8)

Indeed, the whole document is replete with references to extremism:

Respecting and valuing diversity is an essential part of building a successful, integrated society. But respect for diversity must take place within a framework of rights and responsibilities that are recognized by and apply to all – to abide by the law, to reject extremism *and intolerance and make a positive contribution to UK society. Different ways of living our lives, different cultures or beliefs all coexist within this shared framework of rights and responsibilities.*   (p. 7, para 2.6)

Racism and extremism *have no place in modern Britain ... The rise in* international terrorism, *new patterns of migration and the effects of globalization, can all contribute to people's sense of insecurity and fear, which is often profoundly felt in areas suffering deprivation or where change occurs over a short period of time. We need to acknowledge those concerns as valid, while we work to address the*

causes and continue to drive out racism and extremism, political
and religious, *wherever they are found.* (p. 10, para 3.1)

*All political and community leaders share responsibility, working with
local and national media, for tackling the myths and misrepresentation
of facts that can damage cohesion.*
  *Religious extremists who wrongly argue for support for acts of
terrorism in the name of Islam present the same threat to British
Muslim communities as they do to others, compounded by the fact that
they propagate false perceptions about the values and beliefs of Islam.*
(p. 11, para 3.4)   (my emphasis throughout)

In *Confident Communities in a Secure Britain – The Home Office
Strategic Plan 2004-2008*, the Home Secretary argues as follows:

*Realizing our vision of a successfully integrated society requires a
comprehensive strategy; that cannot be achieved through legislation
and the improved delivery of public services alone. It must be underpinned by a sense of belonging to the country and the community, and
by a shared understanding of human rights and values.*

Presumably, it is precisely in order to inculcate the latter in those
who do not behave as if they belong, that the Home Secretary's
citizenship 'passing out' ceremonies have been devised.
  For 'legislation' above, one could read race legislation, and for
'improved delivery of public services' read improved delivery
of public services to black and ethnic minority people. Indeed,
that interpretation is suggested by the statement that
immediately follows, for the Government surely does not
believe that white people suffer from a sense of not 'belonging
to the country'. What is more, the more extreme, xenophobic
and racist of them would argue that that is the very point, the
fact that they feel that 'their country' is being taken away from
them by an alien race, irrespective of whether the latter see
themselves as belonging to the country or not. Similarly, the
notion as implied in that passage that the majority society
demonstrates *a shared understanding of human rights and values* is
fanciful.

All of this is evidence in my view that Government itself is adding massively to the confusion that surrounds these concepts.

'Valuing 'Diversity' is not the same as promoting race equality, gender equality, disability equality, etc. The latter cannot be done without tackling discrimination (in its structural, cultural, institutional, and personal manifestations). It is both misleading and unhelpful to use the term 'diversity' to denote the range of discriminations suffered by historically oppressed groups in society (women, black people, people with disabilities, lesbian/gay/bisexual/transsexual, etc.) While such groups are systematically discriminated against in society, there are other aspects of diversity which militate against inclusiveness, fairness and justice.

Indeed, for generations they have created in communities the very antithesis of 'community cohesion', a concept the Government saw fit to introduce only in relation to its growing fear at the prospect of racially segregated communities and the rise of 'extremism' among British Muslims.

Wealth; social class; socio-economic status; housing; disadvantages and constraints of rural living, especially for the elderly and the unemployed; educational achievement/ underachievement; University attended; area in which you live and the effect of that on decision making in relation to your employability, access to health care and insurance (post code discrimination); are all manifestations of diversity in a highly stratified society where social exclusion mirrors social injustice.

'Valuing Diversity' is about allowing people to be themselves without having prejudice heaped upon them and without denying them opportunity because of who they are, where they live, what their belief system is, or the group to which they belong.

Cuddly, touchy feely concepts such as 'diversity', 'cultural awareness', and 'community cohesion' continue to serve as a reason for not examining the complex structural, cultural, institutional, and personal dynamics that underpin the experiences of individuals and groups in our increasingly complex and atomized society.

'Valuing Diversity' eschews notions of 'tolerance' because tolerance is in the gift of those who have the power:

* to marginalize and exclude
* to define themselves as 'normal' and 'belonging' (the 'in group')
* to define the 'tolerated' as outsiders, and as not conforming to the 'norm'

Those who are tolerating also exercise the right to determine the threshold of tolerance that the tolerated should not seek to surpass.

When one examines the genesis of the phenomenon that has increasingly become known as 'white flight', the concept of tolerance turns out to be much more problematic than it sounds. How many families with all their ethnic diversity could one tolerate before market considerations and your unease at living in a multiethnic community lead you to worry about your house value and other people's attitude to the changing ethnic profile of your area?

Social class, educational qualifications, job status, having or not having a criminal record, employability, type of family unit, parental status, area and type of residence, access to transport, are all aspects of the diversity in any community, district or city, and all have a major impact on the way people regulate their lives or have their lives ordered for them. That list is not complete even when you include gender (1), age (2), race/ethnicity (3), sexual orientation (4), disability (5) and faith and religion (6), i.e., those that typically get included under the banner of 'diversity'. The latter are dynamic factors which cluster with one another within that same group of six and with others in our list.

As with multiculturalism before it, I believe that unless one keeps those basic understandings at the forefront of one's mind, the majority who see themselves as not belonging to these six target groups would be encouraged not to have regard to their own identity, their own experience of oppression and of marginalization if not of exclusion, their own capacity to use power to oppress, deny other people's rights and to exclude.

Policymakers and those charged with the responsibility to

implement policy and encourage active participation by citizens, have a duty to be more careful in their use of terms which are invested with deep meaning and power and are thus incorporated into consensual thinking, the kind of thinking and discourse that make those of us who protest at the liberties that are taken with such terms seem decidedly perverse.

In order to fully comprehend how patterns of discrimination manifest and are sustained in society and its institutions, it is necessary to have an understanding of concepts of oppression, ideology, power, inclusion, and exclusion, and how they relate to the operational and social 'culture' of institutions.

Albert Einstein said:

The problems we have created can not be solved with the same level of thinking on which they were created.

The Government can no more manufacture 'community cohesion' by extracting a pledge of good citizenship from those seeking British nationality than it could separate those people from their concerns about Britain's role in the world, and in the seemingly intractable conflicts and systematic oppressions that it appears to ignore, or in which it is seen as complicit.

My experience with Britain, here and in the Caribbean, has taught me that:

no nation, no group of people, can preside over or give tacit consent to the denial of rights and fundamental liberties to any section of itself, or to any other nation or group without putting their own fundamental rights and liberties at risk.

That fundamental lesson of history is especially apposite at a time when we are all being asked to subscribe to notions of 'an axis of evil' and the belief that if you do not simplistically sign on to the 'war against terror' you are naturally to be numbered among the forces of evil.

Martin Luther King reminded us:

Injustice anywhere is a threat to justice everywhere

Our creative capacity and our fundamental instinct for freedom as human beings empower us to make and remake our histories, shaping and transforming our lives. Throughout history, we have demonstrated our capacity as oppressed and marginalized people to transcend oppression, rise above barbarism, humanize societies and not be defeated morally or spiritually, even when we have been defeated economically.

We must therefore nurture visions of change, especially in young black Britishers. We need to encourage them to be positive about their own generation's capacity to continue to transform this society. I say to them: learn from the experience of past generations, from our successes and our failures, our advances and gains in the society as well as our defeats.

Celebrate the courage, resilience and hope of that heroic generation that came with the *Windrush* and of those who followed in the 1950s and 1960s. They who endured so much 'back home', many of them having already laboured in Aruba, Curacao, Cuba, and Panama, and who still had the courage to face the future in an alien land and the capacity to survive and to build, indeed to rebuild Britain, in the face of untold hostility and deprivation.

Above all, let us endeavour to eradicate for all time the spurious belief in white superiority and assist all children in forging an authentic identity that is not rooted in myths and falsehoods.

Knowledge has no colour. It is neither white nor black. It is the universal creation of all people in all societies, so-called 'advanced' or not. In a society such as this that automatically validates white people and does not regard 'whiteness' as racial identity, black people, British or not, will always have to struggle against bigotry and injustice.

Remember the words of Paulo Friere:

There is one thing I am certain about: Nobody is superior to anybody.

Let us make bold and assert that. It does wonders for your self esteem and it neutralizes the power people feel they have over you because of their class, their wealth, or the extent to which they belong to a group that the society validates.

If we are to equip today's generation to manage the multiethic, multifaith Britain that has evolved in the last half century, we need to ensure that no black or white young person, irrespective of class or socio-economic background, should have to apologize for themselves to anyone. Rather, each should be assisted in embracing values that make them fit for living in, and for building and managing, a fair and just society.

Let me end with an extract from a letter Frantz Fanon wrote to his friend Roger Tayeb, four weeks prior to his death from leukaemia in 1961:

Roger, what I wanted to tell you is that death is always with us and that what matters is not to know whether we can escape it but whether we have achieved the maximum for the ideas we have made our own…

We are nothing on earth if we are not in the first place the slaves of a cause, the cause of the peoples, the cause of justice and liberty. I want you to know that even when the doctors had given me up, in the gathering dusk I was still thinking of the Algerian people, of the peoples of the Third World, and when I have persevered, it was for their sake.

Only one week earlier, Fanon received the published copy of his book: *The Wretched of the Earth*. He 'persevered' long enough to see the evidence that the ideas he had made his own were handed on to us in the pages of that most important book.

With deep humility and gratitude, therefore, I salute him. I salute and pay homage to my Glorious Ancestors and all those other giants of black history on whose broad shoulders I stand, and to whom I owe so very, very much. And, I join you in the continuing struggle for racial equality and social justice in Britain and the world.

8.0

RACE, CIVIL SOCIETY AND CIVIL UNREST

Introduction
The Lozells district of Birmingham was the scene of civil unrest that attracted international media attention over the weekend of 22-23 October 2005. A series of extraordinary events, unprecedented in the history of relations within black and ethnic minority communities in Britain, led to violent conflict between Asians and Africans in which one African male died from stab wounds and several people sustained serious injuries.

This was civil unrest of a different order, not because of the level of violence or the duration of the disturbances. Lozells and the neighbouring district of Handsworth had seen worse. The unrest caused alarm because it took the form of violent clashes between Asians and Africans, mainly youths.

The reported reason for the disturbances was aggression by Asian youths, on the evening of 22 October, against Africans who were peacefully protesting the alleged gang rape of a fourteen year old African girl by a group of Asian men, eleven to nineteen of them, depending on the particular version of the rumour doing the rounds in the community. Reports suggest that following a rally outside the cosmetics store where the rape allegedly took place, the demonstrators were invited, with the encouragement of the police, to attend a meeting at the New Testament Church of God in George Street, Lozells, at which various African and Asian 'community leaders', church leaders and senior police officers would discuss the concerns of the

African and Asian communities, both about the rumours and the respective community's reactions to them. It was expected that the police would tell that meeting what had been reported to them about the alleged 'rape', what they were investigating and what they were able to tell the communities at that stage.

It is suggested that the police who had been keeping a watchful eye on the protest outside the store were more energetic in their control of the movement of African youths who were trying to get into that meeting, keeping most of them out of the church, than they were in dealing with the Asian youths whose conduct towards the people attending the meeting and those being kept outside by the police was described as 'menacing', racially abusive and physically aggressive. It is alleged that that aggression escalated and that the Asian youths let off fireworks outside the church, giving the impression of gunfire and causing a panic and defensive reaction on the part of the young African males.

Thus began a series of clashes between the two groups and the swelling of their ranks once word got round that, as one young man put it, 'something had kicked off'. Two further incidents that evening led to an escalation of the conflict and might have resulted in even worse and more sustained clashes between the communities but for the intervention of some foul weather. In one incident, twenty-three year old Isaiah Young-Sam, who had not been involved in the disturbances and was simply making his way through the area, accompanied by his brother and cousins, was fatally stabbed. His cousin also sustained serious stab wounds. Although the police did not confirm the ethnicity of their attackers, the word in the community was that they were 'a gang of Asian youths'. This turned out to be the most serious of a series of sporadic attacks by members of one community against the other.

The other incident involved a large crowd of Asian men laying siege to a long established African community organization on Heathfield Road. The African community is seeking an explanation from the police as to how it was that an estimated two to three hundred Asian men were able to pass through police cordons and make their way to the premises of that community organization. They allege that the police intervened only when those inside the building took steps to defend themselves, and that they were treated as the aggressors.

Eyewitness accounts suggest that some of the Asians were chanting racist abuse, including 'Kill the niggers', 'Kill the Blacks' and 'Burn the Niggers, Burn the Blacks'.

There are those in the African community who believe that organized Asian gangs were involved in both those major incidents and that their 'attack on the black community' was a direct challenge to the gangs in the African community who would have no option but to come out and defend their community.

The clashes on the street ceased by the early hours of Monday 24 October. Sporadic attacks on individuals or groups of different ages continued, as did rumours about other rapes committed against African women by Asian men. Individuals and groups from both communities met and talked in an effort to sow peace and prevent the communities from becoming further polarized. People talked about bringing the youths from both communities 'under control'. Meanwhile, however, there were threats circulating around the communities of Lozells, Perry Barr, Handsworth, and Aston, that the African community would be dealt with if the protests about the alleged rape and the disruption of trade with Asian shops continued.

There was to be a further escalation of tension in the following two weeks. Inflammatory and racist leaflets inciting hatred and violence against the African community started circulating around the communities. The African community expressed concern both about that material and what they saw as the lack of robust condemnation of it by the Asian community. Then, at the start of the Eid celebrations on 4 November, members of the Muslim faith discovered that the Muslim section of Handsworth Cemetery had been desecrated. Scores of monuments had been smashed or dislodged and leaflets with pejorative statements against Islam were strewn around the cemetery.

In the wake of all that had transpired since the rumour about gang rape started circulating at least one week before the disturbances, a number of groups of Asian and African people, including a large assembly of women and children across the ethnic groups in the Lozells and surrounding districts, met in various settings, and demonstrated in the name of peace and in condemnation of the violence and incitement to racial hatred. There have been calls for Birmingham City Council and the Government to set up 'a public inquiry' into the events of 22-23 October, and particularly the way the police and the emergency services responded.

Meanwhile, rumours of other rapes by Asian men of black, older women continue to circulate, as do rumours concerning the reason(s) for the fact that the alleged fourteen year old rape victim has not personally made a report to the police.

Whatever may have happened between Asian men and African women in the communities of Perry Barr, Lozells, and Handsworth in the weeks or months prior to the gang rape rumour, it is clear that serious tensions pre-existed between Asians and Africans. It is equally clear that, given the conflicts that had erupted in those communities in the previous twenty years at least, over regeneration funding, housing allocation, youth and crime, drug dealing, the treatment of African customers by Asian traders, and much else besides, no mechanisms existed for joint approaches to resolving those conflicts. Furthermore, Birmingham City Council, regional government structures and the police, are seen as complicit in requiring the two communities to compete against each other for funding and access to decision making in matters that affect the organization of their communities. The charge laid by the African community against those bodies, justifiably in my experience, is that they uncritically buy into the organizational structures within the Asian community that are anything but transparent, and that the African community sees as manipulating democratic processes and civic organizations unfairly, and to their disadvantage.

As the events unfolded in the days immediately following the turbulent weekend of 22-23 October, the *Guardian* newspaper invited me to write a comment on those events, against the background of my prior involvement in those communities.

'Gus John Revisits Handsworth/Lozells', (8.1) is the full version of what appeared in the *Guardian* on Wednesday 26 October 2005.

Anger and outrage in any community about the spectacle of a fourteen year old girl being raped by a gang of men, possibly totalling nineteen, is clearly understandable. The crucial issue here, therefore, is the fact that the African community decided that the rape did occur and that it was racially aggravated. The conflation of that alleged incident, with reports circulating in the African community in the preceding months about individual acts of rape by Asian men of 'at least four older black women', intensified the view that those alleged rapes represented a collective attack by the Asian community upon the most vulnerable section of the African community, its women. There has been little or no discussion in all this about the fact that, week by week, men rape women, and other men, within the same ethnic group (Asian, African, white English), and across ethnic boundaries, including gang rape.

Even if the African community took the view that the alleged gang rape of the fourteen year old girl represented the most extreme form of the treatment they had been complaining about as African customers at the hands of Asian shopkeepers, that would not explain why every other rape by an Asian man of an African woman should be seen as a symbol of the vulnerability of the African community at the hands of Asians. Civil society would really be in crisis if mass protests by whites or by Asians were to be triggered by reports of rape by black males of white women or of Asian women, whether those women are minors or the elderly.

As I observed in the *Guardian* article, 'rape' is a barbaric form of sexual predation on women, irrespective of ethnicity. It was gratifying, therefore, to see Asian women and African women joining together to condemn 'rape' within their own community and across all communities. It is even more necessary for there to be a large coalition of Asian and African men, of all age groups, mounting a sustained campaign against rape and the emotional and physical abuse of women of any ethnicity, irrespective of whether or not the alleged rape that sparked off those disturbances actually took place. That, surely, is the issue. It is an issue as important as ensuring that the conditions are created where the alleged victim of the rape could safely come forward and assist the police in taking the most robust action.

There remain deep seated tensions between those two communities which in my view have much more to do with the unequal distribution of power; cultural, religious, and in-your-face male chauvinism on the part of certain sections of the Asian community; privileged access to resources and opportunities; and a deep and worsening lack of mutual respect, than to do with 'race' as such. The African community in those districts of Birmingham clearly feels increasingly beleaguered by their Asian neighbours, I suspect not unlike the way the white community of those working class districts of Oldham spoke of being beleaguered.

The more that elements within either community are encouraged in the view that 'the other' is essentially antipathetic to them and their interests, and should be opposed, the more polarities of superior/inferior, economically powerful/economically powerless, politically strong/ politically weak, aggressors/victims, will flourish, thus displacing any real possibility of mutual cooperation, peace building, and mutual management of affairs in the community and in the city. What is worse, both communities if divided are likely to be able to exert even less control over the growth and activities of gangs among them, especially as those gangs are more than likely to exploit and reinforce racial divisions.

For these reasons, it is essential that the communities themselves take ownership of that conflict and assume responsibility for establishing what lay at the basis of the rumours that led to the disturbances, and how the communities, the emergency services, and the City Council conducted themselves during and after those disturbances.

'Lozells Disturbances – Proposed call for a People's Inquiry' (8.2) is premised upon my firm belief that the communities themselves must be facilitated to conduct and report upon their own Inquiry, to come up with proposals for healing the community and laying the foundations for sustainable development, and equitable access to, and deployment of, resources.

It is essential that the City Council, in partnership with the communities, youth parliaments or local youth councils, the Black Educators' Network, the teaching unions, and religious and faith groups, determine as a matter of urgency what schools should be doing to assist all children in the city to understand the conflict and its implications for them as learners and as citizens.

The disturbances in Lozells occurred twenty years and one month after even more major civil unrest in Lozells, Handsworth and Perry Barr on 9-11 September 1985. On that occasion, the police were primarily the target of the communities' anger. Those involved in the street disturbances then were mainly Africans and white English, with a sizeable group of young Asians also taking part. Of those arrested in connection with the events over those two to three days were 132 whites, 49 Asians and 221 Africans. The profile of the area presented by the West Midlands Police then, was of an area with lots of deprivation, high youth unemployment, little racial tension, but where a small criminal element made up of a 'small minority of Afro-Caribbean males' were causing social disorder. According to the police, they were targeting the growing number of Asian businesses in the community and generally sowing fear and causing tension in the Asian community.

Birmingham City Council commissioned Julius Silverman to conduct an 'Inquiry into the Handsworth Disturbances' and the Silverman Report was published on 27 February 1986. For his part, Mr Geoffrey Dear, then Chief Constable of the West Midlands Police, reported to Home Secretary Douglas Hurd in September 1985 on the 'Handsworth/Lozells Disturbances'. The burden of Mr Dear's report was that the disturbances had been instigated by criminal elements. In a cover article: 'Oh Dear! That Criminal Minority Again' commissioned by the radical journal Race Today for their January 1986 edition, I provided a critique of Mr Dear's thesis (8.3).

The way a problem is defined is generally indicative of the measures considered appropriate to its solution. Both Mr Dear and Mr Silverman rather missed the crucial points in the circumstances that were at the root of the 1985 disturbances, irrespective of whether or not it is believed that a small band of African criminals conspired to ambush the police and start 'a riot'.

There is no doubt that the West Midlands Police and Mr Julius Silverman had a view of urban deprivation and youth unemployment as impacting upon white English, Africans and Asians in the districts where the disturbances took place. However, they tended to rely on the all too familiar characterization of 'ethnic minorities' in those communities, as follows: Africans (African-Caribbean) have less entrepreneuring skills and business acumen, much less of an economic base in the community, much less control of their youth and much more fragile systems of family organization. Their youths suffered from high unemployment and, while their adults were generally law abiding, African youths (males especially) were more involved in crime and drug dealing, and showed greater hostility towards the police. Asians, on the other hand, were thrifty and good at developing and sustaining business ventures, and made a vital contribution to service provision and to the economy of the area. Their family and community organization was more supportive of their youths, provided sharper boundaries and were deeply rooted in their religious beliefs and cultural customs. They absorbed a greater number of young people within family businesses and, consequently, fewer of them were involved in criminality and in hostile encounters with the police.

Take, for example, the section on 'Crime in Handsworth' in the Silverman Report. The report notes:

A substantial number of the offences of robbery and assault have been committed against Asians, often by more than one person. The Asian complaints are made mostly against black youths. One must state frankly that there are a small number of Afro-Caribbean youths who are persistent and active petty criminals, who are a nuisance to other ethnic races [sic] and who bring disrepute to the whole of the Afro-Caribbean community who consist of respectable decent people.

(Silverman 1986, p. 45)

Nothing is said anywhere in the report about young Asians' involvement in crime. The report projects an image of a well adjusted, enterprising Asian community, making provision for its own, absorbing the shock of unemployment in the area that impacts upon other youths, and generally keeping their young in check. The only thing interfering with that totally functional section of the local population is 'that criminal minority' within the African community.

It gets worse. The report devotes a section to a discussion of cannabis/ganja/hashish and its effects. Silverman was concerned to establish the extent to which the smoking of cannabis 'could have been one of the stimulants which incited the riots'. Expert witness Dr Norman Imlah is reported as telling the Inquiry that:

in general the use of ganja tended to produce passivity rather than excitement and activity. He said that whilst this was generally the case, there were occasions when the person taking the drug reacted rather violently. He was not prepared to commit himself as to whether the use of these drugs made any contribution to the precipitation of the riots. He said, 'I was not there, and therefore I am not prepared to say
(p. 86)

The report goes on to discuss 'Rastafarians', observing that:

But then there are the dreadlocks, the people who call themselves Rastas, who wear the same accoutrements as Rastafarians, but whom it would appear are disapproved of by the 'genuine' Rastafarians ...
It is thought that some of the dreadlocks wear these clothes as a mark of rejection of the society in which they live, and it is not surprising therefore that amongst these people there are some who live by crime. *The vast majority, however, are unemployed like the rest of Afro-Caribbean youths.* (my emphasis)   (p. 87)

What on earth does wearing certain clothes have to do with a propensity to 'live by crime'? As the police and any number of prosecutors could have told Mr Silverman, there are vastly more be-suited white men feigning respectability, who are considered to be upright pillars of society, who live by crime than there are 'dreadlocks' who are actively involved in crime. Indeed, the open prisons across the country are full of those be-suited types, let alone those who have so far escaped capture.

Again, one is left with the impression that in middle 1980s Birmingham the only community using 'ganja' or other narcotics that might have incited them to riot was the African community, Rastafarians in particular.

It is on the basis of such a banal analysis of major civil unrest in Lozells and Handsworth, riddled as it is with stereotypes and taken-for-granted assumptions, that Birmingham City Council set about rebuilding those districts in the wake of the 1985 disturbances.

It would be bad enough if such reports were just used to inform civic action in the aftermath of such unrest. Worryingly, however, the media make much of them in seeking to report on causes, the analysis of the events as they unfolded, and especially the recommendations emerging from the Inquiry. One group of people who take an especially keen interest in the findings of such inquiries are the lawyers and courts involved in trials of those arrested and charged for involvement in the disturbances.

It is in one such context that Lord Tony Clarke's report on the Burnley disturbances in 2001 was used. It became clear that the Clarke Report and its observations about those disturbances had played a crucial part in the trial of people charged with serious offences arising from the unrest. In the course of putting together the case for the defence, solicitors acting for four people appealing against their conviction sought my involvement as an 'expert witness', with the brief:

to provide expert advice on the events in Burnley during the weekend of 23 to 25 June 2001 insofar as they relate to the ethnicity of those involved and the possible bearing that might have on the way the events unfolded.

'Disorder in Burnley – Summer 2001' (8.4) is the Witness Statement I prepared and which the court was asked to consider in determining the guilt or innocence of the accused parties. In reaching its decision, the court accepted that the defendants were legitimately defending their community against organized racist aggression.

Following the disturbances in Moss Side in July 1981, Manchester City Council appointed Ben Hytner QC to conduct an inquiry into those events, just as Birmingham was to do four years later with Julius Silverman. The Home Secretary had already appointed Lord Justice Scarman to conduct a judicial inquiry into the Brixton disorders.

'The 1981 Moss Side Uprising' (8.5) gives the immediate background to the disturbances, and the critique of the Hytner Report which was published by the Moss Side Defence Committee of which I was Chair. The Committee was mindful that, as happened in Manchester and was later to happen in Burnley, the Hytner Report was likely to be used by prosecutors and the Manchester courts. The critique of the report was intended to provide an alternative and more informed analysis of the events and their background.

Sir William Macpherson and his team inquiring into the matters arising from the death of Stephen Lawrence heard evidence at their base in South London and then travelled to various locations around the country, including Manchester Town Hall, to receive supplementary evidence. 'Submission to the Inquiry into Matters Arising from the Death of Stephen Lawrence' (8.6) is the second of a two part statement I submitted, dealing in this part with policing matters generally and in Manchester in particular. The report highlights the fact that seventeen years after the disturbances in Moss Side, and events that had caused the death of innocent black people (Joy Gardener, Cynthia Jarrett) and triggered disturbances in other parts of the country, the style of policing in the Moss Side community was still a cause of deep concern and could easily lead to more disturbances.

In that statement, I make the point that there is a culture of racism which is endemic within the police and which can co-exist very healthily with positive initiatives, including those that involve black people themselves. This remains the case today, despite the requirements of the Race Relations Amendment Act, as was clearly demonstrated in the BBC documentary: *The Secret Policeman* in October 2003.

Black communities across the country, and especially in places such as Moss Side, Hackney, and Harlesden that have suffered a high incidence of gun related murders, cannot fail to be vigilant about the way their communities are policed, simply because they are concerned that there are vicious gun toting criminals who are generating fear and anxiety, and causing mayhem in their community. It is precisely in circumstances such as these that we need to ensure that our human rights and civil liberties are not trampled upon in the name of rooting out crime and the fear of crime.

8.1

GUS JOHN REVISITS HANDSWORTH/LOZELLS

Manchester
25 October 2005

Gus John wrote this article at the request of the *Guardian* in the week following the Lozells disturbances on 22-24 October 2005. The *Guardian* edited the article before publication and crucial points were lost. We publish the uncut article here because we consider it to be a specially significant contribution to the ongoing debate about causes and cures.

Whatever may have been the origin of the rumour that led to the disturbances in Lozells last weekend, one thing cannot be denied. 'Gang rape', whether by groups of men or members of gangs, is a barbaric form of sexual predation on women, irrespective of the ethnicity of perpetrators and victims. It causes alarm and revulsion in African-Caribbean communities when the rapists and victims are from that same background, as is increasingly the case, but it doesn't trigger riots. The key issue in Lozells, therefore, is the conditions that led to the racialization of rape, rumour or fact.

The answer lies, among other things, in the strained relationship between the African and Asian communities in Handsworth/Lozells over the last three decades and the way in which Birmingham City Council and various Government funding regimes has fuelled hostility between those communities.

I worked in Birmingham for the Runnymede Trust between 1969 and 1971 and wrote a report titled 'Race in the Inner City'. I lived on Churchill Road, just down the way from Lozells.

Handsworth was a very different place then. The majority ethnic group was white English and the second largest African-Caribbean. When the Birmingham *Evening Mail* wrote in 1969 about 'the Angry Suburbs', they were describing the reaction of African-Caribbean young people and their parents to the treatment they had been receiving from state institutions, the police especially, and from a hostile population that blamed them for pre-existing social ills. Business in the community was conducted mainly by white English and African-Caribbean people and there was a large measure of social cohesion.

By 1985, when police operations in Lozells triggered a massive rebellion that left two Asian brothers dead in their burnt out Post Office, and scores of people injured, the situation was very different. Most of the traders in Handsworth/Lozells were Asian, African-Caribbean businesses were in decline and the highest number of unemployed people in the area were black youth.

Julius Silverman's report on the 1985 disturbances, commissioned by Birmingham City Council, noted that the Asian communities were then expressing resentment at 'attacks by hooligans upon defenceless Asian people, especially women': 'it will be seen that the Asians are major victims of the crimes of robbery: assault and theft from the person by young Black criminals in the Area … there is some jealousy of Indian shop-keepers by Black youths, although most of the Asians are themselves very poor'.

Silverman concluded that 'the bridge between these two communities will be difficult to build, but all efforts must be made to do so'.

The last twenty years have seen the expansion of the Asian business sector across Handsworth, Lozells, and Perry Bar, with traders on whose goods and services the African-Caribbean community increasingly depends. Yet, one of the major causes of resentment within the latter community remains the fact that no African-Caribbean people are employed in these Asian retail outlets or warehouses, even when what is on sale are goods that only African heritage people purchase, e.g., hair products.

What is more, access to business and regeneration funding is anything but equitable. In the last two years there have been inter-ethnic conflicts over the allocation of £49m of Single Regeneration Budget (SRB) funds and the balance of representation of African/Asian people on the SRB Board. African-Caribbean groups complained of losing out because they were required to find £3,000 to match each £1,000 they were given, something which the Asian community found it much easier to do because of the way their communities, religious organizations and businesses were run. Asian communities complained that there were too many Africans on the Board (12 as compared to their 6). As a result of his protest about the unequal allocation of funding, one respected African community activist and member of the SRB Board was charged with aggravated racial abuse and intent to terrorize the Asian community, a charge of which he was acquitted in the Birmingham Crown Court. African-Caribbean individuals or syndicates have had a hard task over the years getting people in power and custodians of the public purse to support their proposals. Financial establishments tend to the view that there is a culture of entrepreneurship amongst people from the Indian sub-continent that African-Caribbean people do not share.

Clan elders exert a great deal of influence in all of these matters and can mobilize communities to lobby decision makers to get the outcomes they want. But, the more local councils do business with 'community leaders' who project themselves as local managers of their communities, the more the young people are prevented from having a say in matters that are important to them. That whole process results in Asian youths being pushed to the margins, and African-Caribbean communities feeling that Asians exert undue influence over decisions concerning local affairs and undue control over community resources.

Silverman in his report highlighted the 'great importance in the strength of the family unit' among Indians, Pakistanis, Bangladeshis, and Vietnamese, as compared to 'the impact of British social conditions on the matriarchal extended family structure of the West Indian immigrant (which) has proved to be very severe'. Would it were that simple. In his TV documentary

'Young, Angry and Muslim', (C4, 24 October 2005) Navid
Akhtar confirmed what some of us had known and protested
about for many years, i.e., the clan system and the exercise of
clan power to exercise control and exert influence in families
and in public life.

I have seen such clan power at work in Manchester in relation
to triggering the deportation of Pakistani women who deserted
their husbands because of sustained domestic violence and
dehumanizing treatment. Those of us in the Black Parents
Movement and the Asian Youth Movement who mounted
campaigns against those threatened deportations were harassed
by organized forces within the Pakistani community. Those
same forces, going by the dubious name of 'community leaders',
regularly sat at the table with the leading group within the City
Council, working out what was best for the youths and how and
where Muslim girls should be educated. When the City Council
decided to elect ethnic minority representatives on to its Race
Relations Committee, the clan system moved into gear and
corralled people from as far away as Bolton and Blackburn to
come and vote for Asian representatives to sit on Manchester
City Council. Navid Akhtar gets to the heart of the matter when
he reminds us that: 'Clan elders have for years provided huge
vote banks for mainstream parties, in return for positions and
influence in local politics' (*Observer*, 23 October 2005).

Political parties have colluded with that system of corruption
and abuse of democratic processes with two major effects. One
is the alienation of a generation of young Asians who have been
made to put up with whatever settlement the community
leaders worked out with local town halls. The other is the
resentment felt by African communities about the access and
influence those organized clan elders are seen to have, and the
tangible results of that as far as control of community resources
is concerned.

The fundamental difference between the Asian and African
communities of 1985 and now, is that both communities have
spawned some very vicious and seemingly uncontrollable
gangs. Those gangs distance themselves from the mundane
squabbles about funding and projects, etc., because they have

bigger fish to fry. The respective communities distance themselves from them and try to rein them in, e.g. in response to the shootings of Charlene Ellis and Letisha Shakespeare in Aston in 2003. They, on the other hand, own the community conflicts and are prepared to insert themselves in those conflicts as a 'third army' when it suits them. The African-Caribbean gangs in Birmingham would no doubt be flexing their muscles on behalf of a community worried about Asians showing dominance over Africans, a community that believes it must either stand up for itself or forever live in fear of them.

If sections of the African and Asian communities, especially the youth, ever allow the gangs to see themselves as being in the vanguard of their struggle against 'that other lot whom the police are failing to control', then we would all have lost the plot. These are therefore not matters for the police alone. They are even less matters for the so-called community leaders. Government will have to invest in some urgent and meaningful, short and long term conflict resolution programmes and structural initiatives that could help apprehend conflict and lay the foundations for a culture of peace and mutual respect within those communities. Such initiatives should focus upon systems of democratic governance that provide young people from all communities with the skills and capacity to make decisions, manage local affairs and apply resources in the interest of the whole community, having regard to the diverse needs and the history of the relationship between those communities.

8.2

LOZELLS DISTURBANCES
22-24 OCTOBER 2005
Proposed call for a People's Inquiry

1.0 Rationale

1.1 The tragic events in Lozells in October have left huge scars, families mourning their dead, a community under threat of more violence and many questions unanswered.

1.2 There has been little scope for those affected within the African, Asian and white English communities to speak about the conflict that threatens to tear the community apart and to work, jointly, towards solutions. Instead, the flames of hostility and racial hatred have been fanned by irresponsible and inflammatory statements made verbally, circulated in literature and aired in the media.

1.3 The community is desperately in need of healing and reconciliation. Each section of our community needs to take responsibility for that and work together with every other section to make it happen. But before healing could begin, lessons need to be learned, causes of conflict identified and wrongs righted.

1.4 We believe that the people of Handsworth/Lozells, the overwhelming majority of whom are committed to living peaceably with one another in a fair, racially just and socially cohesive environment, have:

i. a duty to examine the background to those disturbances
ii. the right to know
   • what caused the outbreak of violence and the stand off between the African and Asian communities

- how the authorities in the City, especially the police, and the local and national media dealt with the events as they unfolded
- whether, and if so how, they have engaged with the traumatized community in picking up the pieces
- the support being given to those individuals and families directly affected by the conflict
- the lessons to be learned from those events and the way they were handled
- the measures that are considered necessary to ensure there can be no repeat of those events and the tragic loss of life to which they gave rise
- how and by whom a process of conflict resolution and peace building would be undertaken

1.5 The typical response to such events on the part of Government, central or local, is to set up an inquiry led by someone chosen by them , typically with little knowledge or understanding of the area of conflict, its people, the dynamics of their social interactions or their day to day realities. We believe that the Home Secretary and Birmingham City Council should break with tradition and support a People's Inquiry.

1.6 The people of the area should be facilitated and financially supported to set up their own Inquiry, with a panel of inquirers constituted mainly by the people themselves, with that panel having the right to choose its own chairperson and any other expert assistance it might need.

1.7 It means, therefore, that The People's Inquiry Panel will be made up of members of the Asian, African and white communities in Lozells/Handsworth/Aston, with a secretariat whom they would choose.

2.0 Terms of Reference

2.1 The People's Inquiry's 'Terms of Reference' could be the 7 points in 1.4 ii. above, or variations on those.

2.2 The two main objectives of the Inquiry must be:
- to provide a mutually agreed forum where people in the community, the police, and other emergency

services could come and say what happened, what part they played in the run up to the events or during the events themselves, what might have been done differently
- how the City and community could work together to isolate and eliminate the underlying causes of the conflict and begin a process of conflict resolution and peace building.

3.0 Funding

3.1 It would be unreasonable and counter productive to expect the community to do this work in a meaningful way just by getting some volunteers to go and sit in a hall a couple evenings per week or on a Saturday.

3.2 The fact that it will be an Inquiry conducted and managed by the people of the area does not mean it should not be done to the highest professional standards, facilitated by an experienced chairperson and a competent and knowledge-able secretariat.

3.3 To achieve this, Birmingham City Council should be asked to fund the Inquiry and its secretariat.

3.4 Why Birmingham City Council? The City Council clearly has an interest in ensuring that conflicts between the African and Asian communities in Handsworth/Lozells do not remain unresolved and festering, thereby providing the basis for further eruptions and even worse community conflict. The City Council will be aware of the danger of such conflict spreading across Birmingham, if not to other cities, were there to be a repeat of the events of 22-24 October.

3.5 The City Council has a Race Equality Scheme that effectively says how it is meeting its legal obligation to implement the Race Relations (Amendment) Act 2000 and in particular the three strands of the General Duty, i.e.,:
- to eliminate unlawful racial discrimination
- to promote equality of opportunity
- to promote good relations between people of different racial groups

There is an obvious danger of things falling apart in

Handsworth/Lozells, resulting in major, long lasting, inter-ethnic violence and community conflict. Pursuant to its duty under the RRAA 2000, the City Council must be seen to take all necessary steps to ensure that this does not happen. It is in its interest, therefore, to work with the communities in the area and come up with local and City-wide solutions in the short and longer term.

3.6 Should the City Council argue that it has the political will to make this happen but not the money, it would be its business to argue with the Home Secretary to be given the money, especially in the light of the Home Office's 'Building Community Cohesion' strategy.

3.7 Details of the estimated cost of the Inquiry could be worked up once a clear commitment has been made to supporting its establishment.

4.0 Next Steps:

4.1 I recommend:

  i. that this proposal is circulated to every member of the Black Educators' Network for information and discussion, following the very successful meeting on 14 November 2005

  ii. that it is discussed with the key community groups and organizations with an interest in working together to put an end to this conflict, with a view to getting agreement that such a proposal should go to the City Council

  iii. that, when there is agreement that the proposal would go forward, it should be copied to Trevor Phillips at the Commission for Racial Equality and to the Home Secretary, Charles Clarke MP, at the same time that it is sent to Birmingham City Council.

I shall be willing to provide any further guidance and assistance.

8.3

OH DEAR! THAT CRIMINAL MINORITY AGAIN
Gus John examines the Police Report on the Handsworth Riots

Race Today
January 1986

I have no doubt that by now every 'O' Level student worth their salt could rehearse the official answer to the set and predictable question 'who and what are the causes of riots in Britain's inner cities, and how should law and order be guaranteed?'

In providing the answer, that student is amply assisted by the report of the Scarman Inquiry and of the Hytner Inquiry, the preaching of umpteen magistrates and judges, the rantings of Margaret Thatcher and of her various Home Secretaries under whose governance those massive revolts have occurred, yards of newsprint from an unashamedly racist media, and now, the latest offering from Mr Geoffrey Dear, Chief Constable of the West Midlands Police.

Mr Dear recently reported to Douglas Hurd (Home Secretary) on the Handsworth events, a taste of which Hurd himself got, and from which not even his obsequious 'obedient servant' Geoffrey Dear and his paramilitary police could have protected him.

Mr Dear's report has all the flavour, common sense and profundity of a lengthy piece written by a *Daily Mail* reporter who, having scurried around picking up half-baked theories here and there, runs off proclaiming to the world that he has got a scoop.

Cloud Cuckoo Land
Let us examine Mr Dear's claims, based on enquiries his officers

have diligently and successfully carried out 'combining the best traditional detective skills with the latest computer technology'. Mr Dear in his covering letter to the Home Secretary states boldly:

The overwhelming majority of the population in Handsworth supported the police before, during and after the disturbances and that one fact reassures me above all others that the position can be retrieved and that normal life can continue in the future.

Normality for Mr Dear equals the absence of overt hostility towards the police, and the absence of riots. The police, in his view and according to the law and gospel of Thatcherism, are representatives of moral authority and, in protecting the very moral fabric of society, they require the 'active and constructive support of all persons of goodwill'. Those who do not readily offer such support are held to be deviant.

Pointing 'the way ahead', Mr Dear warns:

The facts already cited in this report point very clearly to the conclusion that the majority of the rioters who took part in these unhappy events were young, black and of Afro-Caribbean origin. Let there be no doubt, these young criminals are not in any way representative of the vast majority of the Afro-Caribbean community whose presence has contributed to the life and culture of the West Midlands over many years and whose hopes and aspirations are at one with those of every other law-abiding citizen. We share a common sorrow. It is the duty of all of us to ensure that an entire cultural group is not tainted by the actions of a criminal minority.

So, you co-opt the majority on the side of law and order and you coerce them into believing that they have a moral duty to help you control and discipline the 'criminal minority'.

Problems they do have. Mr Dear 'would never seek to minimize the problems of being, young black and unemployed in a decaying inner city environment'. 'These and other ills cannot be ignored and deserve to be addressed by society as a whole. But they can never be taken singly or cumulatively as an excuse for criminal behaviour or as a retrospective justification for rioting, looting and murder'. And what of the 132 whites and 49 Asians who with the 221 blacks were arrested in Handsworth/Lozells and elsewhere in the Force area during the two days of rioting?

By seeking to distance young blacks from the experience of the black working class as a whole, Mr Dear, like others before him, is hoping to transform class warfare into the unfortunate happenstance of an organized group of young black criminals attacking police and property, in Handsworth's case because the police dared to upset their drug dealing practices.

The whites and Asians who were arrested then become opportunistic criminals, not endemic criminals like the blacks, but people who could not resist criminality once such golden opportunities were created by the blacks. The mass uprisings that were visited upon this nation by the forebears of those whites (and which incidentally the forebears of the Asians staged repeatedly on another terrain) are therefore seen as having nothing to do with the condition of Britain today, and the response of this generation to it.

The 'Soft' Approach

But then, Mr Dear's diagnosis is very simple, as is his prescription. He went to great pains to point out how he and his predecessor, Phillip Knight, followed the Scarman catechism to the letter. Their police penetrated youth clubs, schools, tenant's associations, mosques, leisure centres, and the minds of citizens of goodwill, establishing 'an intricate web of community contact'. Not for surveillance purposes, of course. Rather, 'in this way the expectations of the public are heard and an exchange of views is possible'. Similarly, the police ran youth clubs and 'involved the young in leisure activities as [it] was believed that those likely to come into conflict with the police could be reached in this way'.

Convinced that the law and order gospel demands that the police be allowed free rein to represent moral and social authority in this way, Thatcher's government is stipulating that the police must be given the right to work on childrens' minds in schools and steer them away from joining that 'criminal minority'.

For those out of school, for the '90% of 16-18 year olds in Handsworth who've never had a job, [and the] 56% unemployed for more than one year', the message from Mr Dear is clear. Swallow Thatcher's pill. Be disciplined through the Manpower Services Commission Community Programme spearheaded by the West Midlands Police, and when you escape from that, go and be disciplined and guided onto the straight and narrow through leisure activities with the West Midlands Police.

If you don't, you are, in Mr Dear's words, part of 'a minority of dissidents who refuse to participate actively in any community project despite all the goodwill from both the police and community leaders'.

And what of the dissident drug dealers, Mr Dear's scoop? Drug-dealing in Handsworth is as old as Thornhill Road Police Station itself. When I worked in Handsworth in the late1960s the police knew which pubs and shebeens did a trade in drugs and who the pushers were, no less than they do today. They struck deals with shebeen owners and pushers, confiscated drugs, resold some, planted some on unsuspecting victims, and harassed people with their stop and search powers which they whimsically abused no less than they do today. Every drug pusher in Handsworth, first and second generation, knows that as do those who are put upon by the police under the guise of 'needing to identify the criminals in an area of high crime'.

If now drug-pushers have the social instrument of 'riot' to deal with their grievances against the police despite the settlement they make with the police and vice versa – and that is a theory Mr Dear claims to have proven – then that instrument could only be effectively deployed because those whom they 'activate' are already in riot mode.

Having interviewed young people and adults in Handsworth on September 10 and 11, and sat in the magistrates court as scores of those arrested were paraded in front of magistrates determined to see law and order restored at any cost, I am convinced that those drug pushers would have had as much luck getting those men and women to riot in their defence as I would by taking a loud-hailer and walking the streets, summoning people to come out and riot.

When on Wednesday, 11 September, those same drug-dealers who had supposedly marshalled such a well-organized combat force, took to the streets following one of those 'truce' meetings with the police, and were commanding young people and curiosity merchants to clear the streets, they received the length of people's tongues. They wanted people off the streets not because they felt the riot had burnt itself out and people should settle down till next time, but because as one fellow put it: 'I've got a woman and kids to feed, and three days now I man can do no trade. Go to your whatsit yard and mek dem beast an' dem goweh outa dis place'.

It was not a youth but an adult woman aged about fifty who remonstrated with them. The police, she claimed, would not take the defeat they suffered lying down. They would make someone pay for it. So when they come back and start busting down people's doors and picking people off the street, who would be there to see what they're doing and defend those people when you lot make people clear the streets? Why keep the police away from dem streets for two nights running only to go and hide inside now and leave the streets to dem to run riot and do what they like with people?

And, as the young people were produced in the dock from beneath the magistrate's courts, each man and woman of them instinctively looked around the public gallery. And sure enough there were mothers and fathers of that same 45-55 age group sitting there nodding at them and waiting to hear the inevitable remand in custody or remand on bail with a dusk to dawn curfew.

One old man was prompted to exclaim afterwards that he'd never been in a South African court, but what he experienced in that court that day must come pretty damned close to what goes on in South Africa. So there at least were some 'dissident' parents who made a point of standing by 'the criminal minority'.

And what of Mr Dear's way forward?

Coercion as a Deterrent

Terence Morris, writing in *New Society*, 29 November 1985, observed, 'riot confers no license for generalized violence on the part of the agents of the state'. Morris is there arguing, unlike Dear, in favour of a riot squad, and asserting that it will be easier to keep a tight rein on a riot squad in a way that one can't with support groups drafted into a police district from other areas.

If people like Anderton, Newman, Oxford, and others never mind the blood thirstier sections of the British media, believe that lawlessness on the part of the police is excusable in a riot and post-riot situation, then the British courts have shown themselves to endorse that view every step of the way. The whole affair becomes viciously circular.

While Commissions of Inquiry meet to analyse causes and cures, and police and community leaders scurry around demonstrating that theirs is a 'common sorrow' and that they have no fundamental disagreements, not even about what 'returning the situation back to normality' means, the injustice machine accelerates in the cause of law and order, and the safeguarding of people's rights and civic entitlements is considered an almost obscene concern, given the circumstances. In one fell swoop, magistrates and judges, not to mention solicitors and barristers, manage to engender in defendants, their families and their communities the kind of resentment which remains deep seated and festering, ready and waiting to be given expression in full force on another day, whether or not by the same people.

No one is deterred. Others see no one as 'an example'. They do not learn to respect and abide by 'the consensual values' of the society any more than they did before. They don't go running in droves to the nearest community policing facility. They and their communities are subjected instead to more of the vicious treatment which is visited upon the community by an occupying force on whom no checks are imposed in the wake of the warfare on the streets, even as the consultation and the community liaison is stepped up in an effort to restore 'normality'.

And if the law and order gospel and the pilgrims within the

police and the community and inside the courts failed to achieve what they want now, they would be no more successful with the baton rounds, CS gas, and water cannon at their disposal.

Similarly, African-Caribbean and Asian communities must deal with those 'leaders' who seek through their activities to incorporate the black working class into the law and order regime of Thatcherism. They must stand by Mr Dear's 'criminal minority' and assert that black people, young and old, have every right to a stake in the political, economic, social and cultural life of this country, and will not be coerced into swallowing Thatcher's pill.

Contrary to what Chief Officers of Police say, it is crystal clear that they see themselves not as the 'alien wedge' within the inner cities, pushed inexorably to the front line of the class war, but as people on whose shoulders it properly rests to promote an authoritarian if not totalitarian police state.

In forces such as Geoffrey Dear's the police have had a fair measure of success in gaining acquiescence in that belief and the strategies that arise from it. Which person of goodwill would want to argue with the police running MSC work schemes, youth clubs, etc., unless they are criminally or politically 'dissident?'

The police and the courts have had their way with us for generations. So indeed has the British economy and successive British governments.

If Mr Dear's report and the British establishment's response to Handsworth, Brixton, Tottenham, etc., do anything, they compel us, and not least of all the present generation of urban black British warriors, to reassess the political stance we adopt to the British state and its coercive agencies, and it is a task that cannot be delegated or long be delayed.

DISORDER IN BURNLEY – SUMMER 2001
Statement of Gus John, expert witness
Burnley
June 2001

I have been asked to provide expert advice on the events in Burnley during the weekend of 23-25 June 2001 insofar as they relate to the ethnicity of those involved and the possible bearing that might have had on the way the events unfolded.

I do so on the basis of my employment, teaching, research, and publication record which encompasses the experience I bring to this task and is provided in some detail as background to this statement.

1.0 The Burnley Report

1.1 In preparing this Advice, I have drawn substantially on the report of the Burnley Task Force by its Chair, Lord Tony Clarke.

1.2 In his preface to the report, Lord Clarke writes:

Turning to 23rd to 25th June, I have had the opportunity to meet and discuss with a number of people who witnessed those events. As a result of what I have heard, I am convinced that what was described as a 'race riot' was in fact a series of criminal acts, perpetrated by a relatively small number of people. Certainly, racial intolerance played a significant role in those disturbances; the confrontations that took place were clearly identified as aggression and violence by both white people and those from within the Asian heritage communities. However, in my view, the label of 'race riot' does the people of Burnley a grave disservice. p. 8

1.4   Lord Clarke returns to that theme at the end of his report: In a section headed 'Disturbance or Riot?', we read:

> *The Task Force wants to make it clear that Burnley does not deserve a reputation of being a riotous town. It accepts that criminal acts and criminal damage took place during the period 23rd to 25th June. Nevertheless it is felt that, bad as they were, the incidents should not be described as riots. At the same time it respects those who have differing views on the terminology used.*
> p. 85

1.5   The report states that one of the decisions taken at their first meeting was that:

> *a priority for the Task Force would be to focus on obtaining facts about what actually happened and to dispel myths already emerging within the Borough and beyond.* p. 31

1.6   The above quotations are at the heart of what is deficient about Lord Clarke's report.

1.7   'Facts' are not reified entities that stand in isolation from the context in which they occur.

1.8   In their submission to the Task Force, the Lancashire Constabulary makes some rather pertinent observations. For example, they employ a conceptual model to describe different levels of community disorder, along a time continuum of: *normality, high tension, disorder, de-escalation, normality.*

1.9   With respect to *normality*, they make the point that a situation which requires normal policing 'will vary from one area to another. Some areas by reference to levels of crime, illegal enterprise, for example, drug dealing, and a record of hostility to law enforcement, have a much greater potential for urban disorder. Normal policing in these areas generally involves a degree of sensitivity, planning and resolve which would be considered abnormal elsewhere'.

1.10 A record of hostility to law enforcement in these terms could result from, for example, the community's experience of how their area is policed and the manner in which particular groups are targeted by age and ethnicity. A record of hostility to law enforcement was engendered within black communities, for example, as a result of the application in the 1980s of what became known as 'sus' laws, i.e., arrest on suspicion of being about to commit an indictable offence.

1.11 The Lancashire Constabulary are therefore acknowledging a basic fact, i.e., that there is as much a *context* to policing as there is to the commitment of criminal offences. Thus, they describe a condition of 'high tension' as *'the situation in a community when feelings are running high and the potential for disorder is perceived to be considerably increased'*. It is in situations such as these that the police rely on 'high quality intelligence' in order to test the 'perception' that there is a high risk of disorder.

1.12 Parliament finally conceded that there is a context to certain types of offences when it passed the Crime and Disorder Act (CDA) 1998. Damage, burglary, harassment, assault, and murder were all indictable offences prior to the CDA 1998. The racially aggravated nature of such acts is something black communities had experienced and complained about for decades before the criminal justice system acknowledged them as such. Indeed, in the submission from the Lancashire Police that Lord Clarke and his committee considered, an offence profile is given in which no less than 61 crimes with a racial dimension are listed.

1.13 The tendency to deconstruct the racial aggravation in civil disorder such as occurred in Burnley in June 2001 is not a new phenomenon. Lord Clarke is in good company with the likes of former Prime Minister Margaret Thatcher, former Home Secretary William Whitelaw, former West Midlands Chief Constable Geoffrey Dear, among others. Those persons, in respect of disturbances in Brixton,

Toxteth, Moss Side and elsewhere in 1981, and in Handsworth, Birmingham in 1985, sought to focus the country's interpretation of the events and their causes on 'criminal elements' and on 'thuggery', in other words away from their very obvious origins in the way these urban communities had been experiencing institutions of the state and one another for some considerable time.

1.14 That tendency towards consensus, towards normality, aimed as it is towards reassuring the country and the specific area, Burnley in this case, that things are not falling apart, is both misleading and dangerous. When Lord Clarke says he is convinced that what happened in Burnley 'was in fact a series of criminal acts perpetrated by a relatively small number of people', he is:

a. by implication, calling for those apprehended by the police and charged to be treated, first and foremost, as 'criminals' who by their conduct upset the 'normal functioning' of a community, a town, that has the misfortune of having elements within its multiethnic community that caused everyone a deal of anxiety and stress during that weekend in June 2001

b. failing to make a distinction between the Asian heritage people caught up in the disorder and the whites

c. denying the experience those Asian heritage people would have had of racist crimes perpetrated against them, at one extreme, and the ghettoization caused by the process known as 'white flight' and by local authority housing and social policy

d. failing to understand that the 'white flight' phenomenon leads to a sense of ostracization on the part of the Asian heritage people in areas such as Daneshouse, as well as a sense of their vulnerability at the hands of those like the British National Party who then use the very existence of their so-called 'Asian only' area as a reason to incite racial hostility towards them

e. failing to understand that even if one accepts the police view that 'the trigger for the disorder was the clash between two criminal groupings (Asian heritage and white) in Daneshouse during the early hours of Saturday 23 June, and thereafter the indiscriminate attack by white men on the off duty Asian heritage taxi driver' (Lancs Constabulary Submission), an inquiry such as his, and he as the author of the Task Force Report, has a duty to look beyond these precipitating events and be better informed about the 'tinder' that has fostered the bitterness and hatred displayed by both white and Asian heritage people during those events

f. in danger of inducing in Burnley as a whole a false sense of security and cohesion by locating the cause of the racial conflict in the criminal activities of a relatively small number of individuals

g. by focusing on the 'racial intolerance' exhibited by those caught up in the conflict, locating the racial dimension only in the individuals concerned rather than in the wider structural, cultural, and institutional bases of the racism that has infested the communities of Burnley

h. therefore, failing to understand that Asian heritage people's experience of such roots of racism is qualitatively different from that of whites generally and particularly from the experience of those caught up in the conflict

i. failing to have regard to the collective experience of group oppression that Asian heritage people have had and the understandable steps they take to defend their communities as a consequence of that , both in Burnley and elsewhere

j. therefore, limiting himself and, potentially, readers of his report to a singularly unhelpful discourse about 'community relations' and 'valuing diversity' which is unfit for purpose, given the nature of the submissions the Task Force received from the people of Burnley themselves

k. failing to focus Burnley Council and Lancashire County Council on the very urgent need to take active steps to *combat racism* as well as promoting race equality and good relations between people of different racial groups

l. most worryingly, projecting the disturbances as, essentially, a 'law and order' issue, with racial intolerance as a qualifying component.

1.15 The events in Burnley, coming so soon after Oldham and Bradford, and against the backcloth of the many commissions of inquiry since Scarman (Brixton) and Hytner (Moss Side) in 1981, right up to Macpherson on Stephen Lawrence (1999), were such that the people of Burnley and the country as a whole had a right to expect a more informed framework of analysis to be brought to the interpretation of those events.

1.16 The 'cult' of the individual bigot or peddler of race hatred runs through Lord Clarke's report over and over again. That is exemplified most clearly in section 3.1 which, in my view, appears to sum up Lord Clarke's understanding of how racism functions in the society:

It would be easy to dismiss many of the biased and prejudiced views expressed, especially those directed at members of the minority ethnic communities. We believe that the reason for some of the outright racist views held by many, *including some quite young people, have their foundation in the poor communication between the governed and the government in Burnley. That does not in any way detract from the fact that Burnley does have in its midst* a number of people who are committed to racism and the fostering of race hatred. *Tragically, Burnley is not unique in this respect. Many of Britain's towns and cities are targeted by the* bigoted and dangerous people and right wing organisations who preach prejudice and intolerance. *Before and during the period of the Task Force work national media outlets have exposed the* true nature of these people and their organisations. *It is our fervent hope that such evil people do not attract Burnley's young people by their outpourings of hatred and prejudice. All of us have a duty to expose, whenever we can, their lies and deceit. At all times we must remember the past and the sacrifice made by literally millions of good people to preserve our nation's freedom.* (my emphasis)   p. 38

1.17 Earlier this year, the current Head of the Los Angeles Police Department had this to say about an earlier riot:

> *It is ten years (29 April 1992) since the rebellion/civil unrest/riot/uprising took place in Los Angeles.*
>
> *The myth was that the uprising was a black orchestrated 'tantrum' inspired by the verdict against the four police officers on trial for the beating of black motorist Rodney King.*
>
> *In truth, the verdict was the spark, but the tinder was the rage of decades of deprivation, neglect, inequality and prejudice in the poor areas of South LA.*
>
> *We need to look beyond the incident that sparked the unrest.*
>
> *The actual ingredient was the existence of poor communities of colour pitted against each other. The uprising was a manifestation of the despair felt by disaffected people.*
>
> *Years and years of distrust, discourtesy and disrespect is what drives people to react in that fashion'*
>
> – Bernard Parks (chief of the LAPD)

1.18 A significant part of the evidence presented to the Task Force is contained in the submission of the Lancashire Constabulary as follows:

> *that Sunday (24 June), something of a siege mentality developed, with groups drinking and singing football and nationalist songs such as, 'No surrender to the IRA'. Substantial fireworks were also set off at the back of the pub and* racial abuse was directed at passing Asian Heritage motorists, followed by actual damage to some of their cars, mainly taxis.
>
> There is no doubt that any incident involving taxis is instantaneously fed back into the Asian communities via radios and mobile phones, and the communities in general were well aware of events around the public house as they were developing. *Equally, there can be little doubt that some people in the Asian communities were being 'mobilised' as the situation was developing, evidenced by the fact that huge numbers of Asian heritage males very quickly gathered, many armed with weapons such as swords, machetes and clubs.*

The next significant move, however, was made by a white group *from the public house near to the Duke of York, in that about thirty males* decided to walk the relatively short distance from the pub into the Daneshouse area, which is populated mainly by Asian heritage people. *Other white males moved off in the opposite direction, presenting problems for the Police trying to deal with the situation.* Both white groups were fuelled by drink, singing songs and hurling racial abuse, *but the group heading towards Daneshouse was prevented from doing so by Police officers who were now increasing in numbers.*

This group was marshalled along Colne Road towards Burnley town centre. This took them past a number of streets leading into Daneshouse, in which significant numbers of males from the Asian communities, possibly 300 strong, had gathered. *The police ... were faced on both sides by people who were quite literally 'spitting hatred' at each other, armed with weapons, throwing missiles and making every effort to fight each other and the Police.*

Whilst the white faction was on the move, the Asian heritage group remained in and around Daneshouse.

(my emphasis)

1.19 Whatever definition Lord Clarke may have of 'a riot', and I see no evidence of what in his view constitutes one, that police chronology of events suggests to me something much, much more than criminality on the part of the Asian heritage groups. The following factors are especially relevant by way of context:

a. In the early hours of Saturday morning an Asian heritage taxi driver had been viciously attacked with a hammer in what the Police recorded as a racially aggravated crime. That caused consternation, anger, and fear within the black community in Burnley. The police, worryingly, observe that:

There is no doubt that this man was in the wrong place at the wrong time and that he was attacked because of his ethnicity.

b. By that logic, black people have a woeful and lemming-like propensity to be in the wrong place at the wrong time, including Stephen Lawrence. One wonders why the Police saw fit to make that observation in view of what they noted 4 paragraphs earlier, i.e., that:

Taxi drivers in Burnley are a vulnerable group and can be considered repeat victims. They work until the early hours of the morning and are subjected to abuse and crime from customers, *many of whom are the worse for drink. Many taxi drivers are from ethnic minority communities. They have two well organised associations ... who are very active in addressing their members' problems, for example, when they have been victims of crime in the past they have withdrawn their services and on occasions have besieged the police station and town hall. They have excellent lines of communication between themselves and word travels fast between them.* (my emphasis)

c. This would suggest that, collectively, those taxi drivers are in the habit of being 'in the wrong place at the wrong time'.

d. I believe that it signifies something much more fundamental. In Pakistani and Bangladeshi communities up and down the country (Bradford, Bury, Manchester, Leicester, Southall, Oldham), taxi drivers have been murdered or maimed in the course of doing what most white counterparts do without any suggestion that they would be murdered because of the colour of their skin or because of their faith.

e. The level of organization among the taxi drivers in Burnley, therefore, is not just about the protection of trade and general issues to do with safety. It is very much about collective action in the face of known and deadly threats, collective action to make the authorities, including the police, take those threats seriously and to signal to would-be assailants that they would not render themselves vulnerable to attack without protest, albeit they are necessarily single person units of operation.

f. It is significant that the police themselves noted that 'whilst the white faction were on the move, *the Asian heritage group remained in and around Daneshouse'*. This would suggest that rather than being hell bent on causing mayhem and roaming around attacking people indiscriminately, or targeting white individuals and property, people had gathered to defend their communities and prevent Asian heritage people like themselves from being attacked as the taxi driver had been.

g. One can legitimately argue from the particular case of taxi drivers to the experience of black and Asian heritage people across the country more generally. The experience of black and Asian heritage people over the last five decades has been of racist attacks by individuals and groups against places of worship, Mosques especially, dwellings and people. These have taken the form of desecration, firebombing families while they slept, stabbing, abduction and killing, running people off the roads. Indeed, as observed earlier, the provisions of the Crime and Disorder Act with respect to racially aggravated offences have their origins in the struggle of black communities against such crimes that have become endemic.

h. The culture of racism that spawns such activities and is in turn reinforced by them, acts upon white perpetrators no less than black victims and those rendered vulnerable by such practices.

i. Young people of whatever ethnicity have been socialized into a culture in which 'paki bashing', racist bullying of Asian heritage children, racist attacks against Asian heritage women and men, lie on a spectrum with public debates and government pronouncements about immigration controls linked to 'race', illegal immigrants, language and 'integration', language tests, oaths of allegiance, and the rest.

j. That leads whites to see blacks as the people whom the society considers marginal and not quite belonging, and therefore people who could be seen as legitimate targets, and blacks to see themselves as at the receiving end of adverse policies, restrictive practices, discrimination and, at the most extreme, racist violence that too often leads to murder.

k. Where there is a general tendency to violence, bullying, vandalism in an area, the fact that the culture of racism renders black and ethnic minority people vulnerable means that they are often seen as suitable targets for those sorts of activities.

l. That goes for bullying in schools, workplace bullying, bullying in shops, no less than the treatment meted out to black people by institutions such as the police. I have written quite extensively about this over the years, notably in the report: *Murder in the Playground*, the story of racist bullying and the 'robbing of identity' in the treatment of Bangladeshi students at Burnage High School in South Manchester in 1986, which led to the racist murder of fourteen year old Ahmed Iqbal Ullah by fourteen year old Darren Coulburn, himself a white working class Burnage student.

m. Part of that culture of racism in Britain has been and is the existence and activities of neo-fascist and right wing groups such as the National Front, Column 88, the British National Party, and the Independent Group in Burnley. They have operated over the decades to render local black and ethnic minority communities much more open to racist attack and general levels of racist intolerance and bigotry. Their targeting of such communities has been such as to give rise to organized resistance on the part of those communities in their own self defence.

1.20 There has been a debate in Britain for over three decades about the place of self defence in communities' response to the racist threats facing them. The question is put:

When the police whose duty it is to protect all communities fail to carry out their responsibilities, what course of action is there but for Black communities to defend themselves?

1.21 The lack of protection can lead some young people to

adopt the stance that 'self defence is no offence' and thus
to arm themselves against racist attacks (Edwards, Oakley
and Carey, 1987). However, in these cases, youths are
criminalized for attempting to defend communities from
racism, in the absence of police protection and in the face
of ethnic majority communities' tacit consent to the
activities of those organized neo-fascist groups within their
communities.

1.22 That process of criminalization is often boosted by the
insistence that it is a desire to indulge in 'thuggery' or
'wanton acts of vandalism' that drives young black people
to these extremes.

1.23 It is significant, for example, that in the Preface to his
report, Lord Clarke quotes Tony Blair's remarks in a
speech to the Labour Party conference on 2 October 2001:

*The graffiti, the vandalism, the burnt out cars, the street corner
drug dealers, the teenage mugger just graduating from the minor
school of crime: we're not old fashioned or right-wing to take
action against this social menace.*

*We're standing up for the people we represent, who play by the
rules and have a right to expect others to do the same.*

*And especially at this time let us say: we celebrate the diversity
in our country, get strength from the cultures and races that go
to make up Britain today; and racist abuse and racist attacks
have no place in the Britain we believe in.*

1.24 This is not the place to examine those two-edged messages
from Mr Blair, except to say that the juxtaposition of
dealing with criminals and celebrating diversity mirrors
the approach that Lord Clarke has adopted in examining
the events in Burnley, events which, like Bradford and
Oldham, Mr Blair had very much in his sights.

1.25 'The Bradford Twelve'

*Fascists were waging a murderous campaign against our people.
It was necessary to defend our community. It was with this in
mind that we did what we did.*

Those were the words of one of the defendants in the trial of the 'Bradford 12' – twelve Asian youths who were charged with conspiracy to cause an explosion following the discovery of a stash of petrol bombs. The bombs had been prepared to defend black areas in Bradford from National Front violence.

The case became a landmark in antiracism as the youths argued that their militant defence of the community was the only way to stop the planned racist attack. They argued they were acting legitimately in self-defence.

The twelve were all found not guilty in 1982 and their 'self-defence is no offence' argument was an inspiration to black communities and organized groups struggling to contain the rise of right wing groups in Britain.

1.26 'The Newham 8'

In 1982, eight Asian youths were arrested in Newham following action against racist attacks in schools. They were charged with conspiracy, assault and a number of other offences. The Newham 8 Defence Campaign was launched and exposed police racism. Four of the eight were found guilty of the much lesser charge of affray.

1.27 The Duke of York Pub (Burnley 2001)

Historically perceived by the Asian community to be a meeting place for football hooligans accustomed to indulging racism at football matches and in the community, and others determined to attack nearby Asian premises, the disturbances in Burnley culminated in an arson attack on the Duke of York pub.

1.28 The British Crime Survey (BCS) statistics are a useful guide to the level of anxiety there is within black and ethnic minority communities about their vulnerability to crime. BCS asks people about crimes they have experienced in the last year and about a range of other crime related topics.

The Pakistani/Bangladeshi group emerges as a group for whom worry about crime is obvious and highly salient.

1.29 Anxiety about crime: Hough's (1995) analysis of the 1994 BCS found that

- 61% of Asians were 'very' or 'fairly' worried about racial crime compared with 49% of African-Caribbeans, and 15% of whites.
- The annual risk of being a victim of a racially motivated incident varied for different groups. In 1999, the risks for ethnic minority groups were considerably higher, estimated at:
- 4.2% for Bangladeshis and Pakistanis
- 3.6% for Indians
- 2.2% for blacks
- 0.3% for whites

1.30   BCS 2000

- People from ethnic minorities, particularly Bangladeshi and Pakistani respondents, worry more about crime than white respondents.
- Against the background of declining crime there are substantial variations in the risks of victimization experienced by ethnic minority groups. The most up to date figures, (BCS 2000), suggest that:
- 5% of white respondents were 'very' worried about being a victim of a racially motivated assault, as opposed to 28% of black respondents and 33% of Asian respondents
- Pakistanis and Bangladeshis were significantly more likely than white or black people to be victims of household crime.
- Emotional reactions to racially motivated incidents reported were generally more severe than for other incidents. They are not 'just like any other crime': 42% said they had been affected by the incident compared with 19% for other sorts of incidents.
- Ethnic minorities have consistently reported lower levels of satisfaction with the police when they have contacted them than white people. In the 2000 BCS, overall satisfaction with public-initiated police contact was highest amongst white respondents (70% were very/fairly satisfied) and lowest for Pakistanis and Bangladeshis (56% were very/fairly satisfied)

2.0   Task Force Report is Fundamentally Flawed

2.1   Having regard to all the above, the Burnley Task Force report has managed to focus very narrowly on the Burnley events themselves without putting them into their proper context, locally and nationally. With respect to the report's local focus, Lord Clarke does not appear to have analysed the messages coming forth from many of the submissions he received, including that of the Lancashire Constabulary. Similarly, I do not see the very thoughtful and crucial submissions from the Bangladeshi Welfare Association and the East Lancashire Development Unit sufficiently reflected in the main findings and conclusions Lord Clarke produced.

2.2   My professional opinion is that, having regard to the quality of the submissions the Task Force had at its disposal, the report is deficient because of the narrow and poorly informed analytical framework that was brought to the interpretation of them.

2.3   In other words, the people of Burnley could be forgiven for thinking that Lord Clarke projected the Burnley of June 2001 as he felt the people of Burnley had a right to expect it to be, rather than as the most vulnerable groups within it had in reality experienced it.

2.4   As regards the national context, no black community in Britain can afford to take a view of itself that is entirely circumscribed by its own local circumstances and the manner in which its activities are interpreted locally. By removing the black and Asian heritage people in Burnley from the wider context of racism and black resistance to racist oppression over the last fifty years, the Task Force report does a number of things:

- It trivializes their experience and by implication encourages the people of Burnley (Asian heritage included) to see the activities of those who were arrested simply as the criminal activities of people who should be dealt with and isolated (in custody or not)
- It prevents the public authorities and the ethnic majority of whites in Burnley from understanding the connection

between those events and their precipitating causes, and the challenges facing the society as a whole

- It prevents them from asking the right questions and therefore setting an appropriate agenda for ensuring that new generations of Burnley residents, black and white, won't be similarly influenced by the realities of racism as it is constructed structurally, culturally, institutionally as well as personally

- It reduces the bases of these conflicts to a lack of attention to multicultural activities and a failure to 'value diversity', without regard to the fact that a major problem with Burnley and so many other places is that whites, working class whites in particular, are not given any basis in schooling and education or in validated 'culture' for locating themselves and rooting their identity in their own rich working class culture

- It buys in to the notion that there is a unifying majority culture that must begin to mingle with and give space for the expression of the cultures of 'the ethnic minorities'

- It rather assumes that embracing multiculturalism and 'valuing diversity' could be a meaningful substitute for collective action to eradicate racism in all its structural, cultural, and institutional manifestations, and attend to the task of promoting social justice in the process

In this connection, it is worth remembering the words of the Director of the Institute of Race Relations, A. Sivanandan:

Just to learn about other people's cultures is not to learn about the racism of one's own. To learn about the racism of one's own culture, on the other hand, is to approach other cultures objectively.

The courts will deal with matters that concern them. It would be unfortunate indeed, however, if in seeking to do so they were to depend upon the analysis and conclusions of this fundamentally flawed and ill-informed report.

8.5

THE 1981 MOSS SIDE UPRISING

On the evening of 8 July 1981, the community of Moss Side witnessed a rebellion by young people, mainly black but with sizeable numbers of whites (especially Irish) also involved. That rebellion raged throughout the night of 8 July and fizzled out by dawn on 9 July after a night of running battles with the police.

There had been similar rebellions in St Paul's (Bristol), Brixton (London), Toxteth (Liverpool 8) and a number of other areas in England.

Four months earlier, on the 2 March 1981, six coach loads of local people and a large number of cars had left Moss Side before dawn to travel to New Cross in South East London to be part of the Black People's Day of Action (BPDA). The BPDA had been organized by the New Cross Massacre Action Committee (NCMAC) which was formed in the immediate aftermath of the massacre on 18 January 1981 at 439 New Cross Road, Lewisham, of thirteen young black people who were attending the sixteenth birthday party of Yvonne Ruddock. The fire was to claim the life of a fourteenth victim some weeks later.

The Metropolitan Police had told the Ruddock family hours after the fire, which totally burnt out the house, that the house had been firebombed. In the days following the fire, the British Movement and the National Front callously wrote to the relatives of the dead and went around putting leaflets through black people's doors stating that: 'This is just the start of what is to come'.

The NCMAC mobilized people in London and across the country for a day of action in protest against the killings and the failure of the state to protect black people from murderous attacks by racists.

Gus John was a founder member of the NCMAC and its organizer in the North/North West of England. The Manchester Black Parents Movement of which he was then Chair, affiliated to the NCMAC and mobilized support for the families of the New Cross victims, and for the Day of Action planned for 2 March 1981. A series of well attended public meetings were held in Manchester, Preston, Liverpool, Leeds, Sheffield, and Huddersfield at which Gus John and persons in the leadership of the NCMAC in London spoke.

The march from 439 New Cross Road to Fleet Street, Scotland Yard, the Houses of Parliament, 10 Downing Street, and finishing in Hyde Park represented the biggest show of force by the black communities of Britain in response to any single issue before or since. The fact that 25,000 people took to the streets of London on a Monday, the start of an ordinary working and school week, made the national response to that tragedy, the worst in the experience of black people in Britain, all the more remarkable and therefore historical.

In the period between the Day of Action and the rebellion in Moss Side, police activities in various parts of the country, including in Brixton where the Metropolitan Police launched 'Swamp '81', targeted black communities and black youths in particular. Swamp '81 triggered the Brixton Riots in April 1981. Meanwhile, young people in Moss Side continued to bear the brunt of police harassment, the unemployed amongst them were routinely criminalized and the general discourse concerning ' black youth' was couched in terms such as 'alienation', 'disaffection', and 'a lack of respect for authority'.

In the months between the Day of Action and the Moss Side disturbances, the black community in Moss Side was also actively engaged in a campaign against the deportation of a local black woman, a well established member of the community with two British born children. Having lived here for many years she had gone to the Caribbean to care for her mother whose health was failing. Immigration law stipulated that people with resident status in the UK could retain that status as long as they were not out of the country for more than two years continuously. Cynthia Gordon who had given up her employment to go and be a carer, could not afford to take care of her mother and find the fare back to England within those two years just to satisfy that requirement, and then return to caring for her mother. When, eventually, she was able to return some months after the deadline to join her children and get on with her life, she was only allowed temporary stay as a visitor. In due course, the Home Office decided she had to leave the country, taking her British born teenagers with her for all they cared.

The people of Moss Side protested that the threat of deportation was unacceptable and inhumane. For them and communities up and down Britain, it epitomized the worst aspects of racialized immigration legislation and represented an attack on social and family organization within the black communities of Britain, especially given the history of migration from the Caribbean. For, not only were black people contributing to the economic development of Britain and suffering multiple disadvantage in the process, the very process of migration had given rise to a sizeable population of elderly dependents in their homeland for whom they had continuing responsibility.

The Cynthia Gordon Anti-Deportation Campaign was led by the Black Parents Movement and resulted in the Home Secretary granting Cynthia leave to remain and resume her resident status.

There was also a growing and increasingly organized movement against the activities of the National Front, Column 88, and the British Movement in Moss Side and surrounding areas with a sizeable black population. Those neo-fascist organizations sought to whip up hostility amongst poor whites in relation to what they presented as evidence of the government 'favouring the blacks who sponge off the State at the expense of "our" people who have nothing'. They were rounded upon and run out of town by white and black residents alike.

By 8 July 1981, therefore, the black people of Moss Side, youths in particular, had endured neglect, marginalization and aggravation such that they did not need the example of people in Brixton, St Paul's, Toxteth or anywhere else.

I was working at the Moss Side Community Education Centre at the time as a Co-ordinator of Community Education. Not only did that involve me in a close working relationship with the youth and community workers in Moss Side and the central district of Manchester, I also knew, and was known, to most of the young people in the area, if not to their parents and carers.

By July 1981, the communities and organized groups in Moss Side, Hulme, Rusholme, Whalley Range, and Longsight, irrespective of the range of ideological positions and political tendencies amongst them, could have all borne witness to the condition of being black and young in Manchester and to the repeated, sporadic attacks by white racists on sections of the community, Asian and African.

After the rebellion, I was elected Chair of the Moss Side Defence Committee, a development which caused a certain unease in the Manchester Education Department, not least because I was a middle manager in their community education service, and opened up the Moss Side Community Education Centre for the use of the community in its efforts to take stock of what had transpired during the disturbances, and to organize the defence of those adults and young people who had been arrested, many of them students at the Centre itself.

It is against that background and on the basis of our assessment of the terms of reference of the Hytner Inquiry and its approach to the events of 8/9 July that the Moss Side Defence Committee decided not to associate itself in any way with the Inquiry. The following critique of the Hytner Report which the Moss Side Defence Committee adopted, was written on the basis of a careful examination of the report, and was very much informed by that background and my extensive knowledge of the Moss Side community in which I had lived and worked since 1971.

The Hytner Myths – A preliminary critique of the report by Ben Hytner QC on the disturbances in Moss Side, Manchester, on 8/9 July 1981 by The Moss Side Defence Committee

Preamble

The initial informal responses of members of the Police Committee to the Hytner report, its adoption by the policy committee of Greater Manchester Council (GMC), and the generally favourable reception given to its findings by the media, suggest that it is on the way to being accepted as an authorized and accurate account of the 'July Days', and that its analysis and recommendations are being taken seriously as a sound basis for shaping future policy.

These responses are understandable.

The report has a thin veneer of liberalism, humanity, and scholarship. It offers an easy explanation of the riots to offset what it describes as 'the gathering force of rumour'. It contains suggestions for stabilizing the situation in Moss Side, for 'promoting reconciliation between the police and the community' and for dissolving the 'misunderstandings' which have marred relationships between the Chief Constable and the Police Committee. It opens the way to further inquiries into the policing of Greater Manchester. In all these ways, it has the superficial appearance of a balanced and objective analysis which offers the real promise of a harmonious future.

These are not the views of the Moss Side Defence Committee.

In general, the Defence Committee sees the Hytner report as:

- riddled with inconsistencies
- suffused with condescending ignorance about the people of Moss Side and particularly about its black population
- deeply biased in its identification of the cause of the riots
- evasive on all those issues which the people of Moss Side would see as central and decisive, and in its comments and recommendations
- blatantly concerned to conceal those issues behind a façade of cosmetic operations designed to reconcile the people of Moss Side to a form of policing which would remain substantially unchanged

As an interpretation of events, it is therefore no more reliable than many of the rumours which preceded it.

Further, the Defence Committee believes that by emphasizing the lawlessness and supposed irrationality of the rioters, and by publicly stating that their 'criminal offences' should neither be 'disguised by euphemism', nor 'softened' by a consideration of the background out of which they arose, the report places in serious jeopardy all those who have appeared, or are likely to appear, before the courts in connection with alleged offences arising out of the troubles.

It is important that further injustices are not committed against the people of Moss Side and elsewhere in the name of the very 'law and order' which has so badly let them down in the past. And this is particularly so when agents of that law and order on the Manchester streets have so far escaped the consequences of their own violence, before, during, and after the disturbances.

The attitude of the authorities towards the rioters, echoed in the report, has in fact been deeply ambivalent and hypocritical. On the one hand, their motives have been characterized as mindless and their acts as criminal. The significance of their protest has been repeatedly underrated by the press, in official pronouncements, by politicians of every major party, and now in the report. On the other hand, it must be clear from the frantic search for explanations and causes, the breadth and fury of the debate, and the initiation of the Hytner inquiry itself, that the rioters have called public attention to problems which are recognized as severe but which might not otherwise have received the discussion they merited.

It is worth remembering that the credit belongs to the rioters. They spoke very clearly. It would be sad if the distortion, the obfuscations and evasions of Hytner were now to obscure their message.

For all these reasons, the Defence Committee has decided to set out its own considered dissent to a report from which it has happily dissociated itself. The preconceptions evident throughout the Inquiry and the resulting predictability of its report, provide ample justification of the boycott on which the

Defence Committee decided. It may be argued that the Hytner panel did its best within the limited scope it allowed itself. In fact, however, many of the report's conclusions are open to dispute for this very reason. They are based on inadequate inquiry into those very areas which the people of Moss Side would regard as crucial.

The Cause and Character of the Disturbances

Mr Benet Hytner believes that he has identified the cause of the July disturbances. They happened, according to his report, because they were expected. And they were expected because Moss Side was believed to be the kind of place in which rioting was inevitable. That belief, he goes on, was founded largely upon mythology. Moss Side was wrongly regarded as 'a sleazy, down-market Soho with racial tension bubbling not far below boiling point', an area of 'vice, high crime, racial friction and poor social conditions'. The image was outdated, but it led to the belief in the spring of 1981 that 'if trouble were to occur in Manchester it would inevitably take place in Moss Side'.

That first myth was compounded by a second, which held that rioting could happen only in areas of substantial black residence. Following the outbreaks in Bristol, Brixton, Southall, and Toxteth, such myths generated in Manchester a 'mood of inevitability'. It became generally accepted that riots were 'bound to happen' in Moss Side. And so they did.

According to Hytner, a group of black youths who spilled out of the Nile Club in Moss Side in the early morning of 8 July 1981 were greeted by white bystanders with the taunt that 'Manchester blacks were slower than those of Brixton and Toxteth'. Goaded on by drink and lacking 'respect for the property of others and the law of the land', they did what 'they felt was expected of them'. They rioted.

And so it all began; the sad product of ill-founded myths. A tragic misunderstanding.

Once this accidental spark had set Moss Side alight, flames were 'cumulatively increased' by groups who joined in from motives of a quite different kind: some 'to indulge in crime', some to express the total frustration of prolonged unemployment, some caught up in the general excitement, a few to achieve political objectives, some to vent their hostility against the police, some simply to loot. In the case of young blacks there were the added incentives of 'alienation' from their parents and bitterness against a discriminatory white society in which they felt they had no stake. All 'were lacking in a sense of discipline and respect for the law'. Such, according to Mr Hytner, was the explosive 'raw material' detonated by the sparks of 8 July.

The picture, then, is quite clear. Moss Side was a tinder box of different forms of discontent and frustration. All that was required to set it alight was the mistaken belief that the fire was inevitable.

Such an analysis has many attractions for those who are inclined to see rioting as essentially a mindless eruption of unconscious violence. In the first place, it identifies an irrational cause: a sense of expectation based upon myth. In the second, it presents a generalized picture of disaffection in which no particular form of discontent is given priority, and no specific form of malaise is afforded validity, and every form of dissent is tainted by a reckless disregard of the law.

One effect of such an analysis is to debunk the motives and to decry the methods of the rioters. Another is to shy away from the possibility that the riots were a rational and legitimate protest against specific and definable forms of injustice, which can in fact be prioritized and validated.

A report predisposed to believe in the irrationality of the riots and the inherent lawlessness of rioters is unlikely to accept that those who rioted did so because they understood very well the forms of injustice under which they suffered. It is unlikely to conclude that the methods chosen were a rational alternative to the more articulate and constitutional, but unsuccessful, protests which had preceded them. It will be much more inclined to conceive riots as a form of collective madness which puts the law and order of society dangerously at risk, rather than as a symptom of collective sanity which, finally, and in desperation, seeks to promote social justice.

The use by the report of such emotive phrases as 'swarming

mobs', drawn directly from the elitist hysteria of the nineteenth century, underlines such preconceptions.

The Issue of Police Harassment in Moss Side

One of the most revealing aspects of the report is its evasion of the issue of police harassment, a circumstance that most people in Moss Side would see as the basic form of injustice under which they were forced to live. The everyday experience of most young people in Moss Side over many years has been one of an intimidating form of policing deeply stained with racial prejudice. The Hytner report itself refers to the 'deeply rooted' belief of many young people, and particularly many young black people, that such harassment takes place. It makes reference also to the hostile attitudes towards the police which such belief has generated.

How then does the Inquiry deal with this belief?

In the first place, it assumes it to be the belief of only the young, an assumption which is part of the tendency underlying the whole report, i.e., to differentiate generally and sharply between the attitudes of the young black people and the experiences of their elders. These elders are portrayed in the report as 'God-fearing law abiding and disciplined citizens' whose harmony with the police the Chief Constable has successfully promoted. It is only the young who are disaffected. This is partly, the report goes on, because their particular 'habits' inevitably bring them into collision with the police, especially during periods of 'enforced idleness'. They congregate in groups and wander through shopping areas, causing anxiety and giving rise to justifiable suspicion.

It is 'not unreasonable' that the police should seek to break them up or move them on, but such acts create an unavoidable tension. The rebelliousness, indiscipline, and potential lawlessness of black youth has been supposedly exacerbated in the recent years by the demoralizing effect of unemployment, experiences of discrimination, a feeling that they have 'no stake in white society', and 'a general deterioration of discipline' among young people. This deterioration has itself been accelerated by the 'alienation' of many young blacks from their parents and their consequent removal from an area of discipline within the family. They have rebelled against the authoritarian attitudes of traditionally minded parents, and feel let down because parental 'promises' of better jobs and equal opportunity in white society have not materialized.

It needs to be emphasized that in making these judgements the report both seriously underestimates the degree of discontent amongst an older black generation, and totally misconceives the relationship between an 'immigrant generation' and that which succeeds it. Neither harassment itself nor the 'belief' that it takes place is confined to the young. If it is felt more sharply and more commonly by the young, it is only because young people everywhere are more open and vulnerable to the abuses of those in authority.

The claims of 'alienation', which the report makes, are deeply insulting to the black people of Moss Side. Much more evident, in reality, is the solidarity of black families and of the black community in general. If young blacks rebel, it is not against discrimination and abuse, which they alone have felt. It is equally part, perhaps more substantially part, of their parents' experience. But the immigrant generation, new to Manchester society, uncertain of its foothold in Manchester society and inevitably fearful of new forms of authority, was understandably reluctant to protest, at least in public.

What differentiates the young is their sense of belonging to Manchester and their greater willingness to voice and express protest. Much of it is on their parents' behalf. They are unwilling to accept the continuance of injustices which wrought havoc in their parent's lives.

This is a very different perspective from that adopted in Hytner. It is one, which sets discrimination and harassment in a wider and more accurate context, as conditions experienced not by the young alone, but by the black population as a whole. It is one which makes it possible to take a much more favourable view of the motives and actions of the young, before and during the riots. They are not made 'disaffected and rebellious' by their particular circumstances of unemployment, by any general decline in the standards of discipline amongst the young, or by the alienation from law abiding parents. They were led to disaffection and rebelliousness by their knowledge and understanding, and a very clear understanding, of the discriminatory society in which they and their parents live, and the realities of police harassment and abuse from which both generations suffer. And they were proclaiming, clearly and unequivocally, violently even, that such conditions are not acceptable.

Hytner's second response to the belief in police harassment is non-committal. For him, the belief may be wholly unfounded; it may have been induced by political extremists or by the media. It may not even exist at all; interviewees may have been 'mistaken' or unreliable in identifying it. Or the belief may exist and it may be well founded. The report itself suspends judgement, partly to save Mr Anderton from feeling that he has been dealt with 'unconstitutionally, and partly because it did not feel that it possessed the evidence or the expertise from which a judgement might be made'. And so Hytner rests content with the offer of his private conclusions to the Police Committee, and with the recommendation that the Chief Constable and the Police Committee should conduct their own investigations.

Now this is all very well, and we may hope that such an investigation takes place, that it is a searching one, and that it embraces the policing of Moss Side and not simply the police harassment of young blacks. But it is also important to understand very clearly the consequence of Hytner's non-committal stance. The report has sought to identify the cause of the riots. It has identified the cause to its own satisfaction in those expectations, based largely on myth, which made rioting inevitable. At the same time, it has failed to report on those circumstances which most people in Moss Side itself believe to have been the major cause of the outbreaks. The effect of such an evasion, of Hytner's diffused and generalized discussion of the factors which led to the riot's escalation, and his emphasis on 'disaffected youth', is again to place emphasis on the 'irrationality' of what happened, and to direct attention away from the possibility of seeing the riots as a rational response to very grave and very real injustices.

The Defence Committee believes the riot to be have been caused not by outdated myth but by present realities. And in particular the reality of police harassment which is deeply racist in context, and which is in no way new to Moss Side. The Defence Committee itself has ample evidence of this harassment, and it is well known to black people living in Moss Side, whatever their age. Those black people who took to the streets did not simply do so because it was expected of them after Brixton and Toxteth. They took to the streets because they suffer the same brutal realities as the blacks of Brixton and Toxteth. And they did so in Moss Side not because a riot was expected in Moss Side, but because in Moss Side can be found the most glaring and conspicuous examples of those realities.

That is the way that history actually happens.

In the early nineteenth century Chartist protests erupted in sequence in a number of English and Welsh towns. They did so not because of any chain of expectation based upon myth, but because in each town actual conditions existed which provoked justifiable protest. If there was a 'chain reaction' it was one which inspired courage: people who might not otherwise have openly protested were inspired to do so by the example of others. That is a very different kind of sequence from that posed by Hytner. It is one which makes it plain that there were real causes of grievance in each of the areas in which it was expressed.

The second myth, which supposedly triggered the unrest – the myth that rioting is more likely in areas of black residence – needs to be seen in perspective. The factor of importance is not the existence of a black population *per se*, but the fact that wherever a black population lives certain police attitudes and styles are likely to follow.

It is worth emphasizing, in case the reader is led astray by the veneer of scholarship occasionally evident in the report, that it misreads history in its identification of the causes as badly as it misuses sociology in its analysis of black youth. And yet, in contrast to the way in which certain areas of fact [such as police harassment or deficiencies in the complaints procedure] are dealt with in the report only as 'beliefs', which may or may not be true, the results of the panel's own investigations into Moss Side, its black population, and the causes of the riots are laid out in yards of un-attributed jargon as an objective and apparently indisputable analysis.

There may in fact be a myth of Moss Side but, if so, it is one held by the police rather than by the community. The police have identified Moss Side as a neighbourhood in which the likelihood of crime is exceptionally high. It may be suggested that the identification is based substantially on implicit racist assumptions. It also partly rests on the kind of misconceptions about youth in general, and black youths in particular, to which the report lends credence. Once the identification is made and accepted, it serves to legitimize the kind of police surveillance, suspicion, and force to which the people of Moss Side have become accustomed. The result is the policing of an inner city neighbourhood as if it were a dangerous alien colony in an otherwise wholesome society, with the gradual, perhaps even the desired, effect of criminalizing large sections of its population.

The Defence Committee rejects such identification absolutely, and is unwilling to countenance the forms of policing which it has been used to justify. The real divide is not between the young and the mature, or between the law-abiding and the lawbreakers. The real divide is between the community and the police.

And the divide is not only between the police and the black community. Deeply discriminatory policing, coupled with exceptional disadvantages in the labour market, placed black youth in the front line of resistance. But white youths were also deeply involved in the disturbances. Many were arrested. Some have been imprisoned. While the sharpest cutting edge of deprivation and victimization was felt by a doubly oppressed black population, white people in Moss Side have also experienced the effects of generally repressive social and economic policies, and the severity of intimidatory police attitudes and techniques. In July they joined their black neighbours in a common protest.

The Issue of General Policing and the Chief Constable

The reticence, which led Hytner not to report on the realities of police harassment, led also to the portrayal of the Chief Constable of Greater Manchester as a paragon of virtue. The report was 'mindful ... of the danger of being unfair to the Chief Constable' by the use of uncorroborated, unchallenged, and hearsay evidence. It did not feel 'suited' to determining any issue which involved the criticism of any individual; including the Chief Constable. The Chief Constable himself declined to appear before the panel as, naturally, he has every right to do. He gave only limited written answers to specific questions, which the panel found 'disappointing'. He did, however, send the panel 'numerous petitions' in support of the police from the people of Moss Side, including many people 'with Asian' names.

'Disappointing' is a very gentle word to describe the response of the Chief Constable to Mr Hytner's request for his assistance. Many of the main issues, which surround the outbreak of the riots, concern the nature of policing in Moss Side and elsewhere, and some concern the way in which the Chief Constable deployed the forces under his command during the riots themselves. Many people in Moss Side are rightly and deeply disturbed at the nature of policing within the community and about the procedures for processing complaints. Many are equally disturbed by the brutal confrontations and murderous van charge which formed part of the police operations, and by the vicious way in which arrests were conducted after the riots. It is again difficult to understand how the report could reach such conclusions either about the outbreak of the riots, or the way in which they were handled, without a thorough investigation of the nature of policing in Greater Manchester and the tactics adopted by the Chief Constable. In fact, however, no such investigations were conducted and the report contains no conclusions on these central issues.

On the question of policing, the report did not feel that it was part of its task to examine the statutory machinery, to comment upon the efficacy of the complaints procedure, or to generally explore the nature of policing in Moss Side and the rest of

Greater Manchester. On all these issues it was again non-committal. It ended by recommending that the Police Committee should delay consideration of 'general policing' until the appearance of the Scarman Report (on the Brixton riots), and that it should rest content with bringing to the Chief Constable's attention criticism of his handling of the riots. If the Chief Constable held that further information on his operations was 'non-disclosable', the report hopes that the public would be 'satisfied by the reasons for the absence of an explanation'.

It needs to be stated very plainly that the public of Moss Side would not be so satisfied. The police charges and confrontations took place within their community, as did their subsequent arrests. The people of Moss Side will in no way be content until they have received a full explanation of the Chief Constable's motives and strategy. When such an explanation appears, they will draw their own conclusions. They again find it very difficult to understand how the Hytner report can 'generally applaud' the police handling of the situation when it did not possess the evidence of its vital and decisive stages. The report's recommendations with regards to complaints are unlikely to alter a situation the gravity of which the report fails utterly to appreciate. While Hytner chooses to remain non-committal about the procedure, those who have experienced it cannot.

What does Hytner propose?
- A 'community representative', chosen by GMC in consultation with Manchester Council for Community Relations and other relevant bodies, to receive, sift, and pass on complaints
- An experienced, extra-mural police officer in Moss Side to receive and deal with complaints

Hytner's belief is that such mechanisms would ensure the careful consideration of serious complaints, backed by adequate evidence, and the informal handling of less serious complaints, or complaints lacking sufficient evidence, in such a way as to 'placate' (Hytner's own word) the community.

'Placate' is certainly the right word. The aim of the proposed superficial changes is to restore confidence in the complaints procedure, rather than to improve it, just as the recommendations in relation to policing are designed to reconcile the public to the police, rather than to effect radical changes in police attitudes and methods.

The people of Moss Side will not be bought off by such engineering. What they demand is an effective complaints procedure independent of the police, not a new way of seeing their complaints thwarted by the very police force which generated them. The appointment of a community 'middle-man' could only further legitimize the unacceptable. In the same way the people do not seek reconciliation through any extension of community policing with a basically unchanged police force. They want to see steps taken which would fundamentally change the attitudes and methods adopted by the police in Moss Side and elsewhere. Dissatisfaction with the complaints system is only another symptom of dissatisfaction with the police, compounded by a sense of their apparent immunity.

The people of Moss Side reserve judgement on the Chief Constable. The Hytner report felt unable to deal with the very serious criticisms directed against him and he himself did not appear, perhaps understandably, to give account of his actions. We would, however, direct attention to the report's stated intention of not 'passing judgement' on the Chief Constable's 'efficiency and as a policeman'. This needs to be read in conjunction with the many passages of praise, which the report contains.

Mr Anderton is described as 'a man who has a deep and abiding hatred of racial prejudice'. He is said to have done much to promote harmony between the police and ethnic minorities. We are told that he is on warm terms with representatives of ethnic minorities of 'mature years' (again, that supposed generational divide), other than those 'whose political view's create a gulf'. Such relationships are said to result from his Christian convictions and traditional moral values and discipline. He receives praise for his promotion of community policing even against a background of inadequate manpower and community contact police, many 'loved' by young black people. Such strategies have cemented relations between the police and 'maturer members' of the black community. In the report's recommendations it is implied that Mr Anderton's blunt and vigorous style and abhorrence of racial prejudice are preferable to 'a smooth personality, a serpent's tongue and secret prejudices'. Hytner is pleased that Mr Anderton does not favour CS Gas or rubber bullets. The Greater Manchester Police is said to be 'probably better than most in the United Kingdom', due largely to Mr Anderton's efforts. He is both 'informative and accessible' and his relationship with the Police Committee was generally 'good'. No one has ever seriously suggested his removal.

What does it mean, then, that his efficiency as a policeman will receive no judgement? The cumulative effect of the report's refusal to deal with criticisms of the Chief Constable, of its failure to fully investigate the complaints procedure, police harassment, and the operational events of 8-9 July, and of the Chief Constable's non-appearance before the panel, is that Mr Anderton has emerged relatively unscathed. The report simply expresses the hope that he will cooperate in further enquiries and live in harmony with the Police Committee.

Otherwise, what would we do without such a man?

The true answer, perhaps, 'is very well indeed'. The Defence Committee believes that in this respect, as in others, the Hytner report has simply not gone far enough. The Chief Constable is an articulate and powerful public figure, well able to defend himself, and in command of a police force which daily impinges on the lives of Moss Side people. During the July riots and in the weeks that followed, the people of Moss Side bore the brunt of police operations. This committee will not rest content until the nature of those operations are fully disclosed, and until the Chief Constable is called to account fully for the nature of the policing which he so efficiently directs. In the meantime, this committee calls attention to those biases and gaps within the Hytner Report, which might induce unwarranted complacency towards the way in which the Manchester Police are commanded and deployed.

The report's gentle treatment of the Chief Constable is in line with its general attitude of deference to those in authority. There is a marked contrast between the polite comments on Mr Anderton and the reductive view of the motives of the rioters. This same attitude of deference to those 'above', and critical condescension to those 'below', is evidenced by the Inquiry's judgement about, and treatment of, the witnesses who appeared before it. The Haldane Society, for example, is written off as consisting mainly of a handful of young solicitors. Mr Anderton is asked to note that the solicitors whom the panel interviewed 'do not include those he may think are motivated against the police'. There are several other comments on the unreliability of 'anti-police elements' and 'extremists'.

The Chief Constable is said to be on good terms with black leaders other than those 'whose political views create a gulf'. The bias inherent in such comment has affected the whole balance of the report. Is it not possible that those branded as 'anti-police' adopt the attitude not because of any political preconception, but because they have found many good reasons to be critical of police methods? Why should 'pro-police' elements be considered any more reliable? Is it not possible that those black leaders from whom Mr Anderton is divided by a 'political gulf' are more representative of the black community than those with whom he has a 'warm' relationship? Is it not possible that the gulf is created by the realistic appraisal by some black leaders of the oppression from which the black community suffers, including its oppression at the hands of the police?

Racism – Individual and Institutional Forms

In placing emphasis on race relations within Moss Side the report diverts attention from an institutionalized racism, which bears far more heavily upon the black population. Racism can take the form of a blatant and calculated hostility towards black people. But it can also exist in the subtler, but equally dangerous form of implicit and often unaware attitudes of discrimination both within individuals and within established institutions. The Hytner panel does not deal with this form of racial prejudice and racial discrimination. There are in fact passages in their report which suggest that they were not fully alive to its existence and force.

In dealing with Moss Side's schools, the report welcomes the few signs that black studies are being incorporated into the curriculum. But the question must be asked, why have such studies not been introduced already given the black community's long establishment in Moss Side? And further questions need to be asked about the seriousness of Manchester Education Committee's intent, the nature of the black studies it seeks to introduce, and the motives behind their introduction.

The spurious reputation of Moss Side as an area with an especially high level of street crime is another example of a racism implicit in public attitudes promoted by the media, for it rests on popular, but inaccurate, association of mugging with the black young. Although it deals at length (and, many would believe, complacently) with the improved amenities in Moss Side, the report fails to explore the possibility of implicit racial bias in housing, educational and social policies, policies that affect the everyday experiences of all black people.

The report suggests that young black people are 'turning away' from white society, some into black consciousness movements of which the report clearly disapproves. The real question is whether they have ever been seen (and therefore ever seen themselves) as fully and equally part of society. Such a question can only be answered in relation to society's policies towards, and treatment of, their community.

The assertion prevalent throughout the report that young black people are dissenting from, and rebelling against, established society needs to be balanced by the appreciation of the ways in which black people have been implicitly excluded from it. While the report is silent on such crucial matters, it does not hesitate to condemn young blacks for their supposed anti-social behaviour. The context of this behaviour, beyond the immediate impact of police brutality, is the wide-ranging national assault on the black community, symbolized by the proposed Nationality Bill, immigration restrictions, and the Jenkins' proposals. Police harassment forms part of a range of institutional acts designed to define black people as a sub-class in white society.

The most blatant example of the report's failure to understand and confront institutionalized racism is the absence of any comment on the possibility of racism within the police, beyond its bland approval of Mr Anderton's attitudes.

The panel did not feel itself empowered to interview members of the Greater Manchester Police. The result is a serious imbalance. The panel was concerned with a conflict between the Moss Side community and the forces of law and order. Aspects of the Moss Side background are given emphasis in however distorted a way. The background, education, and attitudes of the police remain a mystery. The conclusion might well be drawn that the troubles resulted from the nature of Moss Side society; and that Moss Side is the problem to be solved. But equally valid would be the conclusion that they resulted from the attitudes, including the racist attitudes, and conduct of the police, and that the problem to be solved is the police.

The Moss Side Defence Committee believes this to be the case. At this stage, we would simply draw attention to the fact that police racism has not been explored in the report and to the possibility that such attitudes, well known to any black person living in Moss Side, may well have been decisive. The report's failure in this respect may also influence opinion on future changes which may be necessary. The report makes much of a revision of police training, which would include some introduction to the cultural backgrounds of the minorities with whom the police come into contact. This is all very well, but it is not nearly enough. In the long term, it is the racist attitudes which police training will need to address and counter, and the study of minority cultures will not necessarily achieve this object.

In this training it will be necessary to introduce some means by which police recruits are brought in touch with their own feelings about race and the factors on which such feelings are based. This is a more difficult proposition, not to be fulfilled by a crash course in 'Afro-Caribbean history', but it is one which will need to be worked out and implemented before racist attitudes can be eliminated.

Finally, the report states that the 'hurt' produced by racial prejudice is in inverse proportion to the social status of its victims. Such a generalization needs to be very carefully understood and interpreted. It should in no way be taken to imply that any section of the black community is not hurt by racial prejudice. On the contrary, all black people in Moss Side, regardless of their age or social status, are deeply damaged by racism. The anger, of which one expression was the riot, is both understandable and surely welcome.

Racism was in many ways a crucial factor in the situation that developed in Moss Side. Not, however, racism within Moss Side, but the racism directed against it. Most particularly, the racism inherent in police responses.

Conclusion

The investigations of the Moss Side Defence Committee are still in progress and it would be improper to anticipate their results by setting out a full analysis which would serve as an alternative to the Hytner report. The purpose of this paper has been simply to emphasize the inadequacies and distortions of the report and to highlight those areas of ignorance and evasion which makes nonsense of its conclusions. At a later stage, the Defence Committee will make its own report and formulate its own demands.

In the meantime, it would demand justice for the people of Moss Side, including those people who were involved in the uprising of July. The riots were the loud cry of a desperately oppressed and powerless people. It is a cry that should be heard and taken to heart. The rioters were not the mindless victims of a myth. They did not succumb to an irrational rebelliousness generated by rootlessness, deteriorating discipline, conditioning to 'new levels of violence', or a supposed generation gap. Nor did they respond simply to the enforced idleness of unemployment. They were the protesters, expressing a powerful and rational protest by the only means which lay to hand and directing it against the only appropriate targets available. Far from being ruthless or divorced from the experiences of their parents, their protest was on behalf of the community in which they and their parents lived. They need to be taken seriously. So do the targets of their protest, particularly the nature of policing in Moss Side, with its predominant style of intimidatory harassment and its racist overtones.

Afterword

Whatever happened to the report of the Moss Side Defence Committee's own investigation that was to follow this preliminary response to Hytner?

The Moss Side Defence Committee did continue to investigate the events that led to the full scale rebellion in Moss Side on 8-9 July 1981. In the immediate aftermath of the disturbances, however, it decided to concentrate on the following activities:

1. Ensuring that those who had been arrested and charged following the disturbances had competent legal representation
2. Assisting defendants to find witnesses, take witness statements, and generally take charge of organizing their own defence, briefing solicitors and barristers so that they understood and worked within the principle that defendants and their families were in charge of their own case
3. Working with Haldane Society lawyers and with the Probation Service to draw public attention to potential and actual miscarriages of justice resulting from the way the courts, in collusion with the police, were handling cases arising from the disturbances
4. Networking with other Defence Committees (London, Liverpool 8, Toxteth, Bristol) to share information about the activities of national leaders of state, the media, the police, the courts, and the legal profession in response to that mass rebellion in Britain's inner cities.

We in the Defence Committee faced a number of challenges. Foremost among them was the fact that the then Prime Minister, Margaret Thatcher and Home Secretary William Whitelaw were outraged that people who did not belong here, who had been allowed to make Britain their home, and whom the society had given opportunities to integrate and to identify fully with British norms and values, could want to commit such criminal acts and attack the forces of law and order. As far as they were concerned, it was necessary to send a message to the nation that things were not falling apart, that the centre could hold firm and that law and order would prevail.

The media echoed those sentiments in large measure, suggesting that lack of employment, racial disadvantage, and alienation from their parents' generation and their forms of parenting could in no way justify such criminality.

The courts were sent a strong message that the sentences they imposed upon those found guilty of the charges the police brought against them should both reflect society's abhorrence of such criminal conduct and act as a deterrent to those who might have it in mind to repeat those same acts.

Under those circumstances, the police were keen to be seen to bring to justice as many 'perpetrators' as possible. In Moss Side, for example, the community witnessed the indiscriminate rounding up of residents, young and old, in the days and weeks following the disturbances. The police approach appeared to be that those whom they arrested would have to prove that they had no involvement in the events of 8-9 July or they would have to take the rap for something.

Mindful of the fact that many innocent people were likely to be criminalized as a result of such police activity, the Moss Side Defence Committee mobilized a body of youth workers, progressive solicitors, and custody visitors to keep a watchful eye on what was going on in the police stations in central Manchester.

Another challenge facing the Committee was the fact that many of the defendants had had no experience of preparing a case, or any belief that they had either the right or the capacity to do so. As in other cities, many of the young people (black and white) arrested during the disturbances already had convictions for a string of petty or sometimes more serious offences. Many had been victims of that process of criminalizing the young unemployed, young and excluded from school, and young drivers that has been an integral part of the history of black settlement in Britain.

For them, the most common experience had been going to

court and depending upon a solicitor with whom they had spent very little time preparing their defence, or being allotted a duty solicitor who had even less of a grasp of their case, or a barrister whom they had never seen. Deferring to the professionals' superior knowledge of the court system, not to mention the law, they would agree with whatever advice they were given even when it was not in their best interest to do so.

Time and again, individuals told us of the times they pleaded guilty to offences they had not committed because they were persuaded that it was the police's word against theirs, that the likelihood was that the court would believe the police and that if found guilty they would receive a stiffer sentence than if they pleaded guilty. Or, they would be advised to plead guilty to lesser offences in exchange for the prosecution dropping a more serious charge. All of those charges had arisen in situations where the young person had been part of a group. In some cases the individual charged had simply been part of a group whom the police had tried to move on or had been called to disperse, and they had been arrested with the rest of the group who had protested that they had indeed been talking loudly amongst themselves but had not intimidated anyone. In numerous cases, young people then went on to tell us how such convictions had obstructed their ability to gain employment and had directly contributed to them being long term unemployed.

The concept of taking charge of their own case and ensuring that their solicitor worked according to their instructions was therefore totally new to them. But, as we were to discover, it was no less new to solicitors and barristers and to the courts in Manchester. Unlike London where there had been a number of defence campaigns organized by the African-Caribbean community, Manchester had had no such history. In 1981 Manchester, therefore, solicitors and barristers, with a few notable exceptions, had had no experience of working with communities to prepare cases and seeing those cases not simply as matters between the individual and the criminal justice system, but in the wider context of policing in an area such as Moss Side, the way young people were criminalized and the collusion there was between the court system and the police.

The Black Parents Movement, drawing upon the experience of organizing defence campaigns that our members had gained from work with our sister organization in London, was able to bring a practice to the work of the Moss Side Defence Committee in supporting defendants that politicized both the defendants themselves, and people in the legal profession.

Part of the rationale for that method of organizing was the need to mobilize the public to be vigilant to the fact that it is at times of such crisis that our civil liberties are most threatened, not least by the knee jerk reactions of the state and its control agencies. It is for that reason that we produced leaflets giving the background to cases and highlighted the issues the prosecutions raised.

In organizing in those ways, we were also sending a message to the judicial system. We picketed the courts during the trials, giving out leaflets to all who entered and left. We made it clear to the courts that we, the community of Manchester, were taking a keen interest in what they were doing, in their attitude to the submissions of the police, and of the defence, in the remarks that were being made from the bench, in the extent to which they were taking their cue from the media and the Government or were independently dispensing justice, dealing with each case on its own merit and being as prepared to challenge the veracity of police evidence as that of defendants.

We were very conscious of the fact that the country as a whole was searching for an explanation of the nationwide outburst of anger, frustration, and violence that erupted in England between April and August 1981. In the case of Moss Side, it was very likely that the assessment of Mr Benet Hytner, a Queens Counsel, would carry some weight with those who were having to pass judgement on the guilt or innocence of those arrested for their alleged involvement in the disturbances.

It was on account of all of those factors that the Moss Side Defence Committee committed its energies to defending those brought to court and raising public awareness of the need to deal with the issues raised by the disturbances and the trials that flowed from them.

The 'People's Inquiry' into the disturbances on which the

Defence Committee embarked was able to provide useful information to support the defence in respect of a number of charges. The Inquiry itself was never completed.

8.6

TO THE INQUIRY INTO MATTERS ARISING FROM THE DEATH OF STEPHEN LAWRENCE
Part Two
Manchester
13 October 1998

In 1971/72 I co-authored with Derek Humphry (then a staff reporter with the *Sunday Times*) a book titled *Police Power and Black People*. That book described policing practices in different parts of the country, including Liverpool and Manchester, and highlighted a pattern of police malpractices and abuse of power. It offered an analysis of the positions advanced by the police, and demonstrated the manner in which their stereotypical construction of black people led to actions and decisions which were fundamentally unjust, if not racist, and often to a miscarriage of justice.

The book shocked the British establishment and it is my belief that the Police and the Home Office applied pressure to ensure that the publishers were less than energetic in marketing the book. Within less than a year, Derek Humphry and I were travelling the country giving handfuls of copies of the book to community organizations as we had been informed that 20,000 copies of it were to be pulped.

Reading that book twenty-five years later, I couldn't help but be extremely saddened at how institutionalized the things we had highlighted as worrying trends had become.

Towards the end of that book, I wrote:

Our duty is to lay bare the system not only to those blacks who refuse to see but, more importantly, to the White majority whose inaction and neglect leave the police secure in the belief that they control and contain the Blacks for the greater good of White society.

I say all of this to emphasize one sadly neglected point.

For many years I have been arguing that until such time that the State and the population as a whole come to an understanding of racial attacks and racial murders as not just criminal offences but human rights violations, their impact upon the society as a whole, and the urgency with which they need to be treated, will never be fully grasped.

There surely can be no more fundamental a human right than the right to stand at a bus stop, walk to work, go to school and go about the routine business of living without being maimed or killed for no other reason than that you are black.

The death of Cynthia Jarrett, Joy Gardener, and many of those who have perished in police custody, and of Stephen Lawrence, and the many others are the ultimate in human rights violations. Whenever the police de-racialize such killings and adopt operational practices which deny the hurt the black families and the black communities experience, they send a very dangerous message to the society as a whole and to would-be perpetrators of similar acts.

To fail to recognize that the motives, if not justification for such attacks and murders as far as perpetrators are concerned often lie in their consciousness of the racialization that has become institutionalized vis à vis the people they attack, is dangerous. The racialization of immigration was followed by the racialization of street crimes into 'Sus', the racialization of school exclusions, the racialization of underachievement and of other processes at the interface between black people and the society. This fact of racialization informs the activities of racists no less than of the police.

Insofar as it both emanates from, and further contributes to, the culture of racism within the society and its institutions, including schools, it has to be acknowledged as a given that institutional cultures and practices would have a tendency to reflect that racism, however subliminally it occurs.

My experience of policing in Manchester bears this out.

One of the principal reasons for community displeasure and lack of faith in the police over the years has been their practice of conflating immigration control with investigating crimes committed against black people. The organization which I led here in Manchester frequently dealt with cases where a South Asian family would report a crime of racial attack to the police who would eventually arrive at the scene. They would then proceed to ignore vital clues and witnesses, and concentrate their attention on establishing the immigration status of the complainants or their witnesses. Invariably, that would be followed by statements to the effect that the crime was not necessarily racially motivated.

I have had the personal experience of being burgled and calling the police, only to find them more interested in the political nature of the posters on my wall or the titles of the books on my bookshelf, than in the trauma and loss I suffered as a result of the burglary. Irrespective of whether or not I am considered to be a 'black activist', I surely must expect a measure of protection and service from the police and not have them approach my legitimate need for that service with an armful of prejudices about my ideological predispositions.

In 1987, I joined the commission of inquiry into the murder of Ahmed Ullah at Burnage High School in South Manchester. The inquiry was set up by Manchester City Council and chaired by Ian Macdonald (later QC). I co-authored the Burnage Report, *Murder in the Playground* and then, both as an educationalist and a member of the Inquiry, toured the country trying to assist police forces, local education authorities, schools and communities in understanding and applying the serious lessons of that tragedy.

Manchester City Council refused to publish the report, and even after the Inquiry team decided to use our own funds and publish it ourselves they suppressed it, and introduced such a climate of fear in relation to it that there has been few serious discussions about the lessons of that tragedy within Manchester LEA itself.

I commend the book to you in its entirety, but would draw your attention specifically to Chapters 1-9, and 18.

I have no doubt that issues to do with the *investigation and prosecution of racially motivated crimes* are dealt with in this book in a manner that the Stephen Lawrence Inquiry Team would find extremely helpful.

It is clear that Manchester City Council, the Greater Manchester Police, and a range of community organizations have made, and are making, strenuous efforts to improve police and community awareness of the collective responsibility the society has for creating a climate in which it is more difficult for racial harassment and racial attacks to be perpetrated. Schemes such as the Longsight Pilot Project, the Racial Harassment Monitoring Scheme, etc., are to be very much welcomed.

I fear, however, that these high profile joint initiatives do little to dispel the sense of injustice and neglect certain sections of the community still feel about the quality of policing in their areas. This is especially true of police activities in respect of drug-related crimes and murders in Moss Side and Cheetham Hill.

I was called by a distraught black family at 4.30am a few months ago to come and give them support and advice. They had just had a SAS-style raid on their Council home which left windows at the front and back and their front door completely demolished. There had been a killing of a young black male and the police were trying to identify suspects. In that home lived an eighteen year old male who had not been in trouble with the police before but, not surprisingly, knew the murdered man and might well have known his killer(s).

The mother of that household, a single parent, was racially and verbally abused, her young daughter who had an 'A' level examination later that day was racially abused, physically assaulted, and had all sorts of slurs hurled at her, and the entire family felt they had been treated like animals by that raiding gang, wearing balaclava helmets and armed to the eyeballs. By the end of that day, the young man they half demolished the house to come and arrest in his bed had been released and was eventually eliminated from the police enquiries. A number of other families with young black males in the area suffered the same treatment.

What is worrying about this is that that experience caused

both mother and daughter health problems for many months and, according to them, their complaint to the police was met with a response which effectively said that the community wishes the police to root out those ruthless murderers from its midst and the police cannot do that wearing kid gloves.

What is even more worrying is that the spate of killings in Moss Side has so traumatized that community, and has wrecked so many lives, that the community is now considerably less vigilant than it used to be about the brutality and racism with which the police still go about the business of policing. It is precisely in the absence of that vigilance that tragedies occur.

The mother in that home told me and her brother, that she very nearly had a heart attack when the police came piling in through every door and window in the house and pushed her down as she ran downstairs, rushing to the phone to ring the police. Someone with a weak heart or generally in poor health could easily have died in that situation. One can only imagine what the repercussions of such a death would have been in that community, in Manchester, and in the country.

I have dealt with these issues since 1966 in this country and the overwhelming feeling I still have is that there is such root and branch racism underpinning the manner in which the police view communities and treat black people, especially in situations of stress and confrontation, that too many of their positive initiatives become the finger stuck in the dike.

There needs to be an acceptance that there is a culture of racism which is endemic within the police and which can co-exist very healthily with positive initiatives, including those that involve black people themselves.

I would wish to say a number of things about training and about management in the police, not least of all against the background of my experience of teaching as a Visiting Lecturer on the Command Course at Bramshill, and heading workshops for police forces up and down the country. I would hope therefore to submit a further document that deals with these matters.

Finally, as Frantz Fanon said:

What matters is not to know the world but to change it.

I trust that the knowledge and insights gained from this extraordinary inquiry into this most tragic event would result not just in a better understanding of the issues under consideration but in visible change at institutional levels, underpinned by legislation where necessary, in the society and its dealings with its black population.

SECURE IN OUR IDENTITIES

Introduction

In 2004, the Ealing *Windrush* Consortium, a body of parents, teachers, young people and community activists, invited me to present a paper during their Black History Month celebrations on 'The Role of African and African Caribbean Churches in Britain's Changing Society' (9.1). The event was held at the Priory Community Centre in Acton, West London, a youth and community centre that has served the multiethnic communities of Acton and the Borough of Ealing for many decades. In addition to white English, it has nurtured the educational development of young people and adults in the African and Asian communities originating in Grenada and other Eastern Caribbean Islands, Trinidad, Guyana, Jamaica, and latterly Somalia, Lebanon and West Africa. As such, it has been home to many faiths and religious traditions, Christian and non-Christian. It was therefore a fitting venue in which to ask some searching questions about the role of black churches in today's Britain.

The paper sets out some of the features of Britain's changing society, asks what 'church' is for, examines the role of the mainstream denominations in the lives of people in the Caribbean. It explores the growth of religions that were crafted in that region at the interface between European colonizers and the traditional religious practices and rituals of African slaves, and the way those religions were treated by the colonial regimes in the region. It suggests that we should have the strength and the courage to challenge received wisdom about traditional African religious beliefs and practices, and to be secure in our African identity.

It ends by examining the role of Britain's black churches in the affairs of black people and in relation to the changing features of British society, suggesting that that has to be much less about individual salvation and much more about collective action for social justice and for social change.

In August 2003, while in Port-of-Spain, Trinidad & Tobago, I received a call from the organizers of the Rendezvous of Victory – Remembering Enslavement programme of events that were held that same month. They asked whether I would send a message to their convention since I was out of the country and could not attend. They had experienced some difficulty getting hold of me and therefore needed my 'message' by return. I went into an internet café on Frederick Street and composed and despatched the *Message* (9.2).

At the beginning of December 2005, the University of Bradford hosted a celebration of the Life of Rosa Parks in their newly established Centre for Inclusion and Diversity. I was asked to present the keynote address at that event on 'The Legacy of Rosa Parks and its Impact on Black Struggle in Britain' (9.3).

The paper highlights the historical contribution of people, like Rosa Parks, who take a stand in defence of liberty, thus carving out political space for others to do the same and, collectively, to seek to subvert the whole edifice of oppression. It reminds us that it is part of the dialectics of the struggle for change that the space won by those struggles allows for the incorporation of members of oppressed groups themselves under the guise of inclusiveness, people who then serve to perpetuate those very systems of oppression. It makes the point that fifty years after Rosa Parks' protest, and the civil rights activism it inspired in Britain, there are still an estimated 10,000 racist incidents each year in Britain, black people are still being murdered by white racists for no other reason than they are black, and neo-fascist political parties are gaining increasing popularity amongst the

British electorate.

The paper notes the fact that despite the requirements of the Race Relations Amendment Act, many public bodies are failing to comply with the legislation and take steps to eliminate racial discrimination and promote equality of opportunity. It points to the key role of higher education in combating racism and other forms of oppression and building a just, fair and equitable society. Finally, it argues that the Government should consider making evidence of higher education institutions' compliance with the RRAA 2000 a condition of the funding they receive from the public purse. It calls upon black staff and students to organize themselves and to have the confidence to form alliances with other interest groups and work collaboratively to bring about change.

9.1

THE ROLE OF AFRICAN AND AFRICAN-CARIBBEAN CHURCHES IN BRITAIN'S CHANGING SOCIETY

Ealing Windrush Consortium, London
20 November 2004

Today's programme is part of an increasing range of events that are planned year on year during Black History Month. I applaud the boldness with which the organizers of this event have given expression to the fact that every month is Black History Month and that our history and our discourse about contemporary affairs in the lives of black people across the world cannot be crammed into any one month.

Let us start a campaign, therefore, and have organizations up and down the country, especially schools, colleges, and universities, organize programmes each month in the year and call that month 'Black History Month'. You have organized this event a few weeks after the end of the official Black History Month. Organize even more events in April next year and make April your Black History Month.

Encourage Ealing schools and Thames Valley University to work with you and construct their own programmes to coincide with yours, not as a substitute for but in addition to what they do in October. And let them explain to their own staff and students that it is by ensuring that we keep a continuous focus on black history and its significance for what we do every day that we meet the objectives and fulfil the dreams of those who laid the foundations for what has become Black History Month. But, I digress.

It is right and fitting that we should be examining the role of black churches in Britain's changing society as part of a Black

History Month programme, because in order to place the present in its proper perspective we need to understand our past. It is impossible to consider black churches' current role without examining the role of religion and spirituality in the lives of African people on the continent and in the first diaspora. I suggest that it is only by understanding the part religion played in the first diaspora and our experience with Britain in the last 500 years that we could meaningfully consider the role of churches led by African heritage people in Britain's changing society.

First, though, I want to make clear that my focus in this talk is not only upon black churches, namely the Christian churches led by black people and attended predominantly by black people in Britain, but also upon two other groups:

- The first group comprises those that are part of the established Christian denominations (Methodists, Anglicans, Roman Catholics, Pentecostals, Seventh Day Adventists) and have congregations that are predominantly black. Increasingly, they mirror what is happening in inner city schools, an increasing number of which are 90% black with white headteachers as part of a white administration, local authority or private

- The second is a group which, although they are not organized around churches and are not Christian, nevertheless played a crucial role in the survival of African people in the first diaspora and continue to do so here in Britain in the second diaspora, albeit to a lesser extent than the black Christian churches. That group encompasses practitioners of traditional, pre-Christian African religion, such as followers of the Ifa (Orisa) tradition, the historical and contemporary religion of the Yoruba people of Nigeria.

So much for who it is I am talking about. Now for the context in which I want to discuss their role, i.e., Britain's changing society. What are some of its features:

1. First and foremost, the persistence of racism and the widespread and flagrant denial of the rights of black people, including the most fundamental right of all: the right to walk the streets, go about your daily business and

sleep peacefully in your bed without being attacked,
maimed or murdered for no other reason than that you are
black. Not much change in British society here

2.   The effects of globalization and the movement of
       populations around the world, especially into Britain,
       coupled with the consequences of tyranny, political
       conflicts and civil wars around the world, both giving rise
       to a new migrant population of economic and political
       refugees and asylum seekers in Britain

3.   The steady erosion by an increasingly centralist and
       conservative State of the hard won rights and civil liberties
       for which earlier generations fought, matched by a
       disintegrated labour movement and a black working class
       movement that manifests signs of being defeated,
       incorporated and refocused

4.   The fact that whereas, ever since the brutal, racist murder
       of Kelso Cochrane, a black worker, in Notting Hill in 1958,
       and the sustained torture and murder of David Oluwale, a
       Nigerian vagrant, by the Leeds Police in 1970, the black
       communities of Britain campaigned against racial attacks
       and racist murders, and the brutality visited upon black
       people by the police across the nation, we are now at a
       point where black people are campaigning against gun
       crimes and the mindless destruction of black males,
       predominantly young, by other black males.

5.   The fear of crime and the misery that such fear, let alone
       the crimes themselves, causes to young black people and
       their parents in our communities, is now perhaps the most
       significant feature of our experience of Britain's changing
       society

6.   The fact that many more young black men are progressing
       to Britain's prisons and youth custody institutions than to
       Universities. While black and so-called ethnic minority
       people constitute an estimated 7.6% of the British
       population, we make up 29% of the overall prison
       population. And if we are locked away in the 'secure
       estate', we are not in the colleges and universities, not in
       the labour market and definitely not providing parenting

to our children. This is as true of boys and girls growing up without their fathers as of those who, increasingly, are being parented by grandparents or others carers while their single mothers serve prison sentences.

7. The fact that whereas people of my generation typically associated death with old age or, at worst, with illness at any age, the current generation of black people, especially children of school age, associate death increasingly with violence and youth, and, what is more, are becoming blasé about it

8. The fact that there is a high correlation between the number of black boys excluded from school, and the number of black young men in the 'secure estate'

9. Demographic projections suggest that by the next census but one (2021), Britain will be looking to its black and ethnic minority population to supply its labour market needs more than to the indigenous white population. The black population is growing at a faster rate than any other. School exclusions, educational underachievement, youth crime, and the imprisonment of massive numbers of black people must surely mean that 75 years after the Windrush, we would still be the most socially and economically excluded group in the society, massively over represented in all the negative social statistics in Britain

10. The enlargement of the European Union and the free movement of labour within the Union are already showing signs of having consequences for the employment and housing prospects of British born blacks, young males in particular. We face the spectacle, therefore, of a burgeoning black underclass in the society, characterized by low aspirations, high levels of underachievement, crime, and a growing and pernicious alternative economy

11. The cult of 'the individual' and the culture of materialism which leads increasingly to warped values and a-moral conduct on the part of young and old alike. The tendency, therefore, for more and more of us to seek private solutions to collective, public ills, (like sending our children to fee paying schools so long as there are not too many blacks

already there, or to the Caribbean and the Continent for their schooling) rather than to act collectively to bring about change and to humanize the society. African and Caribbean parents are clearly happy to send their children to majority or exclusively black schools in their countries of origin, but regard the presence of large numbers of black children, even in private schools, as a potential hindrance to their children's learning. When asked to explain this apparent contradiction, many such parents argue that their concern is partly to do with the behaviour and attitude to learning of black boys in Britain, and the peer group pressures to which they are subjected, but mainly to do with the expectations teachers have of black boys

12. The increasing sexualization of the young, and the growing phenomenon of confused and undeveloped minds and values in physically mature bodies and in 'the displaced Self'

13. The crisis of identity, culture and belonging and the attendant mental health challenges faced by multiple heritage children and the fact that there is still a reluctance on the part of black communities to engage with the issue

14. Some 55% of all Caribbean heritage males and 37% of Caribbean heritage females have a white partner. In a society that refuses to confront its endemic racism as Britain does, and with an increasing population from across Europe that has been challenged even less to confront their racism, the issues of identity, cultural rootedness and belonging loom large for multiple heritage children the older they become

15. The fact that British born young people of African heritage are themselves no longer saying it loud: 'I'm Black and I'm Proud' but, rather, are having skirmishes amongst themselves and heaping misery upon one another because of gradations of skin colour.

It would appear that if you are light skinned you are more acceptable. If you are light skinned and are seen as attractive, beautiful or handsome, you are likely to be the target of the jealousy of those who want to be like you. If you are black, African (ebony) black, you risk being bullied, put down and excluded by your own peers. The Black Consciousness Movement appears to have had its day. And, inasmuch as it was not validated by the schooling and education system such that black young people could both know about and understand its origins and its contemporary significance, they have been nurtured within a culture that has largely projected negative stereotypes of black people. In turn, popular culture has reinforced those stereotypes as well as creating new ones. Thus, the majority of black young people are left with few positive reference points, few building blocks for what I call 'constructive self building'

16. The fact that the 'in-your-face' racism that confronted the grandparents of today's young blacks, the Windrush generation, has been largely sanitized but not flushed out. Rather, it has achieved a high level of sophistication and recycled itself as liberal and benign racism, taking on more malignant forms, without warning (such as racial attacks and racial murders) when it will

17. It is an indisputable fact that many more black people have penetrated the system in the last two decades, even at the level of Government and the judiciary. This has given rise to a tendency, even among black people, to argue that every one of us 'could make it' to any level or position in the society we choose, even inside the royal household, if only we have the right attitude, work hard and don't get preoccupied with the issues that 'these frustrated black community activists' keep trumpeting on about

18. The fact that Britain's trade relationship with its former colonies, especially in the Caribbean which it massively underdeveloped and whose natural resources it continues to exploit, has been kicked into touch by its gaze on the USA out of its left eye and on the extended European Union out of its right. The economic interests of the peoples of the Caribbean recede further and further away in the consciousness of the British state and its people, including those of us who are consumers of the very

products that undermine the livelihood of those to whom we send remittances and barrels of goods and foodstuff in the Caribbean every week

19. The fact that there is a rise in the numbers of black people supporting and attending the established Christian churches that is in inverse proportion to the fall in attendance by whites in Britain

20. The fact that the longer we stay here as black settlers and black Britons of African heritage and the more numerous we become, the less capable of developing and sustaining sound, high profile economic institutions we appear to be. We therefore remain producers and consumers of other people's goods and services, and providers of public services

Need I say more? These are just some of the more pertinent features of changing British society which have relevance for the role of churches and organized religion generally and of black churches in particular.

But before we examine the role of Britain's black churches in relation to our changing situation in British society, let us look for a moment at the role of the church in our 'life experience with Britain' in the first and second diaspora. I want to suggest to you that we must make a distinction between what church is for, and what the role of the established and newer churches has been.

So, what is church for?

In the Christian tradition, churchgoers profess to be followers of Christ. But there are contestations within all Christian churches as to which teachings and example of Jesus Christ one should emulate. Few people bear witness to their Christianity by projecting and living principles and values which reflect a holistic view of what has been handed down as the Way, the Truth and the Life of Jesus Christ. What is more, some Christians and some denominations within Christianity display supreme arrogance, un-Christian in their lack of humanity and compassion, professing that man can be whole and fulfil his destiny only by following their way, their doctrine, their dogma. They represent various strains of fundamentalism which sit well with totalitarianism and fascism. That is why it was so supremely easy for the Roman Catholic Church to collude with fascism, and for it and just about all other churches to collude with apartheid.

For me, religion, Christian, Islamic, Hindu or Yoruba, is about belief systems that equip the individual with the capacity to give full expression to the fact that they are mind, body and spirit, and that spirit is indivisible and indestructible.

So, to put it crudely, whether you believe in karma, reincarnation or resurrection from the dead when the trumpet shall sound and all the saints of God gather, there is a connection made between your carnal self and your spiritual self, between how you are and what you do in your carnal life, and how you are in your spiritual life, now, and will be when your spirit has no further use for the shell that is your mortal body and your carnal self.

Religion is therefore the oil, the lubricating oil that allows the engine of life to work in synchrony, without the disintegration of the Self and with full expression being given to the fact that we are all divine, with that universal, indivisible and indestructible spirit dwelling within us. But, religion is neither necessary nor sufficient for us to reach fulfilment and the development of the Higher Self. In that sense, and in my book, that makes spirituality more important than religion. More important in the sense that non-believers as well as believers must give expression to and nourish their spiritual Self and respect all life as sacred.

The moment that respect for life and for the right of people to live life in its fullness as an expression of their basic humanity is sacrificed on the altar of belief, then religion itself becomes oppressive and places everybody at risk. In that sense, also, the conservative Christian fundamentalists that see George W Bush as their champion, and the Israelis who believe that the Holocaust is a justification for their own acts of state repression and genocide are no different from the Christian fundamentalists in Northern Ireland and the Islamic fundamentalists in Afghanistan, Iraq or anywhere else.

There is no denying the fact, therefore, that throughout

history what Karen Armstrong calls 'the Battle for God' and what could crudely be described as arrogant and pompous attempts by man to substitute their will and their prejudices for the will and purpose of God has led to the barbaric treatment of God's people, to the extent of denying to millions the right to life itself.

In the context of our experience with Britain in the Caribbean and here in these islands, the Church has had many functions:

- Colluding with the dominant social order and validating the exploitation of black people
- Actively subjugating traditional African religion and peddling prejudices and stereotypes which we in turn internalize and use to oppress ourselves and one another
- Encouraging the belief that if we take care of our souls and ignore what people are doing to our bodies and to our fundamental humanity and basic dignity, our suffering would be a form of cleansing and lead to greater rewards in heaven
- Encouraging the belief that poverty and suffering is good for the soul only when you are the oppressed and dispossessed; consequently, not preaching to the oppressors that they could reap the same benefits from poverty and suffering and should therefore divest themselves of all their wealth and privileges
- Encouraging a view of morality and of sin which places responsibilities on the poor and needy, particularly with respect to property and to sex, while identifying with the exploitation and sexual predation indulged in by the rich and powerful

Throughout history there have been gradations and variations across the churches with respect to the above. In the islands of the Caribbean, for example, the Church of England typically represented the landowners, former slave owners and the educated elite. The Roman Catholic Church had a following principally among the peasants and workers. And then there was and is the indigenous church in the Caribbean.

For example, whatever disputes there might be about its actual origins, the growth of what we now generically refer to as

the Spiritual Baptist Faith is interwoven with our history as
African slaves, African freed-slaves, African plantation workers,
and as a predominantly working and peasant class, ruled,
controlled and regulated by local colonial administrators acting
on behalf of European colonizers.

And, like colonizers everywhere, classic methods of
domination, control and regulation were employed over the
centuries by those who ruled over us. Those methods included:

- keeping us in economic, cultural and religious bondage
- denying the use of our native languages
- condemning our traditional religious practices and belief
  systems
- getting us to internalize negative definitions of ourselves
  and negative attitudes towards how we look, our beliefs, our
  traditional practices and our African heritage generally
- granting privileges to some of us in order that they might
  help exercise control over the majority of us and act against
  our collective efforts to liberate ourselves from economic
  bondage and from illiteracy and ignorance

It is an inescapable fact of history, however, that cultures of
oppression generate cultures of resistance. It is also a fact of
history that oppressors do not succeed in winning over, or
corrupting the mentality of all of the people. Part of our history,
therefore, has been massive resistance to economic exploitation,
to working excessively long hours in inhumane conditions, to
being kept in poverty whilst the fruits of our labour are shipped
abroad to enrich and develop Europe (the same Europe that
continued to project us as 'underdeveloped') and to nurture a
burgeoning local elite.

That history of resistance has spawned a unique culture, a
culture that encompasses a wide range of art forms, a range of
local languages in the region that sit side by side with standard
English, adapting it, transforming it, adding to it, drawing from
it and making it altogether more expressive and less stilted. That
history of resistance has also generated a religion that is unique
to the Caribbean, i.e., the Spiritual Baptist Faith. Whilst, in most
parts of the English, French and Spanish speaking Caribbean,
there are variations in the practice of the Ifa (Yoruba) and other

African religious traditions, popularly known as Orisa, Santeria, Condomble, Voodun, Pocomania, Kumina, etc., the Spiritual Baptist Faith as we know it appears to have evolved only in the English speaking Caribbean and Guyana in South America. In that sense, it is indigenous to the Caribbean.

The islands of the Caribbean have always had more in common with one another than not, if only because of their economic history and the purpose for which European colonizers fought over them so fiercely from one century to another. The most common feature of our existence was our oppression as colonial subjects and producers of wealth for Europeans. Sufferers on Grenada could identify with the sufferings of workers and peasants in Barbados. Workers in the oilfields of Trinidad could identify with the struggles of workers in the bauxite mines in Jamaica. Sugar cane workers in Trinidad could identify with the struggles of sugar cane workers in Guyana.

Presiding over all of that exploitation and suffering, and apologizing for the plantation owners and the colonial governments in Europe, were the Roman Catholic Church, the Church of England, the Church of Scotland and the Presbyterian Church. The leaders of those Churches had the ear of the colonial establishment both in the islands and in England, Spain, France or Holland.

The established churches exercised excessive power over the organization and provision of education, the running of the local colonial government, and the making of laws to govern the islands. They sought to use that power to control the masses and especially to obstruct the growth of a workers' movement in any one island and across the region. They were always eager and willing to determine that this workers' leader or that was a communist, or was threatening the stability of the local colonial regime and the economic interests of their colonial masters.

Teachers, police officers and other government employees would be summarily dismissed, or would be discriminated against when seeking employment because of their support for labour struggles. What is more, the majority of the people received the most elementary schooling and therefore high status jobs were seen as the preserve of the middle classes, especially the middle classes of 'high colour'.

It is against that background that the action of colonial governments against the indigenous church in the Caribbean in the second decade of the twentieth century is to be understood.

On 28 November 1917, the colonial government in Trinidad passed the Shouters Prohibition Ordinance, forbidding the public expression of the Spiritual Baptist Faith. It was a period of proscription that was to last thirty-four years before being repealed in 1951 after a sustained struggle by elders, members and supporters of the Faith. That was preceded by prohibition in the island of St Vincent, where in October 1912, the colonial government outlawed the practices of the 'Shakers', referred to as Shakerism, an ordinance that was eventually repealed as late as 1965.

Crown colony government in the Caribbean islands, aided and abetted by the established churches, was getting increasingly concerned about the growth of those religious groups known variously as 'Tie Heads', 'Shouters', 'Shakers', 'Spiritualists' and 'Shango Baptists'. They were concerned both about the form of their practices and the beliefs to which they gave expression, but particularly about the influence such groups were having on the ordinary working people. And, indeed, it was the ordinary working people who were the followers of those religions. The middle classes saw them as backward, as perpetuating African 'mumbo jumbo', as encouraging superstition and ignorance, and, at worse, as dealing with the devil himself. For the ordinary working people on the other hand, religious practice was not just about church on Sunday. It permeated every aspect of their daily living.

African retentions in Caribbean societies, be they English, French, Spanish or Dutch speaking, and especially in the religious traditions and practices of those societies are no more evident than in the Orisa Tradition and in the Spiritual Baptist Faith, with all their variety and in all their diversity.

In the Caribbean context, that can be described as the systematic interface between believers and the many identified Spiritual Forces in Nature, (the Orisa and the Ancestors) that operate in relation to, and direct the pattern of the lives of, those believers.

The Orisa Tradition in the Caribbean and Latin American regions has evolved over three centuries and is co-terminus with the Transatlantic Slave Trade and the social and religious practices and forms of organization which bonded and freed slaves effected.

The Orisa Tradition survives in its most extensive form, both as Yoruba retentions and practices in their own right, and as an integral part of Spiritual Baptist practice in certain islands in the English-speaking Caribbean.

Archbishop Monica Randoo, one of the most influential leaders and thinkers in the Spiritual Baptist Faith, estimates that some 75% of Spiritual Baptists in Trinidad and Tobago follow the Orisa Tradition. Yet, the practices of the 'Shango Baptists' as they had become widely known throughout the Caribbean remain shrouded in myth and mystery, to the extent that some Spiritual Baptists, leaders especially, despite their origins and growth within the Orisa Tradition, now seek to distance themselves from it. They make a point of projecting themselves as 'true Spiritual Baptists' who acknowledge the working of the Holy Spirit and only the Holy Spirit in their lives and in God's designs for the Universe.

The period of imperialism and colonialism which defined the relationship, economically, socially and culturally, between Europe, Africa and the Americas, generated a set of attitudes and beliefs in relation to primal African customs, philosophy, and practices which both misunderstood and denied the relationship between man and nature, between the physical and the spiritual, between the temporal and the supernatural, the cosmological and the theological, a relationship which lay at the very basis of the organization of African civilization.

At best, those African beliefs and practices were seen as primeval, primitive, pantheistic, anthropomorphic and, above all, fundamentally unchristian. At worst, they were regarded as savage, barbaric, bestial, as evidence of the African's lack of a brain and as the work of 'human animals' who had not fully evolved to the superior status of 'homo sapiens'.

When I was a boy growing up in Grenada, we had religious observance in our school every morning. One hymn from the Ancient and Modern that was much loved by our headteacher, a fellow who was black like me, was: 'Thy Kingdom Come O God, Thy rule O Christ' begin. I think it was No.117 in the school hymnal. One particular verse which, even then, made me cringe, had the words:

O'er heathen lands afar, thick darkness broodeth yet
Arise, O morning star, arise and never set.

I suppose the 'morning star' was not rising fast enough for the colonizers, so they went with the gun in one hand and the Bible in the other, to take care of business themselves. So, you see, even George Bush and Tony Blair have their ancestors.

Terms such as obeah, ju ju, black magic, devil worship, 'dealing' (in evil spirits), became part of political, academic, and popular discourse. Moreover, the colonialists produced thereby a language and a frame of reference which the indigenous peoples and the former Africans internalized and used to oppress themselves and others. As a consequence, the more events occurred which could not readily and obviously be explained, the more those events engendered fear and distrust among descendants of the African slaves themselves, as well as what was left of the Carib, Amerindian and Arawak population, especially those who were compelled to embrace Christianity.

The more Christianity was imposed, with its roots supposedly in Judaism rather than in African history and civilization, the more those definitions were internalized and African retentions marginalized. Not surprisingly, therefore, those African retentions continued to shape and influence the lives and religious beliefs and practices of the poor and dispossessed, of those in physical, social, and economic bondage.

While, like the Spiritual Baptists, many adherents of the Church of Rome continued to be Roman Catholics and to worship as Roman Catholics, those many among them who believed in the Orisa, and in their place and power in the Universe, would keep Sacri-feasts (the ritual slaying and offering of animals and birds to the Orisa), Osun festivals (feeding of the lakes and rivers), ceremonies for 'Ancestors of Light', Nation Dance, and other rituals originating within the Yoruba and other African religious traditions.

Such folk were as comfortable in those practices as they were in marrying within the Roman Catholic religion, christening their infants, having them receive the sacraments of Confirmation and Holy Communion , etc.

This form of what might be described as 'double indemnity' was a source of constant aggravation to priests, missionaries and Christian zealots generally. In my experience, however, the power of the Orisa, as a force in people's lives and especially as seen in their manipulation of the elements, was felt by those dual believers to be much more awesome, and more greatly to be feared than that of Jesus of Nazareth. For others who see Jesus as the total antithesis of the Orisa, Jesus of Nazareth is a rock of defence against their power. The latter are unlikely ever to accept that the Orisa also see Jesus as a messenger of God, a 'Higher Energy' worthy of our respect and homage, albeit not equal to God.

Be that as it may, the colonial establishment and the established churches alike were becoming increasingly alarmed at the growth of an organized labour movement in the Caribbean in the first decades of the twentieth century, and the role of what I call the indigenous Church in the development of that movement. The Spiritual Baptist Faith was proscribed in Trinidad in 1917 until 1951, and in St Vincent from 1912 to 1965, because in addition to the growth in its following, despite efforts to ridicule it, the activities of the Faith were felt to be fuelling labour unrest.

That refusal to separate their faith from what life was like for them, especially at the hands of their oppressors, gave those workers who were 'Shouters' and 'Shakers' a phenomenal confidence. They asked God and His messengers to take charge of every situation. They looked to Him for guidance and for victory in their labour disputes. They continued to believe in His protection as they worshipped in secret, baptised in secret, mourned in secret throughout the years of prohibition. They continued to derive strength and courage from His abiding presence and abundant grace when they were beaten up, arrested and imprisoned for practising their faith.

It is that faith, added to their common solidarity as workers against colonialism and oppression that led eventually to the lifting of the Prohibition Ordinance in both Trinidad and St Vincent. The end of prohibition both in Trinidad and in St Vincent had a great deal to do with individuals who identified with ordinary working people and their struggles, Elton Griffiths and Albert Gomes in Trinidad, and George Augustus McIntosh and Ebenezer Joshua in St Vincent.

Joshua, like many other Vincentians, had worked in Trinidad and had been a member of Tubal Uriah Butler's British Empire Workers and Citizens Home Rule Party. Butler had himself migrated to South Trinidad to later become the most famous labour organizer Trinidad has known. Organizing in Fyzabad, where over 40% of the population were Grenadian like himself, Butler took on the colonial government and accelerated the growth of the Oilfields Workers Trade Union (OWTU) and the Transport and Industrial Workers Union. Central to his activities and the communities of Fyzabad, La Brea and Point Fortin, was Butler's own practice as a Spiritual Baptist Leader. Wherever they gathered for a trade union meeting, rally or picket, Butler would unfold his white tablecloth, place it even on a tree trunk, somebody would get a glass of water and put a flower or a frond of green leaves in it, and there would be a Bible, however small and battered. It is hardly surprising, therefore, that to this day the song book of the OWTU is full of rallying songs sung to Spiritual Baptist tunes. Songs such as the Union song 'We meet today in freedom's cause'.

> We meet today in freedom's cause
> And raise our voices high
> We'll join our hands in Union strong
> To battle or to die
>
> Chorus

Hold the fort for we are coming
Unionists be strong
Side by side we battle onward
Victory will come.

Fierce and long the battle rages
But we will never fear
Help will come whene'er it's needed
Cheer, my Comrades, cheer.

We remain the only ethnic group in the Caribbean that has not preserved and extended the traditional religion of our ancestral home, the African continent and the coast of West Africa in particular. Our societies have had mosques, temples, and mandirs for generations. We have accommodated Hindus, Muslims, Greek and Ethiopian Orthodox, Moravians, Confucians and more. But in a predominantly African population, we have wholeheartedly embraced Christianity with all its contradictions and its barbaric history, not least in its collusion with imperialism, colonialism, and racism, and refined it beyond belief.

The struggles of black and other oppressed people in South Africa, the USA, and Latin America, principally, gave rise to a Black Theology and a Theology of Liberation from which the black churches in Britain largely distanced themselves. For their part, the established white-led churches with predominantly black congregations adopted a multicultural and ecumenical theology which mirrored the social policy agenda of the State and its institutions. Multiculturalism and community relations represented those parts of the agenda that the churches pursued more energetically than the radical politics of liberation and a theology for the struggle for racial equality and social justice.

Black led churches in African and Caribbean communities in Britain, therefore, have little to say about those twenty features of changing British society I listed above. When they do take a stand, it is invariably reactive and/or focused upon reaching out to those who have lost their way, and seeking to bring them back to a realization of their uniqueness to God and a belief that faith could make them free.

I applaud the involvement of black churches in community efforts to challenge the gun culture and the growing culture of violence in black communities, a sure sign that racism, and the systematic exclusion of, and denial of opportunity to black people in the society have resulted in our communities imploding upon themselves.

I believe, however, that the black churches remain the most organized and potentially powerful social institutions in black communities up and down the land and need, therefore, to develop a theology and a praxis that is much less about individual salvation and much more about collective action for social justice and an end to racist oppression.

The Black Churches need to see themselves as having a historical responsibility to bear witness in this present age, not by enabling their followers to take pharisaic delight in proclaiming that they are born again and therefore not like the great unredeemed masses, but by getting their hands dirty and their shirts bloodied, and confronting the systematic racial and social oppression that the majority of people in the society face.

One songwriter wrote: *Stand up, stand up for Jesus*
Ye soldiers of the Cross.

You cannot stand up for Jesus unless you are prepared to stand up for justice. But, standing up for justice means taking up the Cross and facing the ridicule, the hardships, the recriminations, the denial of opportunity and conferment of favours by the state.

It means taking a stand and declaring whose side you are on. If the black churches were to spend more time doing that, I am sure Jesus Christ would be present to them and find them much more useful instruments of his purpose, a purpose that set great store on defending the defenceless and setting the captives free.

9.2

'AT THE RENDEZVOUS OF VICTORY'
Remembering Enslavement 2003

A Message from Professor Gus John
(*composed and sent from an internet café in Port-of-Spain, Trinidad,
in response to a telephone request from the organizers, August 2003*)

I commend Anti-Slavery International and the Rendezvous of
Victory Committee for planning this timely Convention. I
identify fully with the objectives of the Convention and would
have wished to see the Home Office and the Department for
Education and Skills listed among its sponsors and supporters.

When Jack Straw was Home Secretary, the Race Relations
Forum which he established and chaired, and of which I was a
member, spent a great deal of time discussing plans for a
Holocaust Memorial. A ceremony to remember the industrial
genocide of the twentieth century and its far reaching
consequences has now been held annually for the last three
years. The Race Relations Forum also discussed the Reparations
issue, not least through the campaigning efforts of the late
Bernie Grant MP, also a former member of the Forum.

In due course, the Home Secretary asked a sub-group of the
Forum to consider the issues and make proposals in relation to
a 'Slavery Remembrance Day' to keep alive the memory of the
100 million or so who perished in the Atlantic Slave Trade, as
well as appropriate responses to the Reparations demand. The
results of the deliberations of the sub-group were tentative and
most uninspiring. I therefore applaud the work of Anti-Slavery

International, and of the Transatlantic Slavery Museum at the National Maritime in Liverpool in keeping this issue on the agenda and refocusing attention on the connections between our current realities and the legacy of slavery. I commend especially the pioneering work of Garry Morris at the National Maritime Museum in pushing this agenda forward.

In a period when we are revisiting the circumstances that led to the Haitian Revolution (1791-1804), the unspeakable courage, self confidence, and military skill of a body of people the world had defined as congenitally inferior with the capacity and instinct only of brutes, and the way that historic struggle altered the trajectory of the development of western civilization, the objectives of the Convention could not be more apposite.

I am unable to join you because I am actively involved with a body of people in Trinidad, and in Grenada, whose religious practices have their origins in slavery, and in the insistence of Africans in bondage that the Bible and the gun would not displace their traditional way of relating to the Creator and to the Cosmos. African retentions in the religious sphere, and particularly practices in the Ifa Tradition in the Eastern and Southern Caribbean, provide an important template for examining the intersection of religion, culture, economy, and politics in Post-Emancipation West Indies.

Mercantile and plantation capitalism responded to the stance adopted by freed slaves in a manner that intertwined the lives and fortunes of people from the Indian Subcontinent with that of those from Africa, from Europe, and from the Middle and Far East. Today, some 200 years after the end of the Haitian Revolution, there is a live and divisive debate amongst descendants of slaves in Trinidad and other Caribbean societies about their identity and their origins.

While the former Prime Minister, Basdeo Panday, many generations removed from his Motherland and spiritual home, made a point of visiting India with a sizeable entourage, and reclaiming his roots soon after he became Prime Minister, descendants of Africa were having fierce arguments about being called 'African'. The abiding image that far too many African descendants in the Caribbean region, and in the second African diaspora in Europe and North America, actually hang on to is of Africa as defined by imperialists and colonialists who sought to justify their barbarism by projecting Africans as backward and less than human.

To this day, therefore, more descendants of the African diaspora are content, if not eager, to forge their identity and claim their heritage on the basis of colonial constructions of blackness and civilization, as compared to the conflated image of whiteness and civilization, than on an understanding of their African-ness in all its complexity.

Throughout history, however, a culture of oppression has always given rise to its opposite, a culture of resistance. The most striking example of that is in the determination of those slaves whose fundamental instinct for freedom led them to seek to escape from their dehumanizing treatment, even though they knew they risked being killed or maimed for life by having their feet chopped off.

Cultures of resistance by their very nature engender the most profound examples of creativity, in art, language, literature, songs, music, storytelling, health and medicine and general ingenuity. This is the story of suffering peoples the world over, workers, peasants, populations fleeing genocide as well as national liberation movements. Africans in the transatlantic diaspora and all their descendants have either been creators or purveyors of such living culture.

The challenge for us is in ensuring that we make and sustain those links for present and future generations, not least in order to make it plain that we are in a continuity of struggle and that however much we become incorporated within the social, political, and economic structures of our former oppressors, the legacy of slavery and colonialism is still having a devastating effect upon entire nation states across the world, and not least in the regions from which we ourselves came. Indeed, it continues to impact upon generations of British born black people in the ethnic colonies that have been re-created in Britain itself.

To say that is not to indulge in a mindless form of atavistic sentimentality or to encourage anyone to subscribe to a glorified vision of Africa, past and present, but to remind us all that as the world shrinks in the wake of global technology and the communications revolution, we need to see ourselves more and more as interconnected but *secure in our identities* within that global interconnectedness.

If you don't know who you are, if you have lost your memory of your rootedness as an individual, who you are, where you've come from and where you are headed, the last place you want to be is in a crowd. You get bounced hither and thither and eventually end up being trampled under many feet.

But knowing who you are is about connectedness with your history and your lineage and with your spiritual history. It is that that defines your 'otherness' and provides you with a basis for self affirmation in the face of others and whatever they might represent. That spiritual dimension is critical for one more fundamental reason.

All empires, all imperialistic and expansionist exploits have given rise to and involved barbarism on a massive scale. That was no less true of the British Empire than it was of the Roman Empire or the Ottoman Empire. Ironically, however, we who are descendants of those who survived in the face of such barbarism have historically taken on the task of humanizing the very societies that have been so marred, deep within their collective psyche, by that history of barbarism. And whether or not we articulate it as that, we do so because we genuinely believe that those who resist oppression should be careful not to take on the self-destructive mantle of the barbarous oppressor.

So, yes, let us remove the jackboot that is squashing our windpipe 'By Any Means Necessary' but remember that we do so in order to affirm our right to life, our right to life with dignity, a right we cannot enjoy if we do not collectively create the conditions in which *all* people could live with dignity and not feel that they need to become predators in order to enjoy the basic comforts the rest of society take for granted.

The Anti-Slavery project is therefore pertinent today not just in relation to the barbaric and worldwide growth in human trafficking and its devastating consequences for individuals and societies, but also in relation to the growing number of enslaved minds that lead to wasted lives in each new generation of blacks and whites alike.

Despite erudite discourses on globalization and citizenship, fundamental issues to do with the rooting of identity, constructive self building, ontological dislocation, and understanding difference are ignored in education and schooling and in popular media.

If young black people in the majority black countries of the Caribbean are having heated debates about the role Africa played in determining who they are, and about whether or not it is sufficient for those in Trinidad, let's say, to claim a Trinidadian identity with no other historical antecedents, how much more critical must it be for British born blacks, products of the second African diaspora?

Similarly, without burdening them with the collective 'sins of their fathers', how much more critical it must be for young British born whites to understand how interconnected their histories are with the black people around them with whom they must learn to share and manage the society and, together, deal with the unfinished business of the Legacy of Empire. How much, for example, are they told about the historic struggles of the white working class in Britain and the relationship between those and the anti-colonial struggles of the forebears of today's British black natives?

If the Convention succeeds in raising levels of consciousness around these pressing issues and in pointing out to policy makers, practitioners, and collaborators the extent of their collusion with a conspiracy of silence on, and the structured omission of, those issues, then it will have laid the foundations for a political and educational agenda, driven by the people, that will leave no part of British society untouched.

I wish you success and much inspiration in all your deliberations. May Olodumare, the Orisa and our Ascended Ancestors of Light be ever there to steer your proceedings and inspire you to sound judgement.

Positive Energies, Peace and Nuff In-Courage-Meant

THE LEGACY OF ROSA PARKS
Its impact on black struggle in Britain
Centre for Inclusion and Diversity, Bradford
1 December 2005

I have been asked to share with you some reflections on 'the Equality movement', how far we have come, where we are now and where we seem to be going. I shall be commenting upon the struggle for race equality and its intersection with the struggle for equality for other target groups. I have chosen to call this talk: 'The Legacy of Rosa Parks and its Impact upon Black Struggle in Britain' because that is primarily what I want to concentrate upon. In so doing, I shall examine the progress various sectors in public life have made in promoting race equality, including the higher education sector.

In the first week in November, the world mourned the passing of Rosa Parks and paid tribute to her fearlessness and determination in standing up to a system that perpetrated racial segregation and the dehumanizing of black people by sitting down for freedom in December 1955.

1955 was also hugely significant in the life of someone who helped to lay the foundations and win political space in this society, thus making possible what many of us were later able to do. Contrary to popular belief, she was not one of the Windrush generation of early West Indian migrants. She had come to Britain in 1955, having been deported from that great haven and worldwide defender of democracy, freedom and human rights, the United States of America. What was her crime against the US Government? Why was she considered a threat to national security? She had engaged in political, left wing activities against state racism and US imperialism. She was born in the then British colony of Trinidad and Tobago and borne to the USA by her parents.

She became founder, publisher, and editor of Britain's first black newspaper, the *West Indian Gazette*. Just three years after arriving in this country, she founded our longest lasting, most celebrated social and cultural institution, the Notting Hill Carnival, which now attracts well over a million people to London each year from across the world, and has an annual turnover in excess of £90 million.

Some of you will have attended the memorial lecture in her honour given by Professor Carole Boyce Davies at London Metropolitan University a month ago, at the beginning of November. I speak, of course, of Claudia Jones.

In one single and no doubt unpremeditated act, in the same country that expelled Claudia Jones, Rosa Parks changed the course of history by defying the United States authorities and their racist laws, risking jail and even death itself, and sitting down for freedom.

The mythology has it that Rosa Parks was a tired black woman, forty-two years old, who had simply had enough and refused to give up her seat on a bus to a white man in the then segregated transport system of the USA.

She had had enough alright, because ever since 1932 when she married her husband, Raymond, at the age of nineteen, she had been active in the civil rights movement. Rosa and Raymond were both indefatigable workers in the voter registration movement in the southern states of America, deep down in Jim Crow country. Rosa Parks was one of the first women to join the National Association for the Advancement of Coloured People (NAACP), in Montgomery in 1943.

By December 1955, then, she had seen enough, read enough, struggled enough, put up with enough and, in that one encounter, she decided 'enough is enough. I ain't moving no how, I ain't moving for nobody. If you want me to move, youall go have to move me'. That one act of defiance changed the course of the history of the United States of America and gave new life to black and other liberation struggles across the world.

In 1956, the United States Supreme Court ruled that the segregated bus service was unconstitutional. Rosa Parks' single act of defiance was to change the lives of millions of people, not least that of one Martin Luther King Jr.

It is one of the supreme ironies of history that that same struggle has given us Condolezza Rice and Colin Powell on the one hand and thousands of black, US citizens being brought back home in body bags from theatres of war across the world on the other hand; people who join the US Army and are called upon to go and 'kick the butt' of folk who are often struggling to put an end to the very marginalization and dehumanization from which they themselves sought to escape by joining the US Armed Forces.

But, such is the way of change. History will certainly not hold that against Rosa Parks, any more than it would hold it against us that the struggles here in Britain, which she so greatly inspired, have given rise to black people at the heart of state government in Britain who could be sent by Tony Blair to try and win support among African heads of state for an illegal war in Iraq, and could collude with the US Government over the appropriation of the Chagos Islands, and the expulsion of the people of Diego Garcia from their own land because of its strategic importance to the United Sates of America and Britain. Ironically, it is projected as the surest sign of progress for black people in an open society when a Government Minister, black like me, with origins in a former British colony, British Guiana as it was then, could be in a position to put up a spirited defence of such imperialist plunder.

Rosa Parks, before 1955 and especially after, reminded people of her generation that they were standing upon the shoulders of those who had gone before them, struggled before them, died in the name of freedom so that they could live fuller lives and be respected. She reminded her generation that they had a duty to those who had given so much and endured so much. A duty to continue the struggle and not cease till they cast off the yoke of oppression, till every black man, woman, and child could stand tall and walk free. Rosa Parks gave concrete expression to that famous statement of Paulo Friere:

There is one thing I am certain about: Nobody is superior to anybody

There have been numerous women, and men, in this country who have engaged in struggle with confidence and with determination, because there was a Rosa Parks, because there was a Claudia Jones, and because before them there had been Harriet Tubman, Sojourner Truth, Nanny of the Maroons and many, many more besides.

Like Claudia Jones and Rosa Parks before her, and all those others before them, they took risks, huge risks. Theirs was a life of courage, of conviction, of commitment, and above all, of belief in themselves, and pride in their blackness. They were at ease with themselves and were all driven by a passionate belief in justice and in the right of everyone to live with respect and dignity; driven by that fundamental instinct for freedom with which as human beings we are all endowed, because we are born free and are meant to be free. You might imprison our bodies, you might violate our bodies, but you can never imprison our spirit, especially when we are at ease with ourselves and can make the distinction between our body and our spirit. Our Ancestors knew that, deep within themselves, they knew that. And that is why they were able to endure, able to fight, able to resist the attempts of oppressors to render them less than human. That is why they could have sung with such passion:

Oh, Freedom, Oh Freedom
Oh, Oh Freedom over me
For before I'd be a slave
I'd be buried in my grave
And go home to my God
AND BE FREE.

In reflecting upon the legacy of Rosa Parks, I want to make a connection between what she and others like her stood for and the need for an education movement constructed upon the aspirations and dreams of ordinary people and not just the needs of the economy or the designs of the state, in other words, a genuine 'Education for Liberation'. Let me go back to Rosa Parks for a moment.

In 1988, Rosa Parks said this:

I am leaving this legacy to you all ... To bring peace, justice, equality, love and fulfilment of what our lives should be.
Without vision, the people will perish, and without courage and inspiration, dreams will die – the dream of freedom and peace.

To bring peace, justice, equality, love and fulfilment of what our lives should be.

What a challenge. It is a challenge for our generation and for every generation.

A few weeks ago, during Black History Month, we in Manchester marked the 60th anniversary of the Fifth Pan-African Congress which was held at Chorlton Town Hall, Manchester, in October 1945. Among the many resolutions adopted at that conference was one on the 'Colour Bar Problem in Great Britain', as follows:

To secure equal opportunities for all Colonial and Coloured people in Great Britain, this Congress demands that discrimination on account of race, creed or colour be made a criminal offence by law.

That all employments and occupations shall be opened to all qualified Africans, and that to bar such applicants because of race, creed or colour should be deemed an offence against the law.

Among the key supporters of the resolutions passed at that conference were William Edward Burghardt DuBois, the 'Father of Pan-Africanism' and President of the Congress; James Egert Allen, President of the New York State Conference of the NAACP, and Mary McLeod Bethune, Founder and President of the National Council of Negro Women. The young Rosa Parks was hugely influenced by the scholarly works of WEB DuBois and by the activities of the NAACP. Forty-five years after she joined the NAACP, thirty-three years after she sat down for freedom and seventeen years before her death, she was leaving us the legacy ... 'To bring peace, justice, equality, love and fulfilment of what our lives should be'.

Inspired by those who, in Manchester in 1945, laid the foundations for the independence of African and West Indian nation states from colonial rule, a body of people, blacks and progressive whites, campaigned in the early to late 1960s to make the Pan-African Congress' resolution a reality. The Campaign Against Racial Discrimination (CARD) worked across Britain to produce compelling evidence of the extent of race discrimination in the society and its potential impact on British life generally. That led the Labour Government in 1968, with Harold Wilson as Prime Minister, to pass the first major piece of legislation against race discrimination.

Almost forty years after The 1968 Race Relations Act and sixty years after the 'colour bar' resolution, discrimination on account of 'race' is still widespread, and across the land there are public bodies, including police forces, schools, and Universities, failing to comply with legislation requiring them to eliminate racial discrimination and promote equal opportunity.

I can hear some of you speaking inwardly and saying: but, surely, things have improved significantly. I agree and I shall identify evidence of change on a number of indicators presently, change, that is, in addition to the growing number of black Baronesses and Lords of the Realm that this nation now boasts. Sadly, however, there is overwhelming evidence to suggest that the more things change, the more they stay the same when they don't actually get worse.

Let me take one example and deal for a moment with the issue of human rights, not in Turkey or Zimbabwe, but right here in Britain. I hope you will agree with me that there can be no more fundamental a human right than the right to walk the street, wait at a bus stop, sleep peacefully in your bed, be held in custody when the state has legitimate reason to hold you, and not be killed because other citizens, or people who have a duty to protect you when in custody, don't too much like the colour of your skin and would prefer to see you dead than to see you here.

The most recent racist incident monitoring report from the

Crown Prosecution Service noted that the CPS charged 8,706 people for racially aggravated offences in 2004-2005. Of those, 6,200 were prosecuted, 949 of which were for racially aggravated assaults and 4 for racist murders. The police and CPS themselves acknowledge that, for a whole variety of reasons, many racist incidents are not reported to them. This suggests, therefore, that the 8,706 defendants charged are but a fraction of those perpetrating racist acts.

Of the 6,200 prosecuted, 4,292 pleaded guilty, and a further 937 were found guilty, making a total of 5,229 guilty.

The largest number of defendant cases recorded by the CPS outside the Metropolitan & City area (682) was in West Yorkshire (472). That compares with a total of 126 in South Yorkshire.

The policies of the Far Right are gaining popularity among the British electorate. The British National Party (BNP) stood 119 candidates in the general election of May 2005 winning 192,750 votes, a full 60,990 of them in your region, Yorkshire and Humberside alone, as compared to 3,245 in the same region in the 2001 General Elections.

In 1958, three years after Rosa Parks sat down for freedom, Kelso Cochrane, a black migrant worker from the Caribbean was savagely murdered by white racists on the streets of Notting Hill, sending shock waves throughout this country. In April 1993, Stephen Lawrence was racially attacked and murdered while waiting for a bus in Eltham, South London. His murderers remain free, largely as a result of a bungled investigation by the Metropolitan Police in which racial stereotyping and racist beliefs and attitudes played a great part. Unlike his predecessor, Jack Straw, Home Secretary in the newly elected Labour Government, yielded to demands for a public inquiry into the circumstances of Stephen Lawrence's murder and the police investigation of it.

That Stephen Lawrence Inquiry pointed to institutional failures in the Metropolitan police and institutional racism within the police and other public institutions, including schooling and education, making a host of recommendations in respect of those matters.

On 29 July 2005, in the City of Liverpool, another eighteen year old black student, Anthony Walker, was racially abused as he waited with his white girlfriend at a bus stop, and then murdered after they moved away from their racist attackers. The police acted with commendable speed in this case and liaised with the family in a manner which suggests that they have come a very long way since the Lawrence Inquiry. Two white young men, similar in age to their innocent black victim, having been found guilty are to be sentenced today for his murder.

These racist murders, all given a very high profile, have been punctuated by scores more ever since Kelso Cochrane's in 1958.

For the rest of this talk, I want to concentrate on equality issues as they relate to schooling and education, keeping a primary focus on 'race' in higher education.

If schools have a duty to prepare students for life in multiethnic Britain, assisting them in taking personal responsibility for eliminating racism, then, arguably, Universities have an even more onerous responsibility. For one thing, they produce the people who run the schools, for another, they are in the knowledge business, generating, it, validating it, sifting it, quality controlling it, transmitting it, and much more besides. It is worrying, therefore, that Universities are lagging behind, behind Government, and even behind the police, as far as compliance with equality legislation and proactive steps to promote a culture of equity are concerned.

In 2002-2003, the organization for which I work, The Gus John Partnership (GJP) Limited, reviewed the Race Equality Policy and Action Plan of each of the Universities and HE Institutions in England (and, later, of the 46 colleges and 20 Universities in Scotland). Of the 130 Institutions that submitted their race equality policy/plan to the Higher Education Funding Council for England (HEFCE), 45 were found to be seriously deficient. Of those, 28 were totally non-compliant with the requirements of the legislation. 34 of the total were judged to have submitted exemplary paper policies. Yet, when the GJP team actually visited some of those Institutions for a later exercise, they discovered that eighteen months to two years later, those

Institutions had done very little to translate their first class policy into meaningful action that could make a difference to the learning community, and especially to its black students and staff.

As is the case with schools and colleges, there is a very serious issue about the competence of white managers in higher education to manage black staff and to deal with complaints from black students. There is a prevalent and erroneous assumption that there is, and should be, no difference in the way black and white staff and complaints involving black students and white students should be managed. Erroneous, because you don't treat people equally by treating them all the same, especially in a racist society where institutional cultures and practices could so easily act as a barrier to an individual's performance, or/and the way they are treated by the institution.

For those reasons, I believe that each school, each college and each University should have a vibrant Black Staff Network, working to support its members and to draw upon their experience of the Institution in order to assist it in transforming its culture, procedures, and practices.

One needs to see much more evidence in Universities of an approach to meeting the requirements of the RRAA 2000 which, at least, demonstrates an understanding of the structural bases of social exclusion, 'race' as a dynamic factor in social exclusion, and the extent to which institutions could be implicated in the perpetuation of it unless proactive steps are taken to identify and eliminate the conditions that sustain it.

Among the many things that concerned the GJP team in reviewing the race equality policies and visiting Institutions subsequently were:

- the evidence of an insistence upon reducing the emphasis that the Act places on 'race', race discrimination and race equality and subsuming the intentions of the legislation under broader and more amorphous and ill-defined concepts such as equal opportunities, cultural diversity, ethnicity, and cultural awareness.
- In one instance, an Ethnicity Equality Policy and Ethnicity Equality Action Plan were submitted on the grounds that

'race' was an outmoded and unhelpful colonial concept which the Institution had decided to move away from.

- Time and again they found that, if the material submitted to HEFCE said anything, it was that terms such as diversity, equality, equal opportunity, equity, cultural awareness, cultural diversity are often used interchangeably in a morass of sociological confusion, eschewing notions of power, dominance, ideology, and hegemony.

- Even when that approach to sanitizing 'race' appears, on the face of it, to be coherent and holistic, there is no specific focus on the requirements of the General Duty and the Specific Duties of the RRAA 2000. Indeed, some sustained burrowing is necessary in order to identify the specific, or any, aspects of the policy that are amenable to monitoring and assessment as fulfilling the requirements of the legislation.

The researchers expressed the view that: 'Few, if any, governing Councils of HEIs would adopt a "take it or leave it" attitude to Health and Safety legislation, public indemnity insurance legislation or, increasingly these days, sexual harassment legislation. They should be equally concerned, therefore, that their most senior officers do not appear to be assuming leadership responsibility not only for ensuring compliance with the RRAA but for driving the agenda to grow a culture of equity within their Institutions'.

They found that, in the majority of cases, 'Leadership in carrying forward the aims of the RRAA' was delegated to the Director of Human Resources or, more frequently, the Equal Opportunities Manager.

Equalities legislation, including the RRAA 2000, is best regarded as facilitative. Such legislation enshrines protection for the rights and basic entitlements of the citizen. It does not by itself create an environment in which all people are valued and have their rights respected and their diversity acknowledged and promoted.

The organization and those who lead and manage it are facilitated by the legislation in imparting and applying their vision of a just, fair, and equitable society, and ensuring that staff, students, service users and service providers understand their individual roles in ensuring that policy making, service planning and delivery, and employment practices reflect the ethos of an organization with that vision.

The GJP team concluded that the evidence of non-compliance, grudging and truculent compliance, and the lack of commitment to confronting racism through their statutory functions and powers that many Institutions exhibited, as revealed by the evaluation exercise, raised a major question for HEFCE and for Government.

It would appear that many Institutions believe that it does not really matter whether or not they demonstrate evidence of meeting the requirements of the RRAA 2000. Our discussions outside the specific context of this evaluation project suggest that a good number of public bodies, HEIs included, are of the view that the CRE will never have the level of resources to enable it to perform its monitoring and enforcement functions.

Despite HEFCE's attempts to encourage best practice, aided by appropriate research, the researchers concluded that the Government will need to consider whether, in the same way that it has established a funding link between recruitment of certain groups of students in the population and top up fees as part of its funding arrangements for HEIs, it should link the funding of Institutions to evidence of their compliance with the requirements of the Race Relations Amendment Act 2000, and empower HEFCE to withhold funding until such time that certain specific conditions are met.

Most HEIs depend increasingly upon overseas students for a not insignificant percentage of their annual income. Similarly, home grown black and ethnic minority students are taken into the reckoning like everybody else in the student data that is inputted into funding formulae. For decades, such students and black staff have had their concerns marginalized. The GJP team argued that as a basic business case, it is reasonable for Government to seek to satisfy itself that HEIs are doing what is legally required as a condition of continuing to fund them at the levels that they have come to expect, rather than encouraging them in the view that they will continue to receive that funding irrespective of whether or not they demonstrate evidence of operating within the law.

Were they to adopt a similar 'take it or leave it' attitude to Health and Safety legislation and the practices commensurate with that legislation, the Health and Safety Executive would be entitled to issue compliance notices, take them to court or at worst shut them down. Given the inertia that accompanied the RRA 1976 and the performance of the Sector on 'race' issues prior to the RRAA 2000, it is obvious that self regulation cannot be depended upon to deliver equality and social justice to marginalized groups. All the more reason, therefore, to give HEIs a wake up call by linking their funding to their performance in respect of the duty under the RRAA 2000.

The GJP team saw that as 'a most logical step for Government to take' if it wished to see a joined-up approach to its policies on widening participation, bringing about the learning revolution, promoting race equality and building community cohesion through education.

I strongly believe that financial coercion, added to the self organization of black and progressive white staff and students of all target groups, is the only way we would get the higher education sector to perform that crucial function of eliminating unlawful discrimination and promoting equality of opportunity, such that they could be seen to be playing their part in ensuring that racial justice and social justice could become the hallmark of the society our children will inherit.

Were we to achieve that, we would have truly embraced the legacy of Rosa Parks and all those other beacons of freedom and justice that have criss-crossed our skies.

So, I say to you, the black staff and students at this Institution and at every other Further and Higher Education Institution in the country: 'Seize the Time'. Know and understand what is happening in your own Institution, in the community around you and in the country as it relates to the rest of the world, and hold yourselves and the Institution to account. The situation we are in calls for a resurgence of black self-organization and the self confidence with which to form alliances with other interest groups and work collaboratively to bring about change.

So, be not afraid! Take heart and remember that 'We have

nothing to fear but our fear!'

Our deepest fear is not that we are inadequate.
Our deepest fear is that we are powerful beyond measure.
It is our light, not our darkness, that most frightens us....

There's nothing enlightened about shrinking so that
other people won't feel insecure around you ...
                              (Nelson Mandela, Inaugural Speech, 1994)

I wish the new Centre for Inclusion and Diversity and all who
work in it a long and purposeful life.

FURTHER READING

Acton, T & Dalphinis, M ed. (2000) *Language, Blacks and Gypsies – languages without a written tradition and their role in education*. London: Whiting & Birch

Adi H, & Sherwood, M. (1995) *The 1945 Manchester Pan African Congress Revisited*. London: New Beacon Books

Alleyne, B W. (2002) *Radicals Against Race: Black Activism and Cultural Politics*. Oxford: Berg

Allsopp, R ed. (1996) *Dictionary of Caribbean English Usage*. Oxford University Press

Armstrong, K. (1993) *A History of God: From Abraham to the Present: The 4000 year quest for God*. London: Mandarin

— (2000) *The Battle for God: Fundamentalism in Judaism, Christianity and Islam*. London: Harper Collins

Brathwaite, Edward Kamau. (1984) *History of the Voice*. London: New Beacon Books

Brown, S ed. (2000) *Kiss & Quarrel: Yoruba/English strategies of mediation*. Birmingham: University of Birmingham Press

Cassidy, Frederic. (1961) *Jamaica Talk: Three Hundred Years of the English Language in Jamaica*. London: Macmillan

Christie, Pauline. (2003) *Language in Jamaica…* Kingston: Arawak

Coard, Bernard. (1971) *How the West Indian Child is made Educationally Subnormal in the British School System*. London: Beacon Press

Commission for Racial Equality. (2000) *Inspecting Schools for Racial Equality: OfSTED's strengths and weaknesses*. London: Commission for Racial Equality

Connell, R W, Ashenden, D J, Kessler, S & Dowsett, G W. (1983) *Making the Difference – Schools, Families and Social Division*. London: George Allen & Unwin

Crystal, David. (2000) *Language Death*. Cambridge: Cambridge University Press

Devonish, Hubert. (1986) *Language and Liberation: Creole Language Politics in the Caribbean.* London: Karia Press

Dhondy, F, Beese, B & Hassan, L. (1983) 'Who's Educating Whom?' in *The Black Explosion in British Schools.* London: Race Today Publications

Elton, Lord. (1989) *Discipline in Schools – Report of the Committee of Enquiry.* London: HMSO

Eriksen, T H. (1993) *Ethnicity and Anthropological Perspectives.* London: Pluto Press

Fanon, F. (1967) *The Wretched of the Earth.* London: Penguin Books

Fisher, R. (1998) *Teaching Thinking: Philosophical Enquiry in the Classroom.* London: Souvenir Press

— (1999) *Head Start: How to Develop Your Child's Mind.* London: Souvenir Press

Freire, P & Shor, I. (1987) *A Pedagogy for Liberation: Dialogues on Transforming Education.* London: Macmillan

Gill, Dawn, Mayor, Barbara & Blair, Maud. (1993) *Racism and Education, Structures and Strategies.* London: The Open University & Sage Publications

Gillborn, D & Gipps, C. (1996) *Recent Research on the Achievement of Ethnic Minority Pupils. Report for the Office of Standards in Education.* London: HMSO

Gillborn, D & Youdell, D. (2000) *Rationing Education: Policy, Practice, Reform & Equity.* Buckingham: Open University Press

Goldberg, D T & Solomos, J ed. (2002) *A Companion to Racial and Ethnic Studies.* Oxford: Blackwell

Hall, S, (1978) 'Racism and Reaction' in *Five Views of Multi-Racial Britain.* London: CRE

Hall, S, Critcher C, Jefferson, T, Clarke, J & Roberts, B. (1978) *Policing the Crisis: Mugging, the State, and Law and Order.* Palgrave MacMillan

Hall, S, Hobson, D, Lowe, A & Willis. (1980) *Culture, Media, Language: Working Papers in Cultural Studies 1972–79.* London: Unwin Hyman

Hall, S & Gieben, B. (1992) *Formations of Modernity.* London: Polity Press in association with the Open University

Hammersmith & Fulham LEA. (1997) *Minds of Their Own – School Improvement through Thinking Skills Project Video*

Hesse, B ed. (2000) *Un/settled Multiculturalism: Diasporas, Entanglements, 'Transruptions'.* London: Zed Books

Home Office. (1998) *Human Rights Act.* London: Home Office

Home Office. (2000) *Race Relations (Amendment) Act.* London: Home Office

Hirson, B. (1979) *Year of Fire, Year of Ash. The Soweto Revolt: Roots of a Revolution?* London: Zed Press

Jacobs, W R ed. (1976) *Butler Versus the King – riots and sedition in 1937.* Trinidad: Port-of-Spain: Key Caribbean Publications

James, C L R. (1980) *Spheres of Existence: Selected Writings.* London: Allison and Busby

— (1980) *The Black Jacobins: Toussaint L'Ouverture and The San Domingo Revolution.* London: Allison & Busby

John, Gus. (1981) In the Service of Black Youth – A study of the political culture of youth and community work with black people in English cities. Leicester: National Association of Youth Clubs

— (1986) *The Black Working Class Movement in Education and Schooling and the 1985–86 Teachers Dispute.* London: Black Parents Movement

— (1990) *The Resurgence of Barbarism – Europe, 1992 ... and all that. Working Paper for European Action for Racial Equality and Social Justice.* London

John La Rose Tribute Committee. (1991) *Foundations of a Movement: A tribute to John La Rose on the occasion of the 10th International Book Fair of Radical Black and Third World Books.* London

Kambon, Khafra. (1988) *For Bread Justice and Freedom: A political biography of George Weekes.* London: New Beacon Books

Lewis, W A. (1977) *Labour in the West Indies: The Birth of a Workers Movement.* London: New Beacon Books

Macdonald, I, Bhavnani, R, Khan, L, & John, G. (1989) *Murder in the Playground – the Report of the Macdonald Inquiry into racism and racial violence in Manchester schools.* London: Longsight Press, New Beacon Books

Macpherson, W. (1999) *The Stephen Lawrence Inquiry Report.* London: The Stationery Office

Mamdani, M. (2001) *When Victims Become Killers: Colonialism, Nativism and the Genocide in Rwanda.* Princeton University Press

Mayo, M & Thompson, J ed. (1995) *Adult Learning, Critical Intelligence and Social Change.* Leicester: NIACE

Mayor, Federico. (1995) *Memory of the Future.* Paris: UNESCO

Rampton, A. (1981) *West Indian Children in Our Schools.* Cmnd 8273. London: HMSO

Richardson, B, ed. (2005) *Tell it like it is: How our schools fail black children.* London: Bookmarks and Trentham

Runnymede Trust. (2000) *The Future of Multi-Ethnic Britain – Report of the Commission on the Future of Multi-Ethnic Britain.* London: Profile Books

Social Exclusion Unit. (1998) *Truancy and School Exclusion – Report by the Social Exclusion Unit.* London: The Stationery Office

Stephens, Patricia. (1999) *The Spiritual Baptist Faith – African new world religions, identity, history and testimony.* London: Karnak

Swann, Lord. (1985) *Education for All: Final Report of the Committee of Enquiry into the Education of Children from Ethnic Minority Groups.* Cmnd 9453. London: HMSO

Thomas, J J. (1969) *Theory and Practice of Creole Grammar.* London: New Beacon Books

Vanzant, I. (1996) *The Spirit of a Man: A Vision of Transformation for Black Men and Women who love them.* San Francisco: Harper

Walmsley, A. (1992) *The Caribbean Artists Movement 1966–1972: A Literary and Cultural History.* London: New Beacon Books

Warner-Lewis, Maureen. (1997) *Trinidad Yoruba: From Mother Tongue to Memory.* Jamaica: The Press, University of the West Indies

INDEX

W

Walker, Anthony 2,593
Wark, Kirsty 341
Warner, Norman Lord 33,139,243
Washington, Booker T. 375
Webb 250
Weinstein, Jenny 286
Weinstein, Jeremy 286
West Indian World 423
Whitelaw, William 422,513,548
Williams, Raymond 387
Williams, Shirley 102,190
Windrush 481
Woodhead, Chris 14
Working Groups Against Racism in
    Children's Resources 138
Wright Cecile 219
Wright, Richard 375

Y

Youdell 13
Young Mediators Network 118,175
Youth Justice Board 42,233,234,235,243
Youth Justice Panels 235
Youth Offending Teams 238
Youth Training Scheme 105

Z

Zephaniah, Benjamin 355